The Gendered Screen

FILM+MEDIASTUDIES

Film studies is the critical exploration of cinematic texts as art and entertainment, as well as the industries that produce them and the audiences that consume them. Although a medium barely one hundred years old, film is already transformed through the emergence of new media forms. Media studies is an interdisciplinary field that considers the nature and effects of mass media upon individuals and society and analyzes media content and representations. Despite changing modes of consumption—especially the proliferation of individuated viewing technologies—film has retained its cultural dominance into the 21st century, and it is this transformative moment that the WLU Press Film and Media Studies series addresses.

Our Film and Media Studies series includes topics such as identity, gender, sexuality, class, race, visuality, space, music, new media, aesthetics, genre, youth culture, popular culture, consumer culture, regional/national cinemas, film policy, film theory, and film history.

Wilfrid Laurier University Press invites submissions. For further information, please contact the Series editors, all of whom are in the Department of English and Film Studies at Wilfrid Laurier University:

Dr. Philippa Gates
Email: pgates@wlu.ca

Dr. Russell Kilbourn
Email: rkilbourn@wlu.ca

Dr. Ute Lischke
Email: ulischke@wlu.ca

Department of English and Film Studies
Wilfrid Laurier University
75 University Avenue West
Waterloo, ON N2L 3C5
Canada

Phone: 519-884-0710
Fax: 519-884-8307

Brenda Austin-Smith
and George Melnyk
editors Canadian Women
The Gendered Screen
Filmmakers

Wilfrid Laurier University Press

[WLU]

This book has been published with the help of a grant from the Canadian Federation for the Humanities and Social Sciences, through the Aid to Scholarly Publications Programme, using funds provided by the Social Sciences and Humanities Research Council of Canada. Wilfrid Laurier University Press acknowledges the financial support of the Government of Canada through its Book Publishing Industry Development Program for our publishing activities.

Canada Council for the Arts

Conseil des Arts du Canada

ONTARIO ARTS COUNCIL CONSEIL DES ARTS DE L'ONTARIO

Library and Archives Canada Cataloguing in Publication

The gendered screen : Canadian women filmmakers / Brenda Austin-Smith and George Melnyk, editors.

(Film and media studies series)
Includes bibliographical references and index.
Also available in electronic format.
ISBN 978-1-55458-179-5

1. Feminist films—Canada—History and criticism. 2. Women motion picture producers and directors—Canada. 3. Women in motion pictures. 4. Lesbians in motion pictures. 5. Nationalism in motion pictures. I. Austin-Smith, Brenda, 1958– II. Melnyk, George III. Series: Film and media studies series

PN1995.9.W6G44 2010   791.43082'0971   C2009-906511-8

ISBN 978-1-55458-195-5
Electronic format.

1. Feminist films—Canada—History and criticism. 2. Women motion picture producers and directors—Canada. 3. Women in motion pictures. 4. Lesbians in motion pictures. 5. Nationalism in motion pictures. I. Austin-Smith, Brenda, 1958– II. Melnyk, George III. Series: Film and media studies series

PN1995.9.W6G44 2010a   791.43082'0971   C2009-907079-0

Recycled
Supporting responsible use
of forest resources
FSC www.fsc.org Cert no. SGS-COC-003153
© 1996 Forest Stewardship Council

To women filmmakers everywhere

Contents

Acknowledgements

The editors would like to thank the Aid to Scholarly Publishing Program of SSHRC for its financial support for this book. This project has taken several years and has been helped by various people. In particular we would like to acknowledge the valuable comments made by the anonymous readers of the initial manuscript. Their observations allowed us to improve the editorial content and theoretical framing of the book. We would like to thank our respective families for their support during the preparation of the manuscript. The staff at Wilfrid Laurier University Press has been exceedingly professional in their assistance and we are pleased to have this book included in the Film and Media Studies Series.

1
Introduction

Canadian Women Filmmakers: Re-imaging Authorship, Nationality, and Gender
Brenda Austin-Smith
and George Melnyk

An introduction is a strangely duplex creature. At the same time that it ushers readers forward, preparing them for an encounter with texts marshalled for a particular intellectual purpose, it is inevitably retrospective, constructed from reflection on the reasons for the gathering in the first place. This introduction engages that double task by providing us, the co-editors of this collection of essays on Canadian women film directors, with a chance to revisit our original motives for the collection while situating these pieces in ways intended to make them as useful as possible to readers. In this case, looking back on the process of soliciting, reading, and editing the essays offered here allows us to consider some of the practical and theoretical issues that have shaped the book.

"Specific but not essential" was the phrase that occurred to us as we considered the rationale for a collection of essays on the work of Canadian women filmmakers that in the beginning was conceived as one that would focus on particular works by particular directors but would be wary of advancing sweeping claims about what constituted the feminist or Canadian qualities of the works or the directors under discussion. The phrase itself points to the pixelating effect of feminist, cultural, and post-colonial theory on the topics with which this project immediately engages, though in an expanded and critical sense: auteur theory and national cinema. In the introduction to *Gendering the Nation: Canadian Women's Cinema*, the authors wonder whether "an examination of national cinema necessarily entail[s] an auteurist approach, an emphasis on films and filmmakers" (Armatage et al., 12), a question that the present editors also considered as we put this book together. We found ourselves caught up in interesting political and practical conversations about our own goals for this project, realizing that authorship and nation had not lost their troublesome fascination for us as teachers and scholars of film. Auteurism and nationalism can be easily read in terms of a Canadian-spun homology in which singular and fully intentional subjects emerge from their given surroundings with innate artistic gifts, and proceed to create works through which a similarly coherent national identity gradually takes shape. Even the description of the auteur heroically making art out of the "tensions" between "a director's personality and his material" (Sarris, 562) suggests a tempting correspondence with tales of settler struggles to carve out a country from harsh and resistant landscapes. As mutually reinforcing essentialisms, these notions can rest as well on assumptions about the gender of both the author and the citizen, assumptions that the last thirty years of feminist theory and practice have subjected to thorough critique.

How, for example, would such a conceptual model apply to the production circumstances and screen works of the film and video collectives and studios that have provided the technical training, site support, and collaborative experience for many women screenworkers in Canada? One example that comes to mind is Arnait, an Inuit women's filmmaking collective based in Igloolik. Since 1991 Arnait has produced computer animated videos, video documentaries, docudramas, and the feature film adaptation *Before Tomorrow*, based on a Danish novel, which in 2008 won the Best Canadian First Feature Award at the Toronto International Film Festival and first prize at the ImagineNATIVE Film + Media Arts Festival. Apart from gallery and festival screenings, Arnait's widest distribution is through its association with IsumaTV, which describes itself as "an internet video portal for indigenous filmmakers." Arnait's process, its productions, and its distribution channels conform to no conventional model of single authorship in the service of national affirmation, but in its self-description as an entity working "to value the voice of Inuit women in debates of interest to all Canadians," we find an example of the expanded sense of authorship as cultural agency with which this collection is concerned.

Gender has complicated the close association of auteur and nation by questioning each term in the relationship, revealing critical ambivalence about the aesthetic and political value of these two concepts taken independently as well as in connection with each other. A brief summary of the interactions of feminism and traditional understandings of authorship in film studies is useful at this point. In feminist film scholarship of the 1970s, for example, many feminist critics concentrated on the problem of representation, especially in Hollywood films directed by men. The result was the production of "images of women" articles and extensive critiques of women's status as cinematic spectacle. For other feminist scholars, the content analysis of particular films was beside the point, focusing as it did on the symptom of a more basic problem of signification. A combination of Lacanian psychoanalysis, structuralism, and, later, poststructuralism gave critics like Claire Johnston, Pam Cook, Teresa de Lauretis, Kaja Silverman, and Laura Mulvey theoretical instruments with which to describe women's fundamental exclusion from systems that produce meaning in and through cinema. The interrogation of women's images moved on, under the influence of these critics, to focus on women as viewers of cinematic texts, as well as on the very conditions of cinematic representation. Influential debates during the period of what came to be known as screen theory in the 1980s considered the degree to which viewer agency was possible, given the power of unconscious forces that structured looking relations. The influence of apparatus theory was corrosive not only to the claim that women could escape the "male gaze" but also to the proposition that auteurs had conscious and intentional control over the texts they appeared to create. Meaning arose from relations within the system of the film text rather than from the intentions of a director, whether male or female. Pam Cook and Claire Johnston could argue for example that though several films by Raoul Walsh "appear to present women as strong and independent characters," the gendered meanings of those films had been "fixed by a patriarchal culture" in which woman is "the locus of emptiness" (Cook and Johnston, 26–27). At the same time, feminist scholars looked for evidence of female subjectivity in the gaps and absences in films made by men, as well as in the destabilizing practices of the "spectatrix" who actively read "against the grain" of the film text before her, thereby preserving some kind of agency in the face of the apparatus and its power to articulate and reify female subjectivities.

During this period feminist film scholars worked to excavate a history of filmmaking by women, though they made it clear that their efforts were not additive—that is, the point was not to supplement an existing tradition of male auteurs with female ones. This is the view expressed in Johnston's essay "Dorothy Arzner: Critical Strategies," in which Johnston writes that the intention of feminist scholars like herself is not to install Arzner "as some cult figure in a pantheon of Hollywood directors nor, indeed, in a pantheon of women directors" (Johnston, 37). In examining films by women and in calling for a feminist approach to filmmaking, theorists like Johnston and Mulvey advocated the making of films that would disrupt conventional representational practices. The analysis of women's cinema as "counter-cinema" was one way of justifying critical attention to women directors, of claiming that a woman behind the camera made a difference.

The nature of the difference it made, though, proved a problem that continues to give feminist theorists pause some thirty years after these theoretical interventions in the authorship debate first appeared. Though women's auteurship is in many ways an attractive notion, it can also suggest a return to the intentional auteurism of the past and to gender essentialism. In the face of this quandary, as Geetha Ramanathan writes, feminist theory "insists on the historical author but concentrates more on the ideological traces of the auteur in the text" (3). Auteurship, by this light, is a formalist entity, present in the textual strategies of the film. Keeping the gender of the historical film author theoretically quarantined from any idea of intended effects was one way to avoid essentialism and maintain the emphasis on discourse as the generator of film meaning. However, as Catherine Grant points out, this gave rise to another problem. In an article tracking the idea of film authorship in feminist theory, she writes about the paradox that emerged in the 1980s and 1990s for feminists interested in theorizing female authorship: "If the 'unconscious structures' of a film text cannot usefully be shaped by their directorial authors, why aim to advise women film-makers at all?" (Grant, 117). So concerned were feminist theorists to avoid the taint of essentialism clinging to the spectre of the director as intentional auteur, that authorship became an inside job: the film text took over as the locus of authorial traces. Grant quotes John Caughie to the effect that the danger "'in placing the author as a fictional figure inside the text ... [is] of constructing the text as an ideal essence'" with no ties to a social or historical "outside" (qtd. in Grant, 121).

Grant finds in the work of Carol Watts and Susan Martin-Márquez, who write about the inevitably limited but no less real agency of women as cultural producers, a corrective to the "embarrassed deconstruction" of the last few decades, as well as a useful example of a revised and expanded understanding of women's auteurist agency. Theirs is a critical example that would enable agency "finally to be subjected to analysis in the form of its textual, biographical traces, alongside more conventionally 'legitimate' activities for feminist cultural theorists, such as applying theories to 'primary' literary and film texts in formal 'readings'" (Grant 123). Martin-Márquez's view of agency—"bounded, it is true, by the limits of available subject positions as well as by unconscious processes, but no less a producer of new 'cultural forms'" (qtd. in Grant, 123)—is one that attracts us as editors to this work, and to the work of Geetha Ramanathan as well. In her recent book *Feminist Auteurs*, Ramanathan acknowledges Grant as someone attentive to the unease felt by any critic "about to embark on any study referencing the auteur," and conscious of the encounter with "a 'queasy' moment in a bid to take cover from the charge of essentialism" (3). Nevertheless, Ramanathan builds on the insights of Judith Mayne in order to argue that feminist authorship "entails the impression of feminist authority, not necessarily that of the auteur herself, on screen" (3).

The traces of this critical history are apparent in our editorial procedures and in the methodologies and subjects chosen by those who submitted essays for our consideration. As editors, we had some ideas about filmmakers and films we ourselves would like to read about and teach in our courses, but not all of the areas of our own interest were captured by the "single author of feature film" method of analysis. On one hand, the attraction of an auteurist approach to Canadian women filmmakers that would pay sustained attention to feature-length work or the oeuvre of a specific filmmaker was in part the satisfying counterbalance it offered to the long-established practice of treating films made by men as the work of single authors, even though film is obviously a collaborative art form. Less attractive was the drawback, just as obvious, of conventional auteurism, given the collaborative practices of some of the women whose works are discussed here, and the preference expressed by the writers of the essays for an emphasis on community politics, on certain generative sites of production, and on forms other than the conventional feature. Several of the authors in this collection are critically drawn to the works of those who ally themselves, in Christine Ramsay's words, "with forms of collectivization that have ... to do with valuing the specificities of place, regional cultural expression and local community identities" (210). These writers address filmmakers for whom, as Kathleen Buddle observes, "the *mode of participation*" is itself a performative act crucial to filmmaking's expressive success (160). Then again, to treat some filmmakers largely within the context of their regions or political or creative or sexual communities can attract charges that such approaches diminish the accomplishments of these women. The question we faced in these cases is why some filmmakers in this collection are given sustained individual attention while others are not. Asking ourselves this same question, we revisited debates over whether auteurist treatment constituted some sort of critical "arrival" or imprimatur, while other forms of assessment and analysis did both the filmmakers and the works a disservice. Or did an emphasis on single authorship do equal disservice to themes, patterns, and vital production realities that become apparent only when a larger field is canvassed for its influence and significance? Certainly the institutional study of film has tended to emphasize a focus on single-author studies, as Pierre Véronneau notes in a recent essay on Quebec cinema, thus tending to "disregard the multifaceted reality of film as an industry and a cultural practice" (93).

Our conclusion was that the contest between figure and ground, between different ways of understanding and examining women filmmakers—as a part of, or apart from, their contexts—should remain visible in this collection precisely because these questions cannot be settled by editorial fiat but are embedded in the field of film and screen studies itself. We did not wish to obscure the politics attending any such methodological privileging but wanted these essays to take up the struggle over female authorship articulated by Angela Martin in her essay "Refocusing Authorship in Women's Filmmaking."

In that essay, Martin writes about the necessity to recognize how ill suited traditional auteur theory is to women's filmmaking, but she insists on the need "to claim women filmmakers as auteurs or to define and defend notions of female authorship" (35). She suggests a move toward authorship as a "practice" that "may or may not emerge from a single person but, in terms of film production, will certainly be organized around the director" (36). This collection, we believe, benefits from this variety of critical takes on the practice of women filmmakers in Canada as cultural agents, the methodological cross-currents between and among the essays embodying debates about the relationships between film, gender, authorship, and nation in ways that this introduction can only outline.

As the editors of *Gendering the Nation* write, "Canadian women's cinema is not necessarily an equitably shared tradition," since it is shaped by the vagaries of personal history, region, and access to institutional supports (Armatage et al., 4). While they go on to say that these circumstances affect men as well, they point out that the "*gaps* in women's production repeat a familiar pattern" (4), contributing to the persistent impression of women's cinema in Canada as having to be reinvented every few decades. Adding to this are the well-known funding and distribution challenges facing filmmakers in Canada, forces that Anne Wheeler identifies as having pushed some of her own projects in the direction of television rather than film, a course sometimes difficult to alter (Levitin et al., 211). Related to whether the discussions of the filmmakers in this book tilt toward an examination of an individual career or toward participation in collective expression is the matter of media form, which is often inextricably connected to issues of funding, distribution, and region. It is easy to undervalue the part played by state-supported entities such as Studio D, the Quebec-based Régards des Femmes, as well as various provincial film co-operatives if the only productions that count as part of women's cinema are features. Diane Burgess has made the point most forcefully in her essay "'Leaving Gender Aside': The Legacy of Studio D?" in which she recommends "shifting the criteria of canonical value to encompass the actual diversity of filmmaking" in this country (423). Several of the essays here are responsive to her call to scholarly arms, as our interest in composing this volume of essays was to broaden rather than abandon the definition of "film author" to include a wide range of films by women working in Canada who have made documentaries, experimental films, and videos, and whose authorship involves adaptation. This collection treats Canadian women filmmakers in their multiple contexts as both singular and collective authors, as engaged and creative agents whose works—whether short or feature-length, documentary or fictional, co-produced or domestically produced—embody a particular understanding of what filmmaking means in that probable fiction we know as Canada. This reference to the national entity in turn calls upon the second contested term in the equation between creative activity and nation building referred to earlier in this Introduction.

The relationship between gender and nation is as complicated and ambivalent as that between gender and authorship, and some unpacking of these complexities is useful in making more apparent the larger field of discourse, debate, and experience in which cultural productions take place. Some definitions are in order. Tamar Mayer, in her introductory essay to the collection *Gender Ironies of Nationalism: Sexing the Nation*, reminds us that while the terms "state" and "nation" are often used interchangeably, their crucial differences must be understood in order to grasp the implications of gender in relation to each one. Mayer defines a state as "a sovereign political unit" with "tangible boundaries" that "abides by international law and is recognized by the international community" (2). However, while it "may have tangible characteristics" and "is always self-defined, a nation is not tangible" (2). Rather, the nation is in Anderson's famous formulation an "imagined community," and Mayer cites those who refer to the nation as a "soul, a spiritual principle," something "its members believe must be maintained at all times and at all costs" (2). This intense personal investment in the idea of the nation and the "exclusive empowerment of those who share a sense of belonging" (1) to this constructed community is what connects nation to ego, in Mayer's view, and leads to her claim that this national ego is bound up with both male and female egos. Nevertheless, Mayer sees the nation as "the property of men," and argues that "nationalism becomes the language through which sexual control and repression (specifically, but not exclusively, of women and homosexuals) is justified, and masculine prowess is expressed and exercised" (1).

Mayer's suspicion of nationalism is in keeping with the critical views of nationalism expressed by many feminist scholars. This position is itself subject to critique by scholars such as Vanaja Dhruvarajan and Jill Vickers, who argue in their book *Gender, Race, and Nation: A Global Perspective* that relations between feminism and nationalism are complicated and mutable, and who point out that women have often gained legal and political rights "*because* they participated in nation building and national liberation movements" (247). In the chapter "Feminism and Nationalism," Vickers points to Quebec francophone feminists who have "constructed their identities as feminists within the framework of Quebec nationalism" (248). She observes that while many English-Canadian feminists decry the nationalist movements of Quebec and First Nations women as distractions from, or dilutions of, what feminism "should" be, it was in fact the support English-Canadian women gave to the nationalist "Canadianization" effort during the period 1890–1918 that led to their being given the vote, something denied to other women in Canada at the time (252). Vickers goes on to claim that mainstream feminists who are members of the dominant culture are the ones most likely to criticize nationalism (253). She reminds us that "women's power to reproduce groups physically by bearing children, and to transmit collective identities across time by rearing them, has made nationalisms gendered, in that sex/gender is key to both the material and symbolic dimensions of nationalisms" (255). Nira Yuval-Davis makes similar points in her work *Gender and Nation*, writing of women as "symbolic border guards and as embodiments of the collectivity, while at the same time being its cultural reproducers" (23). They are the "bearers of collectivities," the "transmitters of their cultures." Vickers sums up the connections between her work and Yuval-Davis's by concluding "all of our experiences of gender occur within a national culture, and all manifestations of nation are gendered" (256).

Dhruvarajan and Vickers's discussion of marginalized women in Canadian society and Mayer's account of the imaginary ego identity of the nation combine to provide a political context for understanding the marginalization of screenworks made by women who are regarded as "outside" of the imagined nation—whose works are not Canadian enough because they focus too much on women, on aboriginality, or on sexual identities, as if these identities and concerns were not really Canadian. In a roundtable discussion featuring Canadian documentary filmmakers included in the collection *Women Filmmakers: Refocusing*, Loretta Todd recounts a concrete example of how institutions exclude those who are not really regarded as contributing to the work of affirming or sustaining the constructed entity of the nation. Working on a project for the History Channel, she received a memo telling her that she was "too Native" (Levitin, Plessis, and Raoul, 211). In contrast, it is hard to imagine filmmakers being told they are "too male," "too English," "too white," or "too straight" to be considered truly Canadian in the same way.

Theorists of women's cinema such as Geetha Ramanathan and Alison Butler challenge the "imagined community" of the nation by arguing instead for internationalist approaches to films made by women. Ramanathan's critical gaze is trained on film texts she defines as feminist in the sense that they are not made by men and not made by women who are not feminist. Butler, in a more intriguing move, advances the idea of women's cinema as a "minor" rather than an oppositional cinema. She adapts this idea from Gilles Deleuze and Felix Guattari's concept of a minor literature, "the literature of a minority or marginalised group, written, not in a minor language, but in a major one" (Butler, 19). The function of a minor cinema is to "conjure up" rather than to express a preexisting community, something that allows it to escape charges of essentialism in regard to the existence of a predefined "women's community." As Butler puts it, "The communities imagined by women's cinema are as many and varied as the films it comprises, and each is involved in its own historical moment" (21). Calling women's cinema minor in this sense, claims Butler, liberates it from the binaries—for example popular/elitist—that attach themselves to the idea of an oppositional or parallel cinema (21–22).

Butler's central claim is that "women's cinema is not 'at home' in any of the host cinematic or national discourses it inhabits, but that it is always an inflected mode, incorporating, re-working and contesting the conventions of established traditions" (22). Although the present volume does not share Butler's focus on international woman's cinema, her words capture our sense of the essays assembled here as attentive not only to the specific conditions of filmmaking in Canada that have shaped the cultural agency of the women discussed in these pages but also to the work in its expression of and challenge to the nationalisms within which it has been produced. As Christopher Gittings and others have stressed, gender interrupts Canadian cinema's understanding of itself by introducing difference—difference that works critically and productively in relation to regional practices, institutional sites of production, sexuality, racialized identities, and the reality of emergent and suppressed counter-nationalisms. There is more to this interruption, though, than merely the conceptual diffusion of the idea of gender among and through a host of terms. This collection of essays is politically driven by an interest in the cultural agency of Canadian women directors, and the ways in which what Gittings calls the "cultural co-ordinates used to narrate the nation" (7)—territory, state, language—enable, thwart, and otherwise affect that agency. We have sought contributions that address the possibilities provided by the imagined Canadian community for women's film authorship, influenced in this task by Sean Burke's words that "Authorship *is the principle of specificity in the world of texts*," and that "the retracing of the work to its author is a working back to historical, cultural and political embeddedness" (202).

No collection such as this can be complete or comprehensive. The best one can do is establish workable boundaries around a topic that make sense for the project; the worst one can do is maintain that these boundaries are the best ones imaginable, or that they couldn't have been otherwise. We decided to include essays on a range of filmmakers from across the country, some of them well known (though given new treatment here) and some not so well known. Similarly, we sought both established scholars who have done previous and important work on women's cinema and Canadian cinema, and newer scholars whose essays contribute to an ongoing exploration of Canadian women's filmmaking practices in the light of their own understanding of what authorship in a national context could mean. We see this volume as transitional, as providing a sense of current tensions and directions at play, and we realize that as theory and practice shift, as definitions of screenwork continue to change, so will definitions of authorship, of national cinema, and of film itself.

The issues raised by feminist and poststructuralist critics in their engagement with authorship, nationality, and gender have lead us to create three groupings of essays. The first, "Feminist/feminine Binaries and the Body Politic," contains four essays on the work of women filmmakers from various regions of Canada who critique, unpack, and otherwise explore the connections between the feminine and the feminist in specific cultural contexts. The second grouping is titled "Queer Nation and Popular Culture" and concentrates on the work of filmmakers for whom the representation of sexuality is subversive of conventional narrative and nationhood. The third grouping, "Transiting Nationality and the Battlefields of Otherness," discusses the films of Aboriginal and minority women filmmakers and how these films create new narratives for the female gaze.

Feminist/feminine Binaries and the Body Politic

Andrew Burke's study of former Torontonian and now Haligonian filmmaker Andrea Dorfman introduces the subject of feminist/feminine binaries that constitutes the first section of this book. He does so in a way that unites these ideologically framed oppositional terms into a mutually reinforcing preoccupation with everyday life, which he links to the filmmaker's demand that "we recognize the beauty and creativity latent in ordinary things" (25) as expressed by her idiosyncratic female characters. According to Burke, Dorfman creates female characters with a comic touch, emphasizing their quirky, marginalized natures as they search for emotional fulfillment in a patriarchal environment. Their resistance to conformity becomes an affirmation of female subjectivity and agency. For example, the conventional search for a boyfriend undertaken by the character Phoebe in Dorfman's *Love That Boy* (2003) ends up with Phoebe's correcting and lecturing the candidate. The result is a failed search and a re-channelling of desire into a non-competitive relationship with a fourteen-year-old boy who is her neighbour. The problematic dynamic of this relationship is sensitively explored as an example of women's "counter-cinema," in which female agency is valorized. Burke's discussion of Dorfman emphasizes her magic-realist style, which serves as an engaging aesthetic counterpart to her ideological articulation of the psychological and social complexities that women face in the search for relationships.

The topic of feminine/feminist binaries is continued in Lee Parpart's study of the feminist ambiguities in the film adaptations of Lynne Stopkewich. Best known for her sympathetic portrayal of a necrophiliac in the ground-breaking 1996 film *Kissed*, Stopkewich is portrayed by Parpart as having a complex relationship to feminism through her use of "a carefully cultivated sense of ambiguity around cultural norms and definitions of femininity" (44). Parpart concludes that Stopkewich's work is feminist in its adaptation of "feminist, female-authored, and/or female-centred literary texts" (44). Parpart's main examples are *Kissed*, which Stopkewich adapted from a short story by Canadian writer Barbara Gowdy, and *Suspicious River*, which she adapted from the American novel by Laura Kasischke, both of which portray female sexual nonconformity. Parpart argues that the fidelity of a film to its source is an important way of understanding the ideological transformations that occur between authorship in one medium and authorship in another. Parpart considers *Kissed* "lyrical" and "soothing" (46) in its approach to female sexual deviance, while *Suspicious River* is more "brutal and disturbing" (46). In short, the former may be considered more "feminine" and the latter more "feminist." Even so, Parpart considers *Suspicious River* to be filled with the compromises associated with cinema as a public medium. She attributes this state of affairs to an "industry that actively discourages feminist narratives" (51). Themes of feminine masochism and abjection at the core of *Suspicious River* are also extremely challenging, which leads Parpart to conclude that Stopkewich's work engages the universe of "gendered political positions" (59) through her willingness to address the reader of her films as female. Nevertheless her films have had "to straddle the line between artistic and commercial aims" (59), which means compromise. As a result, fidelity to rendering female subjectivity in complex and contradictory ways has faced and continues to face boundaries/barriers not readily overcome.

The politics that circumscribe the feminist/feminine binary are explicitly addressed in Kathleen Cummins's discussion of the work of Anne Wheeler, which has attracted limited critical attention despite a near forty-year career as a filmmaker, first in documentaries and then in feature films. As a director associated with commercial genre product rather than auteurism, Wheeler has nonetheless been consistently associated with feminism among the few critics who have carefully examined her work. In spite of these occasional and sporadic studies, Cummins considers Wheeler's work devalued by cultural critics, who fail to see the substantive fusion of feminist aesthetics and mainstream narrative in her genre films.

Cummins argues that Wheeler's maternal figures in films from *Loyalties* (1986) to *Bye Bye Blues* (1989) and *Better Than Chocolate* (1999) are figures of resistance, redefinition, and reinvention rather than simply reincarnations of the conventional Hollywood "good/bad" mother dichotomy. These mothers join their daughters in a mutual search for individualized identity. In the foregrounding of women that is central to her films, Wheeler also embraces the grandmother figure as a figure of accomplishment. Outside these generational characters of grandmother-mother-daughter, Wheeler explores the relationship of women to the workplace, eschewing any superwoman characterization in favour of articulating the tensions around identity faced by the working mother. She has done this both in television movies (*Other Women's Children*, 1993) and in television docudrama (*Betrayed*, 2003).

Cummins argues that Wheeler's work with mainstream melodrama and romantic comedy in feature films and her extensive work in television may have contributed to the perception that she is less personal in her work than other women filmmakers. This is unfortunate, she argues, because Wheeler's genre films are informed by issues of race, class, sexuality, age, and ethnicity. Cummins concludes that the feminism of Wheeler's work comes from protagonists who claim their own spaces in a more forceful way than is typically found in the genres with which she works.

While the feminist/feminine binary is first challenged, and then radically transformed, and finally recreated as a unified field of the female gaze in the work of Dorfman, Stopkewich, and Wheeler, the work of these filmmakers exists primarily in the arena of genre filmmaking, which creates challenges and barriers to subverting convention because of the commercial imperative under which they operate. The result is a degree of compromise that some may not care for. Compromise is not an issue in the final essay in this section, by Kay Armatage, who takes up the subject of the feminist/feminine in the avant-garde work of Joyce Wieland and moves it onto the more generalized plane of the political.

Armatage's discussion of Wieland's filmmaking shows the range of Wieland's interests from sexuality to Canadian politics to the environment and the range of her film work from avant-garde shorts in 8mm and 16mm to a dramatic feature in 35mm. Armatage provides a capsule description of Wieland's works from the 1960s and '70s as a background to an extensive scholarly analysis, including Wieland's relationship to the structural mode of avant-garde filmmaking of the period. Armatage shows that Wieland was a feminist who championed women's creativity as art rather than craft, a critical attentiveness that links Armatage's essay to Burke's. The focus on gender alone in Wieland's work could end up marginalizing it, so Armatage prefers to emphasize various national issues, such as labour strife, the representation of history, and self-reflexivity in cinema as examples of Wieland's contributions to other cultural knowledges. Using forms such as quilts, for example, Wieland engaged in a commentary on the political issues of her day in an unexpected fashion, informing traditionally regarded craft practices with political edge and resonance. In films such as *Patriotism II* (1964) and *Rat Life and Diet in North America* (1968), Wieland provided artistic allegories of political strife from a Canadian perspective. Likewise, *Reason over Passion* (1969) provided a vivid critical meditation on the Canadian landscape. By bringing the political to the feminine and the feminist to the political in Wieland's work, Armatage shows Wieland as a feminist artist who demythologized gender, nationality, and artistic representation.

Queer Nation and Popular Culture

While the previous section represents filmmaking that challenges essentialist views of auteurism and nationalism from a gendered perspective, the work explored in this section is more overtly subversive of conventional representational practices because of its attention to mediation and sexual orientation. The filmmakers in this section are cultural producers with distinct and often unconventional approaches to their material who contest established traditions with their own reworking of the art form to embrace issues of sexuality.

Jean Bruce's essay on Canadian New Queer Cinema deals with the interaction between a hegemonic popular culture and the artistic imagination that seeks to break out of its restrictive *in*-scriptions and *de*-scriptions. The essay deals with three independent video artists—Dara Gellman, Thirza Cuthand, and Dana Inkster—who produced short videos in 1999. Bruce shows how these artists appropriated highly conventional images and stories and then transformed them into edgy statements of queer sexuality. The result is a space for new stories that popular culture has been loath to articulate. Gellman's *alien kisses* uses the popular *Star Trek* television and film series as its appropriated form to focus on a scene from a 1995 episode with two "alien" women kissing. Through slow motion, image enhancement, and digitilization, the scene is transformed into a heightened statement of queer desire. The use of intertextual references is also fundamental to Thirza Cuthand's *Helpless Maiden Makes an "I" Statement*, which uses the image of the Evil Queen from Disney's *Snow White*. Dana Inkster's *Welcome to Africville* takes off from Shelagh Mackenzie's 1991 NFB short, *Remembering Africville*. Inkster uses documentary footage as a reminder of the demolition of the community and of the migration that resulted, which in turn serves as a metaphor for the sexuality of the women interviewed in the film. Bruce concludes that Canadian cultural ex-centricity is informed by queer representations, which allow us to reimagine the social and the political.

While Bruce deals with the idiosyncratic universe of the video artist, Agata Smoluch Del Sorbo writes on the cinema of Patricia Rozema, a well-known cultural figure. She too uses the rubric of gender and intertextuality as the basis of her analysis of Rozema as a feminist filmmaker, and she celebrates the contribution of Rozema's authorship to developing female subjectivity. Smoluch Del Sorbo sees Rozema's consistent "exploration of the female artist character" (128) as crucial to representing the female on screen. Rozema further explores female subjectivity through the use of "numerous aesthetic, cinematic, and literary intertexts in her films" (133), which disrupt and rearrange the narrative flow. In this she creates a dialogic text that is women-centred, with a focus on the female artist. Smoluch Del Sorbo develops this theme through an analysis of Rozema's four feature films, *I've Heard the Mermaids Singing*, *White Room*, *When Night Is Falling*, and *Mansfield Park*. According to Smoluch Del Sorbo, "Rozema creates brilliant and complex utopian worlds" in these films (136) that challenge convention and reinterpret lesbian desire. Hers is a reimagining of existing society and cultural forms that liberates female agency and sexuality from constricting traditions.

Florian Grandena's essay considers the work of Léa Pool, a Swiss immigrant who since the 1970s has been based in Montreal. A prolific filmmaker who has made nine feature films since the early 1980s, Pool deals with themes of exile, fluid gender and sexual identities, lesbian eroticism, and, like Rozema, the importance of art. Initially focused on female protagonists and their sense of homelessness in Montreal, Pool's practice has changed, leading her to make three films set outside Montreal, both in other countries and in other parts of Canada. She also shifted her focus from female characters and lesbian relations to male protagonists and problematic gay, bisexual, and heterosexual relationships. Each of these phases has involved a cinematic trilogy. The most recent phase also involves three films—*Emporte-moi* (1999), *Lost and Delirious* (2001), and *The Blue Butterfly* (2004), whose subject matter ranges from teenage girls to a sick child. In each of these coming-of-age stories there is a confrontation with the adult world.

Grandena's emphasis is on the continuity and discontinuities in Pool's gay-themed films, in particular love triangles. He argues that "Pool aims at highlighting the universality of human desires" (142) so as to transcend identity categories. He explores how Pool portrays characters with same-sex desires in such a way as to remove them from issues of sexual orientation. Grandena notes that as the auteur of her first feature—the sixty-two-minute *Strass Café*—Pool was able to create a defamiliarized universal urban space. Her first love triangle appeared in *La Femme de l'hôtel*, in which three women, including a film director, interact during the course of a film shoot. Each character represents a different aspect of the human soul. As in Rozema's *Mermaids*, the female characters are portrayed "as independent individuals free from power relations with men" (144). Nevertheless, sexuality is presented as a confused and problematic issue. In *Anne Trister* the two women who are attracted to each other are both in stable heterosexual relationships. Pool's masterpiece, *À corps perdu*, deals with a bisexual protagonist and a bisexual ménage à trois. Pool's work lies at the centre of Canadian queer cinema. Grandena believes that Pool's European/

francophone background contributes to her attempt to universalize desire rather than categorize it. He states that her take on identities is based on "fluidity and elusiveness" (155), and he questions whether this approach is sufficient to take into account "the specific experiences lived by certain communities and groups" (156) in relationship to the dominant society. Through Pool, Grandena also introduces the subject of the immigrant filmmaker and the cultural streams that inform Canadian cinematic practice through migration, topics addressed by some of the filmmakers written about in the next section of the book.

Transiting Nationality and the Battlefields of Otherness

The otherness represented by sexual diversity in the previous section is echoed by and overlaps with the otherness of Aboriginal and minority filmmakers, who, despite their differences in history and situation in relation to the nation-state, are sometimes regarded by non-Aboriginal and non-immigrant audiences as outside the realms of "Canadian" culture. With the growing importance and influence of minority immigrant populations to the Canadian demographic and the reassertion of First Nations into the national dialogue since 1970, these women filmmakers have reworked our sense of national consciousness through post-colonial critiques that rewrite history and redefine territory, nation, culture, and society. The assertion of formerly silenced voices and their confrontational discourses have undermined the old metanarratives and opened up a multiplicity of newly validated perspectives.

Anthony Adah's discussion of Aboriginal women documentarists is a clear example of this development. He sees their films as a challenge to the "distorted representations of their identity in mainstream cinema and media" (164). The documentarists that Adah discusses include Alanis Obomsawin (*Kanehsatake: 270 Years of Resistance*, 1994), whom he sees as incorporating Aboriginal oral narrative techniques in her films; Christine Welsh (*Keepers of the Fire*, 1994), whom he credits with expanding the Native concept of "warrior" to include women; and Loretta Todd (*Forgotten Warriors*, 1997), who presents the forgotten stories of First Nations' WW II veterans.

Adah argues that the "textual body" of these films is pregnant with resisting discourses about Aboriginal identity, which makes them fundamental texts of post-colonialism. As visualized voices of the Other in Canadian cinema, these films represent a third wave of filmmaking that often draws on indigenous North American cultural traditions for inspiration and expression. The "Native Body" of these films is a politically engaged body, whose redefinition of itself and Canadian history contributes significantly to the multicultural discourse that dominates contemporary Canadian cultural criticism. The Native representation in these films challenges not only earlier stereotypes and replaces them with alternative images but also emphasizes the importance of genre hybridity as a cornerstone of Aboriginality in this cinema. Using Gorzian corporeal feminism and Bakhtinian carnavalization as critical tools, Adah helps us understand the powerful relationship between the Aboriginal body and contemporary politics that, when it is rewritten, becomes a mode of subversion that disrupts and liberates viewers from the colonizing representations of history.

While transnationality is a valid concept for extraterritorial filmmaking and cultural influences, another concept, or concepts, is required for filmmakers like African Canadian Sylvia Hamilton. As a documentary filmmaker that belongs to a 300-year heritage in Canada she has addressed the "institutionalized silence" about African Canadian history. Shana McGuire and Darrell Varga claim that Hamilton's work offers "an alternative model for film authorship" and that it challenges the traditional concept of Canadian nationality. The project of inclusiveness that Hamilton has directed is one that recognizes Canadian diversity from the country's colonization and the racialization that it has spawned in historical narrative. The creation of a counter-hegemonic memory lies at the core of her filmmaking. Another example of transnationality is Mina Shum, who came to Vancouver from Hong Kong at the age of one.

Brenda Austin-Smith notes that Mina Shum prefers to be known as "an independent filmmaker" rather than one with a national identity, and thereby raises the issue of how critics deal with the identities that emanate from authorship, nationality, and gender. Shum's films depict "discontented young women who want to leave wherever they are for somewhere or something else" (199), a state of consciousness associated with transnationality. Using a comedic approach in her three feature films (*Double Happiness*, 1994; *Drive, She Said*, 1997; and *Long Life, Happiness and Prosperity*, 2002), Shum has used the device of the Chinese Canadian family and intergenerational conflict to good advantage as she places her characters squarely in the liminal space that is multicultural Canada. In her world of adaptive struggle, ethnicities become "kitschy rather than exotic" (208), which suggests that transnationality produces novel syntheses, whose hybridity is accessible to other cultures. Shum's depiction of familial negotiations for her protagonists ensures a counter-narrative of frustration, expectation, and problematic liberation. The imagined community of Shum's films seems very Chinese to non-Chinese Canadians because of her near total use of Chinese characters and regular use of Cantonese and Mandarin speech, but to non-Canadian Chinese it must seem very Canadian. The zone of hybridity she has created is rooted in two worlds that have not had a comfortable history with each other. Shum's cinematic conflicts exist in a de-territorialized space in which her protagonists move with a mixture of ethereality and groundedness.

For the binational filmmaker transiting two nationalities and two cultural norms, the appeal of comedy as a genre is strong, if only because it lessens the inherent tension in the situation. In comedy the confrontation with gender roles, familial and community pressures, and traditional values can be ameliorated through humorous characterization and dialogue. Shum animates her work with irony and affection while pointing out how the domestic universe informed by patriarchal authoritarianism is a place of disorienting claustrophobia for women, a place of phobia and dystopia. Drawing on post-colonial theorists like Homi Bhabha and Hamid Naifcy, Austin-Smith confirms both the Asian Canadianness of Shum's films, their feminism, and their contribution to transnational filmmaking in Canada.

The other notable transnational woman filmmaker in Canada is Deepa Mehta, who emigrated from India in the 1970s, when she was in her twenties. Christina Stojanova's analysis of Mehta's transnationality covers both her "Canadian" and her "Indian" films, the former linked to comedy and the latter to tragedy and melodrama. Stojanova raises the political dimension of transnational films and how they are often critiqued in the "old country" as being inaccurate and falsifying portraits because they emphasize issues and problems that some prefer hidden. As a result, Mehta's trilogy *Fire*, *Earth*, and *Water* has been the object of vituperative attack. Because she was raised in an Indian context and educated in Canada as a filmmaker, Mehta is as conscious as Shum is of the conflict between the two worlds and the necessity of a post-colonial narrative that challenges traditions. Stojanova is quick to point out how Indocentric are Mehta's most powerful films and how they made her a lightning rod in the "world of politically charged transnational cinema." Nevertheless, her Canadian films from *Sam and Me* (1991) to *Bollywood/Hollywood* (2002) do play a role in her transnationality because they clearly echo the immigrant preoccupation with generational conflict, comic ethnic family drama, and the tension between traditionalism and modernism, which also characterize the films of Shum.

Stojanova emphasizes the blending of historical and metaphorical time and space in Mehta's Indian films, in which oppressed women emerge as "rational and moral agents" who struggle for self-affirmation. But Mehta's feminism is matched by her grounding in Indian literary classics such as *The Broken Nest*, by Tagore, which was made into the film *Charulata* (1964), by Satyajit Ray, and which inspired *Fire*. In turn, *Earth* was based on a well-known Indian memoir, *Cracking India*. Stojanova also points out the visual symbolism found in *Water*, which parallels that found in the work of Ray. All of which suggests that the transnational filmmaker possesses a shifting blend of cultural influences and attitudes, whose overall trajectory is open-ended.

A very important aspect of nationality in Canadian culture is Quebec and how the work of its women filmmakers informs Quebec's contemporary identity. In "Les Québécoises," Jerry White discusses the recent work of a number of these accomplished directors, who have redefined Quebec nationality through their art, both by challenging its tropes and accepting its post-colonial evolution. White fits the filmmakers into three broad categories. Catherine Martin and Lucie Lambert are avant-garde stylists in both the documentary and the narrative film. Lambert's work captures the real lives of women in a maritime landscape, while Martin expresses an artist's "economy of form" in her storytelling. Louise Archambault and Manon Briand are part of the "art cinema" culture and their works explore the new métissage of Quebec society and its effects on women. They acknowledge the shifts in Quebec's culture as the society becomes more diverse and postmodern in its orientation. The final category is that of pop filmmaking, which is represented by the work of Denise Filiatrault, who has been able to capture "Quebec's very vibrant popular cinema and television" in her work. Although White does not cover every major figure working in the medium he does bring us up-to-date on the achievements of a new generation of women filmmakers and their concerns around Quebec nationality, the role of women, and the contested identities informing post–Quiet Revolution Quebec nationalism. Their work represents the intersection of gender and nationality in interesting and provocative ways.

Conclusion

The transnational filmmaker, the queer filmmaker, the feminist filmmaker, the documentarist, and the video artist are just a sampling of the diverse identities of Canadian women filmmakers working in both commercial and art cinema today. The temptation to label that comes with critical space can be avoided when the full of range of each filmmaker's cinematic accomplishment is explored using a variety of theories that emphasize conceptual multiplicity. We consider this collection of essays such a statement. In this way the authorship, nationality, and gender issues these filmmakers represent become embedded in the historical, the cultural, and the political.

It is important to emphasize that Canadian women filmmakers as cultural producers are not bound by the categories of film theory. Instead, they provide their imagined communities with oppositional and subversive narratives that continue to reference difference and similarity as a continuous phenomenon. The cultural agency of Canadian women directors is not in dispute, but the dimensions of that agency continue to inspire debate.

Works Cited

Anderson, Benedict. *Imagined Communities: Reflections on the Origin and Spread of Nationalism*. London: Verso, 1991.

Armatage, Kay, Kass Banning, Brenda Longfellow, and Janine Marchessault, eds. *Gendering the Nation: Canadian Women's Cinema*. Toronto: U of Toronto P, 1999.

Buddle, Kathleen. "Alterity, Activism, and the Articulation of Gendered Cinemascapes in Canadian Indian Country." *Film, History and Cultural Citizenship: Sites of Production*. Ed. Tina Mai Chen and David S. Churchill. New York: Routledge, 2007. 159–77.

Burgess, Diane. "Leaving Gender Aside: The Legacy of Studio D?" Levitin, Plessis, and Raoul 418–33.

Burke, Sean. *The Death and Return of the Author: Criticism and Subjectivity in Barthes, Foucault and Derrida*. Edinburgh: Edinburgh UP, 1998.

Butler, Alison. *Women's Cinema: The Contested Screen*. London: Wallflower Press, 2002.

Caughie, John. *Theories of Authorship*. London: Routledge/ BFI, 1981.

Cook, Pam, and Claire Johnston. "The Place of Woman in the Cinema of Raoul Walsh." *Feminism and Film Theory*. Ed. Constance Penley. New York: Routledge, 1988. 25–35.

Dhruvarajan, Vanaja, and Jill Vickers. *Gender, Race, and Nation: A Global Perspective*. Toronto: U of Toronto P, 2002.

Gittings, Christopher E. *Canadian National Cinema: Ideology, Difference, and Representation*. London: Routledge, 2002.

Grant, Catherine. "Secret Agents: Feminist Theories of Women's Film Authorship." *Feminist Theory* 2.1 (2001): 113–30.

Johnston, Claire. "Dorothy Arzner: Critical Strategies." Penley 36–45.

Levitin, Jacqueline, Judith Plessis, and Valerie Raoul, eds. *Women Filmmakers: Refocusing*. Vancouver: U of British Columbia P, 2003.

Loiselle, André, and Tom McSorley, eds. *Self-Portraits: The Cinemas of Canada since Telefilm*. Ottawa: Canadian Film Institute, 2006.

"Making Documentary Films: Panel Discussion with Nicole Giguere, Brenda Longfellow, Loretta Todd, and Aerlyn Weissman." Levitin, Plessis, and Raoul 208–17.

Martin, Angela. "Refocusing Authorship in Women's Filmmaking." Levitin, Plessis, and Raoul 29–37.

Martin-Marquez, Susan. *Feminist Discourse and Spanish Cinema: Sight Unseen*. New York: Oxford UP, 1999.

Mayer, Tamar. *Gender Ironies of Nationalism: Sexing the Nation*. London: Routledge, 2000.

Penley, Constance, ed. *Feminism and Film Theory*. New York: Routledge, 1988.

Ramanathan, Geetha. *Feminist Auteurs: Reading Women's Films*. London: Wallflower Press, 2006.

Ramsay, Christine. "Made in Saskatchewan!" Loiselle and McSorley 203–35.

Sarris, Andrew. "Notes on the Auteur Theory in 1962." *Film Theory and Criticism*. Ed. Leo Braudy and Marshall Cohen. New York: Oxford UP, 2004. 561–64.

Vérroneau, Pierre. "Genres and Variations: The Audience of Quebec Cinema." Loiselle and McSorley 93–127.

Watts, Carol. "Releasing Possibility into Form: Cultural Choice and the Woman Writer." *New Feminist Discourses*. Ed. I. Armstrong. London: Routledge, 1992. 83–102.

Yuval-Davis, Nira. *Gender and Nation*. London: Sage, 1997.

2
Feminist/Feminine Binaries and the Body Politic

The Art of Craft:
The Films of Andrea Dorfman
Andrew Burke

In *There's a Flower in My Pedal* (2004), director Andrea Dorfman contemplates the ways in which life's mishaps and lost opportunities serve to make us stronger. Over a lazy, looping, mid-tempo hip-hop beat, Dorfman presents a series of observations about the disappointments—and delights—of everyday life. Pleasures derive from the incidental and overlooked as much as from the monumental and marked. On its surface, this short film is a straightforward paean to how the simple joys of living, such as riding a bicycle or eating asparagus, triumph over moments of despair and melancholic regret. But it is also a kind of manifesto that demands we recognize the beauty and creativity latent in ordinary things and activities. As Dorfman declares in the laid-back, white-girl rap that accompanies the film's blend of animated and live action sequences, "I try to put knitting in every film I make / So if you are thinking you'll get bored / You can take a bathroom break / But if you want to be an artist and make something really cool / I'd be more than happy to teach you how to knit and purl."

This generous offer bears within it the key to understanding Dorfman's larger body of work. Many of her films do indeed feature characters who knit, but the films are themselves the products of a craft aesthetic. They are intimate and feel handcrafted, not so much in the sense of being private, solitary creations (filmmaking is, after all, a collaborative effort, and each of Dorfman's films ends with a long list of friends to be thanked) but in the sense of bearing the idiosyncrasies and individuality of artisanal labour. Through two features, *Parsley Days* (2000) and *Love That Boy* (2003), and several short films, Dorfman has established a distinctive visual style and has also staked out her own unique narrative, thematic, and cinematic terrain. Her films, saturated with colour, distinguished by their light comic touch, and filled with the drama of youthful romance, are an awkward fit in a Canadian film canon that has long privileged darkness, male angst, and transgression. Their quiet optimism, however, shouldn't lead to their dismissal as insubstantial or insignificant. On the contrary, Dorfman addresses fundamental questions about happiness and desire in ways that recognize both the triumphs and the tragedies of the everyday.

Although she hails from Toronto, Dorfman through her film work to date is inextricably tied to the Maritime provinces, especially Nova Scotia.[1] Both *Parsley Days* and *Love That Boy* were shot in Halifax. Even though the city is not named in either film, both traverse an urban landscape instantly recognizable as Haligonian to those familiar with the city. As much as Dorfman exploits Halifax's distinctive vernacular architecture to ground her characters in the everyday lived space of the Maritime city, she also captures the bohemian feel of the place, with her young characters orbiting around the city's university, music, and arts scenes. This is perhaps not surprising, given Dorfman's own experience as a student at the prestigious Nova Scotia College of Art and Design (NSCAD). Dorfman graduated from NSCAD in 1994 and remained in Halifax to make short experimental films and work as an assistant on both local independent productions and Hollywood features shooting in Nova Scotia. She became involved with the Atlantic Filmmaker's Co-operative, an organization which, since 1974, has supported independent filmmaking in Atlantic Canada and such filmmakers as William MacGillivray, Lulu Keating, and Thom Fitzgerald. With films such as *Outside Inside Out* (1996), *Letter to Helen* (1997), and *I Love You This Much* (1997), Dorfman gained experience in almost every aspect of the filmmaking process, from scripting to shooting, directing to editing. These films, each about five minutes in length and shot on Super 8 and 16mm, served as venues for her experimentation with colour, sound, grain, and texture.

Swerve (1998) stands as Dorfman's first major film. Shot in 16mm and nearly three times as long as the experimental works that immediately preceded it, *Swerve* marked the emergence of Dorfman on the festival circuit and as a young Canadian filmmaker to watch. The film tells the story of three friends on a road trip—Louise (Shannon Cunningham), Karen (Ingrid Doucet), and Jess (Marcia Connolly). Over the course of two days, a deep rift develops between Jess and the other two as a relationship blossoms between Louise and Karen. Jess is the focal point of the narrative as the film charts her alienation from the other two. In the voice-over that opens the film, Jess observes, "It's easy to look back at a situation and wonder what went wrong. How things could have been different." That these words are spoken over a shot of Jess as she begins to knit a scarf that will grow at an almost magical pace over the course of the narrative, and will later be integral to the film's denouement, is crucial, as the scene establishes questions of fate and fortune as central to the film. *Swerve* is about the tricky entanglements of friendship, but is also about the ruthless and inexorable teleological drive of narrative patterns.

The title of this short derives from a moment early in the film when Louise swerves to avoid an animal that has run in front of their truck. After the truck screeches to a halt, all three friends look back and, seeing nothing in the road, assume the animal has survived and scurried off. Whether or not this is so, the sequence generates a deep sense of dread and anxiety. Something will go wrong on this road trip, even if at this point it is unclear what it will be. Dorfman does, however, provide a visual hint of the form the catastrophe will take. Aligned on the dash of the truck are three apples, two red and one green. When the truck swerves, the green apple is tossed out of the open window and bounces along the side of the road, leaving the two red ones together on the dash. That Louise is reaching for an apple just as the animal runs in front of the truck is also significant. It is perhaps too hard to resist the idea that the apple Louise reaches for is a red one, symbolizing Karen. In doing so, Louise sets in motion a series of events that leads to Jess's exclusion from their friendship.

The image of the three women in the cab of the truck is one of female friendship and camaraderie. Louise disturbs this closeness when she suggests that someone join Mr. Brown, the dog that accompanies them on the trip, in the back of the truck. Dorfman uses a montage sequence to show that, even though each woman takes her turn in the back, it is Jess who eventually assumes the lion's share of the time alone. Banished with the dog from the warmth of the cab, she continues to knit her scarf, which grows by several feet and soon extends the length of the truck's bed, wending its way around her neck to the outstretched paws of Mr. Brown. There is something compulsive in Jess's actions here, as her knitting serves as a substitute for any recognition of the meaning and consequences of her exclusion. When night falls, Louise and Karen make out in the cab of the truck as Jess continues to knit. She witnesses their betrayal, which is cinematically framed by the back window of the truck, but persists in her knitting nevertheless. A fade-out takes the action to the following day, when Jess's alienation and separation from Louise and Karen is confirmed by her ongoing relegation to the back of the truck.

Swerve concludes with a sequence that capitalizes on the tension between the women Dorfman builds throughout the film. This tension is amplified by Dorfman's use of silence and ambient sound. In the scenes that document Jess's alienation, the women barely speak. Jess sits silently in the back of the truck while Louise and Karen conspire in whispers. Even when Jess asks Louise to stop, because she thinks the dog "has to pee," she conveys her request in writing. Indeed, Jess is silent through most of the film, often failing to respond even when asked questions directly. Her silence is ambiguous. It is unclear whether it is a result of paranoia or catatonia, resignation or the desire for revenge. As Louise and Karen debate telling Jess about the transformation of their relationship into a sexual one and worry about whether "she will be able to take it," Jess crawls along the side of the truck and places her head in front of one of the front tires. In doing so, she imagines herself the victim of this road trip, the substitute for the animal the women had earlier swerved to avoid.

But as soon as the film suggests this bleak and devastating denoue-ment, it retracts it in a jump-cut that shows Jess walking away from the back of the truck while the debate about whether to tell her what she already knows continues. As she disappears into the distance, the scarf she has knitted and which she has tied tautly around her neck begins to unravel, having caught on the tailgate of the truck. When Louise and Karen discover that Jess has disap-peared they follow the yarn, but to no avail. Jess has commandeered a bicycle (from exactly where the film does not specify) and, as she pedals away, her scarf unravels at a rapid pace.

There is a symbolic richness to this unravelling. In one sense, it is the friendship between the three women that has come undone. In her escape, Jess disentangles herself from romantic ties that now bind Louise and Karen. In another sense, it is Jess herself who is unravelling. The scarf is so closely associ-ated with her that it is tempting to read it as representative of her psychic state. She unravels as a result of her friends' treachery. In the opening voice-over, Jess warns, "Never knit a scarf as your first knitting project. Knit something interest-ing, like a sweater or sock or mittens or a hat. But if you knit a scarf, I'll guar-antee you'll never knit again." The scarf she has knitted now threatens, as she cycles away, either to unravel completely or to catch and strangle her. Either way, the warning that began the film, and which made the choice of a knitting proj-ect seem almost a matter of life or death, acquires in these final moments its full fatal force. Once again, however, the film steps back from catastrophe. It seems to offer as its final image the scarf unravelling as Jess cycles down the road. But in a post-credit epilogue, Jess reaches back over her head and snaps the yarn that binds her to the truck, the road trip, her friends, and their betrayal. Severing the yarn also marks the end of her psychic unravelling. As the film fades, Jess pedals freely out of the frame, unbound to her past and its complications.

I have spent a significant amount of time discussing *Swerve* because it anticipates many of the dominant themes and concerns of Dorfman's two features. The focus on female friendship returns in both *Parsley Days* and *Love That Boy*. As well, the way in which Jess sublimates her anger into knitting serves as a model for the various obsessions, compulsions, neuroses, or simple idiosyncrasies that characters exhibit in the later films, ranging from Kate's attachment to her lover's jeans in *Parsley Days* to Phoebe's compulsive list-making in *Love That Boy*. The forms that desire takes, the ways in which it is repressed, channelled, and finds encrypted expression, is a major focus in Dorfman's work, and *Swerve* marks the beginnings of a multi-film investigation of the operations of desire.

But *Swerve* also merits extensive consideration because it contains elements that have not yet been repeated in Dorfman's later work. *Parsley Days* and *Love That Boy* each have heterosexual couples at their centre, whereas *Swerve* is notable for its focus on lesbian desire. Jess's decision to cut the thread that binds her to her friends means that she foils the two most obvious stereotypes associated with thwarted or repressed same-sex desire: she is neither tragic nor psychopathic. Despite its affirmative postscript, the film is distinguished by its tense, even chilling, atmosphere, and draws on the generic features of the road movie to create a sense of possible catastrophe. There is genuine menace in *Swerve*, the threat that some form of violence, whether externalized or self-inflicted, might result from the tangled situation. In Dorfman's subsequent films, she turned away from the tension and unease with which *Swerve* was infused and moved into a more comedic vein. If *Parsley Days* and *Love That Boy* demonstrate a deft comic touch and exemplify the way in which certain psychological and social complexities can be represented only by way of humour, *Swerve* is evidence that Dorfman is capable of creating films that draw on different, and darker, cinematic styles and genres.

While *Swerve* points to different sorts of films Dorfman may yet make, she is primarily known for the quality of observation and attention to psychological and emotional detail embodied by both *Parsley Days* and *Love That Boy*. To say that these films are both quirkier ("quirky" is perhaps the adjective most frequently invoked in reviews of Dorfman's films) and more charming than *Swerve* is not to suggest that they do not merit the same kind of scrutiny or that they do not yield a different set of complexities and insights. Indeed, what makes both films so crucial within a Canadian film culture often defined by its desire for, and fascination with, transgression and despair is that they represent an effort to understand how the texture of everyday life is varied and intricate. The enthusiasms the characters display, even down to the expression of happiness or the recognition of beauty in things, are punctuated by troubles and trials, but both states are understood to be part of life and worthy of cinematic contemplation.

Parsley Days was shot in and around Halifax in the summer of 1999 and premiered at the Toronto International Film Festival in the fall of 2000. It received immediate critical acclaim and saw limited release in Canadian cinemas in the spring of 2001. The film tells the story of Kate (Megan Dunlop), who, while deciding that she must end her relationship with long-time boyfriend Ollie (Mike LeBlanc), discovers she is pregnant. Thwarting narrative expectations, *Parsley Days* does not chronicle Kate's deliberations on whether or not to have the baby; she is firm from the outset in her decision to have an abortion. Instead, the film follows her as she builds the courage to break the news to Ollie that she does not love him anymore. Although the pregnancy presents a major obstacle to her break with him, so do the perceptions of her friends and family. Those around Kate universally agree that she and Ollie make a perfect couple. Indeed, to others, they are a hybrid creature, "KateandOllie," whose separate identities have been subsumed in a shared one. *Parsley Days* documents Kate's desire to reclaim an individual identity of her own, and in so doing the film critiques the social stigma attached to being unattached.

When Kate learns that the earliest appointment available at the abortion clinic is three weeks away, she contacts her herbalist friend Chloe (Marcia Connolly), who provides her with bags upon bags of parsley. Parsley, she explains, is an emmenagogue and is capable of herbally inducing abortion. On Chloe's advice, Kate adopts a parsley regime, eating it straight, brewing it as tea, having it on toast, and bathing in a tub of it. If she wants it to work she must even, as Chloe explains, insert it "down there" each night before she sleeps. The irony of Kate's pregnancy is that Ollie is the "king of contraception." He works for a community program that not only distributes condoms but provides advice to those who seek alternate forms of birth control. The film subjects Ollie's comprehensive knowledge of the subject to gentle satire, but it also suggests a more pointed feminist critique of the ideologies governing the right to conceive and the responsibility for contraception. Because of Ollie's encyclopedic knowledge of the various methods of birth control, Kate assumes that she bears all the responsibility for her pregnancy. She feels she is the one who has messed up. Although this is later shown not to be the case—and that Ollie punctured a condom in the hope that Kate would become pregnant, thereby ensuring the continuation of their relationship—there is from the beginning something unsavoury about Ollie's supposed mastery of contraception. He seems the quintessence of the sensitive man, even meriting the designation of "male lesbian" from Chloe's acerbic girlfriend Pauline (Shannon Cunningham), but latent in this mastery is a desire to control and manipulate. Indeed, Kate feels trapped in the relationship at least in part because Ollie, to others, seems so perfect. He is a nurturing, caring man who, as Kate's sister comments, would make a great father. But to Kate, Ollie's compassion is suffocating, and she, in order to reclaim her individual identity, must risk being the monster who would break the boy's heart.

A particularly striking feature of *Parsley Days* is that it represents a contemporary Halifax and a modern Nova Scotia. Such a thing may seem a minor issue, but given the weight of history and the elisions and ideological mystifications that come with the sentimentalization of Nova Scotian history, it is not simply refreshing when a work resists the thrall of the past, it is a matter of some political import. In *The Quest of the Folk*, Ian McKay argues that anti-modernism has functioned as a powerful ideological force within Nova Scotian culture and politics throughout the twentieth century. McKay explains that anti-modernism in Nova Scotia took a particular form—the invention of the Folk—a concept that mythologizes rural poverty as a privileged state of innocence in order to justify and maintain social inequalities in the present:

> This local variant of antimodernism can be called Innocence. Innocence emerged in the period from 1920 to 1950 as a kind of mythomoteur, a set of fused and elaborated myths that provided Nova Scotians with an overall framework of meaning, a new way of imagining their community, a new core of a hegemonic liberal common sense. Innocence discerned the essence of the society. The province was essentially innocent of the complications and anxieties of twentieth-century modernity. Nova Scotia's heart, its true essence, resided in the primitive, the rustic, the unspoiled, the picturesque, the quaint, the unchanging: in all those things and traditions that seemed outside the rapid flow of change in the twentieth century. (30)

It would be hard to argue that contemporary feature film and television production in Nova Scotia is dominated by idealized representations of the past. After all, perhaps the most influential production to have come out of Nova Scotia in recent years is Mike Clattenberg's *Trailer Park Boys*, a television program (2000–8) and spinoff feature films (2006, 2009) that are set firmly in the present and confront directly, if in a broadly satirical form, pressing social and political issues. Nevertheless, it seems fair to claim that the role Nova Scotia plays in the Canadian cultural imaginary is largely that of a sanctuary, a place that retains some measure of its pre-industrial innocence. This image is, of course, as McKay explains, carefully produced and promoted by the Nova Scotia government to bolster the province's tourist industry ("Canada's Ocean Playground" is the tag line that appears on the province's licence plates), but it is also supported in some measure by film and television productions that, in one way or another, cater to the desire to imagine Nova Scotia as a place of rural innocence and idiosyncrasy. This is not to condemn films like *Margaret's Museum* (Mort Ransen, 1995) and *New Waterford Girl* (Allan Moyle, 1999) or television programs like *Pit Pony* (1997–2001), all of which to a degree sentimentalize rural poverty and provide images of the stoic, heroic folk. Rather, it is a matter of understanding how these films, even if they address important historical and political topics, contribute to the perpetuation of a conservative fantasy of the Nova Scotian experience.

Dorfman's films do not overcompensate by depicting a hypermodern Halifax indistinguishable from other cities but rather directly engage with how the past persists into the present and how old forms can be redeployed in a fashion that neither degrades nor sentimentalizes them.[2] Dorfman's commitment to craft—the determination to include knitting in every film she makes—connects her to the rethinking of the relationship between arts and crafts that has been a key issue in artistic and curatorial practice over the past forty years. Indeed, NSCAD in particular has been a key site of debates about the relationship between arts and crafts, not only in terms of the recent explosion in the market for folk art, which has been transformed into a veritable industry in Nova Scotia (and the pitfalls of which McKay details so persuasively in *The Quest of the Folk*) but also in terms of formulating an art school curriculum that teaches ceramics, weaving, and knitting alongside conceptual and digital art.[3] As such, Dorfman's commitment to knitting signals an open and elastic notion of what counts as creative. In *Parsley Days*, sure enough, a student in Kate's bicycle repair class knits a sweater for the bicycle the class gives her as a present. Such a gesture is both quirky and sweet, but it also signals a set of moral and aesthetic commitments fundamental to Dorfman's work: to craft, community, and creativity.[4]

Parsley Days culminates in Kate's confrontation with Ollie. Throughout the film, she plays psychological games with herself as a way to delay, but also to justify, telling Ollie that their relationship must end. She convinces herself and others that she has had an affair with the "slow student" in her bicycle repair class, though the two exchanged only a kiss; she antagonizes Ollie by forcing him to name the person he'd sleep with if she did not exist; finally, she plays a game in which the moment she will tell the truth to Ollie is perpetually deferred. In the meantime, Ollie has realized that Kate is pregnant and is overjoyed. He gathers all of her friends for a surprise birthday party in her honour, although due to his numeric dyslexia he gets the date wrong. The thought behind this sweet gesture seems to make Kate's task of confronting him all the more difficult. Nevertheless, Kate and Ollie retreat to the backyard and sit in their canoe on the grass. This image is a surreal and powerful one. It visually confirms that their relationship has run aground, but it is also a nostalgic reminder for them of the blissful early days of their relationship.

Ollie confesses to Kate that he had punctured a condom in the hope that she would become pregnant, because he could feel her slipping away. Ollie's betrayal barely registers—Kate's reaction is minimal—but it gives her the courage to tell him at last that she does not love him anymore. The scene is bittersweet and void of recrimination or accusation. Instead, Kate and Ollie lie together in the canoe, just as they had at the lake five years before. In a voice-over, Kate says, "When you think it might be the last time you hold a person you want to make sure you remember exactly how it feels." Such a melancholy sentiment drives home the significance of the film's title. These were Kate's parsley days in the sense that parsley seemed to be the solution to her predicament. But the title also plays on the idea of one's salad days. To have parsley days instead is to recognize that the most important moments of one's young life are those that are bittersweet. And exactly what Dorfman delivers in *Parsley Days* is a portrait of Kate at a transitional moment in her life, when the pleasures of the past confront the problems of the present and temporarily obscure the possibilities to come.

Love That Boy likewise has its bittersweet moments, but the film is more broadly comic than its predecessor. Much of this is down to its protagonist, Phoebe (Nadia Litz), an overachiever who, in the weeks before she is set to graduate from college, is determined to work through a list of things to do. Phoebe's drive and ambition has closed her off from meaningful relationships. Even her best friend, Robyn (Nikki Barnett), grows increasingly frustrated with Phoebe's relentless perfectionism. When Robyn accuses her of being incapable of finding a boyfriend, Phoebe simply adds this task to her list of things to accomplish before graduation. The film's plot revolves around Phoebe's efforts to do so, and she approaches the task with the same determination that she approaches the others on her list.

The list itself is a key component in the film. Handwritten and posted to the door of Phoebe's fridge, it is an indication of those things that an ambitious young person might think are essential to building character and widening cultural experience. Among Phoebe's goals are to "Correct posture," to "Learn basic Japanese, Arabic, or Inuktitut," the very Nova Scotian to "Play bagpipes," and to "Watch all movies considered 'French New Wave.'" Dorfman's treatment of Phoebe and her goals is gently satiric. For instance, Phoebe finds she does not have the time to watch all the films considered French New Wave, so she decides to fast-forward through each one. This short-cutting is indicative of Phoebe's approach to her catalogue of things to do. The experiences themselves are secondary to the pleasure and importance of crossing them off the list. As such, Phoebe misses the substance of each experience by completing it in such a mechanical manner. She approaches the task of getting a boyfriend in exactly the same fashion. At the library, she hunts for a guy who is her intellectual equal, on the understanding that this is more important than any actual attraction to him.

Phoebe's drive is explained in an early flashback sequence that shows her as a child. In a voice-over, she explains that she comes "from a long line of spectacular women: scientists, diplomats, entrepreneurs, artists, who all paid dearly for their intellect and talent." Her mother's ambition to become a geneticist was "thwarted when she suffered a nervous breakdown while doing her Ph.D." During this sequence, the energetic young Phoebe tries desperately to get her mother's attention, showing her all the things she is able to do, from composing music to naming all the world capitals to programming a computer. The disjunction between the world and Phoebe's perception of it is cruelly depicted here. Phoebe, in her retrospective voice-over, comments that "she has fond memories of the times" she and her mother "spent in the garden" during her mother's convalescence. But the images tell a different story. Dorfman shows that while the young Phoebe proudly showcases her accomplishments, her mother lies medicated, irritated by her daughter's precocity.

Phoebe's impulse to glorify her mother, to remember her as "a great role model," underlines the tragic dimension to her neurotic habits. She is an overachiever not because she has learned from her mother that "greatness is only born out of hard work" but because she overcompensates for her mother's failures. As such, Phoebe's compulsive list-making is not simply a humorous foible but rather an indication of her suffering. Likewise, her incapacity to feel and to form meaningful relationships also seems born of the same childhood trauma. *Love That Boy* dramatizes Phoebe's confrontation with her own feelings and desires. An unexpected relationship loosens the grip that relentless ambition has upon her and allows her to feel for the very first time.

In its representation of precocity and the consequences of child-hood trauma, *Love That Boy* is oddly reminiscent of Wes Anderson's *Rushmore* (1998), which likewise features an overachieving protagonist, Max Fischer (Jason Schwartzman), whose ambition derives in part from the loss of his mother. Both Anderson and Dorfman are unafraid of representing intelligent and articulate characters onscreen and their films are set apart by their restless invention. As Richard Kelly argues, Max is "a compendium of prodigious tendencies" (54–55), and *Rushmore* draws its "breakneck energy" from its protagonist's surplus of enthusiasm and élan. The same might be said of *Love That Boy*. Phoebe's neurotic energy is amply represented onscreen. Dorfman, along with co-writer Jennifer Deyell, uses Phoebe's to-do list to structure the narrative. The film follows her as she forages for wild mushrooms and attends kayaking class, but it also sneaks into the nooks and crannies of the story evidence that other ambitions, such as learning the names of the constellations and writing and illustrating a children's book, have been achieved. Phoebe's excess energy is also represented visually. *Love That Boy* is filled with colour. On one hand, this represents Phoebe's unrelenting optimism and zeal. On the other, it expresses the emotions she has buried inside. Phoebe's perfect suburban house is awash with colour, and this colour symbolizes the extent to which she has sublimated her desires and channeled her energies into her to-do list.

This striking palette not only represents Phoebe's repressed emotions but also indicates a degree of eccentricity or "quirkiness," both on the part of the character and of the film as a whole. Reviews of Dorfman's films have long used "quirky" as critical shorthand to express the degree to which they are out of step with mainstream film culture. Indeed, Cameron Bailey, in his review of *Parsley Days*, writes that "'Quirky' is likely the word that Dorfman most hates, but the film trips along on a beam of deadpan idiosyncrasy, and there's no other word for it." But what does it mean for a character, a film, or even the entirety of a director's work to be described as quirky? The word itself suggests the peculiar and the idiosyncratic, but such synonyms do not exhaust its meaning. Quirkiness is associated with an excess of intelligence and creative energy that manifests itself in behaviour, aesthetic forms, or social practices that strike others as unusual or bizarre. But ultimately quirkiness does not seem to have a clear definition. It cannot be pinned down to identifiable characteristics but instead signifies a general, even ineffable, oddness. To describe something as quirky seems, on its surface, to diminish it: to be quirky is to be weird yet harmless. Nevertheless, the uncertainty that characterizes quirkiness is an indication that there may be something more deeply unsettling about it. Indeed, this seems to be the case with the twenty-something characters that populate Dorfman's films. Their quirkiness derives from an excess of creativity and invention in an age that is increasingly standardized, uniform, and guided solely by profit. Dorfman's bicycle-riding art school geeks are as out of step with contemporary capitalist culture as Dorfman's films themselves are from mainstream Hollywood production.

Yet it is not only marginality that makes Dorfman's characters quirky. What makes them quirky is that they persist in their creativity, in making their arts and crafts and in attending to the simple pleasures of their lives in the face of their marginalization. Their peripheral status within society makes their peculiarity both cute and amusing (and, to a certain extent, seems to infantilize them), but their quirkiness, more distressingly, speaks to the seeming exhaustion of options within late capitalist culture for creativity and inventiveness. With quirkiness, there is frequently a retreat to, and remobilization of, older forms and practices in order to find outlets for the pent-up creative energy that gives it its charge. The return to craft is the most obvious example in Dorfman's work, but bicycle-riding or herbalism might serve as others. In *Love That Boy*, Phoebe's lovingly designed and decorated '50s-style suburban house suggests, as do her hand-knit sweaters, that a kind of originality and creativity exist in the compilation and collection of things from the past. Fredric Jameson has argued that nostalgia can be understood as one of the primary symptoms of postmodernism and, as such, constitutes a negative formation that potentially blocks positive political and critical engagement with the present (*Postmodernism*, 19–21). Nevertheless, he also suggests that nostalgia retains some glimmer of political viability, and cites the work of Walter Benjamin as an example of a politically progressive nostalgia that cannot be reduced to a listless fascination with the past (*Marxism*, 82). As such, we can understand nostalgia not to be a purely reactionary formation but rather a more complex process, as it draws on the past in an effort to imagine and construct an alternative to the present. A retro style ironically indicates both the impossibility of originality in the contemporary era and the new forms of originality that living in a postmodern society generates. Quirkiness, as such, seems very much a contemporary phenomenon, or at least one that has particular resonance in a moment defined by the homogeneity and uniformity that contemporary capitalism produces and demands. While the quirkiness of Dorfman's characters, and indeed the quirkiness of Dorfman's films more generally, may seem a retreat from contemporary culture, it actually constitutes a political engagement with it. In an era when direct opposition to capitalism has proved frustratingly ineffectual, the return to craft constitutes a political choice: to be quirky is to refuse the benefits and privileges of conformity.

Perhaps the best way to understand the political dimension of quirkiness is to recognize its conceptual proximity to cuteness. Sianne Ngai argues that cuteness constitutes a kind of resistance to the demands of contemporary capitalism even as it seems part and parcel of the processes of commodification. In reference to the work of contemporary Japanese artist Takeshi Murakami, Ngai writes, "it is possible for cute objects to be *helpless and aggressive at the same time*" (823). Quirkiness, I would suggest, is similarly ambivalent. The quirky is subordinate to the normal but generates uneasiness in the way it is slightly askew in relation to normality. Although Ngai never concretely makes the link between cuteness and quirkiness, her analysis of how the unsettling and disconcerting dimensions of cuteness and cute objects often result in their critical dismissal or a kind of agitated antagonism toward them seems to me to connect with Dorfman's films and their critical reception. Quirkiness is offered up as a description of them with a certain level of critical sheepishness and anxiety. A significant part of this has to do with gender. While quirkiness is not exclusively gendered female, it nevertheless seems very much socially and culturally associated with awkward, adolescent femininity, even when women beyond adolescence perform it. And to invoke a language of performance and performativity is to recognize the way in which quirkiness can be understood as part of a critique of gender and gender roles at the same time that it takes aim at the capitalist culture in which they are produced and reproduced. As such, Dorfman's films, as well as the quirky characters that populate them, not only challenge the banality and boringness of contemporary culture but expose the ways in which gendered performances are routinized and regulated within it. Furthermore, they invite a new understanding of the way in which a folk past might be reinvigorated through its redeployment. While McKay is certainly right in condemning the relentless commodification of the regional past in the manufacture of a folk culture in a Nova Scotia specifically designed for tourist consumption, the small-scale artisanal crafting of Dorfman's female characters in particular represents a return to a regional past, and the handmade aesthetic that defines it, that neither indulges in the uncritical sentimentalization of picturesque poverty nor accepts the gender inequalities that characterize the past.

Phoebe's nonconformity comes less from a conscious refusal of commodity culture than from a general disappointment with those around her. When Robyn returns home with white mushrooms for a stir-fry, Phoebe asks why she did not get wild mushrooms: "We can do better than that, can't we?" This rhetorical question is the basis of Phoebe's relations with the rest of the world. Everybody, to a greater or lesser degree, fails to live up to the high standards she sets. Eventually, Robyn dumps Phoebe as a roommate and as a friend. Phoebe asks, "What about our list?" Robyn's reply—"*Your* list"—drives home the degree to which Phoebe is isolated and alone. She has managed to alienate even her closest friend. This is another example of how Dorfman's work constitutes an ongoing examination of female friendship. While the majority of the film is dedicated to Phoebe's search for a boyfriend, her break with Robyn is deeply moving.[5]

Phoebe's search for a boyfriend is comic. She attempts to flirt with a variety of men, but in each case she cannot restrain herself from correcting and lecturing them. She targets those whom she identifies as suitable boyfriend material, but they ultimately all disappoint. She arranges a date with a student who is in International Development Studies, thinking that this might mean he has some interest in world affairs, but sadly discovers that he picked his major strategically, to get a job, and volunteers with an international development charity only to enhance his CV. When Phoebe tells him she plans to cook Laotian food for their date, he surreptitiously writes in his notebook that he should "locate Loatia." The date is doomed to failure, and Phoebe becomes the object of ridicule among the guy and his friends, who think she is crazy.

Phoebe seems undeterred by this setback, but Dorfman suggests her loneliness by showing her alone at kayaking class, without a "buddy" with whom to train. At this point a relationship develops between Phoebe and Frazer (Adrien Dixon), a fourteen-year-old boy who lives across the street from her. Dorfman depicts the development of their relationship in a deft and delicate manner. They progress from exchanging a few words while Frazer mows Phoebe's lawn to discussing her disappointments in love to being partners in kayaking class. Frazer teaches Phoebe to relax and enjoy herself. He encourages her to eat the white part of an Oreo cookie first, even though it is bad for her. His real accomplishment, however, comes when he pushes her to dance. Phoebe, of course, knows how to dance, probably having learned to do so as part of an earlier scheme of self-improvement, but as she tells Frazer, "I just don't like to." With the unthreatening Frazer, Phoebe is able to have a non-competitive relationship. In a montage sequence, Dorfman depicts the pleasure Phoebe derives from doing things for the sake of doing them rather than for the sake of crossing them off her list. Indeed, the surest sign that Phoebe has changed is that her list of things to do before graduation falls to her kitchen floor and gets trampled underfoot. Gone in this sequence is the steely glint of determination that hitherto defined Phoebe. Instead, her face shows pure enjoyment as it does when she and Frazer lie under the night sky, hold hands, and identify the constellations.

In the throes of enjoyment, Phoebe does not recognize that others might consider it inappropriate for her, a twenty-one-year-old woman, to be spending so much time with a fourteen-year-old boy. She does not realize, even when Frazer invites her over for dinner on an evening that his parents are away, that they have in effect become boyfriend and girlfriend. Phoebe is naive rather than malicious or exploitative. Her attraction to Frazer is sincere as his is to hers. Problems arise, however, when each of them is forced to acknowledge that they have a relationship. Spurred on by the pointed comments by a girl his own age, Frazer goes to a pharmacy to buy condoms for his date with Phoebe. Dorfman skilfully parallels this with the conversation between Phoebe and the recently returned Robyn. Upon her return, Robyn discovers that Phoebe is relaxed, happy, and no longer judgmental. Ironically, their roles shift when Robyn forces Phoebe to concede that "the kid across the street" is her boyfriend and casts judgment on Phoebe's naïveté, calling her "demented." Stung by Robyn's comments, Phoebe decides to let Frazer down gently. She attempts to do so during dinner, but cannot bring herself to hurt Frazer's feelings. When Frazer invites her into his room, Phoebe is confronted by the sports and music paraphernalia that so clearly identify it as the bedroom of a fourteen-year-old boy. Frazer attempts to kiss Phoebe, but she pushes him away and struggles to tell him they cannot be boyfriend and girlfriend. Dorfman shoots this scene with great emotional dexterity, drawing from her two actors precise shades of disappointment. Adrien Dixon, having played Frazer as sheepish throughout, captures the exact shade of desolation that comes with having a bold move rebuffed. Nadia Litz allows the camera to see the extent to which the moment shakes Phoebe. Her intrepid self-confidence disappears in an instant.

Frazer is predictably upset by this turn of events, but it is Phoebe who sinks into a deeper malaise. Drained of her previous enthusiasm, she cannot bear to leave the house. She tells Robyn, "All the colour has drained out of my life." But, as her friend tells her, this is normal, and, more than that, it is a sign that Phoebe has the capacity to feel. In intimate conversation with Robyn, Phoebe confesses that she is upset not about losing the award for most outstanding graduating student but because of Frazer. "Am I that much of a freak because I might have loved him?" she asks. Robyn's response is tender and caring, and signals the restoration of their friendship. Robyn encourages Phoebe to go to graduation, and Phoebe makes a game effort to enjoy herself by drinking at home beforehand with Robyn's rowdy friends. When they leave to go, they pass Frazer outside, who has decided to attend Phoebe's graduation. The film concludes with an embrace between Frazer and Phoebe that suggests that each has recognized both the impossibility and the reality of their love for each another. The ending strikes a melancholic note similar to that of *Parsley Days*. Both films represent the pleasures of love at the same time that they register the obstacles to it or the waning of it.

In 2005 Dorfman directed an hour-long documentary titled *Sluts* that continued her ongoing exploration of female sexuality and the social regulation and restriction of feminine desire. It was not Dorfman's first documentary. In 1999 she directed *Nine*, a half-hour documentary that won the Best Short Documentary award at Toronto's Hot Docs festival. *Nine* focuses on a year in the life of a nine-year-old girl who suffers from separation anxiety. Its attention to childhood neuroses connects it to *Love That Boy*, but it also anticipates *Sluts* in its interest in the psychological. In *Sluts*, Dorfman interviews several women who responded to a print ad she took out in newspapers across Canada seeking women who have been labelled sluts. These women range from teenage girls currently suffering through high school to elderly women who transgressed the gendered expectations of earlier eras. The documentary takes a fairly conventional form, blending interviews with experts and the testimonials of the interviewees. What distinguishes the film is the way that Dorfman connects the women who have been ostracized for their transgressions and yet retains a sense of the specificity of each case. While some of the women in the film have overcome the trauma of having been labelled a slut, and have a clear understanding of the social dynamics of misogyny and hate speech more generally, others, like Phoebe near the end of *Love That Boy*, have a more troubled relationship to their own "freakishness." Dorfman shows that difference, idiosyncrasy, and sexual expression are hazardous, especially for women, who run the risk of social exclusion and isolation if they stray from social norms. *Sluts* shares with Dorfman's fictional works an investigation of the dynamics of desire and the impact being different has on young women's perceptions of themselves and their possibilities in the larger world.

To conclude I want to return briefly to *There's a Flower in My Pedal*, since it represents a condensation of the formal features and thematic concerns of Dorfman's full-length films and has the air of a transitional work. This short film is contemplative in tone, as Dorfman meditates upon the hazards of living. Yet she concludes that, for all the dangers of the everyday, people are surprisingly resilient. This message is conveyed most charmingly in the image of a young girl holding a sign that says: "I was dropped and I'm okay." Such an image points at once to the seeming fragility of individuals (and Dorfman's films do contain characters who have been damaged by the ordinary events of life), to their strength in persevering, and to the quirkiness that sets them apart from the rest of society. This observation speaks volumes about the characters that populate Dorfman's films, but it seems also a reflective comment by Dorfman herself on her career. Three years separated *Parsley Days* and *Love That Boy*, and even though Dorfman did some television work during that time, most notably serving as a director for CBC's popular youth-oriented consumer-affairs show *Street Cents*, such a gap indicates how difficult it remains to secure funding to make feature-length films in Canada. A similar gap has opened up between the 2003 release of *Love That Boy* and its anticipated follow-up, *Crème de la Crème*, a drama set in an all-girls private school. Yet the lesson of *There's a Flower in My Pedal* is that one must persist despite the scrapes and disappointments of life. As such, we should expect future projects from Dorfman to appear over the next few years and to extend the impressive body of work she already has completed.

Filmography

Feature Films
Love That Boy, 2003. 85 min.

Parsley Days, 2000. 79 min.

Selected Short Films
There's a Flower in My Pedal, 2004. 5 min.

Nine, 1998. 24 min.

Swerve, 1998. 15 min.

I Love You This Much, 1997. 5 min.

Letter to Helen, 1997. 5 min.

Outside Inside Out, 1996. 5 min.

Television Credits
North/South, 2006. CBC.

Sluts, 2005. Life/IFC. 48 min.

Street Cents, 2000–3. CBC.

Notes

1

Neither of the two most recent historical overviews of Canadian cinema has mentioned Dorfman's films. This is a matter of both gender and region. Both works—Christopher Gittings's *Canadian National Cinema* (2002) and George Melnyk's *One Hundred Years of Canadian Cinema* (2004)—go some way in acknowledging Canadian women filmmakers and recognize the structural obstacles to women's filmmaking that remain in place today, even if Dorfman's films themselves do not find mention. Each volume does, however, struggle to articulate the Atlantic Canadian contribution to a national film culture. Predictably, *Goin' Down the Road* (Don Shebib, 1970) and its familiar story of out-migration takes centre stage in each book's effort to include Maritime content. Gittings's book includes an extended discussion of Mort Ransen's *Margaret's Museum* (1995), while Melnyk comments extensively on the Maritime films that emerged in the wake of Shebib's classic, including *Wedding in White* (William Fruet, 1972) and *The Rowdyman* (Peter Carter, 1972). An edited collection dedicated to Canadian women's cinema, *Gendering the Nation* (1999), predates Dorfman's two feature films, yet a comment made in the Introduction by the editorial collective certainly applies to her work: feature films by women in Canada have, by and large, been "produced almost entirely outside conventional funding formulas ... or at the low budget end of state support" (9).

2

In 2006, Dorfman directed episodes of *North/South*, a CBC daytime drama set in Halifax. Her work on these episodes exemplifies the way in which Halifax can be represented as shaped by its historical connections but not determined by them. The Halifax represented is modern, but the very structure of the relationships between the characters (geographically and symbolically dispersed between the working-class North End and the wealthier South End) is shown to be historically grounded. In addition to finding expression for these class antagonisms, *North/South* also addresses the racialized geography of Halifax. The North End is historically home to the city's Black community, and *North/South* shows that contemporary Haligonian imaginary is shaped by the trauma of Africville, a Black community that was forcibly relocated in order to make way for the A. Murray MacKay Bridge in the late 1960s. For more on Africville, see Clairmont and Magill; Clarke; Moynagh; and Nelson as well as the National Film Board of Canada documentary *Remember Africville* (1991), directed by Shelagh Mackenzie.

3

For an extended discussion of folk art in Nova Scotia and its connections to the emergence of NSCAD as an art school of international renown in the late 1960s and 1970s, see Cliff Eyland (9–24).

4

For a more detailed reading of *Parsley Days* that compares its commitment to craft to the vernacular architecture of Brian Mackay-Lyons, see Burke (219–33).

5

In its focus on female friendship, *Love That Boy* is reminiscent of *Ghost World*. In both Daniel Clowes's graphic novel (1997) and Terry Zwigoff's film adaptation (2001), the deterioration of the friendship between the protagonist Enid and her friend Rebecca gives the story a tremendous emotional force, even in the face of Enid's ironic detachment and wry cynicism. While Dorfman's work in general does not share *Ghost World*'s cutting sarcasm and its protagonist's occasional maliciousness, Enid's quirkiness and her fascination with the odd and outmoded, ranging from the mask she finds in a porn shop to the blues record she listens to obsessively, makes her a kind of sarcastic cousin to Dorfman's characters. Furthermore, the plot of the film adaptation, which sees Enid initiate a relationship with a geeky older man named Seymour, is a kind of inversion of Phoebe's attraction to younger, geeky Frazer in *Love That Boy*.

Works Cited

Armatage, Kay, Kass Banning, Brenda Longfellow, and Janine Marchessault, eds. Introduction. *Gendering the Nation: Canadian Women's Cinema*. Toronto: U of Toronto P, 1999. 1–14.

Bailey, Cameron. Review of *Parsley Days,* by Andrea Dorfman. *Now.* May 3–9, 2001. http://www.nowtoronto.com/movies/story.cfm?content=127213&archive=20,35,2001.

Burke, Andrew. "Site Specific: Visualizing the Vernacular in Andrea Dorfman's *Parsley Days*." *Rain/Drizzle/Fog: Film and Television in Atlantic Canada*. Ed. Darrell Varga. Calgary: U of Calgary P, 2009. 219–33.

Clairmont, Donald H., and Dennis William Magill. *Africville: The Life and Death of a Canadian Black Community*. 3rd ed. Toronto: Canadian Scholars' Press, 1999.Clarke, George Elliott. "The Death and Rebirth of Africadian Nationalism." *Odysseys Home: Mapping African-Canadian Literature*. Toronto: U of Toronto P, 2002: 288–96.

Clowes, Daniel. *Ghost World*. Seattle: Fantagraphics, 1997.

Eyland, Cliff. "Red Herrings, Clever Horses and the Benefits of Doubt." *Uses of the Vernacular in Nova Scotian Art*. Halifax: Dalhousie Art Gallery, 1994: 9–24.

Gauthier, Jennifer. "Where Is Here?: Local Visions in Three Canadian Films." *Canadian Journal of Film Studies/Revue Canadienne d'études Cinématographiques* 14.2 (2005): 38–53.Gittings, Christopher E. *Canadian National Cinema*. New York: Routledge, 2002.

Jameson, Fredric. *Marxism and Form*. Princeton: Princeton UP, 1971.

—. *Postmodernism, or The Cultural Logic of Late Capitalism*. Durham, NC: Duke UP, 1991.

Kelly, Richard. Review of *Rushmore*, by Wes Anderson. *Sight and Sound* 9.9 (September 1999): 54–55.

McKay, Ian. *The Quest of the Folk: Antimodernism and Cultural Selection in Twentieth-Century Nova Scotia*. Kingston: McGill-Queen's UP, 1994.

Melynk, George. *One Hundred Years of Canadian Cinema*. Toronto: U of Toronto P, 2004.

Moynagh, Maureen. "Africville, an Imagined Community." *Canadian Literature* 157 (Summer 1998): 14–34.

Nelson, Jennifer. *Razing Africville: A Geography of Racism*. Toronto: U of Toronto P, 2008.

Ngai, Sianne. "The Cuteness of the Avant-Garde." *Critical Inquiry* 31 (Summer 2005): 811–47.

Parpart, Lee. "Pit(iful) Male Bodies: Colonial Masculinity, Class and Folk Innocence in *Margaret's Museum*." *Canadian Journal of Film Studies/ Revue Canadienne d'Études Cinématographiques* 8.1 (Spring 1999): 63–86.

Wright, Patrick. *On Living in an Old Country: The National Past in Contemporary Britain*. London: Verso, 1985.

Feminist Ambiguity in the Film Adaptations of Lynne Stopkewich
Lee Parpart

Regardless of what new dystopian visions of deviance and desire Lynne Stopkewich may yet have in store for audiences, her name will probably always be synonymous with necrophilia. The Vancouver director's first feature, *Kissed* (1996),
which told the story of a seemingly normal suburban girl who studies embalming
and sleeps with dead men, was just that sort of seared-on-the-brain debut: a
shocking but also strangely palatable entry into a particularly gothic and taboo-
obsessed moment within English-Canadian cinema.[1]

       Since *Kissed* first appeared, however, and partly as a result of her work
on that film, Stopkewich has begun to acquire a different sort of reputation,
particularly among feminist critics, as a sensitive and astute adapter of women's
fiction.[2] *Kissed* was one such adaptation. Based on Barbara Gowdy's story "We
So Seldom Look on Love," it has turned out to be no anomaly. In a career made
up so far of two features, a smattering of short films, and a growing list of TV
credits on series such as *The Guard, Da Vinci's Inquest, This Is Wonderland,*
Bliss, and *The L Word,* roughly half of Stopkewich's projects to date could be
described as feminist adaptations of feminist fiction. From her well-received
student short, *The $3 Wash and Set,* to her features *Kissed* and *Suspicious*
River (2001), and including her contributions to Canadian series and anthology
projects such as *Bliss, The Shields Stories,* and *The Atwood Stories,* Stopkewich
has consistently sought out female-authored and feminist stories and novels
as material for films and television projects, and she has also made herself
available to direct women-centred adaptations initiated by others.[3] As Linda Ruth
Williams noted in a 2001 review of *Suspicious River,* Stopkewich may not always

"wear her feminism ... on her sleeve," but she does make "women's films (even if they centre on the dark fantasies of necrophilia and rape) which fulfill that old feminist criterion of 'by and for women' (from adapted text to directorial focus to star to audience appeal)" (Williams, 54).

Yet Stopkewich's relationship to feminism has been a complex one, involving shifting allegiances and priorities, difficult negotiations within the frankly patriarchal world of commercial feature filmmaking, and a carefully cultivated sense of ambiguity around cultural norms and definitions of femininity. One goal of this essay is to approach these shifts, negotiations, and ambiguities in Stopkewich's work as a feminist adapter of feminist fiction through close readings of her feature films. Moving beyond narrow textual readings, however, this project addresses Stopkewich's adaptation practices in relation to industrial conditions of production, addressing the filmmaker's attempts to balance commercial and independent artistic aims and situating her work in relation to differences between the comparatively private medium of literature and the more public arena of commercial cinema.[4]

Like other critics working in the small sub-field of feminist adaptation studies,[5] my primary concerns have to do with the political and aesthetic transformations that can occur when feminist, female-authored, and/or female-centred literary texts[6] are adapted to other media. However, unlike the majority of critical work in this area that has focused on the evident betrayals and dilutions by "male Hollywood" of feminist novels and short stories, my focus here is on the often subtle ideological slippages and transformations that can occur even in situations of seemingly greater political alignment between a film and its hypotext—as for example when an explicit commitment to feminist political agendas and/or feminist approaches to representation informs both an adaptation and its primary literary source.[7] Given this focus on narrative, aesthetic, and ideological micro-shifts occurring under conditions of shared feminist and/or female authorship, it has been impossible for me to join the chorus of recent voices in adaptation studies calling for a complete rejection of "fidelity criticism." As well worn and often disputed as it tends to be in contemporary theories of adaptation, the concept of fidelity plays an important role in this essay. However, my use of the term is intended to be relativistic rather than absolute, and includes the recognition that there may be many different possible intentions behind any given adaptation, including a desire to contest or creatively "undo" a beloved or bedevilling story or novel[8] (Hutcheon, xiii, 6–7). Whatever motives might exist for adapting a literary work to another medium, Linda Hutcheon points out, "from the adapter's perspective, adaptation is an act of appropriating or salvaging, and this is always a double process of interpreting and then creating something new" (20). With this observation in mind, I try to use the category of fidelity not as a blunt tool for judging the worth of Stopkewich's adaptations in relation to their sources but as one device among many to help mark and analyze the often significant transformations that can take place in attempts to adapt literary works to film. Moreover, I join a small number of other critics, including Elspeth Tulloch and Peter Dickinson, in arguing that where feminist adaptations of feminist fictions are concerned, attention to the degree of "fidelity" between a film and its source continues to be a valid concern, not least because the analysis of differences and continuities between adaptations and their hypotexts can illuminate historical and authorial shifts in the articulation of feminist discourses, agendas, and aesthetic approaches between texts in different media.[9]

Disney vs. Dante

Drawing on a penchant for "outsider" narratives[10] and macabre themes that she traces back to her childhood friendship with Lynn Crosbie, the fellow Anglo-Montrealer with whom she made up stories and played "weird Barbie games" in their east-end 'hood of Ville d'Anjou during the 1970s,[11] Stopkewich has so far directed two feature films, both of which adapt feminist literary narratives and explore themes of highly unorthodox (if straight) female sexuality, and both of which star the Vancouver/L.A. actor Molly Parker. Stopkewich's breakout film, *Kissed*, made while she was a master's student at the University of British Columbia, stars Parker as a young woman named Sandra Larson, whose lifelong fascination with the rituals and the mysteries surrounding death leads her, as a child, to perform innocently sexual burial rituals for dead mice and other rodents, and later, as a young adult, to seek out a kind of sexual-spiritual union with the cadavers at a local funeral home, where she finds work and studies embalming. At times graphic but rarely gruesome (and always working overtime to soften its own shock value with steady doses of audio and visual lyricism), *Kissed* attracted widespread critical acclaim when it was released in 1996 and won numerous festival and industry honours, including eight Genie nominations, one Genie award (for best actress), and a special jury citation for best new Canadian film at the Toronto International Film Festival, as well as several international film festival awards.[12] Critics praised Stopkewich for her subtle handling of incendiary subject matter, while the media gobbled up Molly Parker's otherworldly good looks with feature stories and double-page spreads.[13] But *Kissed* also captured attention for its low-low budget, guerrilla-style production story. Shot on half a shoestring, with much of the film's $473,850 budget coming from friends and family who are acknowledged in the film's credits as "heroes," "champions," and "patron saints," depending on how much they gave, *Kissed* stands out as a model of what can be accomplished (especially by student filmmakers with access to free equipment) working mostly outside of the usual funding mechanisms and simply insisting on getting it done.[14]

By the time Stopkewich got around to making her second film, there were high expectations from all quarters. And like many a sophomore effort in English-Canadian film, the results were comparatively disappointing. Again funded outside the usual system, with money from several European investors and very little from Canadian sources, Stopkewich's next feature, *Suspicious River*, left many critics and viewers cold (and in some cases angry), with its disturbing and far less palatable story of another "marked woman" with even more severe self-destructive tendencies than Stopkewich's first protagonist, Sandra. Based on a first novel of the same name by American poet Laura Kasischke, *Suspicious River*'s fractured narrative traces the downward spiral of an unhappily married young woman who casually takes to prostituting herself with male customers at the rural motel where she works as a receptionist, only to replay, with predictably grim results, aspects of her disturbing family history by becoming the sex slave of one of her johns.

Of the two films, one might expect *Kissed* to deliver a more shocking cinematic experience. After all, it serves up the taboo spectacle of a woman gratifying herself with male cadavers, whereas, on the surface of things, *Suspicious River* simply introduces us to another ill-fated member of the world's oldest profession. Differences in Stopkewich's approaches to her two hypotexts, however, yield the opposite result; in spite of its subject matter, *Kissed* feels like a gentle roller coaster ride compared with the often disturbing ordeal that constitutes *Suspicious River*'s murky study of feminine abjection. At the level of tone, narrative content, cinematography, editing, and sound, *Kissed* is by far the more lyrical, and watchable, of Stopkewich's features. One important distinction between the two films rests with their narrative and aesthetic portrayals of non-normative (though hetero) female sexuality. Sandra Larson's corpse-loving ways in *Kissed* are so remote from everyday experience that the film functions as a kind of twisted fairy tale for most viewers—a far-off fantasy involving sexual practices that few among us would contemplate—whereas the masochism that fuels Leila's downward spiral is just an extreme example of a far more widespread, and therefore more disturbing, tendency (Stopkewich 2006). Stopkewich plays up this distinction between the two films with the suggestion that while *Kissed* feels to viewers like "the Disney version of a film about necrophilia," *Suspicious River* is more like "Dante on 'ludes" (Stopkewich, 19 December 2006). For the most part, this comparison seems about right. Brutal and disturbing in all of the places where *Kissed* reaches for a soothing aesthetic experience, *Suspicious River* almost seems intended as an ideological antidote to the soft-peddaling tendencies that marked Stopkewich's feature debut—an in-your-face attempt to frustrate audience expectations for another guilt-free experience of female (hetero)sexual transgression. As such, *Kissed* and *Suspicious River* represent not only two very different approaches to straight forms of sexual "deviance" but also two aesthetically and therefore ideologically distinct approaches to feminist adaptation. As we will see, however, *Suspicious River* is not immune to the pressures associated with the highly public medium of mainstream commercial cinema, and as such there are compromises and departures from Kasischke's source text that tend to align *Suspicious River* with *Kissed* rather than maintain its absolute difference.

Kissed (1996)

In order to grasp some of the ways *Kissed* might deserve to be called the "Disney version of a movie about necrophilia," it helps to compare it with Gowdy's short story and to explore details of Stopkewich's narrative and aesthetic approach in the film. As I have argued elsewhere, most of the significant transformations in *Kissed* centre on the character of Sandra, whose history of necrophilia forms the basis of both narratives.[15] In Gowdy's story, Sandra is a blunt-talking, self-possessed middle-aged woman who looks back on her lifelong fascination with death and describes how the attraction, which starts innocently enough with childhood burial rituals for squirrels and mice, ultimately turns into a spiritual-sexual fascination with the mystical and alchemical transformations surrounding dead bodies on their way to the afterlife. Gowdy's worldly Sandra is smoothly self-confident and coolly analytical—even flippant at times about her sexual preferences—despite having been caught by police in the act of making love to a dead man. Cavalier about her activities in the morgue, Sandra defends herself against her sister-in-law Carol's charge that she should be "put away" with the unrepentant comeback "But I'm not bad-looking, so if offering my body to dead men is a crime, I'd like to know who the victim is" (Gowdy, 147). Rejecting what the story tells us is the standard medical view of necrophilia as a defence against being hurt by normal sexual relationships, Sandra argues that her own attraction to cadavers is driven by "excitement" rather than fear, and by respect for the single-minded intentionality of a corpse heading for the next realm: "one of the most exciting things about a cadaver is how dedicated it is to dying. Its will is all directed to a single intention, like a huge wave heading for shore, and you can ride along on the wave if you want to, because no matter what you do, because with or without you, that wave is going to hit the beach" (Gowdy, 149).

Taking full advantage of literature's greater ability to signal temporal shifts, Gowdy tantalizes readers by gradually portioning out information about all of the major phases in Sandra's "career" as a necrophile, including her first job as a hearse driver for a local funeral home; her decision to learn the "art" of embalming; and her halting first sexual encounters with human corpses—an initiation that begins with long, loving looks into coffins and progresses to frenzied, Dionysian episodes of sexual and spiritual communion with the dead men she meets at work.[16] In a key development that coincides with Sandra's first sexual encounters with human corpses, the story describes her ill-fated attempts at a "normal" relationship with an intense former medical student named Matt, a sensitive young man who falls hard for Sandra but finds he cannot compete with her boyfriends at the morgue. In a conclusion that is handled with dark humour in the short story and dramatic seriousness in the film, Matt makes the ultimate bid for Sandra's attention by luring her to his apartment late one night with a cryptic phone call, then hanging himself in the nude when she arrives. Faced with this unmistakable invitation to ravish Matt's still-warm corpse (and feeling an enthusiasm for him that she could never quite muster while he was alive), Sandra takes him up on his proposition, only to be caught by the police. The short story's first-person narrative grows out of Sandra's desire to fill in the gaps in what promises to be a stale police record of her capture: "It was crucial to me that the official report contain more than the detective's bleak observations. I wanted two things on record: one, that Matt was ravished by a reverential expert; two, that his cadaver blasted the energy of a star" (Gowdy, 157). In the final lines of the story we learn that Sandra still "cross[es] over, occasionally and recklessly," and still views necrophilia as a victimless crime more related to transcendence than to sex.

As an adaptation, *Kissed* arguably represents a curious combination of surface fidelity and profound, emotive-ideological transformations of its source. Many of the basic functions, characters, situations, and narrative devices in Gowdy's story survive the transition to film—including the important structuring and focalizing device of Sandra's first-person narration, which takes the form of a voice-over in Stopkewich's adaptation. However the tone of *Kissed* is far gentler, more solicitous, and ultimately more seductive than that of the story, and the film includes a number of narrative shifts that arguably combine to domesticate and at times "de-radicalize" certain features of Gowdy's story, including parts of the text that come closest to articulating a radical understanding of female sexual deviance and outlaw desire.

As mentioned, the most glaring and ideologically significant transformations in *Kissed* relate to its portrayal of Sandra. Whereas Gowdy's female necrophile comes across as an utterly unrepentant older woman who surveys her own sexual history with a frank and unapologetic neutrality, the film shows us only her childhood and her early-twenty-something years (erasing the story's emphasis on middle-aged femininity) and in the process positions Sandra as the world's most inoffensive necrophile—an ethereal, corpse-loving waif who whispers about her spiritual motivation for helping her dead boyfriends "cross over" into the next life and who blushes at the mention of her method of making love to the bodies. In introducing these character traits and temporal changes, I have argued elsewhere, Stopkewich's film version of "We So Seldom Look on Love" ushers in a new and significantly less confrontational female voice. Whereas Gowdy's Sandra "speaks with a frankness that some linguists have associated with the 'masculine' voice of authority or what Cheris Kramarae refers to as 'men's speech' or powerful speech, which is 'capable, direct, rational, illustrating a sense of humor, unfeeling, strong (in tone and word choice) and blunt,'" Stopkewich's Sandra tends toward gentler and more circumscribed forms of speech—"closer to what Lanser refers to as 'woman's language' or a discourse of the powerless"[17] (Parpart, 75). Of the many examples of this tendency in the film, two stand out: the fact that Molly Parker's Sandra never utters the words "necrophile" and "cunnilingus" (both of which appear in the story), and the introduction of a subtle but important narrative shift at the end of the film that clearly removes an element of Sandra Larson's personal and sexual autonomy. Whereas the story concludes with Sandra saying, "I am still a necrophile, occasionally and recklessly. I have found no replacement for the torrid serenity of a cadaver" (159), the film's voice-over narration ends with the line "I still work at a funeral home, and I still cross over. *But now I see Matt when I look at the centre*" (Parpart, 77). As I have argued, this ending contributes to the film's overall tendency to contain Sandra's heterosexual extremism by aligning her with the domestic values of loyalty and monogamy, portraying Sandra as one half of a couple with Matt, even after his death, and as a kind of "necrophiliac widow who will forever be haunted by the memory of her favourite corpse" (Parpart, 77).

As Stopkewich describes it, this shift in overall tone was crucial for helping audiences stay with the film and its lead character: "Reading a story about a girl who has sex with dead bodies is one thing; watching her climb up on a gurney and do the deed is something totally different. The audience had to like Sandra enough to stay with her for 90 minutes. They had to care enough about her to go on this journey with her" (Stopkewich, 29 November 2006). Coaxing audiences into a sympathetic attitude toward Sandra was essentially a triumph of technique over subject matter. With the consistent use of fog filters, halo effects, below-eye-line shots, and a recurring motif of bright white light during each of Sandra's encounters with her corpse lovers, *Kissed* sells its blood-loving lead character as a sensitive figure whose stated motivation for sleeping with dead bodies— a desire to take part in the transformative power of death while helping her lovers make it into the next world—becomes all the more believable and acceptable because she is lit and shot in a way that lends her a kind of otherworldly beauty and innocence. Casting also plays a crucial part in this process; faced with the sublime blankness of Parker's delicately freckled face as she enters into another one of her frenzied reveries bathed in bright white light, it becomes easy to accept her view of necrophilia as a spiritual act of communion rather than a carnal invasion. Helped by Parker's essential effeteness, and drawing on every sympathy-building trick in the annals of cinema, Stopkewich and her co-authors managed to make a potentially sickening subject palatable, and created powerful audience connections with a figure of extreme female sexual transgression.[18] (It probably also helps that all this sexual rule-breaking is clearly contained within a heteronormative context, with Sandra portrayed as unambiguously heterosexual in her choice of cadavers. This is true of both the story and the film. Only Matt, the failed medical student, entertains for a moment the possibility that Sandra might be both lesbian *and* a necrophile, a suggestion that clearly catches Sandra by surprise in the film, and her blinking, startled expression at the thought of sleeping with a dead *woman* rather than a dead man arguably helps to further normalize Sandra's otherwise hugely unorthodox sexual aims.)[19]

The feminist implications of this process of softening Gowdy's portrayal of Sandra and making her transgressions more acceptable to viewers are clearly open to debate. On one hand, Stopkewich clearly achieved a victory of sorts over the forces of conservatism by transporting such an obviously improper figure of desire into public consciousness and popular culture. At the same time, however, *Kissed* ultimately makes Sandra a less challenging figure of female sexual desire than her literary counterpart. One of the things that tends to be sacrificed (or at least subdued) in Stopkewich's adaptation is the sense one gets from the short story of being immersed in female enunciation—of being caught up in the jet stream of a prolonged speech act that establishes Sandra Larson as an unrepentant independent woman narrating the events of her own past, a past capable of establishing and defining her own identity as a social and sexual subject. However, I am increasingly convinced that the film's narrative and audiovisual softening of Sandra's character needs to be read in more complex terms and in relation to Stopkewich's stated aims. Apart from wanting to soothe audiences with a sympathetic portrayal of necrophilia, Stopkewich asserts that one of her reasons for bathing Sandra in light during her lovemaking scenes with the corpses was to deny spectators a chance to escape, either literally from the theatre or figuratively into a voyeuristic stance of seeing-without-being-seen. So if Stopkewich set out, as she claims she did, to make the "Disney version" of a necrophilia movie, she was also inspired on some level by a modernist impulse to submit audiences to a certain amount of intellectual discomfort in the process.[20]

Elspeth Tulloch, in another context, has referred to the "*trans-mute-ation*" of feminist literary narratives within film adaptations that tend to modify and mute instances of "feminist critique, female narrative functions, and female voices" (110). I have suggested that a similar process is at work in *Kissed*.

However, as is suggested by the example of its use of blinding white light during moments of transition, the trans-mute-ations enacted in Stopkewich's adaptation of Gowdy's story are partial and complex. Unlike so many other, less ambiguous, examples of aesthetic romanticism within dominant narrative cinema, the changes introduced in *Kissed* cannot be viewed simply as a politically regressive series of moves designed to smooth out or eliminate the radicalism of an overtly feminist literary source. On the contrary, it seems more productive and accurate to view *Kissed* as embodying a number of contradictory (or at least competing) impulses associated with feminist film production poised between the margins and the mainstream. In it, for example, we can see commercial imperatives (such as Stopkewich's desire to "sell" Sandra to audiences as a sympathetic figure of "goodness" and "light") sharing space with a more politically motivated impulse to unsettle audience expectations (for an appropriately "dark" delivery of a topic considered to be inescapably morbid) and to confront audiences about their own modes of looking, specifically by manipulating the film's lighting in a way that collapses any safe distance between spectators and spectacle. Moreover, such negotiations and contradictions appear to be a routine and probably inescapable part of functioning as a feminist director in an industry that actively discourages feminist narratives from seeing the light of day, or that at least works to tame the most radical elements of such narratives, and in a public medium largely won over to the pleasures of passive and voyeuristic forms of spectatorship.

The wonder, in some ways, is that *Kissed* manages, despite the medium in which it was made, to preserve as much of the story's edginess and core attitude of acceptance toward its corpse-loving main character as it does. In spite of the compromises it enacts in order to find a place on the independent edges of mainstream cinema, *Kissed* remains one of the most radical narrative treatments of non-normative heterosexual female desire in Canadian film. As one of the only necrophilia films ever made in a dramatic genre, it represents a groundbreaking mix of mainstream delivery and subversive subject matter, and the fact that a woman is the protagonist constitutes a feminist statement, even if Stopkewich's portrayal of Sandra arguably dilutes certain aspects of Gowdy's source text. Looking historically at the film's relationship to its hypotext, Stopkewich's approach to Gowdy's story can, for better or for worse, even be seen to usher in elements of third-wave feminism. By transforming the story's protagonist from a mature sexual outlaw into a more youthful and accessible figure of deviant desire, *Kissed* falls into line with late feminism's preference for female icons who combine various degrees of surface empowerment with sexual availability. Sandra's availability may be largely on her own terms, as she ditches her live boyfriend to straddle the bodies of other partners at the morgue. But her gamine good looks and her ethereal presence as a celestial caretaker of the dead during their transition to the next world strikes just the kind of delicate balance for which various strands of third-wave feminism are well known: the balance, in this case, between asserting power and maintaining sexual allure.[21] Moreover, the contradictory impulses contained in this gesture—a simultaneous wish to please audiences and to push them beyond their comfort zone—form a consistent duality in Stopkewich's career, which has been marked by a mixture of feminist experimentation and a determination to make feature films that stand at least an outside chance of gaining a moderately wide release. Just how far outside the strictures laid down by commercial cinema Stopkewich is willing to go became clearer with her second feature film, *Suspicious River*.

Suspicious River (2001)

Five years after her well-received debut, Stopkewich was clearly feeling less inclined (or less constrained) than she had been in the mid-1990s to soothe audiences with a tidied-up portrayal of female sexual extremism. As the director told spectators at a Cinematheque Ontario screening in 2006, part of her goal with *Suspicious River* was to overturn the sympathy-building approach taken in *Kissed* by presenting audiences with a much less obviously palatable protagonist—in her words, "a woman doing dark stuff who you don't have a reason to care a fuck about."[22] And although Stopkewich has since explained that part of her reason for leaving audiences more in the lurch with *Suspicious River* was to explore character and narrative in new ways, the film's pitiless portrayal of its masochistic lead character receives ample inspiration from its source text, a grim feminist cautionary tale and first novel by Michigan-based poet Laura Kasischke.[23]

Like Gowdy's story, Kasischke's novel takes the form of an intimate first-person narrative told in mixed-up time frames by a woman with a complex and often ambiguous personal and sexual history. Unlike the coolly self-aware and unapologetic necrophile of "We So Seldom Look on Love," however, *Suspicious River*'s protagonist is presented in the novel as a self-destructive figure struggling with a semi-repressed legacy of trauma, abuse, and sexual violence. When we first meet her, Kasischke's lead character, Leila Murray, is an unhappily married twenty-four-year-old receptionist at a drab motel on a riverbank in a small Michigan town. The river is a leech-infested tributary that is home to hundreds of dirty and hungry swans, birds whose mate-for-life instincts signal to Leila the romantic ideal that she seeks in the novel but never finds. For reasons that become clear only late in the narrative, Leila has recently begun to cope with her boredom and her traumatic family history with a casual turn to prostitution, selling her body for the price of a room to the mostly slack-jawed businessmen and travellers who pass through the Swan Motel. There is no clear sense of purpose in any of her trick-turning, and from the earliest scenes we are guided to think of her actions in terms of the classic Freudian association between masochism and death: prepping for her latest $60 blow job, she surveys herself "in a mirror the length and width of a coffin—a silver one, lined with mercury and sterling, a stainless steel table in an operating room, or morgue, propped up against a wall" (3). Her encounters bring on bouts of bodily dissociation and self-surveillance that recall John Berger's arguments about women's inability to escape the gaze. Facing one client who is "as thick armed and short as an ogre, hairy" (3), she reflects "That was my own body floating in that mirror, I thought, reflected in sharp triangles of light. My *body* in a closet of pure flat space, like a piece of bent sheet metal abandoned on a beach" (3).

With such strong hints of a desire for debasement and annihilation pervading all of her paid sexual encounters, it comes as no surprise when Leila manages to attract the undivided attention of a bona fide sadist. Posing as one of her johns, the boyishly menacing Gary Jensen comes to the motel looking for "a girl my buddy told me about," then woos and abuses Leila until she falls hard for him, robbing the motel's till and running off with her new lover to a "new life, which waits like a mother at the end of a long, white tunnel of light" (203). Jensen's plans for his latest conquest, however, turn out to be considerably darker than even Leila, with all her capacity for self-destruction, can imagine. After driving her to his bungalow, putting her to bed, and stealing her savings, Jensen, who turns out to be a pimp, sets Leila up in his home as a full-time prostitute—the latest unpaid worker in a kind of backwater gangbanger's club for the region's low-lifes. Finally waking up from her dream of a happy ever after to grasp the full extent of her appalling situation, Leila responds by playing dead during sex, a move that so enrages the group's lead sadist that he threatens to kill her. Leila, however, is one step ahead of her attacker, lurching forward to gash her own throat with the man's knife before escaping through a window.

Woven throughout the narrative, meanwhile, flashbacks tell the story of Leila's mother, a tragic figure whose flagrant infidelities and eventual murder Leila witnessed as a child. Stabbed to death by her lover, who also happens to be Leila's uncle (her father's sexier, more successful, more volatile younger brother), Leila's mother hovers over the narrative like a warning or a premonition, supplying both an explanation for the younger woman's semi-conscious masochistic tendencies and a possible way out. During Leila's escape from Jensen's brothel, the flashbacks begin to bleed into the ongoing action, until the mother's voice briefly takes over the narration, providing Leila with a vision of her own possible death and advising her either to submit to her attackers or to collect herself and run. Amid falling-apart prose that suggests Leila's deteriorating state of mind near the end of the novel, there are indications that she may finally have saved herself, but the ending is deliberately ambiguous. Pursued by Gary and the other men as she runs through a forest, Leila seems to escape by wading across the river and finding her co-worker, Millie, on the other side. But the action is so implausible[24] and the co-worker's response is so static ("'We have to get some help,' [Millie] says, but she doesn't move" [270]) that it could all be a dream—a hallucination of her own rescue. Even if we are to assume she makes it across the river, the novel offers little hope for Leila's survival; the final passage has her surveying herself "from the sky" as she lies at Millie's feet next to the river, with Jensen creeping through the trees on the other side.

As an adaptation, this film, like *Kissed*, offers a combination of surface "fidelity" and carefully considered departures from its hypotext, although this time without pandering as much to industry or audience demands for a sympathetic figure of attachment. Apart from a few omissions of graphic scenes of sexual debasement that were filmed and then abandoned after test screenings with groups of Stopkewich's friends,[25] *Suspicious River* closely follows the novel's portrayal of its troubled protagonist, doing little to soften Leila's character or cushion her fall within the narrative. In many ways the film, although dismissed—even despised—by many critics, arguably does an effective job of echoing and amplifying elements of the novel's exploration of the psychological roots of female masochism. Stopkewich avoids many of the traps and instances of Hollywood-style revisionism in her adaptation, and was presumably able to do so in part because she managed to put together a production plan that maximized her autonomy on set, keeping *Suspicious River*'s overall budget at a low CDN$3 million and bankrolling the film with investments from a small number of foreign media outlets.[26] The results of this European-style co-production formula, which freed Stopkewich from having to make her film in Hollywood *and* from having to rely on a then newly revamped and more commercially oriented Telefilm Canada, are evident in the film's overall adherence to Kasischke's dark analysis of cultural norms of femininity.

Although frankly difficult to watch (even for the director herself, who admits to having a hard time sitting through it), *Suspicious River* arguably succeeds in certain respects *as an adaptation* in part by mirroring the novel's core concern with damaged feminine identity, while dramatically altering aspects of the novel that could not be adequately translated into film—aspects that forced the film to search instead for what Benjamin Rifkin refers to as "equivalences" between texts in different media[27] (Rifkin, 9–10). At the same time, there are other, more problematic, shifts that tend to repress the novel's richly detailed analysis of the wider cultural contexts surrounding Leila's actions and that have the effect of leaving her masochistic tendencies stranded within a narrow reading of the familial and psychological origins of her "disorder." This tendency to individualize Leila's condition amounts to a significant shift away from Kasischke's approach, and can be read as a departure from the novel's investments in feminist re-theorizations of the category of feminine masochism. I will have more to say about this shift below.

In a daring transformation of the book's key structuring device, Stopkewich displaces the entire backstory involving Leila's mother into a series of vignettes that initially read as though they are taking place as part of the film's main narrative (within what might be called its "first" diegesis). Instead of revealing the mother's influence on Leila by alternating between conventional flashbacks and present-day actions—a conservative method of signalling temporal shifts that is ubiquitous in mainstream film—Stopkewich displaces the mother's story onto a new layer of ongoing action that revolves around an entirely new character: a little girl (played by Mary Kate Welsh) who lives near the motel and who befriends Leila over the course of the film. For spectators who have read the novel, this unnamed girl's home life is recognizable as an echo of Leila's own childhood, complete with a narcissistic and inconsistently loving mother (played by Sarah Jane Redmond) who sleeps with men for money and is ultimately stabbed to death by her husband's jealous younger brother. For those who have *not* read the book, the girl's story will initially read like a subplot that takes place alongside Leila's story, one perhaps meant to explore the childhood origins of Leila's irresistible attraction to danger and suffering. Midway through the film, however, a series of coincidental appearances by the girl and some rapid, disorienting edits begin to suggest that she may not be real. By the time Leila is running for her life along the river near the end of the film, this suspicion is confirmed when the girl suddenly appears by her side and describes to Leila the violent end she will meet at the hands of Jensen and his gang. So while the character of the girl in Stopkewich's adaptation is ultimately readable as a figment of Leila's memory work and as a fictional embodiment of her own traumatized childhood self, one effect of this transformation is that audiences are never afforded the simple luxury of being guided from one time frame to another within the film, and must work, instead, to draw the links between Leila's family history and her current mental state.

This strategy of shifting the novel's flashbacks onto a new plane that includes both the past and the present is also noteworthy from the point of view of adaptation theory in that it manages at the same time to depart significantly from its source text and to reproduce and even amplify the novel's investments in non-linear and reflexive storytelling. Given that most of Kasischke's early flashbacks in the novel are afforded a special sense of immediacy and indeterminate chronology by being presented to readers in the present tense, Stopkewich's movement away from a classical relay between past and present actually sets up a series of subtle correspondences with Kasischke's text, echoing the novel's play with time and memory, making Leila's memory work seem all the more pressing and immediate, and preserving the novel's subtle suggestion that part of Leila's project may be the literal recovery of memories lost to trauma.

Another important parallel between the novel and the film rests with the refusal of both to romanticize or eroticize Leila's sexual encounters with johns. This is a crucial rhetorical move in both texts, conveying a feminist rejection of what Marianne Noble describes as a long legacy arising out of literature's tendency to romanticize and eroticize patterns of feminine self-denial and debasement.[28] Kasischke's text avoids any hint of complicity with this historical trajectory by offering short, muscular descriptions of Leila's sexual encounters, and by tilting virtually all of Leila's metaphorical language in the direction of death and disease, creating a pattern of imagery that pushes hard against the romantic idealization of the self-denying heroine. Stopkewich, for her part, drains all hints of sexiness out of Leila's trick-turning by shooting these encounters with all the spontaneity and erotic heat of public service announcements. She favours static, flesh-avoiding compositions, keeping most of the sex off-screen, and relies on frequent cutaways to seemingly minor details such as a bank note being stuffed into a patent leather shoe, boxer shorts dropping to the floor around a middle-aged john's thick, unappealing calves, and shots of the motel's low-rent decor, with its '70s-style lamps and cliché-riddled prints of pastoral oil paintings. In all of these ways, Stopkewich's adaptation clearly announces itself as a rejection of the "hooker with a heart of gold" template that has so often been recycled in Hollywood products as diverse as *Pretty Woman*, *Trading Places*, and *Leaving Las Vegas*, and in non-film narratives from Nancy in *Oliver Twist* to the Hebrew Bible's Rahab. In stark contrast to the highly sexualized and aestheticized portrayal of Molly Parker in Wayne Wang's *The Center of the World*, *Suspicious River* works hard to avoid subjecting her character to a male gaze, even as it shows Leila courting that gaze from the other side of the reception desk at the Swan Motel. There are no lingering or overtly eroticized images of Parker's nude body; the framing and camerawork are stubbornly static, particularly during the film's sex scenes; and the lighting is as unflattering as one would expect in a low-rent motel full of fluorescents. Moreover, Stopkewich takes special care to shoot the film's one suggested gang rape scene in a way that seems designed to discourage spectators from connecting with any of the men's desires, in part by avoiding their points of view. All this distancing action from the film's otherwise erotic premise may be one reason why critics—and according to Stopkewich, male critics and spectators in particular—have responded with open and intense hostility to *Suspicious River*.[29] As the director told her Cinematheque Ontario audience, "A lot of men really don't know what to do with this film, whereas women say 'Get it, got it, need it, want it. Well, don't want it, but glad you made it'" (Stopkewich, 8 December 2006).

Stopkewich's adaptation shares with its source novel a certain recognizable commitment to approaching Leila's story by working through, thematically and aesthetically, some of the major values, ideas, and agendas associated with second-wave Anglo-American feminism. As studies of female abjection and victimization, both versions of *Suspicious River* clearly argue that dominant cultural norms of femininity carry serious consequences for women, ranging from sexual exploitation and debasement to death. As a narrative exploration of the psychoanalytic category of feminine masochism, however, Stopkewich's adaptation can also be seen as departing in subtle ways from one of the novel's primary articulations of feminist thought. Unlike Kasischke's text, which is richly layered with descriptive details that point to a wider cultural context that informs and supports individual expressions of female masochism, Stopkewich's film mostly confines itself to an exploration of Leila's own psychopathology. Whereas the novel includes an array of references to pop cultural icons—Barbie dolls and sexualized princesses, case studies of women murdered and left for dead, and other symptoms of normative femininity in contemporary American[30] culture—the film either compresses these references to the point of insignificance or avoids them altogether, leaving Leila's self-denying tendencies more or less unattached to any wider critique of the cultural roots of female subjugation. Of all the losses and transformations inherent in any attempt to adapt Kasischke's 271-page novel into a 98-minute film, this one is especially significant, because it contributes to *Suspicious River*'s movement away from a feminist analysis of the larger cultural contexts of female masochism.[31]

In keeping with other novels in the so-called Blank Fiction phenomenon of the 1990s—a category of mostly American literary fiction that includes Brett Easton Ellis's *American Psycho* (1991) and Susanna Moore's *In the Cut* (1995)—*Suspicious River* is not afraid to venture into postmodern feminist territory through explorations of dark, violent, and uncomfortable corners of the female psyche, including queasy scenarios of abjection and powerlessness. However, Kasischke's novel consistently does so in ways that are clearly informed by second-wave feminism's value-driven and often prescriptive emphasis on generating a critique of the cultural foundations of normative femininity. In the novel, Kasischke seems to suggest that the masochistic tendencies of a character like Leila can never be adequately understood on psychoanalytic grounds alone, as a disorder of the mind stemming from "essential femininity" (Freud) or a refusal to relinquish the maternal figure as imagined primary object (Lacan).[32] By focusing on the connection between Leila's behaviour and the damage she

suffered within the family, Stopkewich's adaptation privileges an individualized psychoanalytic reading and arguably bypasses an important opportunity to
broaden and enrich its narrative of damaged feminine identity with a fuller exploration of the cultural foundations of female masochism.

One revealing example of the film's tendency to soften Kasischke's
bleak and wide-ranging approach to feminine masochism can be found in its conclusion. Unlike the novel, which closes with Leila undergoing some sort of near-
death, out-of-body experience at the feet of her co-worker Millie, who says she
will get help but does not move, Stopkewich's adaptation has Leila limping out
of the river with her arm slung over Millie (who is heard saying, "Gotta get out of
the water, gotta get some help, just lean on me"), while a brief passage of voice-
over narration by Leila hints elliptically at her survival. "The swans came back
and laid their eggs on the riverbank," we hear her voice say as she is helped out
of the water. "When their babies were born, I went down and watched them pad-
dle around the black water. Every now and then, they'd lift their heads and listen
to that call in the distance, echoed by the river and their will to live." Although
Stopkewich has indicated that she believes Leila dies of her injuries in both the
film and the novel, the film's narration is clearly open to being read as suggesting her possible survival.[33] How, otherwise, does she come back to watch the
swans that have laid their eggs (except maybe as an apparition)? Although not as
dramatic or clear-cut in its narrative consequences as, say, Jane Campion's ideologically loaded reversal of the ending of Susanna Moore's novel In the Cut,[34] the
ending of the adaptation of Suspicious River clearly embraces a more decisive
and optimistic view of Leila's fate than does Kasischke's novel. We may argue
about the feminist implications of this difference, but it seems clear that as an
adaptation, Stopkewich's film, despite having been structured and funded in a
way that allowed the director maximum autonomy, responds on some levels to
commercial cinema's self-censoring pressure for an ending that audiences can
live with, one that might help to sell Suspicious River as an "art" film that is bleak
but watchable because it holds out the possibility of hope, however ambiguously
expressed, for Leila's survival.

Conclusion

Enormous and sometimes insurmountable challenges are involved in any
attempt to preserve, echo, translate, or even contest the types of feminist critical
positions and narrative and representational strategies circulating within novels
and stories when such work is adapted to film. As a constant set of negotiations
within an industry that tends to be openly hostile to any declared political
agenda other than one that will put the greatest possible number of "bums in
seats," the articulation of any sort of recognizably feminist (or postcolonial,

or other) agenda or set of critical ideas within the context of North American industrial filmmaking models is inherently fraught with challenges and obstacles, making it impossible at times to engage meaningfully with the gendered political positions and modes of critique evoked by feminist literary texts. Moreover, as critics as diverse as Bela Balazs, Jean Mitry, and E.M. Gombrich have argued, departures and differences are inevitable in any attempt to transcode material from one medium into another for the simple reason that every medium tends to pull the basic material of a narrative in its own, to some extent semiotically predetermined, direction.[35]

Stopkewich has waded into this complex industrial and ideological terrain multiple times now, directing film and television projects based on novels and stories that fulfill one important definition of feminist narrative by openly addressing the reader as female and potentially also as feminist.[36] However, Stopkewich's experiments in feminist adaptation of feminist fiction have been politically mixed. Never simply transcriptions of their hypotexts, her adaptations sit in a complex and often ambiguous relationship to their feminist literary sources, sometimes amplifying and engaging productively with the political agendas suggested by those texts while in other ways arguably effacing feminist critical positions and analyses or shrinking the space available for feminist critique. Significantly, her films straddle the line between artistic and commercial aims, and tend to explore the representational discourses of gendered identity not freely but rather from within the "cracks of dominant norms" (Kemp and Squires, 387).

Given these pressures, we might easily conclude that the goal of "honouring," "reproducing," or "remaining faithful" to feminist narrative strategies and political positions evoked by adapted texts may be too tall an order, even for a filmmaker like Stopkewich, who shares a basic commitment to the feminist project of exploring (and/or exploding) narrative forms and representational strategies and communicating the complexities and contradictions of gendered subjectivity. As this analysis of Stopkewich's adaptations suggests, close attention to the similarities and differences between films and their hypotexts can help to draw out ideologically significant micro-shifts as well as larger political transformations that a different critical approach to adaptation (one more heavily invested in an exploration of intertextual relations, for example) might easily miss.

Where feminist film adaptations of feminist fiction are concerned, fidelity continues to matter on political grounds. In approaching such texts, however, critics need recourse to a model of feminist fidelity that is capable of bringing into focus the ideological significance of shifts and departures from page to screen while remaining sensitive to the forces that make absolute fidelity impossible to achieve. Perfect "fidelity" to the feminist enterprise of rendering gendered subjectivity visible in all its complexity and contradictions may be impossible under the circumstances shaping commercial cinema, but a critical model of fidelity that understands and makes room for these constraints can help to explore and evaluate the limitations and possibilities of a feminist adaptation practice like the one in which Stopkewich has been engaged since the mid-1990s.

Notes

Author's note: Funding for this research was generously provided by the Social Sciences and Humanities Research Council.

1

It was a moment, in fact, that lasted all through the 1990s and produced a dozen or so films almost as thematically provocative as *Kissed,* including David Wellington's *I Love a Man in Uniform,* David Cronenberg's *Crash,* Jerry Ciccoritti's *Paris, France,* and Jeremy Podeswa's *Eclipse.*

2

Linda Williams drew attention to this aspect of Stopkewich's work in a *Sight & Sound* review of *Suspicious River,* where she pointed to Stopkewich's "growing portfolio as an adapter of women's literary works." For Williams, who was one of only a few critics to champion *Suspicious River* at a time when the majority of male (and some female) critics viciously attacked the film, one of the distinctive qualities of Stopkewich's work is her strong attraction to women-centred stories. Linda Ruth Williams, "Suspicious River," *Sight & Sound* 11.9 (September 2001): 54.

3

Stopkewich has come close to adapting other literary works and, as of this writing, has plans to adapt others. In the category of adaptations that almost happened, Stopkewich was slated

to adapt Barbara Gowdy's novel *Falling Angels* in the late 1990s before reducing her role on the film to that of co-producer in order to direct *Suspicious River.* More recently, she planned to direct an adaptation based on stories by Patricia Highsmith but walked away from the project after a rewrite by her friend and co-author Doug Fraser took a direction that didn't interest her (Stopkewich interview, December 2006). Stopkewich was also chosen to adapt a short story by Alice Munro for Shaftesbury Film's planned anthology series The Munro Stories, but that project died, in 2005, due to lack of support and changes in the funding structure adopted by the Canadian Television Fund.

4

For more on the public–private split as it functions in Hollywood adaptations of feminist fiction, see Deborah Cartmell, I.Q. Hunter, Heidi Kaye, and Imelda Whelehan, *Sisterhoods: Across the Literature/Media Divide* (London: Pluto Press, 1998), 13. For a persuasive dissenting view on the viability of this distinction as applied to adaptation studies, see Simone Murray, "Materializing Adaptation Theory: The Adaptation Industry," *Literature Film Quarterly* 36.1 (2008): 4–20. Murray rejects any characterization of literature as the product of isolated authors, and focuses attention on the processes by which

contemporary literary fiction is "created, published, marketed, evaluated for literary prizes and adapted for screen" (5). I became aware of Murray's important work too late to incorporate it into this project in any depth, but her arguments about the need for a more materialist approach to book-to-film transformations are reshaping my thinking about literary fiction and the cultural economy of adaptation.

5

See for example several of the entries in Deborah Cartmell and Imelda Whelehan, eds., *Adaptations: From Text to Screen, Screen to Text* (London: Routledge, 1999); Cartmell et al., *Sisterhoods* (London: Pluto Press, 1998); and Barbara Tepa Lupack, ed., *Vision/Revision: Adapting Contemporary American Fiction by Women to Film,* ed. Lupack (Bowling Green, OH: Bowling Green State University Popular Press, 1996). See also numerous entries in Barbara Tepa Lupack, ed., *Nineteenth-Century Women at the Movies: Adapting Classic Women's Fiction to Film* (Bowling Green, OH: Bowling Green State University Popular Press, 1999). Within *Vision/Revision,* see especially Lupack, "History as Her-Story: Adapting Bobbie Ann Mason's *In Country,*" 159–92; Jennifer Ross Church, "The Balancing Act of *Fried Green Tomatoes,*" 193–210; Janice Doane and

Devon Hodges, "In Love with Consumption: From Anne Rice's Novels to Neil Jordan's *Interview with the Vampire*," 227–48; and Rebecca Summer, "Smoothing Out the Rough Spots: The Film Adaptation of 'Where Are You Going, Where Have You Been?'" 85–100.

6

The attempt to define and distinguish between these three quite separate but often overlapping categories is complicated by decades of critical discussion (and an inevitable lack of consensus) on what constitutes a "feminist text" (or, for that matter, "feminism"). In keeping with Teresa de Lauretis's brilliant theoretical explorations of feminist cinema and semiotics from the late 1980s, my sense is that a feminist text is one that works with contradictions and attempts to specify the modes of consciousness of female and feminist subjectivity, often in ways that help to reshape established narrative and aesthetic categories. Such films, according to de Lauretis, develop conceptual and formal means to represent the contradiction that is constitutive of the female subject of feminism: "to speak, like Cassandra, a discourse that elides woman as speaker-subject, and hence will not be heard by most; to tell stories resisting the drift of narrativization (the operation of narrative closure, or the 'family plot,' as Hitchcock had occasion to call it); to make films against the plot that frames woman as narrative image, object, and ground of cinematic representation. In short, to reread, rewrite, remake all cultural narratives striving to construct another form of coherence, one that is, alas, founded on contradiction." Teresa de Lauretis, *Technologies of Gender: Essays on Theory, Film, and Fiction* (Bloomington: Indiana UP, 1987), 114. Having said this, though, my definition of a feminist text does not depend in any strict sense on the modernist-feminist demand for an aesthetics of alienation or contradiction as the basis of its revolutionary politics. Advances in reception theory and new critical and historical approaches to popular culture have exploded this formalist assumption to such an extent that it now seems impossible to argue that feminist films *necessarily* call attention to the cinematic apparatus or *necessarily* engage in an aesthetics of edifying alienation.

7

Hypotext is Gerard Genette's term for any "source" or prior text within a textual palimpsest, a general category that includes but is not limited to adaptations. Gerard Genette, *Palimpsests: Literature in the Second Degree*, trans. Channa Newman and Claude Doubinsky (Lincoln: U of Nebraska P, 1997). My use of the term "primary literary source" is intended as a compromise between the need to acknowledge when adaptations base themselves on one particular hypotext and the equally pressing need to acknowledge that all texts, including adaptations, are fundamentally intertextual. As Kristeva puts it, "Every text builds itself as a mosaic of quotations, every text is absorption and transformation of another text." Julia Kristeva, quoted in C. Hugh Holman and William Harmon, *A Handbook to Literature*, 6th ed. (New York: Macmillan, 1992), 251.

8

See also Robert Stam, *Literature through film: Realism, Magic, and the Art of Adaptation* (Oxford: Blackwell, 2005), and Robert Stam and Alessandra Raengo, eds., *Literature and Film: A Guide to the Theory and Practice of Film Adaptation* (Oxford: Blackwell, 2005).

9

On this point, see Elspeth Tulloch, "Yves Simoneau's Rewriting of the Troubled Manhood Script in Anne Hébert's *Les fous de Bassan*," *Essays on Canadian Writing* 76 (2002): 83–116, esp. 111. Tulloch argues, "although disparate and even idiosyncratic readings are to be expected in the interpretation of a text as poetic and complex as Hébert's, fidelity still looms as an issue in this adaptation [of *Les fous de Bassan*]—as it does for texts by women and for texts containing feminist critique" (111). Peter Dickinson reiterates this argument and develops it in relation to the "female gothic" in *Screening Gender, Framing Genre: Canadian Literature into Film* (Toronto: U of Toronto P, 2007), 49–76, esp. 51. Unlike Tulloch, however, Dickinson approaches feminist fidelity as a complex and fragile phenomenon that can too easily backfire. He identifies this as a problem in Anna Benson Gyles's 1996 adaptation of Carol Shields's *Swann*, which he sees as taking Shields's "gentle satire of scholarly ambition, literary fame, and social place" and transforming it into a "heavy-handed indictment of the violence perpetrated by men against women, both textually and physically" (74).

10

Despite the well-analyzed limitations of the biographical fallacy, it is tempting to think of Stopkewich's attraction to narratives involving female outsiders in relation to her upbringing as an anglophone in a francophone suburb of Montreal. She has written: "I grew up in Ville d'Anjou ... speaking English but since my neighbourhood was 99% French, picked it up. I'm not as bilingual (trilingual) as my parents. I wish I'd been more but it never happened ... since my education was in English with only one French class and not French immersion ... I know that I felt I didn't fit in as an Anglophone who didn't speak perfect French in Montreal—an outsider in her own home town ... and uncomfortable with the fact that I didn't." Lynne Stopkewich, e-mail exchange with the author, 20 February 2007.

11

Crosbie, who was one grade ahead of Stopkewich in school, went on to write and edit a series of provocative books on subjects ranging from female erotica to Canadian schoolgirl killer Paul Bernardo. Stopkewich and Crosbie fell out of touch after Crosbie's family moved away from Ville d'Anjou in the late 1970s, but Stopkewich remembers their friendship vividly and credits Crosbie with helping to fuel her imagination during long storytelling sessions on their walks to and from school. Stopkewich, interview with the author, 28 November 2006.

12

Kissed won three awards (for best actress, best director, and best film) at the 1998 Málaga International Week of Fantastic Cinema and was nominated for best film at the Sitges-Catalonian International Film Festival in 1996. Back home, Stopkewich was named Best New Western Canadian Director at the 1996 Vancouver International Film Festival. Internet Movie Database, http://www.imdb.com/title/tt0116783/awards.

13

Reviews of *Kissed* were for the most part very positive. (To use one blunt measure of success, the film rated a Tomatometer score of 78 per cent, certifying it as "fresh" rather than "rotten" on www.rottentomatoes.com.) *Variety* praised Stopkewich for showing "an assured hand with the controversial material, never stooping to sensationalism," and described *Kissed* as "an innovative, hard-to-forget meditation on a difficult subject." Branden Kelly, review of *Kissed*, *Variety* (16 September 1996), http://www.variety.com/review/VE1117911096.html?categoryid=31&cs=1. Even *Spirituality & Practice*, a publication billing itself as offering "resources for spiritual journeys," found a lot to like about the film: "*Kissed* is carried by the sensitive, moody, and well-modulated performance of Molly Parker, who makes Sandra's sexual taboo into a sacred search for meaning, embodied ritual, and mystical connection in the face of death." Frederic Brussat and Mary Ann Brussat, "*Kissed* (Review)," *Spirituality & Practice*, n.d., http://www.spiritualityandpractice.com/films/films.php?id=4876.

14

As of 2007 *Kissed* had earned back approximately $1 million, allowing Stopkewich to reimburse herself, her cast and crew, and the friends, family members, and investors who pulled together much of the film's budget. Interview with Lynne Stopkewich, 19 December 2006; and Lynne Stopkewich, "*Wide Awake*: That Necrophile Movie," M.F.A. thesis, University of British Columbia, April 1996, 21. One of the distinctive features of *Kissed* is its funding structure. Unable to secure pre-production grants from either the arts councils or Telefilm Canada, Stopkewich turned to family and friends for help and assigned each investor to a category depending on contribution size: Champions gave $500 per person, Heroes $1,000, and Patron Saints $5,000 to $20,000. The University of British Columbia contributed a student production grant of $3,400, and the Canada Council later kicked in a post-production grant of $47,000. British Columbia's B.C. Film contributed $162,000 and Telefilm finally contributed $25,000, allowing Stopkewich to have the film blown up to 35mm. Stopkewich, "*Wide Awake*," 18–21.

15

Lee Parpart, "Adapting Emotions: Notes on the Transformation of Affect and Ideology from 'We So Seldom Love on Love' to *Kissed*," *Essays on Canadian Writing* 76 (Spring 2002): 51–82. Some of what I say about *Kissed* in this chapter summarizes arguments made in the essay.

16

"If the cadaver was freshly embalmed, I could usually smell him from the basement. The smell is like a hospital and old cheese. For me, it's the smell of danger and permission, it used to key me up like amphetamine, so that by the time I reached the prep room, tremors were running up and down my legs." Barbara Gowdy, "We So Seldom Look on Love," 154.

17
The passage quotes Cheris Kramarae, "Proprietors of Language," 58–68. Qtd. in Susan L. Lanser, "Toward a Feminist Narratology," *Style* 20.3 (1986): 340.

18
As Stopkewich said recently, her "whole task" during the making of *Kissed* was to get audiences to like Sandra enough to follow her out onto a long, fragile limb: "We were literally choosing or rejecting shots based on whether Molly looked good in them, whether she looked soft or empathetic, or whether she came off looking harsh, or if her delivery of a line was at all edgy … it all had to go in that direction. That was the task of the movie: getting the audience on side with a necrophile." Stopkewich, interview, 20 December 2006.

19
I am grateful to one of the referees on this project for drawing my attention to the heteronormative quality of Stopkewich's portrayals of extreme female sexual behaviour in both of her features so far. Stopkewich's fascination with sexual extremes could perhaps be seen as aligning her work with queer and lesbian cinema's long tradition of representing and avowing similarly "outlawed" forms of desire, but in *Kissed* and *Suspicious River*, the

depiction of sexually extreme behaviour (necrophilia, casual prostitution) is contained within a heteronormative context. The situation is a little different in Stopkewich's commissioned television work, where she has mined this subtle connection to queer cinema numerous times and added to her own repertoire by directing scenes of lesbian desire and lesbian sex. She has, for example, explored this territory as a director for hire on four episodes (between 2004 and 2006) of the long-running LA lesbian series *The L Word*, which features *de rigeur* scenes of often highly suggestive lesbian sex. And in her 2002 adaptation of Emily Shultz's short story "The Value of X," for the former Showcase series *Bliss*, Stopkewich approaches the subject of sexual norms and "deviancy" as a kind of juggling act involving as many different varieties of criss-crossing desire as can fit into a half-hour time slot. *The Value of X* centres on the highs and lows of a popular high school student, Jeanette (played by Tara Spencer-Nairn in Stopkewich's adaptation), who sublimates her latent lesbian desire for her oldest and best friend by falling into a sexually ambiguous relationship with a gay young goth named Zachary (Jason MacDonald). Although Stopkewich softens the story's ending by transforming Zach's suicide into an ecstatic scene of spinning, her adaptation captures something ineffably moving in Shultz's portrayal of Jeanette and Zach's relationship and handles their one sex scene with breath-catching intensity. It is possible to view this commissioned work as a kind of continuation and

complication of Stopkewich's work in *Kissed*, another project that explores the sublimation and expression of powerful female desires in a context that includes depictions of radically passive male bodies. Zach in *The Value of X* is not quite a corpse, but Jeanette is clearly in the driver's seat during their sex scene, which features Zach as a willing but passive "bottom" to Jeanette's lesbian top.

20
Stopkewich is quoted as saying: "When I shot the film and when I edited it, especially, I wondered, 'What is the audience going to think at this point? If I was someone watching the film, how would I feel here? Would I still care about her? Would I be walking out at this point?' I liked the idea of the white light, because I thought, 'If I have it at really critical moments where people might be walking out, then the theatre will be filled with bright light and you'll be able to see who's leaving—so they'll feel really embarrassed! It's like 'You can run but you can't hide!'" Steve Biodrowski, "Necrophilia: Director Lynne Stopkewich's *Kissed* Takes a Light Look at a Dark Subject," unknown publication, located in director file for Stopkewich at the Film Reference Library in Toronto, 58.

21
Brenda Longfellow has pointed out that *Kissed* is not just a reflection of third-wave feminism but may be viewed as a response to currents and debates within 1980s feminism in North America, including feminist reconsiderations of the role of pornography and censorship. Personal correspondence, Brenda Longfellow, February 2010.

22
Lynne Stopkewich, question-and-answer session following a screening of *Suspicious River* at Cinematheque Ontario, Toronto, 8 December 2006. The screening took place as part of the Cinematheque series on British Columbian filmmakers, *Only Happy When It Rains: The Roots and Rise of the Vancouver New Wave*, curated by Steve Gravestock.

23
Laura Kasischke, *Suspicious River* (Boston: Houghton Mifflin, 1996).

24
Leila may escape and cross the river to an uncertain end on the other side. Stopkewich's own reading of the ending of the novel (and her intended meaning for the end of the film) is that Leila does not survive: "Her throat is slashed. I think she dies." Interview, 19 December 2006. In the novel, Gary and his friends have announced that they are going to kill Leila when she is apparently saved by the screeching of the swans leaving on their annual fall migration. Making her way to the river, she meets her co-worker, Millie, but the action quickly breaks down, leaving the outcome ambiguous. "Millie's fingers are warm and bony on the back of my neck. 'We have to get some help,' she says, but she doesn't move. I see us from the sky. Frozen'" (270). Leila's observation of her own body "from the sky" suggests that she is, at the very least, already out of her body.

25
Stopkewich, interview, 20 December 2006. The material that was filmed and later cut

included a series of sex scenes with patrons at a strip club where Jensen takes Leila in order to test her willingness to prostitute for him. The novel presents these scenes as key turning points in Leila's move toward abjection. With little prompting from Jensen, she allows multiple men to have sex with her in a back room of the bar and then wanders into the bar itself half-clothed, no longer caring who sees her. Stopkewich says her test audiences consistently found these scenes too difficult to watch: "They said, 'What are you trying to do, kill us?' It was just too much for them." In the end, she said, "we decided it was more effective to leave it out, and to rely more on suggestion." Stopkewich's film also omits a long scene from the novel in which Leila seeks out sex with a local pastor. Stopkewich, interview, 20 December 2006.

26
Investors included Kinowelt, Italy's Key Films, Bac Films of France, and Beyond Films of Australia. Kathy Barthel, "The Future of Feature Financing? *Suspicious River*," *Playback*, 1 January 2001: 49.

27
Rifkin argues that although pure fidelity between texts is impossible because the codes involved in film can never be "entirely identical with … [those] used by the author of the literary text to encode that text," such acts of transcoding can at times produce meaningful resonances between cinematic and literary texts. Benjamin Rifkin, 9–10.

28
Although her position has been

simplified here, Noble's larger approach to nineteenth-century American's women's sentimental literature puts forth a complex argument about women's complicit use of patriarchal constructions of eroticized female suffering and abjection. Rather than simply being the victims of improper desire, female authors have managed to take real pleasure in—and produce real pleasure for readers by—following their own "weird curves" in relation to dominant cultural depictions of female suffering: "The eroticism of sentimental suffering was a double-edged sword, functioning both as a discursive agent for the proliferation of oppressive ideologies and as a rhetorical tool for the exploration of female desire. In other words, to the extent that such literature influenced women's understandings of their own sexuality, training them to experience their desire vicariously through that of a man, or prompting them to be attracted to violent men, it was an agent of the construction of oppressive gender roles. Yes, to the extent that eroticized representations of suffering made available a language of passion, desire, and anger, they were an important form of literary agency." Marianne Noble, *The Masochistic Pleasures of Sentimental Literature* (Princeton, NJ: Princeton UP, 2000), 6.

29
Mainstream reviews of the film were mostly negative. Christopher Null quipped that spectators would "have trouble tracking down a more unwatchable movie this year than *Suspicious River*, which both firmly installs Molly Parker as the unequivocal

goddess of freak-out not-quite-porn movies and will have you wondering just how bad a script has to be in order to get a movie made." Kevin Courrier wrote that *Suspicious River* "explores ... sexually obsessive material [similar to that in *Kissed*] but it isn't as well thought out," and argued that despite "ethereal" and "charming" performances from Molly Parker and Callum Keith Rennie, the film has "too many bends in the stream." Christopher Null, "Suspicious River, review," Filmcritic.com, 2004, http://www.filmcritic.com/misc/emprium.nsf. Kevin Courrier, "*Suspicious River* review," Boxoffice.com, http://www.boxoffice.com/boxoffice_scr/movie_reviews_result.asp?terms=5141.

30
Kasischke's novel is set in northern Michigan, while the film was shot in Hope, B.C., and set in a semi-rural anywhere.

31
In one evocative passage that touches upon the wider context of Leila's descent, Kasischke alternates between a description of one of Uncle Andy's attacks on Leila's mother and some dreamy business about a collection of Barbie dolls that come to Leila's mind while she free-associates, trying to block out the sounds of domestic abuse. A little later, Leila recalls that those dolls made of "rigid plastic" sometimes "slap each other for no reason—jealousy or spite—with their outstretched zombie arms," while at other times they "take off all their clothes and dance around and around in circles, their pointed feet pressed together as if their ankles are tightly chained" (71–72).

32
As Ellie Ragland-Sullivan explains, Lacan's reformulation of "feminine masochism" centres on his notion of "the human hope for completeness" as based on "a structural refusal to relinquish the loss of the mother as imagined primary object" (241). According to Lacan's schema, "masochists identify with jouissance, with the Real of their suffering, which is the fundamental truth of the dissatisfied human subject—the loss of the undifferentiation that a union with the mother represents" (241). Ellie Ragland-Sullivan, "Masochism," *Feminism and Psychoanalysis: A Critical Dictionary*, Elizabeth Wright, ed. (Oxford: Blackwell, 1992), 241. Leila's compulsion to revisit and repeat her mother's fate suggests both Freud's work on trauma and a Lacanian understanding of masochism as rooted in a damaged imaginary relation to the primary m/Other.

33
Regardless of Stopkewich's intent, it is worth noting that at least one critic read the ending as asserting Leila's survival. In a summary of the film's plot, Sameer Padania writes that Leila "escapes back to the other side of Suspicious River, and lives to see the swans come back." Sameer Padania, "Suspicious River," film review, Kamera.co.uk, http://www.kamera.co.uk/reviews_extra/suspiciousriver.php.

34
Unlike Moore's novel, which closes with its masochistic female protagonist dying of knife wounds in an abandoned lighthouse, murdered by a serial killer whose *modus operandi*

is to play to women's culturally inculcated thirst for romance and marriage, Campion's film (adapted by Moore from her own novel) rewrites this bleak analysis of the dominant cultural templates of femininity and romantic love by having Meg Ryan's character shoot her attacker and return home to her sexy homicide detective lover.

35
E.H. Gombrich offers a useful analogy about the differences between media when he suggests that "if an artist stands before a landscape with a pencil in hand, he or she will 'look for those aspects which can be rendered in lines'; if it is a paintbrush that the hand holds, the artist's vision of the very same landscape will be in terms of masses, not lines" (1961, 65). Qtd. in Linda Hutcheon, *A Theory of Adaptation* (New York: Routledge, 2006), 19.

36
One of Teresa de Lauretis's many attempts to define feminist cinema and/or women's cinema (she uses both terms) involves this notion of gendered address. In "Rethinking Women's Cinema," de Lauretis defines as feminist any film whose "visual and symbolic space" is organized in a manner that *addresses its spectator as a woman*, regardless of the gender of the viewers." By this she means that "the film defines all points of identification (with character, image, camera) as female, feminine, or feminist." Teresa de Lauretis, "Rethinking Women's Cinema: Aesthetics and Feminist Theory," *Technologies of Gender: Essays on Theory, Film and Fiction* (Bloomington: Indiana UP, 1987), 133.

Elsewhere, de Lauretis argues that the term feminist cinema evokes "a process rather than an aesthetic or typological category" (115), and involves a wide range of different strategies for representing the contradictions constitutive of the female subject of feminism. De Lauretis, "Strategies of Coherence," 114.

Works Cited

Barthel, Kathy. "The Future of Feature Financing? *Suspicious River.*" *Playback* 1 January 2001: 49.

Gowdy, Barbara. "We So Seldom Look on Love." *We So Seldom Love on Love: Stories.* By Barbara Gowdy. Toronto: Somerville House, 1992.

Hutcheon, Linda. *A Theory of Adaptation.* London: Routledge, 2006.

Kasischke, Laura. *Suspicious River.* Boston: Houghton Mifflin, 1996.

Kemp, Sandra, and Judith Squires. *Feminisms.* Oxford: Oxford UP, 1997.

Kramarae, Chris. "Proprietors of Language." *Women and Language in Literature and Society.* Ed. Sally McConnel-Ginet, Ruth Borker, and Nelly Furman. New York: Praeger, 1980.

Noble, Marianne. *The Masochistic Pleasures of Sentimental Literature.* Princeton, NJ: Princeton UP, 2000.

Parpart, Lee. "Adapting Emotions: Notes on the Transformation of Affect and Ideology from 'We So Seldom Look on Love' to *Kissed.*" *Essays on Canadian Writing* 76 (Spring 2002): 51–82.

Rifkin, Benjamin. *Semiotics of Narration in Film and Prose Fiction.* New York: Lang, 1995.

Stopkewich, Lynne. Interviews. 28 November 2006, 8 December 2006, 19 December 2006, 20 December 2006.

Tulloch, Elspeth. "Yves Simoneau's Rewriting of the Troubled Manhood Script in Anne Hébert's *Les fous de Bassan.*" *Essays on Canadian Writing* 76 (Spring 2002): 83–116.

Williams, Linda Ruth. "Suspicious River." *Sight and Sound* 11.9 (September 2001).

On the Edge of Genre:
Anne Wheeler's Interrogating
Maternal Gaze
Kathleen Cummins

> You know I'm on the edge of being a genre filmmaker, but not enough
> for the distributors. And yet, there is all this pressure not to do that.
> — Anne Wheeler[1]

By identifying herself as being "on the edge of genre," Anne Wheeler is acknowledging, and lamenting, her curious insider–outsider status within Canadian film
culture, where her work has been deemed either too commercial by cultural critics or not commercial enough by mainstream distributors/exhibitors. Despite
Wheeler's extensive body of film and television work, her many filmmaking
awards, her six honorary doctorates, and the Order of Canada,[2] Wheeler's status
as a Canadian woman/feminist film auteur has been curiously delimited, resulting in a devaluing of her work both critically and commercially. Her outsider status has meant that she has flown below the feminist and non-feminist film criticism radar, with a few notable exceptions.[3] In this sense, Wheeler has experienced a fate similar to that of Hollywood filmmaker Kathryn Bigelow, who until
recently has been mainly dismissed by critics.[4] Wheeler's critical marginalization
is a familiar story for women filmmakers and artists who fall outside the high-
art/low-art dichotomy that persists to this day within cultural criticism and that
Brigitte Rollet insists has "indirectly reinforced male predominance over culture"
(Rollet, 129).

For over three decades feminist film culture has sought, albeit without
consensus, to define the parameters of feminist film practices, aesthetics, and
spectatorship. One of the central questions has been, and continues to be:
How can women/feminist filmmakers construct female subjectivity through
"an apparatus so fundamentally structured according to masculine logic?"
(Flitterman-Lewis, 2). Historically, this fundamental question has been applied
primarily to women filmmakers working within art- house or avant-garde

cinemas, resulting in the marginalization of women working in mainstream commercial media. Due to this privileging of counter-cinema work within feminist film culture, and even arguably within Canadian film culture itself, mainstream women filmmakers like Wheeler have either been ignored or dismissed by critics for being not only too commercial but complicit in the problematic representation of woman and femininity within the dominant cinema.

Wheeler's notion of herself as on the edge of genre is an apt point of entry into a discussion of her work because it encapsulates the very essence of Wheeler's feminist signature. Three imbricating strains—ideological, regional, and aesthetic—mark Wheeler's extensive body of film and television work over numerous decades and within various Canadian industrial and institutional con-texts. Ideologically, Wheeler's feminist sensibility and vision, informed by the second-wave women's movement, is expressed through her privileging of the female point of view and female desire. In stark contrast to the mainstream com-mercial cinema, Wheeler's (desiring) female subjects are often cast as moth-ers or maternal figures over the age of thirty and even forty, struggling to main-tain control over their own bodies and voices in a world plagued by colonial and patriarchal violence. Wheeler's film aesthetics have leaned toward traditional genre storytelling forms, particularly melodrama, but also the family films and the romantic comedies often demarcated as "women's films" that have been dis-avowed historically by cultural critics. However, it is Wheeler's nuanced, sub-versive use of genre narrative traditions that position her as a film auteur—tra-ditions in which she destabilizes essentializing notions of femininities and mas-culinities at the narrative level. In addition to embracing genre narrative struc-tures, Wheeler's work is marked by her engagement with realist cinema,[5] consis-tently and enduringly conveying everyday stories about women, men, and chil-dren. Wheeler's feminist aesthetics are rooted in representations of the every-day rather than the edgy de-aesthetics advocated by Teresa de Lauretis or the anti-pleasure/anti-narrative strategies professed by Laura Mulvey.[6] In this sense Wheeler's feminist authorship echoes Claire Johnston's advocacy for the "enter-tainment film" as a means of countering "our objectification in the cinema."[7] With regard to the regional strain of her feminist signature, Wheeler's identity as an Albertan is at the root of her undying commitment to telling Western Canadian (feminist) stories. Hence, Wheeler is not only on the edge of genre as a femi-nist, she is also on the (western) edge of the Canadian film centre. As Canadian critic Jerry White writes, "Alberta filmmaking is not exactly at the forefront of the Canadian cinematic imagination."[8]

Although Wheeler does not always practise all levels of feminist interrogation within any one individual film, her work as a whole tells a certain kind of Canadian feminist story, a story told through an interrogating maternal gaze, a device enabling her to construct female (maternal) desire differently. With regard to the represention of everyday female subjects, Wheeler has given Canada some of its most defiant, complex, and transgressive maternal screen heroines, among them mothers, and often single mothers, such as *Bye Bye Blues*'s grass widow Daisy Cooper (Rebecca Jenkins), belting out the blues to soldiers waiting to be shipped off to war; *Loyalties'* Aboriginal battered wife Rosanne (Tantoo Cardinal), aiming a gun at a white male pedophile and rapist; *Better Than Chocolate*'s middle-aged homemaker Lila (Wendy Crewson), wielding a dildo to the soundtrack of Puccini; *To Set Our House in Order*'s stoic labouring mother (Maureen Thomas), gently assuring her daughter all will be well, though we know this may not be the case; *Marine Life*'s aging lounge singer June (Cybill Shepherd), wrestling her lover to the floor of her messy kitchen.

In opposition to mainstream cultural representations of motherhood, Wheeler's feminist vision defies what E. Ann Kaplan calls the three main mother paradigms: the "all-sacrificing angel in the house, the over-indulgent mother, satisfying her own needs, and finally the evil, possessive and destructive all-devouring one" (48). The dramatic tensions and conflicts in Wheeler's films—most of which are in traditional women's film genres, particularly melodrama and romantic comedy—are politicized through progressive representations of mothers as resisting figures, as well as the construction of female desire through a maternal point of view and gaze. Kaplan sees many maternal melodramas as "resisting texts." "These resisting texts shift the balance between the realism and melodrama in the direction of the cognitive voice not heard in melodramatic texts" (126). Wheeler's texts are not only resisting texts, however; they are progressive texts of the kind advocated by such feminist critics as Linda Williams (1987). Indeed, it is Wheeler's thematic threads and her depictions of resisting maternal figures, rather than issues pertaining to form, that identify her most as feminist auteur.[9] In this sense Wheeler's feminist vision is similar to that of Marie Epstein, the French director from the 1930s, (re)discovered by Sandy Flitterman-Lewis in her seminal *To Desire Differently*. Flitterman-Lewis identifies Epstein's ability to "subvert the dominant Hollywood model" through her use of "populist milieu and location shooting (29)," a straightforward narrative structure, and melodrama, while focused on mother–child relation storylines.

A secondary element of Wheeler's feminist signature is her destabilization and interrogation of masculinity through her depiction of two male figures, the disenfranchised and/or marginalized romantic catalyst and the afflicted, fallen, and/or absent father. Wheeler's male figures function within the narratives on two levels, both as melodramatic devices and as realistic complications of mainstream Hollywood tropes, such as the cowboy (alcoholic ex-rodeo star Josh in *Cowboys Don't Cry* and Aboriginal ex-con cattle rancher

Bill in *Betrayed*), the working-class hero (drifter Max in *Bye Bye Blues*), and the medical professional (the imprisoned Dr. Wheeler in *A War Story* and the rapist/pedophile Dr. Sutton in *Loyalties*). Although much has been written about depictions of male (anti-)heroes as either losers or victims in Canadian literature and cinema, by critics such as Robert Fothergill (1977), Margaret Atwood (1972), and Christine Ramsay (1999), Wheeler's depiction of masculinity is complicated by its use of a maternal lens.[10] Like Bigelow, Wheeler is a woman filmmaker who has dared to make movies about men, and as early as 1981. Unlike Bigelow, however, most of these films have been in the family-film genre, a genre rarely considered prestigious.

This brings us back to Wheeler's stated problem of being considered not commercial enough for mainstream distributors/exhibitors. The regional, political, and aesthetic strains that would traditionally posit Wheeler as a film auteur have perhaps rendered her projects less identifiable to the wider audience sought by theatrical big-screen distributors, forcing her to seek financing and distribution in television, primarily through the CBC but also the Hallmark Channel in the US. Wheeler's marginalization within the industry mirrors the plight of her forceful, subversive, and enigmatic maternal heroines. Casting Wheeler as a heroic figure of resistance is perhaps a bit melodramatic, but Wheeler's edgy place within the mainstream Canadian film context has trapped her in a kind of open-ended vicious circle.

In order to trace Wheeler's enduring feminist vision, I focus on three time periods and industry contexts in Wheeler's extensive oeuvre[11]—her documentary and short dramatic work with the National Film Board of Canada, from 1975 to the late 1980s; her feature film work in the Canadian independent cinema, from the late the 1980s to 2002; and her television work, from 1993 to 2009.

The Early Years: Maternal Divas and Lost Fathers

> Do the films that form the body of 'feminist cinema' say something
> different, speak a different desire, desire in difference? In short, does
> feminist cinema posit a way to *desire differently*?
> – Flitterman-Lewis (2)

Wheeler's earliest significant films were the documentaries and dramatic shorts she made through Studio D and the Prairie Region of the National Film Board of Canada, either in association with Film West Associates, Atlantis Films, or the CBC. The documentaries *Great Grand Mother* (1975), *Augusta* (1976), *Happily Unmarried* (1977), and *A War Story* (1981) would establish the realist aesthetic and thematic foundation for Wheeler's future film oeuvre. Her dramatic shorts *Teach Me to Dance* (1978), *One's a Heifer* (1984), *Change of Heart* (1984), and *To*

Set Our House in Order (1985) would establish her feminist aesthetics through her use of narrative and genre, namely the maternal melodrama. Through these early films Wheeler foregrounds and/or privileges a female (maternal) point of view, while exploring such themes as female autonomy and agency, gender relations, afflicted males, failed fathers, domestic violence, immigrant experiences, the costs of war, mother–daughter bonds, interracial relations, and aging amid Western Canadian communities and landscapes. Wheeler's NFB work would also position her in a particular feminist film practice camp, in which the use of realism and the foregrounding of women's issues as associated with the second-wave women's movement (e.g., equal pay, female independence, domestic abuse) were primary. However, throughout Wheeler's career with the NFB, she would also make films whose narratives revolve around male characters who interrogate masculinity in the process.

It is important to consider the socio-historical contexts for these early films in order to clarify the birth of Wheeler's feminist film practice. When Wheeler made her first films for Studio D, the women's movement in Canada was well under way. White middle-class women were entering the workforce in large numbers for the first time and challenging patriarchy through feminist collective activism, cultural production, and scholarship. Studio D, the first and only feminist film unit in the world, was a new, albeit underfunded, initiative implemented by the federal government under the direction of Kathleen Shannon. Its purpose was to give Canadian women the opportunity to bring their voices and experiences to screens across Canada, though those voices and experiences belonged primarily to white, middle-class, anglophone, heterosexual women, like Anne Wheeler.[12] The "personal is political" mantra of that movement was a core value at the Studio D. Studio D historian Gail Vanstone writes,

> From the outset, Studio D established two main objectives: to protect women's perspectives in its documentaries and to create filmmaking opportunities for Canadian women in a field traditionally dominated by men. The Studio's documentaries captured emerging feminist debates, shadowing such topics as women and work, pornography, sexuality, identity, female spirituality, peace initiatives, the colonizing of race and the celebration of women artists. (36)

Overall, the NFB was committed to counteracting the Hollywood model, reflecting everyday Canadians for Canadians. Its aesthetics were rooted in social realism. Traditional documentary techniques and practices such as the disembodied (male) voice-of-God narration, talking heads, and the use of archival footage were established in the 1940s by "founding father" John

Grierson. For the most part, Studio D inherited Grierson's aesthetics, only to find itself caught up in the feminist film theory wars of the 1980s and '90s, in which it was attacked not only for its realist aesthetics but also for its inherent racism and classism. Gail Vanstone writes, "Studio D aligned itself resolutely with 'realist cinema' and activist feminism throughout its existence, holding a certain skepticism for 'theoretical feminism'" (113). This skepticism would divide feminist film critics and filmmakers into different schools of feminist practice. Teresa de Lauretis writes,

> The accounts of feminist film culture produced in the mid- to late seventies tended to emphasize a dichotomy between two concerns of the women's movement and two types of film work that seemed to be at odds with each other: one called for immediate documentation for purposes of political activism, consciousness raising, self-expression, or the search for "positive images" of women; the other insisted on rigorous, formal work on the medium—or better, the cinematic apparatus, understood as a social technology—in order to analyze and disengage the ideological codes embedded in representation. (128)

Wheeler's work would fall into the former category. Film producer Kim Todd, describing Wheeler's feminist approach, explains, "There is nothing theoretical about Anne's feminism. I think she thinks of people and their stories before she thinks of any *ism*" (qtd. in Dafoe, C6).

Also worth mentioning in regard to Wheeler's identity as a Western Canadian, and her commitment to representing her Prairie culture and iconography on screen, is her involvement in Film West Associates. An independent cooperative and ad hoc film school, Film West Associates was formed in 1971. Wheeler was one of the founding members and the only woman among nine men. Their mantra as a group was to tell stories about Western Canada. It was through Film West that Wheeler learned all aspects of film production and was able to hone her filmmaking skills. While in the collective, Wheeler made about twenty short films. After five years the collective dissolved (http:// www.collectionscanada.gc.ca/women/002026-719-e.html).

Produced by Film West Associates and the NFB, *Great Grand Mother* (1975), co-directed and co-written with Lorna Rasmussen, was inspired by Wheeler's grandmother's personal experiences on the Prairies at the turn of the nineteenth century (Cummins, 30). Privileging the voices of ordinary rural women, through the use of diaries and letters, as well as dramatic re-enactments, the film lovingly renders visible Prairie (white) women's experiences from early European immigration to their struggle for suffrage. Wheeler foregrounds the plurality of female voices, rejecting the traditional (male) voice-of-God nar-ration in the process, thus privileging female experiential knowledge. Through the film's plural voice-over narration the film resists what Kaja Silverman refers to as the disembodied male narration in the dominant cinema, a "voice on high" that speaks from a position of superior knowledge" (48). In her seminal work on the female voice Silverman interrogates how patriarchy has imprisoned the female voice, and hence subjectivity, through specific technical sound devices of the mainstream cinema, an ideological acoustic mirror of Western culture and society. Through Wheeler's use of women's voices we experience and empathize with their isolation and dislocation as immigrants, the physical and psychologi-cal demands of reproductive labour and motherhood, their endless domestic and back-breaking farm work, as well as the emotionally unfulfilling, and sometimes violent, domestic environments. Through her great grand mother's gaze Wheeler resists romanticizing marriage and gender relations of the past.

However, Wheeler's historical female subjects are never represented as passive victims. They do resist, mainly through the formation of community networks among other rural women. Despite their often oppressive and confin-ing lives Wheeler's subjects speak lovingly of the community among women. Amid harsh prairie landscapes these women, across generations, determinedly gather to form essential social networks, all laying the groundwork for univer-sal suffrage. By constructing spaces and places for political organization and community, these women defy victimization and defeat, serving Wheeler's and Rasmussen's story as inspirational figures of resistance. Female bonds amid oppression, isolation, adversity, and harsh western landscapes will be a recur-ring thread in much of Wheeler's later dramatic work.

In her second documentary for the NFB, *Augusta* (1976), Wheeler continued to explore female resistance and resilience in the face of adverse circumstances and settings through the figure of Augusta, an eighty-eight-year-old non-status Shuswap woman and grandmother living alone in her modest isolated backwoods home in the Williams Lake area of British Columbia. Augusta has rejected reservation life and the confines of a nursing home in favour of autonomy. Filmed in the style of traditional documentary realism in the rugged west-coast landscape, the film recounts Augusta's life story as she invites us, and Wheeler, to listen to her eyewitness testimony about colonial genocide. Again, there is no disembodied voice on high delimiting Augusta's point of view. Augusta gives us ordinary life lessons about her experiences as a survivor of the brutally racist Canadian mission school system under which she was torn away from her beloved mother, the difficulties she endured in an abusive marriage, her pride in her work as a volunteer midwife, and the fulfillment and pain she experienced as mother, not only to her own children but to many abandoned

Aboriginal children who had no one at all. We learn that most of these children are no longer living, due to both poverty and alcoholism. Augusta saw many of her children die, and she witnessed the tragic near extinction of her native language and culture. Through Augusta's powerful storytelling she emerges not as victim of oppression and racist violence but as an agent of resistance. Augusta is another "great grand mother," adopting a maternal oppositional gaze and voice in her resistance to the ideological legacy of patriarchal and colonial domination over her people. As in Wheeler's *Great Grand Mother*, Augusta wields not only a maternal gaze but a gaze informed by a subaltern subjectivity. Echoing Gayatri Spivak's seminal "Can the Subaltern Speak?" Wheeler's film carves out space for Augusta to speak her experience and knowledge about the female Aboriginal experience in the Canadian nation-building project. In this sense Wheeler does not attempt to speak for Augusta.[13] Like Wheeler's other (white) great grand mothers, Augusta is to be listened to, not studied under some cold ethnographic colonizing gaze. Wheeler would revisit the figure of the subaltern mother/grandmother in *Loyalties* and *Edge of Madness*.

Produced and written by Lorna Rasmussen, Wheeler's third NFB documentary was *Happily Unmarried* (1977). Set in Edmonton, the film focuses on the themes of female autonomy and the mother–daughter bond. It features an unmarried Lorna Rasmussen and her newly divorced mother, Joyce. Wheeler films the two women living their lives as single women. Wheeler's frame moves through domestic spaces, workplaces, and sites of leisure, as Lorna and her mother discuss marriage, sexuality, autonomy, work, loneliness, depression, and female friendships. The crux of the film is the conversation and connection between daughter and mother, who was only nineteen when she had her first child. Although the women are represented as a positive mother–daughter couple, neither is idealized by Wheeler's gaze. When Joyce tells her daughter, and us, about the isolation and limitations of motherhood, and her resultant bouts of depression, it is clear that she aims to present herself not as the ideal mother but as a human being. Lorna, and Wheeler, listen carefully to Joyce's cautionary tale about the heterosexual marriage and bourgeois bliss. Although the film reflects some of the second-wave white elitist feminist theorizing about the home as women's primary source of oppression, epitomized in the work of American feminist Betty Friedan, Wheeler and Rasmussen do not render invalid domestic work and spaces. Rather, mother and daughter are framed in kitchens doing "women's work" as they talk about the highs and lows of single-hood, and in this sense the representation of the feminine and motherhood is not essentialized.[14] The honesty with which Lorna and Joyce try to make sense of their lives may stand as a meaningful point of identification for the viewer today, male or female.

The NFB short *Teach Me to Dance* (1978) marks the beginning of Wheeler's journey into dramatic work. From an original script by Myrna Kostash, the film explores the theme of cultural and ethnic intolerance in a small Prairie community through the story of two young girls, Ukrainian immigrant Lesia and English Canadian settler Sarah. Ethnic prejudices and patriarchal domination erupt when the girls—who are best friends—decide to perform a traditional Ukrainian folk dance together at their school's Christmas concert. The Anglo-Saxon male community leaders prohibit the girls from performing their dance and publicly disavow their friendship. Wheeler's female gaze interrogates this oppressive patriarchal measure through the trope of the folk dance, a form traditionally associated with the celebration and/or expression of ethnic values and histories as embodied by a performative female body. Wheeler's critical frame depicts how patriarchy deploys gender as a tool for oppressing marginalized groups. Here, non-English—hence non-Canadian—customs and cultural practices are disavowed by the community, through the severing of female bonds and delimiting female subjectivity. Hence, the interconnected relationship between patriarchy and empire are interrogated here, and, significantly, from a female child's point of view. A number of Wheeler's films would be structured from the child's point of view, a perspective commonly silenced or trivialized in mainstream cinema, not unlike the female voice.

In 1981, with the assistance of the NFB, Wheeler returned to the documentary form with her highly personal *A War Story*. Serving as writer, director, and producer, she based her film on letters her father wrote from Japan during his internment as a prisoner of war in World War II. Wheeler (re)tells her father's war story using a variety of devices, such as archival war footage, dramatic re-enactments, and current-day interviews with WW II veterans, her deceased father's surviving fellow prisoners.[15] As in *Augusta* and *Great Grand Mother*, Wheeler rejects the (male) voice-of-God narration technique used routinely in war documentaries. Rather, she uses multiple voices to reconstruct the past, including her own. Appearing onscreen in interviews with aging, haunted veterans, Wheeler casts herself as a daughter figure in search of a lost father, both on a personal level and an allegorical level. Interrogating the tragedy and the human cost of war, Wheeler discovers there is no valour and no glory, only isolation, death, fear, and fragility. Wheeler's father is no war hero but rather a desperate and vulnerable man who struggled to survive starvation, disease, and despair. He found solace only in letters from home, from Wheeler's mother. Despite that she tells a male-centred tale, Wheeler rejects the "band of brothers" trope so commonly used in the war picture genre. *A War Story* would mark the beginning of Wheeler's interest in telling male-driven narratives and working in the more "male genres" (e.g., crime, war), as well as her ability to revision popular genre codes to foreground and critique the problems with patriarchal projects such as war. It is perhaps her tendency to tell stories about men, particularly fathers, that has impeded the passage of Wheeler's work into feminist canons, in the context of both national and international cinema.

Wheeler continued to explore masculinity and paternal figures in her next dramatic short, *One's a Heifer* (1984), produced by Atlantis Films and the NFB, as part of a Canadian short-story film series. This film would mark the beginning of a long-time connection with Atlantis Films, an independent production company that would help produce a number of Wheeler's later theatrical and television films. *One's a Heifer*, co-written by Wheeler and Donaleen Saul, is based on a Sinclair Ross short story set on the Prairies during the Depression. The film is told from thirteen-year-old Peter's point of view and focuses on the troubling encounter between Peter and Arthur Vickers, a strange and lonely frontier man. When Peter sets out to recapture two calves that strayed during a storm, he meets up with Vickers, who seems to be suffering from paranoia and alcoholism and is apparently hiding something mysterious in his barn shed. Fatherless, Peter becomes a kind of surrogate son to the childless predatory figure of Arthur, who, though he is the right age to be Peter's father, is severely lacking in mental stability or wage-earning ability. Filmed forebodingly like a mystery/thriller, the story is rife with the threat of (sexual) violence. Placed in a vulnerable marginal position, the child Peter finds himself the victim of an oppressive (male) gaze. And yet, framed by Wheeler's interrogating lens, Arthur's gaze is not all-powerful or normalized. In this child–father context Wheeler renders the male gaze a dangerous and a monstrous thing.[16] Wheeler would return to her examination of the troubled/afflicted paternal figure later, particularly in the family dramas *Change of Heart* and *Cowboys Don't Cry*.

Wheeler next adapted Margaret Laurence's *To Set This House in Order* (1985), also part of the Canadian short-story series produced by the NFB and Atlantis Films. The film is important because it marks Wheeler's first real foray into the maternal melodrama. As in *Teach Me to Dance* and *One's a Heifer*, the narrative is related from the child's point of view—in this case, that of Vanessa, albeit Vanessa as an adult. Set during the Depression in a small western town, the story centres on an unhappy cash-strapped middle-class family haunted by the death of the girl's uncle—"the gunner with one eye" who died fighting in WW I. The central narrative arc is a coming-of-age story in which the adolescent Vanessa is forced to confront an adult world in which sacrifice is gendered. In the more public "masculine" form of sacrifice, (male) war causalities are memorialized as war heroes, whereas the more feminine invisible sacrifices are represented by Vanessa's mother's near-death experience during labour and Vanessa's grandmother's debilitating grief over the loss of her son. Both maternal figures are figures of stoicism and defiance, though both are rendered seemingly passive by their housebound lives. Vanessa's voice-over functions in a way that is similar to that of the narrating voices in *Great Grand Mother.* Vanessa's question "What kind of God is in charge of this world?" is a female voice interrogating not only the order of Gramma's stifling Protestant household, where the girl lives with her impoverished parents, but the whole of patriarchy and empire, in which organized violence is institutionalized. The film, like Laurence's story, offers no resolution to this question.

Melodrama would prove a very rich form for Wheeler, one in which she would be able to express feminist views about patriarchy and colonialism. Although melodrama has historically been the genre most often disregarded and dismissed by (male) critics, feminist film critics have validated melodrama as the form most open to "progressive texts." Peter Brooks, in his landmark study *The Melodramatic Imagination* (1976), argued for melodrama as a valid genre, equal in cultural value to tragedy, and one to which the modern novel is deeply indebted. Brooks identifies melodrama as a "theatre of the grandiose" but within the reach of the people (Brooks, 43). He uses Freudian analysis as his theoretical foundation, and he uses the non-verbal forms of gesture and music to describe the power of melodrama and its use of excess dramatization. Melodrama was born of the French Revolution, and Brooks traces the genre's strong activist role among the underprivileged and illiterate masses. Jacky Bratton, Christine Gledhill, and Jim Cook, in their introduction to *Melodrama: Stage, Picture, Screen*, write, "Rather than displacing the political by the personal, melodrama produces the body and the interpersonal domain as the sites in which the socio-political stakes its struggles" (1). This is how Wheeler has engaged with melodrama—as a political form.

Wheeler moved into longer-format drama with *Change of Heart* (1984), a one-hour CBC drama produced in association with the NFB and written by Sharon Riis. It chronicles the political and emotional awakenings of Edna, a middle-aged farm wife and mother who bravely leaves her unhappy marriage when she discovers a shocking secret—her husband, Bob, is responsible for the death of her beloved first-born son. We learn through emotionally charged domestic scenes that Bob not only bullies Edna but relishes in bullying his sons, both as children and later as men, revealing the most tragic secret of all—that Edna was denied maternal desire. She couldn't be the kind of mother she really wanted to be in a house (one that she doesn't own) instilled with fear, guilt, and shame. When Edna leaves, the family is thrown into chaos, emotionally and economically. Although Edna escapes an abusive relationship, Wheeler's stoic heroine does not find blissful independence. She remains an undereducated middle-aged low-waged worker who can barely afford the rent. Although she is released from daily put-downs and domestic servility, Edna is not free from patriarchal oppression outside her husband's household. She is, after all, no longer young. Aging and ageism are central threads in much of Wheeler's work. Like Joyce in *Happily Unmarried*, Edna must find her voice and her place in the world as a subject who no longer reproduces or is deemed desirable by a patriarchal culture.

From *Loyalties* to *Edge of Madness*

> Well, everybody says if you're going to have a female lead then it's television, which is probably why I've struggled most of my life to stay on the big screen.
> – Anne Wheeler (Cummins, 22)

Wheeler's theatrical feature debut was *Loyalties*, an independent film written by Sharon Riis and co-produced by Wheeler. Regarded by many critics as Wheeler's best work, the film won numerous awards, including the Grand Prix at the Créteil International Women's Film Festival (1987) and the Canadian Genie for Best Picture (1987). *Loyalties* put Wheeler on the feature filmmaking map, both as a Canadian director (the one from Alberta) and as a woman filmmaker alongside such international luminaries as Jane Campion, Sally Potter, Maggie Greenwald, Agnieszka Holland, Julie Dash, and Kathryn Bigelow. *Loyalties* marked Wheeler's move into the realm of independent theatrical film production/distribution and her departure from the NFB, although she would return to direct two more features with them—*Bye Bye Blues* and *Angel Square*.

Set in the quiet beauty of Lac La Biche, Alberta, *Loyalties* engages with the melodramatic, and with what Brenda Longfellow refers to as "Gothic devices," to interrogate the violence of colonization within white settler society and civilization (Longfellow, 172–73). Initially, when Lily, the white, privileged but neglected wife of Dr. Sutton, hires Rosanne, a local working-class Aboriginal single mother, to be a nanny for her children, the women are divided along lines of class and race. Colonial violence and genocide haunt them and limit any hope for solidarity. However, despite their racial and class differences, and their initial disdain for each other, Lily and Rosanne find common ground when they realize they are both victims/survivors of domestic violence. Rosanne's boyfriend and father to her children is an underemployed Aboriginal man with a drinking and anger-management problem. Frustrated by his marginalized status, he uses Rosanne as his proverbial punching bag. In the case of Wheeler's (white) Lily, she must live with the horrible secret that her husband is a pedophile (the reason they have relocated to a small remote Alberta community). In this sense Lily is not just a victim, she is also complicit in patriarchal colonial violence. Lily's silence is rooted not only in fear, shame, and guilt but in her white upper-class privilege. Her silence is what keeps the two women (mothers) divided. *"What kind of woman are you?"* These are the chilling words that Rosanne Ladouceur (Tantoo Cardinal) screams at Lily Sutton (Susan Aldridge), her white upper-middle-class employer, moments after Lily's husband, Dr. David Sutton, has brutally raped Rosanne's thirteen-year-old daughter. What Rosanne really means by her damning question is What kind of *mother* are you?

It is through female solidarity and maternal desire that Lily is able to discover her own voice and subjectivity and in the end turn her husband over to the authorities. Wheeler and Riis both resist framing Lily and Rosanne as maternal martyrs or tragic romantic figures. Without descending into sentiment, the women seek support and solace from each other rather than from "the system" (e.g., the law, the medical establishment). In one sense, Rosanne is Lily's saviour, but it is clear that Rosanne could be no one's saviour without her own mother, Beatrice (Vera Marin), by her side. Beatrice is a native elder woman who is linked to old ways of knowing and a suppressed language, a language constructed outside colonial patriarchal knowledge. In this sense Beatrice signifies an ancient non-white feminine knowledge and matrifocal power, a power long ago othered and silenced. Beatrice is an Augusta figure, mothering not only her children and grandchildren but also eventually Lily and her family. The final frames of the film are shot in Beatrice's little house, in which Lily is invited to live, without judgment or fear. Indeed, Beatrice, another of Wheeler's great grand mothers, serves the narrative as a saviour of sorts. It is this solidarity among mothers, and along the lines of the maternal, that is foregrounded in the frame and the narrative. The usual female competitiveness and good-versus-bad depictions of mothers that keep all women segregated, isolated, and unfulfilled are virtually absent in the film's *mise en scène* and point of view.

Brenda Longfellow and Susan Lord have identified Wheeler's "resisting" melodramatic texts. Longfellow examines how "*Loyalties* appropriates melodramatic generic conventions to a feminist critique" (173). Lord identifies Wheeler's use of melodramatic conventions as a "deployment of melodramatic structures as they engage with the realms of law, medicine, and government" (315). Often Wheeler's depictions of mothers focus on the complex nature of mother–daughter relations rather than mother–son bonds, still so prevalent in mainstream cinema and in television. The complexity of the mother–daughter bond often manifests itself in Wheeler films through the recurring theme of the search for identity and subjectivity. Both mother and daughter must navigate the difficult terrain of finding their own voice, often in oppressive situations, while struggling to preserve, salvage, and protect their bonds of love and their identification/connection.

In Wheeler's work, and that of many of her Canadian contemporaries, the role of landscape, both rural and urban, features as a prominent trope. Discussing *Loyalties*, Longfellow articulates Wheeler's dramatic engagement with landscape as having an "ethnographic quality": "Her landscapes include the gritty interiors of bars and the kitschy order of suburbia, places marked by particular class distinctions and by the dialectic of relations between metropolitan centres and the margins, North and South stages of development" (173–74). Navigating and (re)imagining these centres and margins are how Wheeler's mothers and daughters find their voices and agency.

Throughout Wheeler's mother–daughter depictions, rape, the threat of rape, or other brutal violations against the daughter are prevalent.[17] Such patriarchal violence is explored through Wheeler's frame without becoming a mere dramatic device and without engaging in sentiment or sensationalism. Through these depictions of violence, Wheeler diverts the traditional mainstream representations of female rape victims through her engagement with motherhood. In Wheeler's films daughters are never saved by some romantic catalyst or all-protecting father figure. It is the figure of the mother that comes to the aid of the daughter, even if only to soothe the pain after the violence is committed.

Wheeler followed *Loyalties* with the family film *Cowboys Don't Cry* (1988), based on the book by Albertan children's author Marilyn Halverson and produced with Atlantis Films. Wheeler served as screenwriter as well as associate producer. Male affliction and paternal dysfunction are revisited here in a father–son story, which Wheeler says she imagined as a mother-and-daughter narrative (Cummins, Wheeler interview, 2002). Conceived through a female point of view, *Cowboys Don't Cry* has a thematic structure similar to that of Wheeler's maternal melodramas, depicting the troubled relationship between single parent Josh Morgan (Ron White), a fading and alcoholic rodeo star, and his emotionally neglected teenage son, Shane (Zachary Ansley). Mired in self-hatred and grief over the death of his wife, Lucy (Rebecca Jenkins), Josh rejects all domestic feminine spaces, and hence any hope for happiness and for a sense of his own self-worth. Josh forces his reluctant son to live amid masculine spaces, the dusty rawhide realm of the rodeo circuit, a sphere that brings with it numerous tropes associated with such "male genres" as westerns, road movies, and gladiatorial pictures. Yet in Wheeler's frame these spaces provide neither solace to the father and son nor resolution to their troubled relationship. Unlike those rawhide western heroes, Josh is unable to find meaning in the limited and oppressive concepts of masculinity. In this sense, Josh's fatherhood is confined and delimited by those male spaces. The traditional signs of manhood and the heroic, which Josh clings to desperately, stifle all possibilities of desire for a meaningful father–son connection. As a means of survival, Shane rejects his father's masculine ways by rebelliously quitting bull riding. Contrary to his father's self-obsessive dreams for his son, Shane pursues not only an education but the company of women through his friendship with Casey (Candace Ratcliffe), a girl his age, and her mother, Lindsay (Janet Laine Green), who is also a single parent. Lindsay takes Shane under her wing, offering him his first glimpse of a home and emotional stability since the death of his mother. Wheeler's positioning of the single mother as a source of wisdom, strength, and autonomy echoes the figures of Augusta and Joyce in *Happily Unmarried*, Rosanne in *Loyalties*, and foreshadows the grass widow Daisy in *Bye Bye Blues*, asserting Wheeler's commitment to a privileging of the maternal even in films ostensibly about men.

Wheeler's next film, the dramatic feature *Bye Bye Blues* (1989), perhaps her best known (and best loved), was co-produced and written by Wheeler and is based on the wartime experiences of her mother, a Prairie grass widow who worked as a musician to support her family during WW II (Thompson, 108). The NFB would serve as the film's distributor. Returning to a more personal form of filmmaking, Wheeler revisits the themes and figures introduced in *Great Grand Mother* and *A War Story*. During the writing-and-researching phase of her script Wheeler interviewed elderly Prairie women, including her own mother, about their experiences as war wives who did what they had to do to keep the home fires burning. Wheeler gleaned much drama from those testimonials (Thompson, 102–3). Told from the point of view of Daisy (Rebecca Jenkins), a young middle-class housewife and mother, *Bye Bye Blues* focuses on women's lives on the home front. When her doctor-husband (Michael Ontkean) goes missing in action, Daisy must find a way to support her young children. Daisy finds a job as a singer, much to the dismay of her disapproving relatives. Daisy hikes across the epic prairie landscape to her late-night music gigs, shedding her middle-class feminine demeanour in the process. Wheeler's Western heroine is forced to do two things she never dreamed she could ever do—find her own voice and return the gaze. She must do both in order to feed her two children.

Paid to belt out heart-wrenching tunes in overcrowded dance halls and bars, Daisy does find her voice, not only as a singer but also as a subject, and a *desiring* subject. Daisy's primary job is to perform for young Prairie boys before they set off for war to fight for Canada. Although Daisy, an attractive young woman, may be the object of the soldiers' gaze, Wheeler's frame enables Daisy to return the look, positioning the stage as a place of empowerment. It is on the stage that Daisy discovers her passion for music and another man. Wheeler's narrative trajectory focuses on Daisy's discovery of her own pleasure through her desire for music[18] and her desire for the sexy drifter-musician Max (Luke Reilly), a man who is *not* fighting for his country. Romance here is not framed within a domestic setting or within the confines of heterosexual marriage; rather,

Daisy and Max realize their desire for each other in dingy bars and broken-down pickup trucks, and it is certainly not tied up with the trappings of the classical Hollywood war romances in which male heroism is privileged over female subjectivity. As with Wheeler's own mother, Daisy's husband returns home from war, forcing her to give up the singing and Max. Sadly, patriarchy is restored.

A year later Wheeler followed *Bye Bye Blues* with the family film *Angel Square* (1990), based on the popular youth novel by Brian Doyle, co-written by Wheeler and James Defelice, best known for his film adaptation of the novel *Why Shoot the Teacher?* The film was an independent production, distributed through the NFB. Although there is very little writing about this film, it signifies some important shifts in Wheeler's work. First, *Angel Square* is Wheeler's first collaboration with male writers (although this would hardly signify a new trend in her career, which would continue to be based on collaborations with women screenwriters, novelists, and producers). Second, the film represents Wheeler's first and perhaps only attempt to depart from classic film realism, incorporating a more stylistic approach rooted in comic-book aesthetics. Third, *Angel Square* marks an iconographical shift in Wheeler's work, from an Albertan western rural aesthetic to the more urban west-coast aesthetic of British Columbia. (This was due primarily to Wheeler's relocation with her family to B.C., where she was forced to find work and where she continues to live [Thompson, 109].) The film is significant also because it marks Wheeler's first foray into comedy.

As in the boy-centred narratives *One's a Heifer* and *Cowboys Don't Cry, Angel Square* is told from the point of view of a child, through a boy's gaze that destabilizes masculine spaces and male bonding practices (e.g., children's war games) across lines of ethnicity and class. In a tough multi-ethnic west-coast urban environment in the 1940s, Tommy imagines himself an adult-like detective figure, in the mould of a sleuth on the serial radio program *The Shadow*, who must discover who committed the brutal assault on his friend's father, an ordinary working-class Jewish man. Far from the superhero world of comic books, detective novels, and war pictures, Tommy must learn to navigate the stark reality of the male world, in which men, as historical subjects, not as masculine icons, work at lousy jobs they hate and get beaten up by anti-Semites. Mr. Rosenberg's Jewish ethnicity represents a marginalized masculinity, exiled and punished for being outside of the heterosexual Anglo-Saxon boys' club.

Ten years passed before Wheeler directed another theatrical feature— the commercially successful *Better Than Chocolate* (1999), written by Peggy Thompson (Wheeler is credited as the script consultant). Although marketed by the film's distributors as a lesbian-themed romantic comedy, the story concerns the relationship between a middle-aged housewife Lila (Wendy Crewson) and her teenage daughter Maggie (Karyn Dwyer), whose expression of her lesbian identity, through her romance with Kim (Christina Fox) and her lesbian-bookstore job, acts as a catalyst for her mother's own repressed and suppressed desires. Though Wheeler seems to be venturing into the new territory of lesbian desire, the film's central point of view is rooted in maternal desire and engages with the maternal gaze, as with Wheeler's films such as *Happily Unmarried, Change of Heart, Cowboys Don't Cry*, and *The Diviners*.

Both Lila and Maggie desperately need to love each other unconditionally, but both are constrained by the fictional identities, imposed by a patriarchal bourgeois family paradigm. Lila, recently separated from her husband and having stifled her dream of becoming an opera singer, cannot truly connect with her daugher Maggie and accept her lesbianism until she sheds the trappings of her suburban housewife role, a bourgeois role for which she is tragically miscast. Again in this film, Wheeler's nuanced use of space and landscape is a key aesthetic. Mother and daughter are empowered to salvage their relationship only outside the confines of the traditional domestic realm, when they room together in an artist's gritty warehouse loft. Anxiety-ridden, Lila initially tries to stake a visual and ideological claim on this new and strange abode by hanging frilly curtains and fussing with flower arrangements. But when she sees her daughter and girlfriend making love, and discovers a box of sex toys under a bed (toys that she ends up using), the notion of home and desire is reimagined for Lila, giving her the space to discover her voice both as a singer and a desiring (maternal) subject. The title *Better Than Chocolate* is a reference to Lila's addiction to chocolate, which she eats to quell her unfulfilled maternal, creative, and sexual desires. Distributors were perhaps uneasy with the prospect of marketing this film as one that centred on a middle-aged housewife and decided instead to market it as a romantic comedy on a young-lesbian theme, perhaps riding on previous American indie successes such as *Personal Best* and *Go Fish*. In many ways Lila mirrors Wheeler's other aging single mothers, particularly Joyce in *Happily Unmarried* and Edna in *Change of Heart*.

The subplot in *Better Than Chocolate* featuring Judy/Jeremy (Peter Outerbridge) is worth discussing because it addresses transgendered maternal desire. An outcast, an "other" to be despised, Judy, like Lila, is a marginalized "woman"—unemployed, middle-aged, and unmarried. Like Lila playing housewife, Judy performs a version of femininity, too, albeit a transgression, a subversion of his maleness, a rejection of masculine ways. Mirroring Lila's journey toward subjectivity, Judy demands to be seen and to have her voice heard as well. This is signified by the song Judy performs as part of her nightclub act, in which she belts out the lyrics "I'm not some fucking drag queen!" In this songrant she is reminiscent of Daisy in *Bye Bye Blues* and of Rosanne in her cry of rage, *What kind of woman are you?!* Both women—Lila and Judy—discover that being feminine is not about twin-sets, pearls, and floral arrangements. Indeed, the essentialized notion of femininity imposed by Western patriarchal ideology and even second-wave feminism is here destabilized.

Following on the commercial success of *Better Than Chocolate*, Wheeler directed her next feature, *Marine Life* (2000). It featured American star Cybill Shepherd and was based on the book by Linda Svendsen. Co-written by Robert Forsyth and Lori Lansens, the film is a comedy-drama that focuses on another mother–daughter relationship, this one featuring June, a flighty divorced middle-aged lounge singer, and Adele (Alexandra Purvis), her rebellious twelve-year-old. It is told from the point of view of Adele and set in a working-class neighbourhood of Vancouver. The film depicts an aimless and confused Adele as she struggles, like Shane in *Cowboys Don't Cry*, to make sense of her chaotic household and the complicated and unhappy relations among the adults in her life.

June is perhaps Wheeler's most flawed mother. Disorganized, self-absorbed, and sometimes apathetic, June is, despite her limitations, never passive, never a victim, never a martyr, and never defeated. Like Daisy and Lila, she insists on having a voice, a passion, and a sex life, and her insistence is perhaps her gift as a maternal and feminine role model to her daughters. When June's eldest daughter returns home to escape an abusive relationship, June accepts her and cradles her in her arms. Like Beatrice in *Loyalties*, June does not have the power to defeat patriarchal violence, but she resists and defies it through maternal love. As in other Wheeler films, domestic spaces prove too confining and sometimes too dangerous for the female characters. Wheeler's frame frees her characters from their domestic prisons, letting them inhabit dark environments like June's dimly lit nightclub or the wide-open spaces of the evening cityscapes. In this sense, Wheeler's female characters "take back the night." Adele finds her inner peace, and a measure of hope, in a city aquarium, hanging out with dolphins. In that space—a watery ocean-inspired seascape, yet a confinement nonetheless—Adele makes a connection with her mother's working-class lover, Robert (Peter Outerbridge), yet another disenfranchised paternal figure, albeit a present and caring one.

Wheeler continued working in the romantic comedy vein with *Suddenly Naked* (2001), written by Elyse Friedman. Wheeler is credited here too as the film's script consultant, as well as executive producer. Set in a more chic urban setting than her previous films, which had tended to foreground working-class neighbourhoods, this film focuses on the May–December romance between twenty-year-old Patrick (Joe Cobden), a talented, impoverished writer, and thirty-nine-year-old Jackie York (Wendy Crewson), a famous and wealthy author who is Patrick's more worldly creative-writing mentor. The film represents a noticeable shift for Wheeler in that it is one of her few films that does not explicitly dramatize motherhood and maternal desire, although two teenage girls do mistake Jackie for Patrick's mother, much to her dismay. Like many of Wheeler's aging female characters, Jackie is plagued by self-doubt and an ageist culture, which contains and delimits female desire within the confines of a patriarchal logic. Jackie, like past Wheeler heroines, has lost her "voice," both as writer/artist and as desiring female subject. Joe serves as a catalyst in Jackie's journey back to subjectivity, like the figure of Max in *Bye Bye Blues* or Judy/Jeremy in *Better Than Chocolate*. Like Max in *Bye Bye Blues* and Josh Morgan in *Cowboys Don't Cry*, Joe is an under-privileged white male, residing in a grotty basement apartment, barely surviving off cheap wine and pasta, and making his living working in a fast-food take-out stall. Unlike the sophisticated and privileged Jackie, Joe has no social status, yet the film resists objectifying him as Jackie's mere boy toy. Joe's masculinity is destabilized. Outfitting Joe in Jackie's sexy feminine silk robe, Wheeler allows her characters to defy oppressive gender categories tied to notions of age, enabling them to find their desiring voices.

    Edge of Madness (2002) is an adaptation of Alice Munro's short story "A Wilderness Station," co-written by Wheeler and Charles K. Pitts. Here Wheeler returns to the historical maternal melodrama, and, with the exception of *Loyalties*, produces perhaps her darkest film. Relocating Munro's story from Ontario to the Manitoba's Red River Valley, Wheeler returns to her beloved prairie iconography, revisiting the themes and tropes of *Great Grand Mother*. Set during the mid-nineteenth century, *Edge of Madness* tells the story of Annie (Caroline Dhavernas), a distressed eighteen-year-old pregnant woman who claims she has murdered her husband. Annie's story is told through various devices common to the "woman's film," such as confessional letters (addressed to a lost female friend) and flash-backs (re-enactments of the past), which reveal the truth about Annie's mysterious identity. We learn of Annie's plight as an impoverished orphan who is sold to the brutal Simon Herron (Brendan Fehr), a frontiersman who lives in a secluded unfinished homestead with his gentler younger brother, George (Corey Sevier). As a wife, Annie is treated like a slave, repeatedly raped and beaten by her psychotic husband. Lonely and unhappy, Annie turns to the younger George, and they become secret lovers. Their desire for one another, however, ultimately leads to more violence, and Simon's death.

    While a prisoner, Annie is further degraded and violated by a British doctor, who performs a forced internal examination on her. He later attempts to rape her. There is no respite from exploitation and male violence for Annie except in the figure of Ruth (Tantoo Cardinal), a caring Aboriginal woman who serves as the prison den mother. It is Ruth who feeds Annie, bathes her, and finds her clothes to wear. Despite their victimization by a harsh settler society, neither Ruth nor

Annie is represented as a passive victim. Interestingly, the Ruth character does not appear in the original Munro story, and she is reminiscent of earlier Wheeler representations of Aboriginal women, such as Augusta as well as Rosanne and her mother, Beatrice, in *Loyalties*. Like her predecessors, Ruth is a positive and powerful maternal figure, but she also carries dramatic agency. It is Ruth, after all, who discovers Annie's talent for sewing, giving her a sense of purpose as well as a means of earning a living. Most importantly, however, it is Ruth—not the investigator assigned to Annie's case, the British police magistrate Henry Mullen (Paul Johansson)—who discovers the truth about Annie. Even when Ruth has no dialogue or action, Wheeler ensures she remains in the frame, always watching, her gaze a continual presence and the source of meaning. The storyline of the implied "romance" between Annie and Henry is subverted by the daughter–mother relationship between Annie and Ruth. Again, maternal desire usurps heterosexual male desire.

Small-Screen Stories: The Television Mould

> Because of our distribution problems in this country and, with only thirty million people, there seems to be more of an emphasis on television. So, a lot of my projects became television rather than features, though I felt some of them should have been features, and that put me into a mould that I really didn't want to get into, and it's been very hard to break out of the television mould and get back into features.
> – Anne Wheeler (Levitin, 1999)

Wheeler spent the decade 2000–2009 in television. In many ways her television years are representative of what's happened to women's cinema in recent years, and perhaps a reflection of women's current declining participation in the mainstream film and television industry (as concluded by the Celluloid Ceiling Report).[19] Although Wheeler has remained productive, television work rarely receives critical attention. Despite the difficulty she has in finding theatrical financing, Wheeler's work continues to reflect a commitment to a feminist agenda. This commitment was established early on in such television projects as *The Diviners* (1992), *Other Women's Children* (1994), and *The War between Us* (1995). In the period 1992–2008 Wheeler directed eleven television movies, the multi-award-winning miniseries *The Sleep Room* (1998), and numerous episodes of various Canadian television series, most notably seven episodes for CBC's award-winning *Da Vinci's Inquest* (1998–2003).

The Diviners (1992), based on the classic novel by Margaret Laurence and scripted by Linda Svendsen, was a special three-hour CBC movie of the week. The story is another mother-daughter–driven drama centred on single motherhood and interracial relations. Morag (Sonya Smitts) struggles to navigate parenthood as a single mother to her Métis singer-songwriter teenage daughter, Pique (Jennifer Podemski), while carving out for herself a successful writing career. Mother and daughter are plagued by feelings of anger, confusion, resentment, and guilt, primarily because of Morag's strained, intermittent relationship with Pique's absent and troubled Métis father, Jules (Tom Jackson). The quest for one's own identity, one's own voice (both as artists and female subjects), proves a dangerous one for them, represented by Pique's rape. And like Rosanne in *Loyalties*, Lila in *Better Than Chocolate*, and June in *Marine Life*, Morag is unable to protect her daughter from a violent and racist patriarchal culture. Despite the mother's delimited ability to save and protect, the mother–daughter bond is rendered a powerful core for inner knowledge and truth. It is a bond rooted in resistance.

The War between Us (1995), written by Sharon Gibbon, deals with the shameful history of Japanese internment camps in the British Columbia interior during WW II. As in *Loyalties*, the issues of gender, race, and class are foregrounded in the narrative, in which educated middle-class Japanese prisoners, robbed of their homes, privilege, and status, are forced to work as servants for rural and working-class white families. Peg (Shannon Lawson), a young mother who opens a general store, hires Aya (Mieko Ouchi), a displaced Canadian-born woman of Japanese heritage, as her babysitter and cleaning woman. As in *Loyalties*, the women initially distrust and dislike one another, divided as they are by race, class, and the chaos of war. Like Roseanne, Aya is a disenfranchised though well-educated urban woman of colour. Peg is a stifled, unfulfilled rural housewife, undereducated and unsophisticated. Amid the majestic and untamed B.C. landscape, the women form a deep bond, one that tests Peg's relationship with her racist husband, family, and friends, and ultimately challenges Peg to find her voice through her resistance to racial and ethnic intolerance in a so-called democratic and peaceful nation. Indeed, notions of nation are destabilized throughout the film and called into question explicitly by both female characters. Though the usual Wheeler romantic storylines are followed—one involving a forbidden interracial relationship—the crux of the story echoes Rosanne's condemnation "What kind of woman are you?," from *Loyalties*. Aya, because of her racial and cultural heritage, is constituted by her government as the wrong kind of Canadian woman. Peg is "othered" in a similar manner, although with less dire consequences, when she is shunned for her bond with Aya and her mothering abilities called into question. The ending is tragic and yet historically accurate: Aya is forced to relocate to Japan, a country in which, no less than Canada, she is not recognized as a citizen. Aya is a displaced other forced into exile and "else-where-ness." Peg, worldlier and sadder, reluctantly returns to her life in the B.C.

interior. The women will never see each other again. Like the two girls in *Teach Me to Dance*, they are victims of a patriarchal and colonial oppression that sets out to dislocate the feminine and sever female bonds.

In between television movies, Wheeler remained productive, directing series such as *North of 60* (1992–93), *Jake and the Kid* (1995), *Cold Squad* (1998), and the (Gemini Award–winning) CBC miniseries *The Sleep Room* (1998), concerning the CIA-funded drug experiments in Canadian psychiatric wards in the 1950s. Also in 1998 Wheeler was invited by Baner-Alper Productions to direct the three-hour pilot for the coroner/cop series *Da Vinci's Inquest* (a critically and commercially successful series that ran from 1998 to 2005). Written by series creator Chris Haddock, the episode "Little Sister" focuses on an investigation of a cold case involving a serial killer, still on the loose, who preys on female runaways and prostitutes in downtown Vancouver.

"Little Sister" is shot in the style of film noir and told from the point of view of hard-boiled coroner Dominic Da Vinci (Nicholas Campbell), who straddles, somewhat unsuccessfully, two seemingly contrasting worlds: the nighttime underworld of serial killers, prostitution, and bad cops, and the messy operations of his chaotic domestic life. Da Vinci is a familiar Wheeler masculine figure—a hard-drinking, irresponsible single father who echoes Josh Morgan from *Cowboys Don't Cry*. "Little sister" refers to a number of feminine figures and tropes, very familiar to Wheeler. The eponymous little sister, Roxanne Flowers, is a single mother, an Aboriginal woman and sex worker who has mysteriously disappeared, echoing the ongoing real-life tragedy in which hundreds of Native women across Canada—many "little sisters"—have been brutally murdered or have gone missing.[20] As Margot Leigh Butler writes,

> In Vancouver and the Lower Mainland many of the unaccounted for and murdered women are First Nations; together, along with and between all women, they are overridingly being publicly described and pictured as prostitutes and drug users, or else they are shoehorned into various mobile stereotypes of the "bad girl" who's in the wrong place, in the wrong company, doing the wrong work, living the wrong lifestyle, wearing the wrong clothing, doing the wrong thing at the wrong time— just being wrong. (Butler 161–62)

The episode subverts the noir tradition of punishing or converting the femme fatale figure by privileging a more social-realist narrative in which Roxanne is represented as someone we might actually know. This representation of the familiar is powerfully expressed in a photograph of Roxanne gazing directly at the camera, and at us, while posing with her young daughter, now motherless. This silent visual device inscribes Roxanne not as a victim or as the "wrong" kind of woman but as someone's mother. Roxanne's silent maternal oppositional gaze haunts the narrative of "Little Sister."

Further generic and gender transgressions are rooted in the central point of identification, in which our white male hero, the investigator Da Vinci, is rendered passive and impotent in an elitist bureaucratic legal and justice system. The actual hero of the story is Goose Flowers (Byron Chief-Moon), elder brother of Roxanne and a disenfranchised Aboriginal. Avenging the murder of *his* beloved little sister by a white man (Eric Peterson), a Willie Pickton figure,[21] Goose hunts down her killer with the deep-seated knowledge that a racist justice system will do nothing for an Aboriginal woman.

After directing episodes for the series *Hope Island* (1999), *Beggars and Choosers* (2000), *Mysterious Ways* (2000), the television movie *The Investigation* (2002), the television documentary *The Orkney Lad: The Story of Isabel Gunn* (2001), as well as the four theatrical features discussed earlier, Wheeler directed *Betrayed* (2003), a television docudrama about a water-contamination scandal in a small western town. Co-written by Wheeler and Jeremy Hole, *Betrayed* centres on Judy Bryce (Kari Matchett), a single mother who becomes embroiled in a deadly public health crisis while trying to sort out her domestic troubles with her former lover, Bill Lebret (Raoul Trujillo), and her alcoholic father, Doug Bryce (Michael Hogan), who happens to be the town's incompetent water treatment manager. With *Betrayed* Wheeler returns to familiar ground: Western Canadian iconography, domestic melodrama, romantic subplots, and, echoing her NFB days, a story driven by a social issue.

Central to Wheeler's story of deception and corruption is the figure of the fallen father, represented both by Doug, Judy's irresponsible and racist dad, and by Doug's nemesis, Bill, the biological father of Judy's teenage son. Bill, a cattle rancher, has been forbidden to know and raise Judy's son, mainly because of his subaltern status as both Aboriginal and ex-convict, two elements of his identity that render him an "unfit" paternal figure. However, Judy in her crusade to save the town from more water-related deaths uncovers the troubling reality of her father's white patriarchal world of good ol' boys. A recurring visual metaphor in the film is microscopic images of deadly E. coli bacteria, although the scientific gaze holds no real power in the film and does not help us see. Rather, it is through Judy's interrogating maternal gaze that the sins of the (white) fathers are literally unearthed, revealing a deadly toxic mess in good soil. As in *Loyalties*, bad fathers wreak havoc on the daughter.

Since *Betrayed*, Wheeler has remained in television. With the exception of CBC's *A Beachcombers Christmas* (2004) and some episodic directing work,[22] she has primarily directed projects for American networks such as Lifetime

Television, a network aimed at women viewers, and the Hallmark Channel, a brand known for family-friendly entertainment. For Lifetime Television Wheeler directed the comedy-drama *Christmas on Chestnut Street* (2006) and the family drama *Mom, Dad and Her* (2008). For the Hallmark Channel Wheeler directed the historical romance *Mail Order Bride* (2008) and *Living Out Loud* (2009), a drama about breast cancer. All of the works cited above are genres Wheeler has become associated with—the family drama and the romance, genres more often found in television than on the big screen. Although these recent productions were filmed in Wheeler's native British Columbia, and cast, in supporting roles, respected Canadian actors such as Tantoo Cardinal, the narratives are set in American cultural and historical contexts and feature American TV stars. Despite this national/regional shift, the narratives are driven by strong female protagonists over the age of thirty, struggling to overcome obstacles and adversity in a patriarchal society amid western landscape iconography.

Conclusion: Wheeler's Maternal Gaze

> Sometimes I haven't fought hard enough for my work, or taken a big enough risk aesthetically. Mostly I think I've been so lucky to have had this opportunity to explore and express.
> – Anne Wheeler (Thompson, 114)

Part of the purpose of this survey was to highlight Wheeler's prolific contribution to Canadian cinema as well as to trace certain ideological, regional, and aesthetic strains in her work in order to foreground her voice as a feminist auteur. Although Wheeler has worked in various industrial and institutional contexts and with different film forms, her use of the maternal gaze has remained a key tool for interrogating patriarchy and colonization and is essential to her reimagining and reconstructing female/maternal desire within the structure of the narrative genre film. Wheeler has given Canadian cinema her own western regional take on the maternal melodrama, a genre that has given her the wide-open space to destabilize conventional cinematic representations of masculinity and femininity and to provide us with progressive texts. Due to Wheeler's longevity in the film and television industry and her extensive body of work, further study is much needed. This piece points to topics, texts, issues, and theoretical concepts that can and should be further explored and expanded in the context of Wheeler's Western Canadian feminist vision.

Notes

1

Wheeler goes on to say: "There's always that period when they're [Toronto International Film Festival] deliberating on whether they are going accept my film or not, and then they always say the same thing 'it's a bit too commercial.' You can't win. And they have all these American commercial films here. But if you're a Canadian filmmaker you're suppose to be ... what? I don't know! We're all completely confused by what we should be." Kathleen Cummins, "Northern Divas and Romantic Catalysts: The Films of Anne Wheeler," *Take One: Film and Television in Canada*, March 2002: 22.

2

"Celebrating Women's Achievements: Canadian Women in Film—Anne Wheeler," Library and Archives Canada, http://www.collectionscanada.ca/women.

3

Feminist film critic Susan Lord has contributed significantly to examining and validating Wheeler's feminist and Western Canadian authorial voice. See Lord, "States of Emergency in the Films of Anne Wheeler," *North of Everything: English-Canadian Cinema since 1980*, ed. William Beard and Jerry White (Edmonton: U of Alberta P, 2002). See also Susan Lord, "Canadian Gothic: Multiculturalism, Indigenity, and Gender in Prairie Cinema," *Canadian Cultural Poesis: Essays on Canadian Culture*, ed. Garry Sherbert, Annie Gerine, and Sheila Petty (Waterloo: Wilfrid Laurier UP, 2006). Brenda Longfellow writes insightfully on Wheeler's use of melodramatic devices in

Longfellow, "Gender, Landscape, and Colonial Allegories in *The Far Shore. Loyalties* and *Mouvements du desir*," *Gendering the Nation: Canadian Women's Cinema*, ed. Kay Armatage, Kass Banning, Brenda Longfellow, and Janine Marchessault (Toronto: U of Toronto P, 1999), 165–82.

4

"Kathryn Bigelow," in Christina Lane, *Feminist Hollywood: From Born in Flames to Point Break* (Detroit: Wayne State UP, 2000). See also Deborah Jermyn and Sean Redmond, eds., *The Cinema of Kathryn Bigelow: Hollywood Transgressor* (London: Wallflower Press, 2003). This collection of essays examines Bigelow's "troubling authorial signature," as she works primarily with male-driven narratives and traditionally masculine genres such as the action film (*Point Break*), the thriller (*Blue Steel*), the horror picture (*Before Dark*), and most recently the war movie (*The Hurt Locker*). One of the central ideological strains in Bigelow's work has been the privileging of androgyny.

5

The term is problematic and debated, and I use it in a fairly loose way. The definition by Ira Konigsberg is somewhat helpful to this discussion: "In its most uncomplicated meaning, realism in film refers to a direct and truthful view of real world through the presentation of characters and their physical surroundings with minimal distortion either from the filmmaker's point of view or from the filmic technique."

Konigsberg, *The Complete Film Dictionary*, 2nd ed. (Toronto: Penguin Canada, 1997), 321.

6

See Laura Mulvey, "Visual Pleasure and Narrative Cinema" (1975), *Feminism and Film*, ed. E. Ann Kaplan (Oxford: Oxford UP, 2000), 34–47; and Teresa de Lauretis, "Rethinking Women's Cinema" (1985), *Figures of Resistance: Essays in Feminist Theory*, ed. Patricia White (Chicago: U of Illinois P, 2007), 25–47.

7

"At this point in time, a strategy should be developed which embraces both the notion of film as political tool and film as entertainment. For too long these have been regarded as two opposing poles with little common ground. In order to counter our objectification in the cinema, our collective fantasies must be released: women's cinema must embody the working through of desire: such an objective demands the use of the entertainment film." Claire Johnston, "Women's Cinema as Counter-Cinema," *Feminism and Film*, ed. E. Ann Kaplan (Oxford: Oxford UP Press, 2000), 32. Johnston wrote her seminal piece 1973, at the birth of feminist film criticism and only two years before the release of Wheeler's film *Great Grand Mother*.

8

"If pressed most Canadian cinephiles could probably come up with a filmmaker or two that hailed from or seemed vaguely connected to, Alberta (um, yeah, isn't Anne Wheeler from Alberta? ... *The War Bride*, that was, um, Albertan, right?). This is not good." Jerry White, "A Typically Canadian Cinema: Filmmaking in Alberta, Its Institutions and Authors," *Self Portraits: The Cinemas of Canada since Telefilm*, ed. André Loiselle and Tom McSorley (Ottawa: Canadian Film Institute, 2006), 306–8.

9
Alison Vermee also notes the thematic nature of Wheeler's authorship. "Spanning television commercials, instructional shorts, NFB documentaries, feature films, episodic television, and work for the CBC, Wheeler's oeuvre can be seen as that of an auteur, foregrounding key themes regardless of the form question." Qtd. in "Anne Wheeler and the Art of Everyday Life," *Take One: Film and Television in Canada* 9 (Fall 1995): 40.

10
There is now a body of writing focused on the representation of masculinities in Canadian cinema. See Robert Fothergill, "Coward, Bully, or Clown: The Dream-Life of a Younger Brother," *Canadian Film Reader*, ed. Seth Feldman and Joyce Nelson (Toronto: Peter Martin Associates, 1977), 234–71; Christine Ramsay, "Dead Queers: One Legacy of the Trope of 'Mind over Matter' in the Films of David Cronenberg," *Canadian Journal of Film Studies* 8.1 (Spring 1999): 45–62; Lee Parpart, "Pit(iful) Male Bodies: Colonial Masculinity, Class and Folk Innocence in *Margaret's Museum*," *Canadian Journal of Film Studies* 8.1 (Spring 1999): 63–86; and Thomas Waugh, "Cinemas, Nations,

Masculinities" (Martin Walsh Memorial Lecture, 1998), in *Canadian Journal of Film Studies* 8.1 (Spring 1999): 8–44.

11
Wheeler has to date directed eight theatrical features, eleven movies for television, one television miniseries, five dramatic shorts, four documentaries, and numerous television episodes. She has also written and produced some of this work. http://www.annewheeler.com.

12
See Gail Vanstone, *D Is for Daring: The Women behind the Films of Studio D* (Toronto: Sumach Press), 2006.

13
See Breda Gray on Spivak in Lorraine Code, ed., *Encyclopedia of Feminist Theories* (London: Routledge, 2000): "Spivak's main concern, then, in relation to the question of, can the subaltern speak?, is with the meaning transaction between speak and listener. Even when the subaltern makes an effort in death to speak she is not able to be heard. It is speaking *and* hearing that completes the speech act" (460). See also Gayatri Chrakravorty Spivak, "Can the Subaltern Speak?" *Marxism and the Interpretation of Culture*, ed. Cary Nelson and Lawrence Grossberg (Urbana: U of Illinois P, 1988), 271–313.

14
"Friedan set out to investigate the lot of US women in the 1950s, an era in which it was claimed women's involvement in the public sphere declined as they succumbed to 'the feminine mystique' which defined women as 'healthy, beautiful, educated (up to a point), concerned only

with her husband, her children and her home' (1963, 13)." Joanne Hollows, *Feminism, Femininity and Popular Culture* (Manchester: Manchester UP, 2000), 11.

15
Wheeler's father died when she herself was a teen, and she claims she knew very little about him. Interview by Peggy Thompson, *The Young, the Restless, and the Dead: Interviews with Canadian Filmmakers*, ed. George Melnyk (Waterloo, ON: Wilfrid Laurier UP, 2008), 102.

16
See Thomas Waugh's paper on Wheeler's short NFB film *One's a Heifer* (1984) and her feature *Cowboys Don't Cry* (1988) in "Queering the Canon," a conference paper given at the Annual Meeting of the Film Studies Association of Canada, University of Alberta, May 2000.

17
Katherine Monk discusses Wheeler's horrible experience with rape in her book. Monk writes, "Shortly after the death of her father, she was raped and impregnated, and told it was illegal to have an abortion. Wheeler's entire worldview shifted, and she began to question the status quo." Katherine Monk, *Weird Sex and Snowshoes and Other Canadian Film Phenomena* (Vancouver: Raincoast Books, 2001), 84.

18
Both Wheeler and her mother are trained musicians. Wheeler worked as a music teacher and was about to pursue a graduate degree in music. "Celebrating Women's Achievements: Canadian Women in Film—Anne Wheeler," *Library and Archives*

Canada, http://www.collections
canada.ca/women.

19
"In 2007, women comprised
15% of all directors, executive
producers, producers, writers, cinematographers, and
editors working on the top
250 domestic grossing films.
This represents a decline of 2
percentage points from 1998
and represents no change from
2006. Women accounted for 6%
of directors in 2007, a decline
of one percentage point since
2006. This figure is almost
half the percentage of women
directors working in 2000 when
women accounted for 11% of
all directors." Martha Lauzen,
2007 Celluloid Ceiling Report
(Center for the Study of Women
in Television and Film, School
of Theatre, Television and Film,
San Diego State University).

20
http://missingwomen.blogspot
.com.

21
Robert Pickton, a pig farmer
from Port Coquitlam, B.C., was
found guilty on six counts of
second-degree murder related
to the scores of missing women
from Vancouver's impoverished
Downtown Eastside. *Globe and
Mail*, 9 December 2007.

22
Wheeler's recent episodic
television work includes CBC's
This Is Wonderland (2004–5)
and *Jozi-H* (2006), as well as
Bravo!'s *Godiva's* (2006) and
GlobalTV's *The Guard* (2008).

Works Cited

Armatage, Kay, et al., eds.
*Gendering the Nation: Canadian
Women's Cinema*. Toronto: U of
Toronto P, 1999.

Atwood, Margaret. *Survival:
A Thematic Guide to Canadian
Literature*. Toronto: Anansi,
1972, 34.

Bratton, Jacky, et al., eds.
*Melodrama: Stage, Picture,
Screen*. London: British Film
Institute. 1994.

Brooks, Peter. *The Melodramatic
Imagination: Balzac, Henry
James, Melodrama and the
Mode of Excess*. New Haven, CT:
Princeton UP, 1976.

Butler, Margot Leigh. "I'm in
There! I'm the One of the Women
in That Picture." *Killing Women:
The Visual Culture of Gender and
Violence*. Ed. Annette Burfoot and
Susan Lord. Waterloo, ON: Wilfrid
Laurier UP, 2006.

Cummins, Kathleen. "Northern
Divas and Romantic Catalysts:
The Films of Anne Wheeler."
*Take One: Film and Television in
Canada* (March 2002): 22.

Dafoe, Chris. "Face to Face—
Anne Wheeler: Every Picture Tells
a Story." *The Globe and Mail* 12
January 1993: C6.

de Lauretis, Teresa. *Technologies
of Gender: Essays on Film,
Theory and Fiction*. Bloomington:
Indiana UP, 1987.

Flitterman-Lewis, Sandy. *To
Desire Differently: Feminism and
the French Cinema*. New York:
Columbia UP, 1996.

Fothergill, Robert. "Coward,
Bully, or Clown: The Dream-Life
of a Younger Brother." *Canadian
Film Reader*. Ed. Seth Feldman
and Joyce Nelson. Toronto:

Peter Martin Associates, 1977,
234–71.

Gray, Breda. "Spivak, Gayatri
Chrakravorty (b. 1942)" *Encyclopedia of Feminist Theories*. Ed.
Lorraine Code. London: Routledge, 2000.

Kaplan, E. Ann. *Motherhood and
Representation: The Mother in
Popular Culture and Melodrama*.
London: Routledge, 1992.

Levitin, Jacqueline. "Making
Feature Films. Panel discussion
with Helma Sanders Brahms,
Caroline Eades, Patricia Plattner,
and Anne Wheeler." Moderated
by Jacqueline Levitin. *Women
Filmmakers Refocusing*, ed.
Jacqueline Levitin, Judith Plessis,
and Valerie Raoul. New York:
Routledge, 2003.

Longfellow, Brenda. "Gender,
Landscape, and Colonial
Allegories in *The Far Shore*,
Loyalties, and *Mouvements du
desir*." Armatage et al.

Lord, Susan. "States of
Emergency in the Films of Anne
Wheeler." *North of Everything:
English-Canadian Cinema since
1980*. Ed. William Beard and Jerry
White. Edmonton: U of Alberta
P, 2002.

Ramsay, Christine. "Dead
Queers: One Legacy of the
Trope of 'Mind over Matter' in
the Films of David Cronenberg."
*Canadian Journal of Film
Studies* 8.1 (Spring 1999):
45–62.

Rollet, Brigitte. "Women Directors
and Genre Films in France."
Women Filmmakers: Refocusing.
Ed. Jacqueline Levitin et al. New
York: Routledge, 2003.

Silverman, Kaja. *The Acoustic
Mirror: The Female Voice in*

Psychoanalysis and the Cinema. Bloomington: Indiana UP, 1988.

Thompson, Peggy. "'I like to work one-on-one': Anne Wheeler." *The Young, the Restless, and the Dead: Interviews with Canadian Filmmakers.* Ed. George Melnyk. Waterloo, ON: Wilfrid Laurier UP, 2008, 95–114.

Vanstone, Gail. *D Is for Daring: The Women behind the Films of Studio D.* Toronto: Sumach Press, 2006.

Vermee, Alison. "Anne Wheeler and the Art of Everyday Life." *Take One: Film and Television in Canada* 9 (Fall 1995).

Wheeler, Anne. *Library and Archives Canada.* http://www .collectionscanada.ca/women.

Williams, Linda. "Something Else besides a Mother': *Stella Dallas* and the Maternal Melodrama." *Home Is Where the Heart Is: Studies in Melodrama and the Women's Film.* Ed. Christine Gledhill. London: British Film Institute, 1987.

Fluidity:
Joyce Wieland's Political Cinema
Kay Armatage

Joyce Wieland's filmmaking was only one component of her production as an artist in many media. As well as films, she has produced paintings, sculptures, fabric, earthwork, stuffed plastic collages, wall hangings, bronze sculptures, lithographs, enormous installations, and small coloured pencil drawings. The important subjects of her work—in film as well as other media—remained feminine subjectivity and sexuality, the genealogy of women's art traditions, the environment, Canadian and international politics, and the signification of representational forms.

Wieland (1931–1998) studied commercial art and design at Central Technical High School under noted artists such as Doris McCarthy. For a short period after matriculation she worked as an animator at Graphic Films (Toronto), resulting in a few short pixilated films co-authored with Maynard Collins.[1] After her marriage to Michael Snow, she moved to New York, the centre of contemporary art in the 1960s. There, with Betty Ferguson, Wieland resumed filmmaking.[2] Initially they deployed montage of found images (e.g., *Barbara's Blindness*, 1965) and pixilated stop-motion, moving objects around in the domestic space. These works would later become known as her kitchen-tabletop films.

Wieland's film work encompasses short pieces in 8mm and 16mm, a feature-length avant-garde film in 16mm as well as a dramatic feature in 35mm. They are polyvalent in structure and materiality and wide-ranging in their subject matter. Many of these films are loved by the spectators who know them, but they are unknown to many.[3] Before moving to the political and critical issues that the films generate, therefore, I'll convey briefly the variety of structures and concerns of a sample of the films.

At the outset, *Water Sark* (1964–65) composes a still life of objects on a table: a blue teapot, some pink plastic roses, a broken mirror, and several vessels of water. The vibrant hues and reflecting surfaces are shot with a variety of hand-held devices (jiggling the bowl of water, the light over the table moving in circles, the camera lens panning and zooming). A series of ludic encounters with ordinary household objects devolves to a sybaritic interlude with her own body in the bathtub in a sensuous montage involving rippling water. The film eventually moves to an examination of corporeal objects, including her own breast and mouth, through magnifying lenses and prisms that she holds in her fingers. The effects of light, reflection, and movement inflect the montage structure. The soundtrack consists of water sounds and a spontaneous percussive composition.[4]

Hand-Tinting (1967–68) was composed from outtakes of a documentary on which Wieland had collaborated with Shirley Clarke.[5] Apparently never finished, the film was commissioned as an industrial project, documenting a retraining program for disenfranchised women. Wieland reprinted some images (young women at a swimming pool or dancing) so that small actions recurred (flipping a bathing cap, exiting the dressing room, "hallelujah arm-flailing") and edited them very tightly to execute a rhyming structure of rhythmic seriality, finally tinting them with fabric dyes and perforating the negative to produce random sparkles of light (Banning, *Textual Excess*, 130). The film is silent.

Catfood (1968) is a humorous piece about desire and plenitude.[6] The frame encloses the tabletop, whereupon fish after fish appears for a cat to eat. The principal technical device is stop-motion cinematography. The animal devours the fish repeatedly until satiated, at which point he can only lie on his back and gaze, upside down, at the final offering. It is impossible to describe either the tenderness, generosity, and humour that the film comprises or the glazed intoxication of the gratified cat. Feline jouissance.

Dripping Water (1969) is a minimalist still life in black and white. Made in conjunction with a radio piece by Michael Snow that consisted simply of the musical sounds of water hitting a shallow watery surface, the film is a modernist work, a static image of a white plate in a white porcelain sink. The film consists of one continuous ten-minute shot (the length of a standard 16mm roll).

A & B in Ontario (shot 1967, completed 1984) was co-directed with Hollis Frampton and later edited by Wieland.[7] Shot in black and white on hand-wound Bolex cameras, the film depicts two intrepid filmmakers spying on each other. The soundtrack, composed almost exclusively of camera sounds (whirring, winding, reloading), may arguably have been the first to foreground—rather than to mask—camera noise.[8] Playful, witty, and tightly edited, the film contrives a chase narrative around the process of filmmaking as suspense.

Birds at Sunrise (shot 1972, completed 1986) begins with a segment of black leader, over which the twenty-third psalm is spoken in Hebrew ("The Lord is my shepherd, I shall not want"). After this opaque opening (for the words are not translated), a rack focus shot of a cyclamen on a windowsill devolves to a series of annular vignettes of birds alighting in a tree outside the window in the cool light of early morning. The shots were made with a cardboard toilet-roll centre taped to the lens, creating a luminous circular image in a field of black, like the iris optical effect common in silent-era cinema. Birds flit from branch to branch. Somehow the orange dot of light (continuous throughout the film) that was placed, in post-production, in the top right-hand corner of the frame, comes to serve as a luminous visual mantra. *Birds at Sunrise* enacts an exquisite meditation, a reverent and yet thoroughly quotidian contemplation of the creatures.

As I hope these descriptions indicate, Wieland's filmmaking lexicon and world view were capacious, inventive, and diverse. I love these films. The pluralities of form, subjects, references, and political tendencies of these films are the foundations of my argument in this essay.

In her 1982 dissertation, Lauren Rabinovitz discusses Wieland's films in terms of structural film, the dominant American avant-garde movement of the period.[9] Rabinovitz used P. Adams Sitney's characterization of the structural avant-garde as demonstrating a cool (i.e., low-tech, artisanal) treatment of the medium, materiality, absence of narrative, abstraction, the static image, and duration.[10] The structural avant-garde film movement was high art: a modernist, minimalist discourse that required education, attention, indeed subservience; the films were shown in art galleries, museums, and the revered spaces of the educated elite, such as the Collective for Living Cinema (New York) and the Institute for Contemporary Art (London).[11] As Janine Marchessault writes, "The reified tenets of modernism in Canadian Experimental cinema are derived from a Fine Art tradition and, supported by its institutions, are founded on an adversarial relationship between high art and mass culture" (138). Marchessault notes, "while the historical avant-garde reacted to the commodification of art by seeking to reintegrate art into the social ... modernist art works continued to be characterized by a contradictory insistence on autonomy, on hermetic forms which could not be readily consumed" (138).

Rabinovitz's approach placed Wieland's films in the structural mode while simultaneously charting her differences from her male confreres, particularly through her celebration of femininity. Countering this view, Marchessault sees Wieland's work in the context of other Canadian women experimental film-makers. She writes: "With very few exceptions films produced by women have not conformed to the rigours of an international modernism. Nor can they be seen to correspond to the structural concerns generally identified with the names of Michael Snow, Jack Chambers and David Rimmer" (137). Marchessault distinguishes experimental from avant-garde works on exactly that basis: "[The adversarial relationship between high art and mass culture] is what distinguishes Experimental from avant-garde films. It is expressly in their relation to popular culture, its institutional supports and the pleasures of its promise that feminist avant-garde films are often antithetical to the Experimental tradition in Canada" (138).

At the time of her dissertation, Rabinovitz's analysis seemed apt: it rescued Wieland from the fringes and placed her firmly within the defined regime of structural avant-garde practices. Yet in the early 1980s, when I was once again teaching Wieland's films in a course on avant-garde cinema, *Water Sark* seemed to speak to issues that outdistanced the concerns of structural cinema. I wrote a short piece about *Water Sark*, situating it in relation to *l'écriture féminine*, the 1980s movement in French feminist psychoanalysis that emphasized the feminine body as a corporeal inscription of sexual difference (Armatage, *Films of Joyce Wieland*, 135–46). I hoped to show that the film had resonance beyond its period of production: in its vivacious beauty, subject matter, libidinous gratification (jouissance), and cinematic aesthetic, Wieland's work could not be consigned to that minimalist moment of the 1960s. Johanne Sloan offers yet another reading, citing the film as subverting the postwar "domestic goddess" figure through its strategy of "investigating and defamiliarizing the housewife's everyday world, opening it out to aesthetic, social, and sexual connotations" (Sloan, 101). The film continues to offer rich material for multiple readings.

Wieland's exploration of the feminine in the 1960s was a bold foray into unknown realms. Refusing to compete with the dominant male artists on their terrain and rejecting the role of the "artist's-wife-type artist," she researched the history of women's creative activity, looking especially at artistic production based in the home: embroidery, quilting, knitting, even cake decorating, and—in the films—the objects on her kitchen table and her own body.[12] Rabinovitz coined the phrase "the domestic altar" to describe these works. These films and artworks are now read as evincing an early feminist politic, championing forms of women's creative production that had routinely been dismissed as craft rather than art.

Wieland's work in all media has been embraced by feminist scholars, who generally ascribe to them a pre-feminist politic. Thus, most of the criticism of Wieland's works has centred on the feminine as a defining analytic.[13] Janine Marchessault, for example, writes:

> In [Wieland's] films the feminine is more than allegorical, more than a
> rhetorical device of sublime negation—the feminine constitutes and

is constituted through ... Wieland's experiences and perceptions as a woman. Working within a prefeminist context, Wieland's films espouse a feminist sensibility by making the personal political, by seeking new ways to represent those aspects of women's lives and consciousness inconsequential to the grander narratives of history, *Water Sark* and *Hand-Tinting* being the exemplary films here. It is in the fragment and through the gaps that Wieland finds the stylistic lexicon to build on a tradition of women's culture. (Marchessault, 140)

Brenda Longfellow also sees Wieland's art as pivoting on femininity and the gendered qualities of nature and landscape: "On one level at least, imagining Canada as female recapitulates a classic trope in which the affinity between the nation and the female is their shared victimization.... For her, the feminine is an elemental principle of life, fertility and eroticism, an embodiment of all that is abjected by masculinist technological modernity. Within her archetypal consciousness, gender is powerfully related to differential attitudes toward nature and landscape" (Longfellow, 167).

The approach that genders Wieland's work as feminine is well known and respected in Canadian scholarship. Throughout the first decades of feminist scholarship, such emphasis was considered the important critical framework for discussion of women's cultural production.[14] In a radical intervention, on the other hand, Kass Banning argues that the insistent gendering of Wieland's work as feminine effectively marginalized her throughout her career ("Mummification," 32–38). In a recent article, Kristy Holmes-Moss also advocates reconceptualizing Wieland's "artistic production as authored by a cultural producer rather than woman artist" (25), thus making "a radical departure from the biography-laden, essentialist, and formalist examinations that consistently have difficulty accounting for such properties as sarcasm, humour, wit, and the overt materialization and manipulation of the corporeal that are so integral to Wieland's work" (23–24).

While the feminine is certainly relevant to Wieland's work in all media, her political capacities also reached beyond single-issue determinants to embrace other urgent issues of her day. In this article I emphasize Canadian national issues, labour strife, Quebec terrorism, the representation of history, and the conceptual self-reflexivity of cinematic discourse as constituting cultural knowledge.

On this last topic—the political meanings of cinematic form—I do not mean to suggest that Wieland embraced the ideological theorizations of the Anglo-French film studies movement of the time. Kass Banning argued long ago that deconstruction or negation of representation (the revelation of the film image as illusory) were not Wieland's principal points of interrogation of formal conventions ("Textual Excess," 129). On the contrary, as Marchessault writes, "Rather than foregrounding ideological questions related to the institutions of Art, experimental films affirmed the formation of a new genre" (138). As Paul Arthur notes, references to cinema as a specific and historic medium regularly inflect Wieland's films, along with ruminations on the complex mediations of the cinematic apparatus and their role in the production of cultural knowledge. Banning adds, "And to the extent that her work embodies an interrogation of formal conventions, this interrogation is always intersected by an abiding and persistent concern with the political" ("Textual Excess," 129). Moreover, although the intellectual conversations of the New York art scene were certainly familiar to her, Wieland publicly eschewed theory and often characterized her work as spontaneous emanations from the unconscious.[15] Yet her intentional statements need not proscribe contemporary readings of her work. Indeed, as Banning has pointed out, such "overdetermined contextualisation" has often obviated the necessity of dealing with the most "unsettling" elements of Wieland's work, specifically the demythologization of identity, naming, and representation ("Mummification," 32–38). Paul Arthur offers a wide-ranging and comprehensive summary of Wieland's "abiding strength," which "is to foster deft exchanges between indexical and figurative image qualities just as, in a similar spirit of confrontation, she yokes narrative cues to aleatory structures, parries looming sentimentality with political anger, counters allegory with pictorial literalism, and uses historical reference to slice through experimental cinema's romantic obsession with the phenomenological present" (47).

I intend, therefore, to treat Wieland's characteristic reflections on filmic materiality and representational practices as one of her political concerns. Wieland combined a variety of media, intermedia, and structural conceptualizations with equally heterogeneous subject matter to present a complex and wide-ranging political perspective. In the great *True Patriot Love/Véritable amour patriotique* exhibition (National Art Gallery of Canada, 1971), she transformed the hallowed expanses of the gallery into a space that welcomed visitors with irreverent wit, historical sagacity, and commanding execution. The exhibition included a duck pond, "Sweet Beaver" perfume, giant quilts, an enormous "cake" decorated to emulate the wilderness terrain of the Canadian north, replicas of letters exchanged between Wolfe and Montcalm rendered in the most precise gold-thread embroidery, and the Canadian flag knitted in a variety of simple stitches (imagine the flag in plain knitting, popcorn stitch, or shrunk horizontally in stocking stitch—irreverent and funny—the sort of desecration for which Americans were arrested in the same period).[16] As Johanne Sloan writes, "The artworks addressed Canada's political and economic sovereignty, ecological damage to the North, and the American war in Southeast Asia; and did so in the guise of conceptually-wrought photographs, cinematic fragments, objects that mimicked the plastic-wrapped world of commercial pop culture, as well as various stitched, hand-crafted, or otherwise feminized and low-tech artifacts. With this material heterogeneity, Wieland set in motion a process by which the attributes of nation-hood could be continually unmade and remade" (81).

Although the *Reason Over Passion* quilt, in its reference to Trudeau's well-known motto, has generally been considered the centrepiece of the exihi-bition, for me the point of convergence was *The Water Quilt*, "a simply remark-able work."[17] The square quilt is composed of small muslin squares, each embroi-dered with an image of a Canadian wildflower and fastened together with rope and metal grommets. The fabric, embroidery, and images are delicate, entic-ing, and "feminine," while the high-tech fastenings bespeak an industrial puis-sance that gives the quilt inordinate reach. Each of the small squares is in fact a flap that could be lifted up to reveal a page of a book (encased in plastic) about the selling of Canada's water resources to the United States.[18] "In Wieland's art-work as in Laxer's book, the newly emerging 'picture' of environmental dam-age challenged artistic representations of the Canadian north—as a vast region of untouched wilderness, forever beautiful in its wildness and forever a trea-sure-house of untapped natural resources.... With *Water Quilt*, Wieland histori-cized the representation of nature and showed how contemporary border poli-tics could have repercussions throughout the national territory, even hundreds of miles north of the 49th parallel" (Sloan, 93–94). This sublime artwork is typical of Wieland's greatest strengths: her understanding of the materials of art, invit-ing presentation, masterful execution, and an acute awareness of the political issues of her time.

Her great films (and they are many) share these same qualities. And these qualities were rare at the time, not only in the art world but also in the cinematic structural avant-garde. To a hermetic art scene that was characterized by a "subject-less" attention to the materiality of the medium—sprocket holes, zoom lenses, static shots, duration, and time—Wieland brought irreverence, painterly intensity, humour, and politics.

One of the earliest of Wieland's overtly political films takes on masculinity and American patriotism. In *Patriotism II* (1964), a close-up of a man occupies the left side of the frame. In a static sequence shot, he gazes at the camera while a large American flag moves repeatedly around his head, sometimes obscuring his face. In a tour de force of performance, he maintains an expression of complete impassivity. His lack of affect—a studied tableau of stoical masculinity—negates the annoyance of the marauding patriotic symbol. Hilarious.

Rat Life and Diet in North America (1968) is an animal fable, which Michael Snow likened to the work of Beatrix Potter.[19] Snow's comparison is consistent with treatment of Wieland's films as referencing the "domestic altar"; Marchessault, for example, assigns *Rat Life and Diet in North America* to "domestic genres such as the structural conventions of the fairytale" (139). Certainly, as Marchessault notes, "it is film's capacity to isolate and magnify details from the everyday that has served Wieland's practice" (140). Yet *Rat Life and Diet in North America*, to my mind more reminiscent of Aesop's morality fables than of Potter, charges the personal domestic space with political allegory to take up a pressing international issue—resistance to the Vietnam War. As Sloan writes, "Rat Life and Diet in North America more than any other work earned Wieland the 'political artist' label" (86).

Pet gerbils are the draft-resister protagonists. Their cage is a "political prison," overseen by hungry cat guards, their torture a repeating blast of a horn. After a lengthy episode of "suffering" through wild free-form jazz on the soundtrack, the gerbils escape and make their way to Canada. The film celebrates Canada as a progressive, countercultural, and peaceful haven for the protagonists, aligning an emancipatory form of nationalism with the claims of the Canadian New Left (Sloan, 93–94). A series of comic tableaux of their new life ensues, until a title card announces that the CIA has read in *Newsweek* that Canada is 3% communist. The military invasion that follows is signified by the loud sound of a knockout punch, ending the idyll and the film.

The narrative throughout is indicated on intertitle cards, and from time to time the image is layered with superimposed red lines, sometimes as crosshairs as in a gun sight, sometimes as dashes across the bottom of the image, suggesting subtitles. Also marking the work are references to cinema as a specific and historic medium: the use of intertitles to convey the narrative (suggesting the silent era of cinema), the superimposed red lines, and, in the gerbils' cage, the reference to Muybridge's scientific grids. Thus marks on the surface of the image not only amplify the sense of threat in the narrative but implicate the cinematic apparatus in a history of surveillance and scientific detachment. At the time, the film was dismissed by the high-art mavens and the radical left alike. For the former, it was the incursion of narrative and the social subject into modernist abstraction that offended, while for the latter it was the opposite—the treatment of a serious political subject with humour and an elitist avant-garde format.[20]

Reason Over Passion (1969) is a feature-length landscape film in the mode of poetic postcard films, a staple of the avant-garde since the 1920s. *Reason Over Passion* documents the Canadian terrain from east coast to west coast; but rather than use the classic (usually static) compositions of the photographic tradition, such as are seen in *Canadian Pacific* (David Rimmer, 1974), the film conjoins the cross-country journey to the rhyming cinematic technique of hand-held tracking shots from moving vehicles (cars, trains). Shots of Wieland reading a light meter and holding the camera to her eye are occasionally interposed, sometimes accompanied by an overexposure or refracted light that defines and then eliminates the image. This is a work that engages the specificities of film as a medium and exacts its capacities in an inceptive manner. The beauty of its individual frames and the brilliance of its structure and conception seem to emanate directly from its subject matter.

Yet apparent disjunctures belie any apparent organicity. Like those of *Rat Life and Diet in North America*, the images of *Reason Over Passion* are marked by superimposed subtitles—computer-generated variations of the phrase "reason over passion." This breaking-down and re-forming of the words literalizes the deconstruction and reconstitution of notions of nationalism, or, as Sloan puts it, "a process by which the attributes of nationhood could be continually unmade and remade" (81). The soundtrack consists of repetitive short automated beeps at regular intervals, which—somewhat paradoxically, in light of the mechanical source—produce a soothing, meditative, and idyllic mood. Wieland's rendering of industrial technology as an element of the poetic is evident here, as it is in much of her work (e.g., the combination of large metal grommets and delicate embroidered muslin in *The Water Quilt*). Holmes-Moss argues that the mechanical and industrial elements in the works constitute the "realm of the *techne*—reason, technology, rationality, logos," which Wieland regularly "interferes" with through the authorial specificity of feminine corporiality (26). Although Holmes-Moss makes an important contribution to studies of Wieland through her archival work and meticulous contextualization, in my view she clings too steadfastly to oppositional binaries (reason versus passion, *techne* versus corporiality). It is worth noting that in the computerized permutations of the subtitles, neither term is privileged; both reason and passion are subjected to encryption. I would argue, on the contrary, that it is precisely the non-hierarchized heterogeneity of elements that marks Wieland's work: the dissolving of boundaries between the industrial and affective, technological and poetic, materiality and corporiality, high art and the sensorium.

This consummate fluidity fuses disparate, even oxymoronic, approaches to construct new ways of thinking about the materials of art and seeing the world. Such active and ongoing negotiation with and between a diverse range of artistic, political, and commercial paradigms has recently been ascribed to women artists working at the interstices of production modes. To assess the fruits that such syncretic labours yield, suggests Corinn Columpar, one must call into question the boundaries that have been drawn around various artistic, industrial, political, and

critical practices in the field of film studies. For both material and ideological reasons, Columpar announces a new theoretical appraisal of filmmaking that is specifically tied to and celebratory of feminist notions of fluidity and reinvention, as
well as their intellectual and affective potential.[21] Wieland's body of work is exemplary of such "flows." Yet this fluidity, this constant interfaciality, too frequently
has been reduced in the critical discourse to a confluence of traditional women's
forms with the history and identity of Canada as a nation. Paul Arthur de-genders
such plurality, stating simply that, "the trajectory of [Wieland's] rather brief career
can be mapped across a bundle of alternative, historically vibrant stylistic options
that remain always fluid and plural" (48).

   Reason Over Passion pauses in its cross-country journey in what is
known as the "Ontario" segment. The east-coast seascapes, bucolic sheep-
dotted fields, and Precambrian forests of Quebec are behind us, and now the
images are concentrated on the face of former Prime Minister Pierre Elliott
Trudeau during the 1968 convention to determine leadership of the Liberal
Party. Trudeau's visage, in close-up, impassive and charismatic, returns again
and again as an icon.

   The installation of Trudeau as a liberatory figure was consistent with
the national tenor of the time, and yet the filmic discourse brooks no celebratory
naïveté. Trudeau's face is often framed in an iris, equally often traversed by optical wipes and overlays. Although structurally the film situates Trudeau as central
to Canada, the interlude, as Dennis Reid suggests, "unmasks him" through the
cinematic artisanal and laboratory devices that the film employs.[22] This section of
the film, substituting images of Pierre Elliott Trudeau for the Upper Canada landscape, has been described as naively celebratory and iconizing. Such readings,
however, can surface only at the expense of the symmetricality of the construction of the film, its highly abstracted imagery, and the multitudinous innovations
of its exploration of cinematic perception. Indeed, Kristy Holmes-Moss argues
that "Wieland's depiction of Trudeau in the film reiterates ambivalence toward
him and his policies. By re-shooting the original footage from the Liberal convention, using different lenses, tinting the celluloid, and playing with camera speed,
focus and iris, Wieland produces a distorted and obviously manipulated image
of the prime minister" (31). Asked about Trudeau by Hollis Frampton a few years
later, Wieland replied, "I feel that he is not as much concerned and impassioned
about Canada as I thought" (Frampton and Wieland, 178). Ironies and ambiguities
abound in *Reason Over Passion*, as in all Wieland's work, in any medium, but-
tressing a mature understanding of the complexities of political machinations,
media savvy, national vicissitudes of identity, and cinema semiotics.

   After Canada's originary love-in with Trudeau as prime minister, an enormous upset occurred in 1970. Trudeau, a Québécois, had insisted on Canadian

unity, instituting French–English bilingualism as national legislation. Meanwhile, the "silent revolution" in Quebec, upon which Trudeau's primacy was significantly buttressed, had become much more vocal. As with revolutionary movements in many parts of the world at the time, the Front de Libération du Québec (FLQ) had participated in terrorist activities.[23] In 1970, Quebec nationalists and FLQ members kidnapped Quebec provincial cabinet minister Pierre Laporte, who was later murdered, and British diplomat James Cross. What is now referred to as the October Crisis (a.k.a. Black October) raised fears in Canada of a militant terrorist faction rising up against the government. At the request of the mayor of Montreal and the government of the Province of Quebec, and in response to general threats and demands made by the FLQ, the federal government, led by Trudeau, invoked the War Measures Act. This was the only use of the War Measures Act in a domestic crisis in Canadian history, when (in October and November 1970) a state of "apprehended insurrection" was declared to exist in Quebec and emergency regulations were proclaimed. Accordingly, police had unfettered power in arrest and detention, so they could find and stop the FLQ members. As the act was a direct threat to civil liberties, its invocation gave rise to considerable concern. Many innocent people were incarcerated without charge.[24]

Upon her return to Canada in 1971, Wieland sought out Pierre Vallières, a founding member and intellectual leader of the Front de Libération du Québec and a journalist and writer of militantly polemical essays and books in support of the Quebec sovereignty movement. Vallières had been imprisoned for four years, during which time he wrote *White Niggers of America* (1968), his most famous book on French-speaking Canada as a colonized nation.

Pierre Vallières (1972) was produced almost immediately upon Vallières' release from prison. The single image of the film closes in on the lips of the eloquent separatist, echoing and expanding Wieland's embroideries and lithographs featuring lips engaged in articulation.[25] The precise frame, an extreme close-up around Vallières' mouth, necessitated the holding of his head in an assistant's tight grip in order to keep the image in focus. In close-up, Vallières' heavy moustache, glistening teeth, and dark red tongue take on monumental proportions. The imagistic qualities of the film—lush, almost monstrous, and yet rigorous in the concentration of attention—take the avant-garde mode of the single-image film into new dimensions of signification. The materiality of the image also enacts its own passion, as it was shot in Ektachrome reversal, a cheap 16mm film stock that required no work print and whose gorgeous fabric-like grain and highly saturated colours were prized. The film material itself gives the image a painterly depth and sensuality that Wieland referred to as "Géricault's colour," citing the early Romantic painter.[26] So vivid is the image that Kristy Holmes-Moss imagines that she can smell the stale cigarette smoke on Vallières' breath (34). What Arthur describes as "a thrilling blend of politics and cinematic reflexivity" (54) is another example of the fluidity of Wieland's art, the transmutation of the material into the corporeal.

In conception, as in so many of Wieland's artworks, the film is astute in its directness, as Vallières' mouth was the corporeal embodiment of his political discourse. Vallières' speech, translated in bright white surtitles, is an essay in three parts: Québec history, race and racism in Canada, and women's equality. As a political work, *Pierre Vallières* offers a militant rejoinder to the accusations of naive "Trudeaumania" in *Reason Over Passion*.

Solidarity (1973) combines Wieland's immutable occupations with women's work and equality and the mediations of representation with an almost documentary application of avant-garde operations. Its form—held-hand camera on location at a labour demonstration—echoes the cinema verité documentary movement of the National Film Board of Canada. The film was inspired by a strike for higher wages at the southern Ontario Dare Cookie factory, which employed women workers. Wieland took her camera to the picket line to film, once again, the telling image: the feet of the strikers, endlessly circling a barren patch of grass around a makeshift platform. In a consistent hand-held tracking shot, the film provides touching glimpses of the women workers' condition. Down-at-the-heels is the general tenor of the film. A montage of calluses, swollen ankles, bunions, limps, and worn-out shoes tells an elementary tale of penury. If, as has been said, the Canadian avant-garde has been marked by the documentary tradition, then this is the foremost of Wieland's films that could be ascribed to such a rubric.[27] Yet the film reduces to a minimum the parameters of the documentary. The sound-track is unembellished; it offers only random dog barks, snatches of songs, and fragments of rousing speeches ("Don't buy Dare cookies," "The Union keeps us strong"), and the images (scrupulous in their single-image attention) belie the general tenets of cinema verité as a fast-moving multi-image form. As Lianne McLarty points out, the continuous point-of-view shot suggests the subjective perspective, belying the traditional claims of documentary to objectivity (88).

The title of the film, *Solidarity*, holds on the image throughout. Unlike *Sailboat* (1967), in which the large title at the top of the image was also held throughout, creating a sense of the Platonic solidity of the word (*logos*) in contrast to the fragility of the tiny pale images of sailboats crossing the frame, here the word (solidarity) is centred in the frame, melding the logos with the affective image. In its spatial disposition and constancy, the title serves as an omnipresent reminder of the significance of the political aspiration.

This is the film that motivated me the most as a filmmaker. Simple and direct in conception, emotionally stirring without sentimentality, evincing the mate-riality of the film medium, eschewing the divisions between cinematic modes, and melding the avant-garde with the political: these were the qualities that spoke to me and that forever characterize Wieland's achievement as a filmmaker.

The Far Shore (1976) was Wieland's last great work in film. Although in the 1980s she completed several avant-garde films she had begun earlier, notably A & B in Ontario (1984) and Birds at Sunrise (1986), Wieland effectively left filmmaking after The Far Shore. This film was the culmination of her political deliberations on Canada as a nation of two cultures and on Canadian art, the history of Canadian modernization, environmentalism, and the role of media representation in the construction of the popular imaginary.

Revoking the conventions of artisanal avant-garde production, Wieland wrote and directed a sumptuously budgeted (for its time) period piece in the melodramatic mode. Feature-film production had only recently begun in Canada when Wieland wrote and directed The Far Shore. It was a rare species in Canada, not only as a dramatic feature by a woman director but as a genre film that aimed for a popular audience.

The generic form attests to Wieland's political aspirations on a broad scale. The Far Shore is a classic melodramatic weepie, a tragic tale of star-crossed lovers—a cinematic dramatic mode dating from the early days of cinema, precisely the period in which the film is set. Loosely characterized by a cluster of constitutive factors, melodrama may incorporate any or all of the elements of pathos, overwrought emotion, moral polarization, sensationalism, expressionist excess, and nonclassical narrative structure.[28] Traditionally associated with mass audience appeal, the genre nevertheless encapsulates a feminist politic, as Brenda Longfellow points out. From Jane Austen on, she argues, "the attraction to melodrama lies in the ability of the genre to give form to the repressed torrents of female longing while simultaneously (and this is crucial) critiquing the bourgeois institution of marriage and the property relations on which it is based. Rooted solidly in a heterosexual romantic tradition, melodrama pitches the spiritual values of love and sexual fulfillment against a debased material world in which the rights of patrilineal inheritance and capitalist accumulation take precedence" (167–68).

Eulalie, a beauteous Québécoise, settles for marriage with an English-Canadian industrialist who whisks her to his home in Toronto. His Victorian mansion and crass aesthetic sensibility stifle her cultured modernism, but here she meets an as-yet-unappreciated artist, with whom she forms an inevitable bond. Eulalie's lover is a thinly fictionalized character based on iconic Canadian artist Tom Thomson, who first exhibited his paintings in 1913.

Thomson was not only the quintessential Canadian artist, whose death remains a mystery, but also the harbinger of the post-colonial period in Canadian art. Although Thomson died before the inception of the Group of Seven as a movement, he is regularly associated with it. It was part of the Canada

First movement, which insisted that Canadian artists break away from the old European styles and paint their country in a novel way. Thomson, unlike previous Canadian artists who had sought instruction in Europe, was self-taught, and, in keeping with the future members of the Group of Seven, he refused to accept European art as superior to Canadian art. Thomson shunned the delicate styles of the dominant art scene of the early twentieth century, preferring instead raw, heavily impasto brushwork to convey the vibrancy of his subjects.[29]

Through the characters of Tom and Eulalie as well as through polyvalent forms of narrative and textuality, the film examines Canadian regional differences. Thus Tom and Eulalie not only come from different linguistic cultures but also from conflicting aesthetic formations. While Tom, an English-Canadian naturalist, significantly diverges from European styles in his paintings, Eulalie is an educated Québécoise and a lover of European modernism, from her taste in music to her fashionable orientalist boudoir apparel (the garb of the moment in Paris). In the treatment of the Québécoise character, the film conceives a contemporary conjunction of the "two solitudes" through the savvy accomplishments of the woman protagonist. Moving to English Canada, Eulalie adapts quickly to the English language and to urban life, performs appropriately in corporate situations, and reveals a complex understanding of modern art, not only through her appreciation of contemporary paintings, but also through her cultivated musicianship, especially in performances of such modernist composers as Debussy. In the guise of an old form (melodrama), Wieland constructs a radical understanding of Canada's political and cultural history throughout the period of industrial modernization.

Through the sophisticated urban figure of Eulalie, *The Far Shore* not only revisions notions of Quebec as a rural and small-town world such as depicted in the classic *Mon Oncle Antoine* (dir. Claude Jutra, 1971) but challenges the typical representations in other contemporary Canadian costume dramas as well, such as *Who Has Seen the Wind* (dir. Alan King, 1977). Another Canadian classic, in production close to the same time as *The Far Shore, Who Has Seen the Wind* is set in a Depression-era small town in the Prairies, augmenting the dominant representations of Canada as rural and ignorant yet ultimately good-hearted. It is worth invoking Eric Hobsbaum's notion of "invented traditions" here. Hobsbaum sees the nation as a creation of the nineteenth century, a period in which national mythologies, symbols, rituals, and histories were invented. Imaginative nationalist fabrications—largely fictive—were new themes for artists, writers, and, shortly thereafter, for filmmakers.[30] These period films, meticulous in their archeological verisimilitude, can be seen, as Anthony Smith suggests, as an aspect of historical national mythopoesis, tied to "a desire to engage a wider range and greater depth of emotions by evoking and representing the panorama of nationhood in all its historical and geographical variety" (51).

On the other hand, Pam Cook suggests that costume dramas can be seen in terms of destabilizing history and national identity. Acknowledging the instability of national and other identities—"identity formation is a fluctuating, fractured affair which militates against any final settlement"—Cook argues that popular, escapist dramas played "on the fluidity of identity," setting the stage for "an adventure in which identities are tried and tested rather than simply bolstered" (Cook, 2–4). Eulalie's period-perfect wardrobe, including her splendid hats, lace collars, elegant lace-up boots, and delicate underwear, poses another challenge to fixed notions of national and regional identities. And lest we forget for a moment the knowing deployment of the excesses of melodrama, Banning reminds us that Wieland's works "never comprise simple celebrations of identity." Rather, "Wieland decodes the fixed consignation of sameness and thus points to the inherent contradictions underlying our engraved national consciousness" ("Mummification," 31).

Convincing historical reconstruction is a passionate concern of *The Far Shore*, from Eulalie's Quebec country house and Ross's Rosedale mansion to the Muskoka log cottage and the precise replication of Tom Thomson's cabin. Often, as Smith points out, such archeological verisimilitude may be accompanied by pictorial tableaux (influenced by historical paintings, a tradition of which Wieland was certainly aware), and which appear in the film in many sequences, such as Eulalie's descent of the grand staircase, Ross's speech to his employees, Tom and Eulalie's duet in his cabin. Such moments come to epitomize something greater than the narrative event or transitional sequence; in their fidelity to period details, foregrounded by the tableau structure, they point to a national and historical specificity as the foundation of national mythmaking. *The Far Shore* effects this grand style as a challenge to understandings of the period of modernization in the early twentieth century.

Echoes of Wieland's persistent artistic practice throughout her career are present in the film. For example, the gorgeous iris-in on Eulalie's face recalls Wieland's recurrent motif of circles, found in the irises of *Birds at Sunrise* and the Trudeau section of *Reason Over Passion*. There remains, however, no trace of the artisanal techniques that the earlier films employed. In *The Far Shore*, the iris is a laboratory-produced effect—a technically perfect red halo encloses the close-up portrait of Eulalie that dissolves to a shot of Tom in his canoe, precisely bisecting the circle, which then widens to fill the frame. This device performs a narratological function (linking Eulalie's reverie to its subject, Tom) while at the same time referencing the cinematic apparatus of the silent era, the period in which the film is set. The film as a whole enacts an elision of painterly high art (the perfectionist account of historical props, settings and costumes, vehicles and music) and popular modes (melodrama, pathos, excess).

Wieland's consummate understanding of the mediations of cinematic representation and the materiality of the film medium performs an operation that situates the period as already cinematic, effectively challenging traditional realist
assumptions about the construction of history. *The Far Shore* is thus consistent
with the complexity of Wieland's treatment of women's equality, Canada as a
nation, Canadian politics, and the representation of history in her other artworks.

In all of this work, Wieland accomplished her grand conceptions without
didacticism or literalness; on the contrary, her work in all media is brilliant in conception and masterful in execution. All of her films are beautiful in an aesthetic
sense—rapturous colour, painterly *mise-en-scène*, and sophisticated invention.
They evince Wieland's keen understanding of the politics of her period.

Notes

1

Tea in the Garden (1956) and *A Salt in the Park* (1958).

2

Betty Ferguson was married at the time to Graeme Ferguson (one of the founders of IMAX). As a documentary producer for television, he had access to many archival movies, which at the time were considered to have little value. Wieland and Fergu-son used such "found footage" to co-direct *Barbara's Blindness* (1965), a montage film. Betty Ferguson also used similar mon-tage techniques in *Kisses* (1976). Her son, Munro Ferguson, made *June* (2004) in memory of Joyce June Wieland.

3

Wieland is not included, for example, in Jean Petrolle and Virginia Wexman, eds., *Women and Experimental Filmmaking* (Champaign: U of Illinois P, 2005).

4

By jazz musicians Carla Bley, Michael Mantler, and Ray Jessel.

5

Shirley Clarke (1919–1997) directed *Ornette: Made in Amer-ica* (1985), *Ornette Coleman:*

A Jazz Video Game (1984), *The Box* (1983), *Performance* (1982), *Tongues* (1982), *Savage/Love* (1981), *A Visual Diary* (1980), *One-2-3* (1978), *Trans* (1978), *Portrait of Jason* (1967), *The Cool World* (1964), *Robert Frost: A Lover's Quarrel with the World* (1963), *The Connection* (1962), *Skyscraper* (1960), *Bridges-Go-Round* (1958), *Brussels Loops* (1957), *Moment in Love* (1956), *In Paris Parks* (1954), and *Dance in the Sun* (1953).

6

I cannot agree with Lianne McLarty, who sees *Catfood* as a critique of consumption, capital-ist values, and the bougeois order. Lianne McLarty, "The Experimental Films of Joyce Wieland," *The Films of Joyce Wieland*, 98.

7

In addition to *A and B in Ontario*, Frampton (1936–1984) directed *Hapax Legomena II: Poetic Justice* (1972), *Hapax Legomena VII: Special Effects* (1972), *Hapax Legomena VI: Remote Control* (1972), *Hapax Legomena V: Ordinary Matter* (1972), *Hapax Legomena IV: Travelling Matte*

(1971), *Hapax Legomena III: Criti-cal Mass* (1971), *Hapax Legom-ena I: Nostalgia* (1971), *Zorn's Lemma* (1970), *Artificial Light* (1969), *Carrots & Peas* (1969), *Lemon* (1969), *Palindrome* (1969), *Prince Ruperts Drops* (1969), *Works & Days* (1969), *Maxwell's Demon* (1968), and *Surface Tension* (1968).

8

According to sound editor Michelle Moses.

9

The dissertation considers the work of Maya Deren and Shirley Clarke as well as that of Wieland. Subsequently published as *Points of Resistance: Women, Power & Politics in the New York Avant-Garde Cinema, 1943–71* (Champaign: U of Illinois P, 1991).

10

See P. Adams Sitney, *Vision-ary Film* (New York: Oxford UP, 1974).

11

In some ways, the spaces were not so hallowed. I remember going to a New York screening of *La Region Central* (Michael Snow, 1971). The spectators had brought pillows and expected to use them during the 180-minute film, throughout which, at the back of the room, the Gaggia machine hissed.

12
See Kay Armatage, "Kay Armatage Interviews Joyce Wieland," *Take One* 3.2 (November–December 1970): 23–25, reprinted with additions in Karyn Kay and Gerald Peary, eds., *Women and the Cinema: A Critical Anthology* (New York: Dutton, 1977), 246–71.

13
See Lauren Rabinovitz, *Points of Resistance: Women, Power & Politics in the New York Avant-Garde Cinema, 1943–71* (Champaign: U of Illinois P, 1991); Janine Marchessault, "Feminist Avant-Garde Cinema: From Introspection to Retrospection," *Points of Resistance*; Kay Armatage, "The Feminine Body: Joyce Wieland's Water Sark," *Points of Resistance*; Barbara Martineau, "The Far Shore: A Film about Violence, a Peaceful Film about Violence," *Cinema Canada* 27 (April 1976): 20–23; Brenda Longfellow, "Gender, Landscape and Colonial Allegories in *The Far Shore, Loyalties,* and *Mouvements du désir*," *Gendering the Nation: Canadian Women's Cinema*, ed. Kay Armatage et al. (Toronto: U of Toronto P, 1999), 165–82.

14
In the past, I have contributed to the concentration on the feminine in Wieland's (and other women filmmakers') work. Kay Armatage, "The Feminine Body: Joyce Wieland's *Water Sark*," *The Films of Joyce Wieland*.

15
Joyce Wieland and Michael

Snow, *Artist on Fire: The Work of Joyce Wieland*, documentary film by Kay Armatage (1987). Wieland referred to the unconscious as "whatever that place is."

16
In October 1968, Abbie Hoffman was arrested in Washington for wearing a shirt that resembled the design of an American flag.

17
Joyce Semons, *Artist on Fire: The Work of Joyce Wieland*.

18
See James Laxer, *The Energy Poker Game* (Toronto: New Press, 1970).

19
Kay Armatage, *Artist on Fire: The Work of Joyce Wieland*.

20
See Mike Zryd's excellent article on reception, "'There Are Many Joyces': The Critical Reception of the Films of Joyce Wieland," *The Films of Joyce Wieland*, ed. Kathryn Elder (Toronto: Cinematheque Ontario), 195–212.

21
Corinn Columpar and Sophie Mayer, "Introduction," *There She Goes: Feminist Filmmaking and Beyond,* ed. Columpar and Mayer (Detroit: Wayne State UP, 2009).

22
Dennis Reid, *Artist on Fire: The Work of Joyce Wieland*.

23
The Baader-Meinhof Gang in Germany, the Red Brigades in Italy, and the Weathermen, the Symbionese Liberation Army, and the Black Panthers in the US.

24
Among the films on the subject

are *Les ordres* (Michel Brault, 1974) and *Action: The October Crisis of 1970* (Robin Spry, 1973).

25
As in, for example, *The Squid-Jigging Grounds* (lithograph) and the "Oh Canada" segment of *Reason Over Passion* (film, 1968). Holmes-Moss considers Wieland's lips in extended analysis.

26
Quoted in Holmes-Moss, Joyce Wieland fonds, CTASC, 1994-004/003, File 3.

27
"The visual arts in Canada have generally been marked by the simple and reductive exposition of a very clear idea…. This approach is exemplified in the films of Chris Gallagher, David Rimmer, Ellie Epp, and Chris Welsby on the West Coast and Joyce Wieland, Michael Snow, John Porter, and Jack Chambers in Ontario. Each of these filmmakers' works also demonstrates a strong affinity with the Canadian tradition of documentary filmmaking. Indeed much of the Canadian avant-garde cinema could be characterized as experimental documentaries." Martin Rumsby, in an amended version of an essay originally published in *The Invisible Cinema*, 1989 Exhibition Catalogue, Govett-Brewster Art Gallery, New Plymouth, New Zealand, http://www.rumsby.net/martin/writing/beyond-the-wax-museum.

28
See Ben Singer, *Melodrama and Modernity* (New York: Columbia UP, 2001), 37–58.

29
Longfellow points to

contemporary critiques of the work of the Group of Seven, which suggest that their depiction of landscape in no way contradicted the aims of the business community in the first decades of the twentieth century to expand the extraction of natural resources from the north. Not only were economic links forged between the Group and industry, through the Massey-Harris enterprise and through significant patronage, but there was a smooth alignment of their joint vision of nation building. Longfellow, 171.

30
See Eric Hobsbaum and Terence Ranger, eds., *The Invention of Tradition* (Cambridge: Cambridge UP, 1983).

Works Cited

Armatage, Kay. "The Feminine Body: Joyce Wieland's *Water Sark*." *The Films of Joyce Wieland*. Ed. Kathryn Elder. Toronto: Cinematheque Ontario, 1999.

—. "Kay Armatage Interviews Joyce Wieland." *Take One* 3.2 (November–December 1970): 23–25. Reprinted with additions in *Women and the Cinema: A Critical Anthology*, ed. Karyn Kay and Gerald Peary. New York: Dutton, 1999.

Arthur, Paul. "Different/Same/Both/Neither: The Polycentric Cinema of Joyce Wieland." *Women's Experimental Cinema: Critical Frameworks*. Ed. Robin Blaetz. Durham, NC: Duke UP, 2007.

Banning, Kass. "Textual Excess in Joyce Wieland's *Handtinting*." *The Films of Joyce Wieland*. Ed. Kathryn Elder. Toronto: Cinematheque Ontario, 1999.

—. "The Mummification of Mummy: Joyce Wieland as the AGO's First Living Other." Elder, 29–44.

Columpar, Corinn, and Sophie Mayer. "Introduction." *There She Goes: Feminist Filmmaking and Beyond*. Ed. Columpar and Mayer. Detroit: Wayne State UP, 2009.

Cook, Pam. *Fashioning the Nation: Costume and Identity in British Cinema*. London: British Film Institute, 1996.

Kathryn Elder, ed. *The Films of Joyce Wieland*. Toronto: Cinematheque Ontario, 1999.

Frampton, Hollis, and Joyce Wieland. "I Don't Even Know about the Second Stanza." *The Films of Joyce Wieland*. Elder

Hobsbaum, Eric, and Terence Ranger, eds. *The Invention of Tradition*. Cambridge: Cambridge UP, 1983, passim.

Holmes-Moss, Kristy. "Negotiating the Nation: 'Expanding' the Work of Joyce Wieland." *Canadian Journal of Film Studies* (Fall 2006): 20–43.

Longfellow, Brenda. "Gender, Landscape and Colonial Allegories in *The Far Shore, Loyalties,* and *Mouvements du désir.*" *Gendering the Nation: Canadian Women's Cinema*. Ed. Kay Armatage et al. (Toronto: U of Toronto P, 1999).

Marchessault, Janine. "Feminist Avant-Grade Cinema: From Introspection to Retrospection." *CineAction* 24–25 (1991): 30–37.

McLarty, Lianne. "The Experimental Films of Joyce Wieland." Elder.

Rabinovitz, Lauren. *Points of Resistance: Women, Power, and Politics in the New York Avant-Garde Cinema, 1943–71*. Carbondale: U of Illinois P, 1991, 150–215.

Singer, Ben. *Melodrama and Modernity*. New York: Columbia UP, 2001.

Sitney, P. Adams. *Visionary Film*. Oxford: Oxford UP, 1974.

Sloan, Johanne. "Joyce Wieland at the Border: Nationalism, the New Left, and the Question of Political Art in Canada." *The Journal of Canadian Art History* 26 (2005): 80–107.

Smith, Anthony. "Images of the Nation: Cinema, Art and National Identity." *Cinema and Nation*. Ed. Mette Hjort and Scott MacKenzie. London: Routledge, 2000.

Zyrd, Michael. "There Are Many Joyces: The Critical Reception of the Films of Joyce Wieland." Elder, 195–212.

3
Queer Nation and Popular Culture

The Art of Making Do: Queer Canadian Girls Make Movies
Jean Bruce

Popular culture is made by the people at the interface between the
products of the culture industries and everyday life. Popular culture
is made by the people, not imposed upon them; it stems from within,
from below, not from above. Popular culture is the art of making do
with what the system provides.
– Michel de Certeau[1]

Nationalism is itself queer inasmuch as it works to reconcile that which
can never be reconciled: the heterogeneous national body.
– Jason Morgan[2]

In the context of New Queer Cinema ... lesbian camp is on the agenda.
Parody, performance and subversion have largely replaced positive-
images feminist politics with "riskier" images of "queer" sexuality.
– Paula Graham[3]

In *The Practice of Everyday Life*, Michel de Certeau (1984) suggests that popular
culture denotes an attitude toward cultural products and industries and their
place in everyday life. His theory of the making of popular culture acknowledges
a paucity of "friendly texts," and it identifies both the hegemonic terms through
which "the system provides" for the people and their limited opportunities for
critical engagement. De Certeau describes the art of making popular culture as
"the art of making do."[4]

But does the "art of making do" render the creation of popular culture
a passive act created more by default than intention? Must it conform to the
expectations of dominant cultural industries of the nation? On the contrary.
Rather than merely being like a charged magnet that picks up the detritus of
mass culture as though it were so many iron filings, popular culture can, in de

Certeau's analysis, be a complex process of critical and artistic negotiation. More significantly, it can be transformative.

This is the case with independent Canadian video artists Dara Gellman, Thirza Cuthand, and Dana Inkster and the constellation of three of their short videos produced serendipitously in 1999. The directors' particular brand of "making do" involves seizing images and highly conventional stories from mass culture and recreating them in the unruly image of lesbian sexuality. The trio of 1999 films—Gellman's *alien kisses*, Cuthand's *Helpless Maiden Makes an "I" Statement*, and Inkster's *Welcome to Africville*—results in an overtly queer Canadian popular culture.

In these three films, Cuthand, Gellman and Inkster detail a queer moment in which certain pressures, pleasures, and possibilities coincide to produce eloquent statements on what it is to be a young Canadian lesbian attempting to make culturally meaningful movies. Many of these films are experimental and use different means to address the cultural fallout that results from being constantly subjected to mainstream content and conventionally told stories. This style of film and video production can be categorized as "new queer cinema," which Ruby Rich describes as a "fresh, edgy, low-budget, inventive, unapologetic, sexy and stylistically daring."[5]

Each of the three videos is informed by a postmodern critical agenda. By isolating certain cultural assumptions upon which the stories are based and offering their own previously untold tales alongside them, they remind viewers what it is like to be excluded on the basis of gender, sexuality, and race. The result is narratives that not only "make do" but "talk back" to conventional idioms and make space for stories that had once been lost to popular consciousness. Each of the films is thus a meditation on dominant modes of storytelling, and together they invoke identifiable cultural references, even while they retain their experimental and analytical edge. Gellman highlights thirty seconds from an episode of a popular science-fiction television show. Cuthand samples images from popular culture to depict the classic sexy-evil character of witch/queen/dominatrix, while Inkster deals with the absence of personal stories in cultural tourism narratives.

Dara Gellman: *alien kisses* (1999)

Gellman's *alien kisses* (1999) "makes do" with what the Star Trek system provides, which arguably is a considerable array of queer material, if the amount of slash fiction written in response to Star Trek is any indication. Slash fiction involves rewriting episodes to include desirable romantic and/or sexual pairings imagined by the Trekker faithful. In keeping with this practice, Vtape, the online database of video, describes *alien kisses* as follows: "A brief moment of two women kissing, reclaimed from the lesbian subtext of a popular science fiction television program, is transformed into a sexy epic of queer desire."[6] The "popular science fiction television program" is *Star Trek: Deep Space Nine*, the third in the Star Trek series. It takes place on a space station where science, commerce, and political intrigue can occur simultaneously. The episode in question is from the fourth season (it aired in November 1995) and is titled "Rejoined."

The episode focuses on a Trill science team that arrives on Deep Space 9 to test ways to create artificial wormholes. The Trill are, in effect, hosts to symbiont parasites who can potentially live forever. The leader of the team is Dr. Lenara Kahn, a joined Trill whose symbiont was once borne by Lelanny, the former wife of one of DS9's officers, Jadzia Dax, who at the time was Torias, a man. Trill society has a strict taboo against "re-association" with past lovers, the penalty for which is exile for the duration of their lives, and the symbionts will die with their current hosts. Dax and Lenara must be careful about interacting, therefore. Despite their best efforts, they nonetheless find themselves reawakening old emotional bonds.

The episode begins with a magic trick with which Dax wows her audience. This sleight of hand immediately opens up the notion of deception; on one hand it produces the pleasurable surprise that is the basis of all magic tricks, but on the other it foreshadows the duplicity in the reconnection of Dax and Lenara. Close-ups juxtaposed with long shots and shot reverse shots convey physical distance and the desire to bridge it. These tender moments culminate in the romantic kiss to suggest that the love between Dax and Lenara is so great it transcends death, identity, gender. Yet the moment is informed by the fact that Dax was a man in her past life. It is as though the Star Trek producers wanted to have the kiss and eat it too. Once the encounter occurs, however, it can never be taken back, and the image is still one of two women kissing, which opens up the possibilities of queer desire on its own terms. And, like a heat-seeking missile, *alien kisses* targets the sexual ambiguity of "Rejoined." Gellman appropriates this single detail of the episode, adds sexy trance music and thereby strips away the gender equivocation by imposing a new queer vision.

The first transformation of the image by Gellman relies on the readily available technology of the VCR. The VCR allows home viewers a closer examination of fleeting images. A TV show on VHS tape can be played over and over. It can be paused, fast-forwarded, slowed down, rewound. These techniques are employed by Gellman, Cuthand, and Inkster in different ways to capture and manipulate images, transforming them into image referents for their own videos as well as providing a how-to manual for independent video production. In the case of *alien kisses,* the techniques include slow motion, cropping, image enlargement, and the conspicuous digitization of the image, which is

underscored by revealing the pixels. All of these manipulations represent significant departures from the original footage.[7]

Thus the very existence of *alien kisses* is built on what might previously
have been considered a contradiction: it is a queer, experimental art video whose
existence *depends* on the already established cultural playfulness of Star Trek
slash fiction and the consumer "need" to manipulate space and time constraints
with the VCR. At the same time, the video constitutes another critical intervention: it is diatribe against the equivocation on sexuality that is central to maintaining the Star Trek brand. As such, *alien kisses* functions as an antidote to Star
Trek's ultimately tame treatment of the potentially queer subject matter that the
various series have for years presented to audiences.[8]

In an age of audience interactivity, Gellman seems to suggest that,
considering the queer audience for Star Trek is in some part responsible for
sustaining the brand, perhaps it is high time there was acknowledgement of
the desires of this group beyond the occasional titillating episode. *alien kisses*
shares a playful-critical intervention not only with slash fiction but with queer
independent art practice generally, which has often borrowed ambiguous
images from straight culture. By recontextualizing, heightening, or reframing
such images, queer cultural artifacts are created by teasing out the queerness of
selected texts. And, as with slash fiction writers, queer visual artists often invite
viewers to both share alternative readings and engage in their own reading or
re-creation strategies.

This habit of reading and making narratives and images against the
grain did not of course originate with Star Trek. Women, gays, non-whites, and
the working class—to name just of few of those who have inhabited the outskirts
of mass culture—have always had to make do, to adjust their stride in order to
navigate unfriendly textual paths. But their reading strategies have increasingly
become incorporated as common textual strategies of postmodern consumer
culture, and they too have become part of the system. As postmodern textual
elements entered the mainstream culture of television, for example, alternative
reading strategies lost their subversive edge. In other words, the so-called
transgressive act of stealing pleasure is built in to many TV shows. Everything
from *Seinfeld* to *The Simpsons* contains some feature that offers the media-
savvy viewer access to such postmodern pleasure.[9]

Thus the frequent deployment of multiplicity and intertextuality, which
have been identified as sites of potential alternative readings in postmodern
texts, have become televisual conventions. When they are understood by
audience members, intertextual references amplify meanings and disarm wary
viewers with their inclusiveness. These understandings create a community of
viewers, because implicit in them is the statement You get this, you are one of us,

aren't we clever? In many television shows referentiality is so common, however, that it has become an authorized use of the medium itself. Whether it operates within the constraints of the sitcom genre and the conventions of animation, these situations arguably encourage viewers to occupy a ready-made ironic position in relation to the subject matter of the shows. But what happens when the filmmaker is a self-confessed baby dyke bottom (Cuthand) who positions herself as visually and culturally central to the circulation of popular images of female domination?[10] Perhaps context is the more important consideration in determining the impact of so-called transgressive acts.

Thirza Cuthand: Helpless Maiden Makes an "I" Statement (1999)

In *Helpless Maiden Makes an "I" Statement*, Cuthand's image in medium close-up reveals a head and bare shoulders with the odd peek at her leather wrist cuffs. This image is intercut throughout with animated and live-action televisual and cinematic references to images of what may be generally classified as femmes fatales. Cuthand's direct address gaze and commentary acknowledge her complicity in the construction of the images and guide our engagement with them in a complex play between desire and tedium. For example, when she discusses her desire for older white women, we are shown the Evil Queen from Disney's *Snow White*. Because Cuthand is not the presumed original audience for such fare, the video implicitly questions the status of these images. Whom are these images designed for? Why are they in this video? In most cases, the evil witch/queen is a character from animated films made for children. Other live-action images Cuthand references are more ambiguous in their address to an adult audience, while still others are already appropriated by an alternative culture for the express purpose of parodying such images of straight society.

Taken from a variety of sources and placed together, these images form a kind of paradigm of potential desire for Cuthand and "violate" the tacit agreement between producer and audience member as to how they *should* be consumed. Cuthand is clearly depicted as a woman talking about her own desire for other women. Meanwhile, she complains about her own stupidity, is bored, and hints at her own lack of imagination when it comes to such clichéd depictions of women and, in the end, wants the consensual bondage to stop.

But Cuthand goes further than to suggest that she too, as a baby dyke bottom, is susceptible to the pleasure-fear these images generate. Because she positions herself as the viewer-creator of such representations, the video becomes an interrogation of misogyny and ageism by way of queer desire. It asks why the image equates evil with the sexy older dark-haired white woman, and, furthermore, why it is so prevalent. It is in this way that the aesthetic intervention of the film is anchored in a history of feminist critique and pushed toward a new queer politics. Given that the video makes reference to its own incompleteness— the "puny" image of Cuthand is not "well balanced" and often hints at what is beyond the frame—this video represents a serious and playful attempt to create a new language for expressing queer desire and generating criticism.

Dana Inkster: *Welcome to Africville* (1999)

Fans and video artists seem to have a lot in common. Those whom de Certeau more broadly refers to as "the people" turn mass-mediated images into popular culture. As fans, we do what Henry Jenkins describes as "transforming personal reaction into social interaction."[11] This concept of constructing a community of like-minded viewers by reframing extant images and creating new stories is perhaps most relevant to analyzing *Welcome to Africville*. Like *alien kisses* and *Helpless Maiden Makes an "I" Statement*, it too provides referent images in the form of archival footage, but the video focuses on telling the personal stories of four Africville residents in the period immediately preceding Africville's demise. In fact, the film's title might suggest that we will see a tourism or commemorative film about Africville, but what we get are fleeting glimpses of Africville prior to its infamous demolition in 1969. These details are provided courtesy of *Remembering Africville* (1991), the short NFB-directed film by Shelagh Mackenzie. In Inkster's film, the personal stories take the forefront in this new "re-enactment-commemoration," and *Welcome to Africville* quickly disabuses viewers of their expectations about documentary or cultural tourism.

Overall, the documentary images function in at least in two ways. First, they provide an immediate backdrop to the stories and timeline of the characters depicted. Second, as archival indices of Africville intact they are a stark reminder of its very real and controversial demolition. The images thus create a tension between the documentary and fiction as well as provide a bridge from the past to the present. Thus, these black-and-white archival images rendered in long shot carry significant weight on their own, imbuing the story with sober, observational authenticity. They contrast strongly with the highly saturated medium close-ups that begin the film and the smoky images of the bar that we see later. While the neighbourhood and implied community of Africville are equally important to the characters, they vie for their attention on the subject of sexuality, with which each character is preoccupied.

All of the characters convey an ambiguous sexuality that can perhaps be compared with the ambivalence that has always informed both the existence and destruction of Africville. The twin concepts of ambiguity and ambivalence can be extended to consider the influence of storytelling decisions on the final film. How best to tell the story of Africville—via documentary or fictional means? The treatment of the subject matter is, as with *alien kisses* and *Helpless Maiden Makes an "I" Statement*, complicated by the technological choices on how to treat the images themselves—as film, video, DV, and so on—to enhance the story.

Arjun Appadurai discusses the importance of the relationship between aesthetics and subjectivity vis-à-vis migrant technologies and migrant subjects. He claims that the "story of mass migrations (voluntary and forced) is hardly a new feature of human history."[12] Mass migration is also a condition of contemporary culture: where films are substituted by video, which becomes DV, and so on. Meanwhile, straight images are queered to become lesbian.[13] For Inkster, sexuality and cultural and geographical migration are all manifestations of the Black woman's alienation and sense of dislocation in her environment. Relocating the stories by imposing her own authorial aesthetic—technical and technological decisions—perhaps provides a sense of comfort and control while it pauses the grand sweep of history to address the fact of personal alienation. Inkster's practice has been to engage in a form of cultural biography: part ethnography, part personal fiction.[14]

Nation, Interrupted

It is precisely within the dynamism created by these moments of cultural and textual intervention that the videos of Gellman, Cuthand, and Inkster can be claimed as a queer national politics of representation. The 1990s, with its explosion of queer filmmaking and its various degrees of cinematic experimentation, led to moments of "making do" that are worth recalling and reclaiming. These moments represent an attempt at post-national points of contact, where queerness—more than simply an effect of nationalism interrupted—provides an opportunity to consider anew the parts of ourselves that constitute who we are socially, historically, culturally. Moreover, these moments remind us that the issue of generic cultural appropriation is not as straightforward as it may seem. The relationship between aesthetics and subjectivity blurs the boundaries between the industrial system of television and video production and mass-cultural consumers, passive viewing and interactivity, art video and television. National borders are not the least of these concerns but form part of the list of sometimes permeable, sometimes fixed, elements of subjectivity. For the queer fan, the relationship between aesthetics and subjectivity can provide an opportunity to reconstruct characters in her or his own alien image.

Appadurai suggests that "when [mass migration] is juxtaposed with the rapid flow of mass-mediated images, scripts, and sensations, we have a new order of instability in the production of modern subjectivities."[15] This, I would argue, is the perfect occasion for migrating technologies and subjectivities to overlap and interact; in this case, altogether they provide the means for a transformative popular culture to occur. The practice of gathering or poaching mass-mediated images of national subjecthood (ours or others) by slowing them down, repeating them in a new context, or enlarging their details entails a transformation of ownership of meaning production that is created by new, migrant subjectivities. I would suggest that this is a queer struggle against subordination, but it also represents an alliance among other subject positions that refuses essentialist identity categories whether these are formed through gender, sexuality, or ethnicity. Dislocating identity challenges us to reconsider the definition of nationalism, as Jason Morgan (2000) suggests, by the very heterogeneity of its subjects.

Understanding the idea of a queer nation and popular culture is more than semantics, and their link is not merely rhetorical. Canadian cinema, video, and new media may occupy a unique position in the world of contemporary culture, in part because our version of nationalism and our depictions of sexuality are unusual.[16] Whether these works are overtly declared queer or not, they are—to use a familiar Canadian social-policy term—ideas that are receptive to harmonization. Like queer, Canadian culture has often signified the abject in all its hopeless, apologetic, and despicable variations. Whether celebrated or scorned, these slightly off terms of reference have been deployed to denote both queer sexuality and Canadian cultural eccentricity. Most artists hope that while they contribute to revitalizing the immediate aesthetic landscape, the effects of their work will migrate beyond their own imagined communities. They, like mainstream television and film producers or national policy-makers, cannot legislate all the meanings that images generate or foresee the uses that their "texts" will be put to. This is perhaps especially obvious for queer artists, whose work invites us to reconsider the status quo, which has tended to exclude them. As excentrics they often offer new ways of imagining the social and political realm; the space for marginal subjects within these realms needs unpacking, after all.

While there are obviously differences between expressing queerness and Canadianness in any medium, there are also interesting points of contact. It is worth remembering that the history of filmmaking like all art is in large part about rethinking the boundaries between geopolitical locations, medium, and genre, and more recently have foregrounded class, gender, and sexuality, as the examples I have discussed all do.[17] What we encounter is not a unified programmatic vision of nation or sexuality but rather with these small films an acknowledgement of the discursive leaks in the system, the un-dammed forms of subjectivity in process. When deployed as a critical gesture aimed at countering acceptable ways of representing things—with its disruptive potential momentarily isolated—queer (gay, lesbian, transgendered, bisexual, theorosexual, etc.) and Canadian (migrant, aboriginal, postnational, transnational, diasporic, exiled, etc.) *can* go hand in hand. But this may occur only if the true complexity of the terms "queer" and "Canadian" are acknowledged and incorporated into the terms of subject positioning. This opening up and out is what the films of Gellman, Inkster, and Cuthand are offering to us.

Appendix

Thirza Cuthand

Thirza Cuthand was born in Regina, Saskatchewan, in 1978, and, as she puts it, "grew up a Cree-Scottish-Irish bipolar butch-lesbian two-spirited boy/girl thingamabob in Saskatoon." She has produced experimental videos and films on low to no budget, exploring issues of identity, race, sexuality, relationships, ageism, and mental health. Her work has been shown worldwide. She has won awards for her videos *Untouchable*, *Helpless Maiden Makes an "I" Statement*, and *Anhedonia*. She majored in film and video at Emily Carr Institute of Art and Design. Currently Cuthand is writing a feature screenplay and scrounging video resources to continue self-producing her short works. She also works in performance, new media, and comics (http://www.vtape.org).

Videography

Film duration is given in minutes and seconds.

My Sister, 1996. 5:00. With Danielle Ratslaff

Colonization: The Second Coming, 1996. 3:30. With Danielle Ratslaff

Working Baby Dyke Theory: The Diasporic Impact of Cross-Generational Barriers, 1997. 4:00

Bisexual Wannabe, 1997. 2:30

Untouchable, 1998. 4:14

Anhedonia, 1999. 9:30

Helpless Maiden Makes an "I" Statement. 1999. 6:00

Through the Looking Glass, 1999. 13:54

Manipulation/Dictation, 1999. 4:00

Love & Numbers, 2004. 9:00

Dara Gellman

Born in Sydney, Australia, Dara Gellman is based in Toronto and works as a video artist, curator, writer, and cultural organizer. She is a founding member of the curatorial organization VVV, which is one of the co-founders of the Tranz Tech Toronto International Media Art Biennial. Gellman was the director of the 3rd Tranz Tech Biennial. Her video and installation work has been exhibited in Canada and internationally (www.vtape.org).

Videography

Subterranean, 1996

Dream of Her in White, 1997

Hold Up, 1997

Territory, 1997. 3:00. With Barbara Gretzny and Leslie Peters

The Bright Sun, 1997. 2:00

Disassemble, 1997

alien kisses, 1999. 3:00

Pearl, 2002. 3:30. With Leslie Peters

That's Pretty Special, 2003. 1:05

Deliberate, 2003. 6:17

Interference, 2003. With Leslie Peters

Impossible Landscapes, 2006. With Leslie Peters

Dana Inkster

Dana Inkster is an Alberta-based media artist and cultural producer. Her art practice experiments with the bounds of cultural representation and our expectations of narrative. Her work has won critical acclaim and awards in Canada and internationally. Dana has produced and directed short films and videos that range from experimental video art to broadcast television. She has been profiled by numerous critics, journalists, and cultural theorists. Her films and videos have been exhibited in galleries and festivals and have been acquired on all continents. Her *24 Days in Brooks* was the winner in 2008 of the Alberta Motion Picture Industry Award for Best Production Reflecting Cultural Diversity (http://www.cinesalon.ca/danainkster.html).

Videography

Electric Dreams, 2008. 45 sec.

24 Days in Brooks, 2007. 42:03

The Art of Autobiography: Redux II, 2006. 3:00

The Art of Autobiography: Redux I, 2006. 3:00

The Art of Autobiography: Redux I, 2006. 5:00

The Art of Autobiography, 2003. 47:30

From Billie ... to Me ... and Back Again, 2002. 4:20

1. We Can Go Anywhere 2. Know Your Sound 3. Words Can Make a Difference, 2000. 3:00

Welcome to Africville, 1999, 15:00

Notes

1
Michel de Certeau (1974), *The Practice of Everyday Life*, trans. Steven Rendall (Berkeley: U of California P, 1984), 32.

2
Jason Morgan, "'Do You Ever Get Tired of Being a Professional Faggot?': 'Perversion Chic,' Queer Nationalism, and English Canadian Cinema," *Confluence* 1.1 (2000), http://confluence .athabascau.ca/content/vol1.1/ nelprocpaper.html.

3
Paula Graham, "Girl's Camp? The Politics of Parody," *Immortal Invisible: Lesbians and the Moving Image*, ed. Tamsin Wilton (London: Routledge, 1995), 163.

4
Michel de Certeau, 29–42.

5
Ruby B. Rich, "Queer and Present Danger," *Sight and Sound* 10.3 (March 2000): 23.

6
alien kisses entry in Vtape, http://www.vtape.org/ catalogue.htm.

7
According to Gellman, the VHS tape was first rescanned and then run through a time-based corrector. Rescanning helps to give texture to the image, softening it and foregrounding the pixels. The time-based corrector helps with contrast and allows the colour to be drained from the tape and the blue-lavender to be added later. Finally, the home-video VHS tape was transferred to professional-grade Betacam tape and then to DV (digital video) format. The specific segment was cut using the Avid media composer, and the speed was slowed down. Author interview with Dara Gellman.

8
Much has been made of Star Trek's creative genius Gene Roddenberry and his progressive gender and racial politics. Roddenberry's famously placing a female second in command way back in 1968—the network objected and pulled the pilot—is often cited as evidence of his progressiveness. But I see no reason to continue to applaud Star Trek's policies. They wear thin when it takes twenty-five years to write in a black man as ship captain (*in Deep Space Nine*) and almost thirty years to write in a white woman as captain (in the *Voyager* series). Equivocation on the subject of race and gender parity becomes clearer when one considers that Captain Benjamin Sisko of *Deep Space Nine* is really only a middle-management commander of a space station going nowhere—that is, he is not an explorer—while Captain Kathryn Janeway of *Voyager* gets lost in space her first day on the job.

9
The Simpsons, for example, is well known for its intertextual references to classic Hollywood cinema, 1960s television, and jazz, among other things.

10
This was true as of 1999, at least. Recently, however, Thirza Cuthand has been "transitioning from a famous unemployed lesbian video artist to a famous

unemployed tranny filmmaker." thirzacuthand.blogspot.com.

11

Henry Jenkins III, "Star Trek Rerun, Reread, Rewritten: Fan Writing as Textual Poaching," *Television: The Critical View*, 6th ed., ed. Horace Newcomb (New York: Oxford UP, 2000), 473.

12

Arjun Appadurai, *Modernity at Large: Cultural Dimensions of Globalization* (Minneapolis: Public Worlds, 1996), 4.

13

It is perhaps worth noting in this context that Gellman was born in Australia, Inkster is Afro-Canadian with white parents, and Cuthand's heritage is Cree-Scottish.

14

See Internet Resources, below, for the aim of Inkster's most recent film in production, *Brooks, AB*, for example.

15

Appadurai, 4.

16

See Katherine Monk, *Weird Sex & Snowshoes and Other Canadian Film Phenomena* (Vancouver: Raincoast Books, 2001).

17

See, for example, Néstor Garcia Canclini, "Remaking Passports: Visual Thought in the Debate on Multiculturalism," *The Visual Culture Reader*, ed. Nicholas Mirzoeff (London: Routledge, 2004). Canclini points out that Latin American art is not limited to local influences and needs to "rethink its own cultural heritage," because, as he argues, "innumerable artists fed on Cubism, Surrealism and other Parisian vanguards to elaborate national discourses" (183). Even a cursory glance at the films of the CFMDC and Vtape reveal acknowledged influences from local educators and institutions like the Ontario College of Art and Design, York University, and Ryerson University to philosophers and film and from cultural theorists to informal film instruction at domestic and foreign post-production houses.

Works Cited

Appadurai, Arjun. *Modernity at Large: Cultural Dimensions of Globalization*. Minneapolis: Public Worlds, 1996.

De Certeau, Michel. *The Practice of Everyday Life*. Trans. Steven Rendall. Berkeley: U of California P, 1984. [1974.]

Graham, Paula. "Girl's Camp? The Politics of Parody." *Immortal Invisible: Lesbians and the Moving Image*. Ed. Tamsin Wilton. London: Routledge, 1995. 163–81.

Jenkins III, Henry. "Star Trek Rerun, Reread, Rewritten: Fan Writing as Textual Poaching." *Television: The Critical View*, 6th ed. Ed. Horace Newcomb. New York: Oxford UP, 2000, 470–94. Morgan, Jason. "'Do You Ever Get Tired of Being a Professional Faggot?': 'Perversion Chic,' Queer Nationalism, and English Canadian Cinema." *Confluence* 1.1 (2000). http://confluence .athabascau.ca/content/vol1.1/ nelprocpaper.html.

Rich, Ruby B. "Queer and Present Danger." *Sight and Sound*. 10.3 (March 2000): 22–25.

Internet Resources

Vtape: http://www.vtape.org

Canadian Filmmakers Distribution Centre: http://www.cfmdc .org

Groupe Intervention Vidéo: http://www.givideo.org

Feminist Filmmaking and the Cinema of Patricia Rozema
Agata Smoluch Del Sorbo

I'm distinctly feminist. My films assume feminism. That's the best way
I can say it. They assume feminism, it's in their foundation. All of the
assumptions of the characters and everything that happens assumes
that women clearly have the right to do whatever they want to do—
clearly have the right to own property, to run the world, whatever. I'm
very, very much a feminist.
– Patricia Rozema, 1993[1]

There's a strain of feminism that seems to suggest that you can only
create heroic female characters.... I could never write a film where
people would say, "My films assume feminist principles." It's so clear to
me that there have been major injustices against women for centuries.
That has to be changed is changing and hasn't changed enough. That's
feminism. That's all.
– Patricia Rozema, 1997[2]

Patricia Rozema has for over twenty years been one of Canada's most significant
and internationally acclaimed woman filmmakers. Examining her work within
the context of feminism presents a particularly intriguing undertaking, given
Rozema's conflicted relationship with the idea of feminism and because film
critics and feminist theorists have responded strongly to her work on this front,
querying whether her films are in fact feminist. While there may or may not
exist an avowedly feminist intent in her work, and while women's filmmaking
by no means necessarily implies feminist filmmaking, Rozema's films can be
interpreted as being informed by feminist film practice and feminist discourse.
In her feature films *I've Heard the Mermaids Singing* (1987), *White Room* (1990),
When Night Is Falling (1995), *Mansfield Park* (1999), and her handful of short
films, Rozema consistently constructs women-centred narratives that position

her female characters in strong, complex, non-heterosexual and nontraditional roles. In addition, Rozema's whimsical and unique filmmaking style, particularly her aesthetic and formal strategies, represents a conscious effort to reinvent traditional narrative structures and formal techniques. In light of this, her work can be contextualized within the rich history of feminist criticism and positioned within a legacy of feminist film praxis in Canada and abroad.

Female Authorship

Currently in its third wave, and possessing its own conflicted history, feminism—and feminist criticism—has continually valued the significance of female subjectivity, agency, and authorship. Given that the notion of authorship has been historically male dominated, the significance of female authorship and the interpretation of women's cinema function, in part, as a strategic intervention and recuperative practice of denied and unrealized agency.[3] What is really at stake, however, "is whether the adjective female in female authorship inflects the noun authorship in a way significant enough to challenge or displace its patriarchal and proprietary implications" (Mayne, 95). Judith Mayne argues that it does indeed challenge these implications, in its presence not only as a political strategy but as a notion "crucial to the reinvention of the cinema that has been undertaken by women filmmakers and feminist spectators" (Mayne, 97). As Janine Marchessault suggests, female authorship now needs to be reconsidered in the context of both political collectivity, women's oppression under patriarchy, and individual subjectivity, thus respecting the diversity among women (Marchessault, 89). It is precisely this process of reinvention and this idea of political collectivity that recast the individuality of the traditional nineteenth-century Romantic patriarchal author. Further contributing to the disruption of the idea of the author as the originating source of transcendent meaning, and providing a useful approach with which to consider female authorship, is Lucy Fischer's formulation that women's cinema can be seen as an ongoing intertextual debate with men's cinema (Fischer, 12). Hence women's cinema and female authorship represent not only a reclaiming of denied agency but a confronting and de-centring of both patriarchal film tradition and the notion of the patriarchal author.

(Re)presenting the Female Artist

Female authorship plays a productive role in the interpretation of Patricia Rozema's work, not only with respect to the gendered filmmaker as the source of meaning but in her focus on female self-expression and creativity in her use of the artist figure. As Kaja Silverman in "The Female Authorial Voice" suggests, there is a close relation between authorship and subjectivity, so much so that cinematic discourse can "provide mechanisms through which an author 'outside' the text could 'speak' her subjectivity" from within the filmic interior (Silverman, 207). The director of the film may therefore "constitute *one* of the speakers" in her film and there may be at times a compelling political basis to maximize what is said from this specific authorial voice (Silverman, 202).

The female artist figure has consistently held an important place in the imagination of female English Canadian feature filmmakers. In fact, two of the earliest dramatic features featured artists as central characters. In Sylvia Spring's *Madeleine Is ...* (1971), the first female-directed English-language feature film ever made in Canada, the title character struggles to find herself and, in the end, discovers her identity and voice as a painter. In Joyce Wieland's *The Far Shore* (1976), newly and unhappily married Eulalie is a pianist whose deep connection to her music stems from an early period of deafness. Her music becomes a site of strain between Eulalie and her husband but remains one of her only outlets of self-expression. The female artists' struggle in both of these films is connected to their intense desire for self-expression and selfhood, which is compromised and stifled by the male characters in their lives. Success for these women lies in the ability to express oneself and in the liberating act of producing art, regardless of whether that art is deemed "acceptable."

In almost all of Rozema's shorts and her features, she presents a meditation on the artist figure who can be interpreted as metaphorically representing Rozema's authorial voice—a voice that addresses the complexities of female, lesbian, and Canadian authorship, the relationship of women to language and Rozema's own development as a filmmaker. Her authorial subjectivity is established "through identification with an anthropomorphic representation which is not, strictly speaking, his or her 'own,' but that of an other who also happens in this case to be a fictional character" (Silverman, 214). As the author "outside" the text, Rozema is constituted "inside" the text via "secondary identification." It is precisely this consistent presence and exploration of the female artist character in Rozema's work, through which her subjectivity is constituted, that demands maximizing.

Rozema's first short, *Passion: A Letter in 16 mm* (1985), is structured as an intimate love letter composed by the artist figure Anna Vogel, a documentary filmmaker, to an unidentified genderless lover. Anna attempts to balance and negotiate passion in both her personal life and her work life, with uneven success. Passion in her work results in a passionate documentary that is described in a voice-over commentary as an "unusually poetic exploration of humanity's relationship with the sky, [that] is a striking departure for a director well known worldwide for elegant and exquisitely logical science documentaries." Her dedication to her work, however, eventually contributes to the breakup of her relationship, and her intersecting success and failure is related in this filmic love letter that allows Anna to come to terms with the end of her relationship. In *Passion* the idea of female authorship is dealt with in terms of the artist's struggle to prioritize and navigate public and private life as well as the importance of truly passionate artistic creation, even if the consequence may be a lonely personal life. As Rozema's first film, *Passion* can also be interpreted as metaphorically marking Rozema's own movement from journalism,[4] a world in love with facts, to the passionate fiction of narrative drama.

Rozema's second film, her internationally acclaimed debut feature *I've Heard the Mermaids Singing*, confronts the notion "that objectivist standards in art have any meaning" and was, in part, a response to a scathing review of *Passion* in *The Globe and Mail* that Rozema was particularly affected by (Posner, 3). With *Mermaids*, Rozema presents the lives of three artist figures—Gabrielle, Mary, and Polly—and their relationships with art and self-expression. Gabrielle—a worldly, intellectual, sophisticated gallery curator and an upholder of conventional highbrow art standards—can be seen as representing the traditional Canadian male artist unable to create, her patriarchal status signalled by her last name, "St. Pères."[5] Mary is a brilliant artist by conventional standards and her work is unanimously praised, but she dislikes public attention and therefore encourages Gabrielle to deceptively claim Mary's artwork as her own. Polly, who of the three is the most closely aligned with Rozema's authorial voice, has two modes of creative self-expression—photography and fantasy, both of which are presented as unacceptable by traditional standards. Although Polly's creative expression is outside the realm of acceptable art practice, it is tremendously satisfying for Polly and wins the respect of others when, in the film's final magical scene, Polly shares her photography and fantastic internal landscape with Gabrielle and Mary.

In *Mermaids*, a distinction is drawn between institutionalized art and the subversive self-expression of fantasy, between "good"/canonized art and "bad"/unconventional art. The historic treatment of women's artmaking—muted, undervalued, deemed trivial—is re-enacted in the relationship between Polly as "other" and the patriarchal Gabrielle St. Pères, their relationship underscoring the history of silencing women's self-expression. Polly "expresses" from a place of double "otherness," as both female and Canadian, and, like the ostensibly silent subject in English Canadian film,[6] Polly is not silent; rather, her desire and self-expression simply do not speak the same "language" as patriarchal or dominant codes prescribe.

In her second feature, *White Room*, Rozema presents us with another group of artists; Jane, a singer; Madeleine X, "the face" of the singer; Norm, an aspiring writer; and Zelda, the environmental artist. Unlike the previous two, this film directly addresses the relationship between the artist and her audience.

Madeleine X describes the love/hate embrace between the star and the audience, both amazing and frightening. Jane, like Mary in *Mermaids*, is unable to handle the public life of an artist and prefers to have Madeleine X be her public persona while Jane remains a recluse. Zelda, on the other hand, is presented as the attention-loving artist who produces only for the sake of attention, while the male character, once again, is unable to produce any credible art. Norm initially cannot find the words to write, but once he does, he can reproduce only clichés. His fantasies are also suitably enigmatic, problematizing rather than elucidating his character.[7] After the tremendous amount of attention that Rozema received with *Mermaids*, which won the Prix de la Jeunesse at Cannes and was both a critical and commercial success, *White Room* speaks to the excitement and the pressure of being embraced by the public, as shown by the necessity of the "split subject" of Madeleine X/Jane.

In her third feature, *When Night Is Falling*, the artist figure is Petra, a circus performer in the subversive "Sircus of Sorts." In this film, Rozema connects creative expression with sexual expression. When Camille decides to choose her lesbian relationship with Petra over her heterosexual relationship with Martin, Camille runs off with Petra to join the circus, her creative expression coinciding with her sexual liberation. *When Night Is Falling* marks Rozema's most overt exploration of lesbianism and, as a loosely autobiographical film, represents an artistic self-expression of her own sexuality.[8] The film can be interpreted as replicating Rozema's own move from a world of religious restrictions (she was formerly a devout Christian), to one significantly more liberal and inclusive.

Though the subjects for the compilation features *Montreal Vu Par* (1991) and *Yo-Yo Ma: Inspired by Bach* (1997) were not chosen by Rozema, her short-film contributions to them are nevertheless much in line with her preoccupations with artistry and self-expression. Given the opportunity, in *Montreal Vu Par*, to reflect on that city, she naturally gravitates toward issues of expression, language, and Canadian bilingualism, as suggested by the short's title, *Desperanto*, a play on the name of the international language Esperanto. Anne Stewart journeys on what she hopes will be an exciting weekend in Montreal armed with a French–English dictionary and a suitcase of not-so-chic clothing. Inspired by the joie de vivre in Denys Arcand's *Decline of the American Empire*, Anne crashes a Montreal house party, pretends to be a professional dancer, and excitedly dances the night away, to the disdain of the other partiers. Her true self-expression and creativity, however, are not fully realized until she slips into her fantasy world to escape an embarrassing moment.[9] It is in this internal space that she literally plays with language, physically manipulating and taking advantage of the film's subtitles and then, finally, celebrating with Denys Arcand and Geneviève Rioux from *Decline*. Once again, when unable to enter into the dominant language, Rozema's character escapes into her more hospitable creative internal landscape.

Rozema's experimental short film *Six Gestures* is part of the *Yo-Yo Ma: Inspired by Bach* series and deals with artistry, which is perhaps why Rozema was drawn to the subject matter. Like the other films in the series, the film is partly an interpretation of the music of Bach as performed by the cellist Yo-Yo Ma. Rozema extends the rendering, however, to include an attempt to understand Bach as an artist via dramatic monologues performed by the character Bach, who describes the private hardships that coincided with the composition of his music. Once again, Rozema addresses the complexities of both private and public in relation to creativity, and thus speaks to the multiple facets of the artist.

Rozema's most intriguing exploration of female artistry materializes in her Jane Austen adaptation, *Mansfield Park*. Diverging from the novel, and confirming Rozema's proclivity for artist characters, Rozema altered the character of Fanny Price by turning her into a writer modelled on Austen herself. Timid and retreating in the novel, Fanny becomes in Rozema's telling strong, clever, irreverent, and the persuasive moral centre of the narrative. This turn allows Rozema to explore the status of females and female artists in early-nineteenth-century England. Fanny struggles for self-expression and a right to a voice through her writing and within her family. Her efforts are met with categorical disapproval and she is forced to negotiate the oppressive expectations and strict gender hierarchies of English society. Unlike the superficial artistry of the Bertram sisters and Mary Crawford, who play musical instruments only for diversion in the parlour, Fanny's art has something to express beyond the traditional artistic limits set for women of that time. Breaking with custom with her tomboyishness, outspokenness, and wicked and daring writing, Fanny represents the historic female artist's desire for voice, her desire to wrestle free of societal gender expectations. Eventually, Fanny's subversive self-expression is, like Polly's, accepted, and her progression represents the transition for women away from the oppression of voicelessness.

Cousin Tom, also an artist, presents an interesting parallel figure, one who provides further commentary on the mores of the time. In his being silenced throughout the film, and his drawings depicting the brutalities of slavery in Antigua, Tom represents the mute, castrated artist carrying the burden of white male colonialism and its mistakes. It is Fanny who brings Tom's drawings to light and liberates his voice and the horrors of slavery.

Although Fanny is Jane Austen's character and many of the events are those of the novel, Rozema has moulded the protagonist into an artist and the story into something very much her own, foregrounding, minimizing, and altering aspects of the original text. In light of this, *Mansfield Park* might be read as a representation of Rozema's own progression as an artist. In much the same way that

Fanny escapes the limited options of Portsmouth for the opportunity and adventure of Mansfield Park, so Rozema departs from production in the struggling Canadian film industry for the adventure and more richly funded opportunities of film production abroad. Like Fanny, who in the end remains closely tied and rooted to her home in Portsmouth, Rozema remains closely tied to and rooted in Canadian filmmaking, but her world and opportunities have grown, and whether she will make films in Canada again is yet to be seen.

With Rozema's following film, the short *This Might Be Good* (2000), commissioned for the twenty-fifth anniversary of the Toronto International Film Festival, she returned to the subject of artists and audiences. A wordless experimental piece set to dance music, the film evokes a moment when the artist is most vulnerable: when her work first makes contact with the public. After a movie actress, played by Sarah Polley, introduces the film in which she stars, she sits in the audience for a few moments and then escapes to the safety of the projection booth. In a surprising twist, the audience begins to file into the booth and gather around her. Like *White Room*, the film speaks to the pressures and pleasures of being an artist, the nervous anticipation of reception, and the desire to be embraced and appreciated by the public, with Polley functioning as a stand-in for Rozema in these concerns.

Rozema's next film was a quickly made adaptation of Samuel Beckett's *Happy Days*, for the Beckett Film Project. Though the guidelines of the project were strict (no changes to the original text were permitted), it is not surprising that Rozema chose the most female-centred of Beckett's plays to adapt. This absurdist play about a middle-aged woman who lives partly buried in sand while her husband comes and goes from a mound located behind her, can be read as a commentary on women, marriage, and voice.

As we have seen, Rozema has, in her films, consistently constituted her subjectivity through the character of the artist figure, who stands as a metaphoric representation of female expression and authorship as well as an articulation of self that parallels Rozema's own life. By extension, this subjectivity can be seen as reflective of the larger theory of art and expression that motivates Rozema. Filmmaking is for Rozema a search for answers, a revealing of hidden truths about humanity, a wish for what society might be like, and, ultimately, a journey to enlightenment. To this end, Rozema's films engage in a dialogue with culture; her films are meditations on society and its cultural forms, particularly traditional belief systems, orthodox views, and the role of the artist. Her artist figures embark on contemplative journeys of their own, questioning, searching, and pushing boundaries to create new realities. The artist figures assume Rozema's own meditative style by challenging and exploring society's traditional expectations and cultural forms.

Intertextuality

As Kaja Silverman suggests, the female authorial voice can take on various guises in the text and the author may in fact "find the mirror for which he or she is looking in the body of the text—in the way in which his or her films choreograph movement; compose objects within the frame; craft, disrupt, or multiply narrative; experiment with sound; create 'atmosphere'; articulate light and shadow; encourage or inhibit identification; use actors; or work with color" (215). The most notable way in which Rozema expresses her subjectivity in the body of the text is through the guise of intertextuality. Rozema alludes to, quotes, assimilates, re-accentuates, and reproduces numerous aesthetic, cinematic, and literary intertexts in her films. She draws on various genres, such as romance in *When Night Is Falling*, comedy, romance, and melodrama in *Mermaids and Desperanto*, as well as the psychological thriller in *White Room*. She quotes specific films—for example, *The Decline of the American Empire* in *Desperanto* and Hitchcock's *Psycho* and *Rear Window* in *White Room*. Rozema incorporates specific filmmaking traditions— for instance, documentary, experimental, narrative, classical Hollywood, and art cinema—as well as different media such as black-and-white film, video, and photography. She also imports various cultural texts, such as poetry, classical mythology, fairy tales, the Bible, novels, and journal writing.

From *Passion* to her commissioned films, Rozema has developed a highly intertextual style by which she assimilates and incorporates various signifying practices into her films. In this regard, it is useful to consider Mikhail Bakhtin's notion of the dialogic text. In *Discourse in the Novel*, he describes the multi-voiced character of language and discourse, the existence of competing and merging voices functioning in a dialogical manner:

> All languages of heteroglossia, whatever the principle underlying them and making each unique, are specific points of view on the world, forms for conceptualizing the world in words, specific world views, each characterized by its own objects, meanings and values. As such they all may be juxtaposed to one another, mutually supplement one another, contradict one another and be interrelated dialogically. As such they encounter one another and co-exist in the consciousness of real people—first and foremost, in the creative consciousness of people who write novels. (Bakhtin 291–92)

For Bakhtin, the novel—and by extension the film as "text"—does not exist as a reflection of the real but rather as a representation of various languages and discourses. A film, therefore, is only a refraction of a refraction of the real, a "mediated version of an already textualized socio-ideological world"

(Stam, 50). Although all texts can potentially be interpreted as intertextual,[10] Bakhtin's approach seems particularly relevant in interpreting Rozema's work, because in her films the multiplicity of conflicting and dialogically interrelated voices and discourses, aesthetic and otherwise, are literal and foregrounded.

Passion represents the combining of two discourses—filmmaking and letter writing—to create a new and inventive mode of expression. The protagonist essentially writes a letter to her lover in the form of a film, directly addressing the intended and the audience, while dramatically recreating moments from the past. *I've Heard the Mermaids Singing* consists of a plurality of socio-ideological positions, artistic discourses, and narrative discourses. More traditional forms of filmmaking, cultural texts, and ideological positions are disrupted by subversive texts and positions. Film is disrupted by video, narrative drama is disrupted by self-reflexive direct address sequences and experimental fantasy sequences, colour is disrupted by black-and-white, and traditional attitudes toward art are disrupted by Polly's unconventional expressions. Rozema draws on all of these various cultural positions and texts, as well as poetry, the Bible, and many others, to create an intensely intertextual film.

Significantly, the notion of the dialogic text also allows for contradictions, conflicting voices, and inconsistencies, to exist within the text. This may help to illuminate what some audiences, critics, and theorists have identified as problematic depictions and contradictions in Rozema's films. In the case of *Mermaids*, the character of Polly has ignited debate over whether she is a positive or negative female representation. Some see her as "bumbling idiot" (O'Toole, 48), while others see her as claiming the active subject-looking position usually reserved for men. The film has also been criticized as being anti-feminist and a negative representation of lesbianism,[11] but it has also been praised by others as strongly feminist and a positive representation of lesbianism.[12] Rather than explaining away these contradictions, the dialogic text accommodates the presence of contradictions as a necessary component of multi-voiced discourse.

With *White Room*, Rozema draws on a disparate range of intertexts, including fairy tales, the psychological thriller, romance, the poetry of Emily Dickinson, and experimental filmmaking, in an effort to interrogate society's relationship with fiction and narratives. Though the film is more sophisticated than *Mermaids*, Rozema's strategies seemed to work against her when it came to audience reception. The film was poorly received. Many critics felt it was a darker, more difficult, and muddled version of *Mermaids*.[13]

With *When Night Is Falling*, Rozema assimilates the heterosexual Roman myth of Cupid and Psyche and the traditional romance genre and recasts them with a lesbian couple. Unlike the rest of Rozema's work, the film appropriates these texts with less interrogation, converting the two characters "as is" into a lesbian couple. Though still representative of Rozema's intertextual style, her strategies in this film, as I have argued elsewhere,[14] raise issues around the representation of lesbian sexuality. The film is contradictory in that it is simultaneously progressive in its subject matter and reactionary in its approach to lesbianism, treating it as a threat that requires mitigation by employing traditional texts without attempting to disrupt traditional meanings. Audiences and many critics similarly found the film heavy-handed and superficial.[15] As is the case with highly intertextual films, however, conflicting voices can often be found subsisting in the same text.

In *Six Gestures*, which takes on the structure of an essay, even to the inclusion of footnotes, Rozema combines different voices, artistic discourses, and modes of filmmaking to create a polyphonic film. She mixes dramatic enactments with documentary-style interviews, the highbrow art of Bach and Yo-Yo Ma with figure skating, and the lowbrow art of graffiti. The past and present, the old and new, the culturally elevated and the popular are all represented.[16] By incorporating Jane Austen's journals, early writings, and biography as well as using key cultural texts on slavery to strengthen the political subtexts of the original novel, Rozema in *Mansfield Park* goes beyond simply adapting the novel. She strategically incorporates a number of intertexts that re-accentuate the film in dramatic ways, including reading the novel against the grain to reveal a subtle lesbian subtext and dramatically bringing to the foreground the issue of slavery. Austen purists were ruffled by the liberties Rozema took with the novel,[17] but the film is a fine example of Rozema's skilful intertextual strategy at its best.

Although the mirror in the body of the text that facilitates "recognition" of a filmmaker's work "is in this case a formal or narrative 'image,' it is not any less complexly imbricated with gender, ideology, or history" (Silverman, 215). In this respect we can interpret Rozema's practice in light of Lucy Fischer's suggestion that we envision women's film culture "as engaged in an ongoing *intertextual debate*" with patriarchal film culture (Fischer, 12). While Fischer primarily constructs a synthetic or induced intertextual debate between female and male film culture, she does dedicate one chapter to the literal practice of intertextuality. Here she analyzes Yvonne Rainer's *The Man Who Envied Women* (1985) and its literal intertextuality, which Fischer finds compelling because it crystallizes and validates her fundamental argument "that an intertextual approach is a compelling means of figuring the feminist cinema" (Fischer, 302). Rozema's particular form of authorship, however, not only reinforces Fischer's theory but extends beyond it in two significant ways. First, Rozema's dialogue with culture is not limited to men's cinema but represents a diffuse and exploratory vision that draws on a wide range of cultural texts, including those produced by males and females, insiders and outsiders. Second, Rozema's particular brand of authorship presents a complex and sustained literal and foregrounded dialogue with culture evident across an entire body of work.

Conclusion

The legacy of women-centred narratives about female artists and authorship continues in English Canadian women's filmmaking and can be seen in films such as Anne Wheeler's *Bye Bye Blues* (1989), Mina Shum's *Double Happiness* (1994), and Anita McGee's *The Bread Maker* (2003). While these films may, directly or indirectly, engage in their own type of intertextual debate with patriarchal culture, Rozema's filmmaking does reveal similarities in subject among Canadian women filmmakers: the female artist and the importance of female authorship. Though it has been argued that Rozema has "avoided the representational strategies associated with feminist counter-cinema" (Parpart, 296), I would argue that her intertextual strategies are clearly aligned not only with the aims of feminist filmmaking but with the larger world of international feminist art practice.[18] The political strategies of feminist artists, their process of questioning, debating, and overturning patriarchal culture in creative and productive ways, are very much a part of Rozema's artistic motivations. Rozema's filmmaking, and specifically her intertextual strategies, share similarities with the work of filmmakers such Sally Potter and Kira Muratova, artists such as Cindy Sherman and Nancy Spero, and writers such as Jeanette Winterson. All of these artists provide a reimagining of art using established cultural forms as a point of accessibility to audiences, but bend them to suggest new ways of seeing and thinking. Like Rozema, they engage in a dialogue with culture, but use the materials, processes, and intertexts specific to the aims and subjectivities of each.

Through her filmmaking, Rozema creates brilliant and complex utopian worlds; in one, a gauche temporary secretary with an astonishing fantasy life becomes a hero; in another, a dazzling Sircus of Sorts provides the setting for two women to fall in love; in yet another, a rebellious nineteenth-century writer changes stubborn and long-held attitudes toward slavery and women. Rozema fashions these worlds out of existing society and its cultural forms, through which she reimagines society and is able to subtly put forward alternate ways of thinking and seeing. She consistently interrogates traditional modes of address and the representation of women. As a female filmmaker, a Canadian filmmaker, and a lesbian filmmaker, Rozema's films directly engage in an intertextual dialogue with numerous cinematic and cultural discourses: patriarchal, heterosexual, and foreign. Thus, the female authorial voice in Rozema's work can be interpreted as speaking not only through the recurring artist figure but from the body of the highly intertextual film and across the intersections of appropriated and assimilated texts embedded in her work. Given that Rozema's aesthetic and formal strategies are strongly involved with the importing of previously claimed territory that Rozema reclaims and re-accentuates as her own, this practice may help us to disentangle the idea of authorship from its patriarchal implications.

Bakhtin's concept of the novelist provides a productive refocusing of the idea of authorship, particularly with respect to filmmakers such as Rozema. Rather than seeing the author as the pure source of originality, Bakhtin draws on a musical metaphor and sees the author as an orchestrator. The author arranges and engages in a dialogue with existing languages, discourses, genres, and conventions, thus orchestrating the elements of an already textualized world. Given the intertextual character of Rozema's filmmaking and the legacy of feminist art practice, Rozema and feminist filmmakers might be better understood not in terms of the graphological trope of the filmmaker as "writer," as implicated by the notion of the phallic "caméra-stylo," but rather in terms of the musical trope of filmmaker as "orchestrator," one who utilizes, arranges, re-accentuates and engages in a strategic dialogue with a number of already existing discourses to create anew.

Notes

This essay has been significantly revised from its origins as a component of my master's thesis, "Con(Texts) of Hybrid Authorship: Canadian Cinema, Feminism, Sexual Difference and the Dialogic Films of Patricia Rozema" (York University, 1999). I am grateful to Brenda Longfellow for her supervision of my thesis and for her comments on this essay.

1
Janis Cole and Holly Dale, *Calling the Shots: Profiles of Woman Filmmakers* (Kingston: Quarry Press, 1993), 183.

2
Judith M. Redding and Victoria A. Brownworth, *Film Fatales: Independent Women Directors* (Seattle: Seal Press, 1997), 210–11.

3
Judith Mayne, looking at cinema and authorship, notes the exclusion of female agency in Alexandre Astruc's phallic equation of the camera and the pen in his phrase "caméra-stylo." Judith Mayne, *The Woman at the Keyhole* (Bloomington: Indiana UP, 1990), 94. In general, those deemed worthy of the status of "great director" or "auteur" have historically been male directors.

4
Rozema started out on the career path of journalism but turned to filmmaking after being laid off from her job at CBC's *The Journal*.

5
Margaret Atwood identifies the paralyzed artist as a major figure in Canada's literary imagination. In describing this artist figure she writes: "We speak of isolated people as being 'cut off,' but in fact something has been cut off from them; as artists, deprived of audience and cultural tradition, they are mutilated." Her discussion of the "cripple, mute or castrated" male artist who is unable "to produce any credible art," and who has figured in numerous novels, poetry, and journals, is counterpointed in her final discussion of the female artist as a significantly more successful functioning artist than her male counterparts. *Survival: A Thematic Guide to Canadian Literature* (Toronto: Anansi, 1972), 184.

6
See Seth Feldman, "The Silent Subject in English Canadian Film," *Take Two*, ed. Seth Feldman (Toronto: Irwin Publishing, 1984).

7
After completing *Mermaids*, Rozema commented that she still did not feel ready to tackle male central characters, hence the extremely peripheral treatment of male characters in *Mermaids*. In fact, Rozema's second film was originally intended to be a more women-centred film called "Zelda: High Priestess of the Universe." See Ron Base,

"Canada's Hottest Film-maker Chalks Up Hit to Beginner's Luck," *Toronto Star* 8 September 1987, and Ron Graham, "A Canadian Director Bursts on the Scene …," *New York Times* 6 September 1987: 20.

8
In several interviews Rozema has commented on the semi-autobiographical character of *When Night Is Falling*. For example, see Ed Nyman's article/interview "Going Out on a Limb," *XTRA!*, 27 April 1995: 27. It is worth noting that although the lesbian community has tried to claim Rozema, she has resisted.

9
Rozema evokes the taboo of menstrual blood here. Anne has unknowingly sat on a strawberry, but she believes the stain on her white dress is blood.

10
The notion of intertextuality was introduced as Julia Kristeva's translation of Bakhtin's conception of the "dialogic"—"the simultaneous presence, within literary works, of two of more intersecting texts that relativize one another." Robert Stam, *Reflexivity in Film and Literature: From Don Quixote to Jean-Luc Godard* (New York: Columbia UP, 1992), 20.

11
See Teresa de Lauretis, "Guerrilla in the Midst: Women's Cinema in the 80's," *Screen* 31:1 (Spring 1990).

12
See George Godwin, "Reclaiming the Subject: A Feminist Reading of *I've Heard the Mermaids Singing*," in *Cinema Canada* 152 (May 1988), and Judith Roof, *A Lure of Knowledge:*

Lesbian Sexuality and Theory (New York: Columbia UP, 1991), 73.

13
See Shlomo Schwartzberg's review of *White Room* in *Screen* 22–28 September 1990: 22, and Rich's review of *White Room* in *Variety* 1 October 1990: 86.

14
See Agata Smoluch, "Lesbian (In)Visibility, Sexual (In)Difference and *When Night Is Falling*," in "Con(Texts) of Hybrid Authorship: Canadian Cinema, Feminism, Sexual Difference and the Dialogic Films of Patricia Rozema," unpublished master's thesis, York University, 1999, 79–107.

15
See Bruce Kirkland, "Tender Is the Night," *Toronto Star* 5 May 1995; Brian D. Johnson, "Sex and the Sacred Girl," *Maclean's* 8 May 1995; and Rick Groen, "Send in the Clowns," *Globe and Mail* 28 May 1995: C2.

16
Rozema herself has said that with this film she wanted to "emulate Bach's tendency towards polyphonic structures." See Patricia Rozema, *Sixth Suite* video cover notes.

17
As Keith Windscuttle argues, Rozema's infidelity to Austen's novel, particularly with respect to the political commentary on slavery, is upsetting to Austen readers "because it imposes a controversial political issue onto the quintessentially domestic concerns of their favorite author." "Rewriting the history of the British Empire," in *The New Criterion* 18.9 (May 2000), www.newcriterion.com.

18
As Carolyn Korsmeyer explains, feminist artists share "a sense of the historic subordination of women and an awareness of how art practices have perpetuated that subordination…. With such issues in mind, not only do feminist and postfeminist artists participate in the complex self-reference that characterizes virtually all postmodern work, but they challenge and overturn patriarchal traditions, often with highly theoretical agendas aiding their creative production…. This sort of play with tradition calls attention to the norms of the genre that are being queried or subverted, and hence a 'knowledge of the history of art' is a special necessity." *Gender and Aesthetics: An Introduction* (New York: Routledge, 2004), 118.

Works Cited

Atwood, Margaret. *Survival: A Thematic Guide to Canadian Literature*. Toronto: Anansi, 1972.

Bakhtin, Mikhail. *The Dialogic Imagination: Four Essays by M.M. Bakhtin*. Ed. Michael Holquist. Austin: U of Texas P, 1981.

Cole, Janis, and Holly Dale. *Calling the Shots: Profiles of Woman Filmmakers*. Kingston: Quarry Press, 1993.

Fischer, Lucy. *Shot/Countershot: Film Tradition and Women's Cinema*. Princeton, NJ: Yale UP, 1989.

Goodwin, George. "Reclaiming the Subject: A Feminist Reading of *I've Heard the Mermaids Singing*." In *Cinema Canada* 152 (May 1988).

Korsmeyer, Carolyn. *Gender and Aesthetics: An Introduction*. New York: Routledge, 2004.

Marchessault, Janine. "Is the Dead Author a Woman? Some Thoughts on Feminist Authorship." *Open Letter: A Canadian Journal of Writing and Theory* 8.4 (Summer 1992).

Mayne, Judith. *The Woman at the Keyhole*. Bloomington: Indiana UP, 1990.

O'Toole, Lawrence. "Murmurs of the Heart." *Maclean's* 28 September 1978.

Parpart, Lee. "Political Alignments and the Lure of 'More Existential Questions' in the Films of Patricia Rozema." In *North of Everything: English-Canadian Cinema since 1980*, ed. William Beard and Jerry White. Edmonton: University of Alberta Press, 2002.

Posner, Michael. *Canadian Dreams: The Making and Marketing of Independent Films*. Vancouver: Douglas & McIntyre, 1993.

Redding, Judith M., and Victoria A. Brownworth. *Film Fatales: Independent Women Directors*. Seattle: Seal Press, 1997.

Roof, Judith. *A Lure of Knowledge: Lesbian Sexuality and Theory*. New York: Columbia UP, 1991.

Silverman, Kaja. "The Female Authorial Voice." In *The Acoustic Mirror: The Female Voice in Psychoanalysis and Cinema*. Bloomington: Indiana UP, 1988.

Stam, Robert. *Subversive Pleasures: Bakhtin, Cultural Criticism and Film*. Baltimore: Johns Hopkins UP, 1989.

—. *Reflexivity in Film and Literature: From Don Quixote to Jean-Luc Godard*. New York: Columbia UP, 1992.

Léa Pool:
The Art of Elusiveness
Florian Grandena

Swiss-born Léa Pool is one of the most distinctive film directors to have emerged in Canada in the last twenty-five years. Difficult and enthralling at the same time, her cinematic production has attracted much attention from critics, film theorists, and audiences alike. Based in Montreal since the mid-1970s, Pool has produced an interesting body of work that is both intellectually challenging and difficult to pinpoint.[1]

Considered "Quebec's pre-eminent immigrant female director" (Melnyk, 180), Pool became involved in filmmaking in a specific socio-cultural context during the late 1970s. Many Quebec filmmakers were at that time moving away from the realist film trend that had developed over the previous two decades. Characterized by film directors such as Pierre Perrault, this cinema repatriated "national identity by the use of images of a country and the people who make it up" and became the locus in which "the French-Canadian defining himself more and more as a Quebecker, [sought] and [expressed] his own distinctive way of living Americanness" (Bachand, 27). A shift from auteur cinema to more market-oriented film productions then occurred and, despite uneven artistic results, contributed to the greater visibility and success of Quebec cinema both at home and abroad. Following "the coming to power of the Parti Québécois in 1976, the intellectuals and the artists turned their energies to other pursuits than those with which they had been preoccupied during the rise of nationalism in the '60s and the '70s" (Bachand, 30).

Quebec cinema thus slowly became less preoccupied with, and dominated by, questions related to the nationalism debates and started to open itself up to the representation of, for example, ethnic groups and women. It was during the following decade (particularly the post-referendum period) that some Quebec and foreign filmmakers contributed to "a new individualist cinema that [was] willing to be the reflection and the memory of a society shaken by an impetuous quest for identity" (Prud'homme, 272; my translation).[2] Moreover, during that time, the Quebec film industry started to devote more attention to women filmmakers such as Anne Claire Poirier and Micheline Lanctôt, who made audacious and personal works.

In Quebec, women came to filmmaking late. Prior to the 1970s, the Montreal-based Office National du Film du Canada (ONF) employed many Québécoises in technical positions such as film editor and assistant director, but very few women were involved in the direction of feature films and documentaries. One of these was Dorothée Brisson, who shot several documentaries in the 1950s, including *Camp Marie-Victorin* and *Zoo*, released in 1956 and 1957, respectively; she also made several works together with Suzanne Caron, such as *Au printemps*, released in 1958. The first short film by a woman from Quebec was *La Beauté même* (Monique Fortier, 1964), closely followed by Anne Claire Poirier's *La Fin des étés* (1964).[3] The vast majority of films directed by women in the 1970s were documentaries and docudramas (see Pallister, 96–117). The key figures of this tradition of feminine/feminist documentaries are Sophie Bissonnette, Sylvie Groulx, Dagmar Guissaz-Teufel, Suzanne Guy, and Diane Létourneau.[4] Thematically speaking, "feminist issues are indeed the proper domain of a great many documentaries" (Pallister, 96).

Anne Claire Poirier played a central role in the promotion of women filmmakers from Quebec. In 1971, she co-wrote with Jeanne Mozarin a text titled "En tant que femmes nous-mêmes," in which they expressed the desire and the necessity to create and coordinate a film program by and for women.[5] The text was sent to the ONF in March 1971, which responded positively and effectively by implementing a new film program, "En tant que femmes." The program marked the beginning of a new era for women filmmakers from Quebec. Six works (four medium-length and two feature films) were produced: *J'me marie, j'me marie pas* (Mireille Dansereau, 1973), *Souris, tu m'inquiètes* (Aimée Danis, 1973), *À qui appartient ce gage?* (Suzanne Gibbard, 1974), *Les Filles, c'est pas pareil* (Hélène Girard, 1974), and two films by Poirier herself, *Les Filles du Roy* (1974) and *Le Temps de l'avant* (1975) (Jean, 78–80). As Yves Lever underlines, the "En tant que femmes" film program has to be seen as an actual school of cinema, in which women were able to familiarize themselves with production management and master the various technical skills involved in filmmaking (Lever, 309).[6]

Poirier played a central role in the "En tant que femme" program (both as an initiator and as a producer) and is praised as one of the major women cineastes from Quebec. Her first feature film, *De mère en fille* (1967), deals with specific feminine themes (pregnancy and motherhood), but it is her 1979 feature film, the formally and thematically challenging *Mourir à tue-tête*, that has generated much interest.[7] Other important female filmmakers from Quebec include Mireille Dansereau and other artists who were not involved with the "En tant que femmes" program, such as Louise Carré (*Ça peut pas être l'hiver, on a même pas eu d'été* and *Qui a tiré sur nos histoires d'amour?*, released in 1980 and 1986, respectively), Brigitte Sauriol (*Rien qu'un jeu*, 1983), Micheline Lanctôt (*Sonatine*, 1983), and Marquise Lepage (*Marie s'en va-t-en ville*, 1987). (See Pallister, 139–45.)[8]

It is precisely at this cultural crossroads that Léa Pool's first film, *Strass Café* (1980), appeared. Both a foreigner (Swiss francophone of Catholic and Jewish descent) and a woman, Pool could have fit particularly well in a cinema opening itself up to Quebec's then emerging gender, sexual, and ethnic multiculturalism. However, instead of treading the paths of so-called feminist or women's cinemas, Pool decided to trace her own itinerary by staying away from, if not rejecting, all-embracing labels and identity categories.

Influenced by the works of European filmmakers such as Chantal Akerman and Robert Bresson, as well as legendary writer-turned-director Marguerite Duras, Pool's feature films are characterized by slow and fragmented narratives in which character motivations are often disregarded; such a disjointed type of cinematic storytelling is often balanced by a prominent non-diegetic soundtrack and recurrent musical themes. This point is particularly valid for the director's film career up to the early 1990s, a period during which she started to integrate her recurrent themes of alienation and uprooting into conventionally coherent narratives. As Janis L. Pallister remarks, "[Pool's] films are not culturally based or bound.... Of course, since Pool is of Swiss origins, her use of Québec cultural materials is in a sense slight, even though the skyline of Montréal and other views of the city serve as a backdrop in her works" (Pallister, 121).

As far as subject matter is concerned, Pool's cinematic oeuvre is both personal and unconventional. Physical and metaphorical displacement, exile, homelessness, floating gender and sexual identities, lesbian eroticism, the expression of desires (be they same-sex or not), urban alienation, madness, art as a revelatory and cathartic mode of human expression—these are some of the main themes present in Pool's works, which are intensely personal films usually privileging characters' emotional turmoil. Moreover, "like most feminist works of art, Pool's films present the woman's cosmos; men are characteristically marginal to the storyline or to the visual preoccupations of the work" (Pallister, 122). In sum, the combination of an enthralling yet minimalist *mise en scène* with interiority-oriented problematics has led to an atypical artistic production that could be described as intensely introspective but also, by Pool's own admission, "autistic" and claustrophobic (Grugeau, 17; Beaulieu, 13).

Since the early 1980s, Pool has made nine features films,[9] which can be grouped into three trilogies. The first of these, the In-Transit Trilogy, focuses almost exclusively on female protagonists and their feeling of homelessness, uprooting, and exile. It includes *Strass Café*, *La Femme de l'hôtel* (1984), and *Anne Trister* (1986). The second triptych, the Shifting Trilogy, marks an evolution as the director started to change locations. Montreal is the only location used in the first trilogy, whereas the following three films are set in South America (*À corps perdu*, 1988), Switzerland (*La Demoiselle sauvage*, 1991), and in a train travelling through the Canadian hinterland (*Mouvements du désir*, 1994). The term "shifting" also indicates a change of attention from female characters and lesbo-erotic relations to male protagonists and (often problematic) man-to-man, bisexual, and heterosexual romances. The third trilogy, the Passage Trilogy, is made up of Pool's three most recent films, which concentrate on a sick child (*The Blue Butterfly*, 2004) and teenage girls (*Emporte-moi*, 1999, and *Lost and Delirious*, 2001). "Passage" here refers to Pool's three coming-of-age stories, which deal with sexual awakening as well as with a shift from an innocent state of mind to an often destabilizing and alienating confrontation with the world of adults.

The following pages provide the reader with, on one hand, a formal and thematic description of the trilogies in question and, on the other, an account of the continuity and changes between these three sets of films. I mostly focus on the representation of gender and sexual identities in Pool's gay-themed feature films. More precisely, my main interest is the (love) triangles systematically presented in the films that deal with lesbo-/ homoerotic concerns. Some space is dedicated to Pool's original yet often problematic take on homosexual desires. I show that, by firmly placing herself outside gender/sexuality-based categories, Pool aims at highlighting the universality of human desires and, consequently, at transcending identity categories. In other words, I pay much attention to the ways Pool portrays characters expressing same-sex desires without anchoring them in specific identity categories. Indeed, Pool's art of elusiveness constitutes the backbone of the present chapter. To underline the evolution and the increasing explicitness in same-sex depictions in Pool's cinematic production, I discuss these films by respecting their chronological order (for reasons of pertinence, it is possible only to touch on *Strass Café*, *La Demoiselle sauvage*, *Mouvements du désir*, and *The Blue Butterfly*).

The In-Transit Trilogy

Pool's first three feature films have been described as a symbolic triptych stamped with a quest for identity. More precisely, these three cinematic works focus on a similar narrative structure, that of a melancholic woman who, through artistic creation, expresses her eagerness to meet her soulmate (the latter being of any gender) (Prud'homme, 273).

Her first feature film, the sixty-two-minute-long *Strass Café*, was made on a shoestring budget and was written, shot, and edited by Pool herself. An experimental and demanding work, her black-and-white cinematic piece is "avant-garde in form, obviously disrupting any expectations the viewer may have, but it is not visibly feminist in content—if indeed, it is possible to speak of content at all" (Green, 52). Pool's first cinematic work contains some of her interests in urban places and fluid identities that will recur in other works. In *Strass Café*, some emphasis is put on urban locations and, by focusing on these places when deserted, Pool succeeds in emptying them of their familiar content and turning them into "a foreign milieu, evoking a European red-light district" (Green, 58). This "defamiliarization" also concerns the protagonist, a nameless woman (referred to only as "elle" throughout the film) characterized by her evanescence. Such a sense of elusiveness was to be explored in more depth in Pool's next two works, *La Femme de l'hôtel* and *Anne Trister*.

With *La Femme de l'hôtel* Pool attracted attention from critics and audiences alike. Formally more accessible than *Strass Café*, *La Femme de l'hôtel* focuses on a trio of female protagonists. The themes of alienation and unfixed identities found in Pool's film (and indeed her overall oeuvre) are underlined from the opening sequence, a panorama of Montreal's urban landscape accompanied by a monologue dispassionately delivered by a female voice:[10]

> I'm looking at and listening to a city where I spent eighteen years of my life. It's strange, I feel I'm in a foreign city, a foreigner in a hotel somewhere. I used to say that this was home, but this is not home, no more here than elsewhere. And that could be why I have chosen to shoot my film here, in order to discover the foreigner I have become. The filming starts within a few days. There'll be streets, places of transit, places that remind me that, once, I was here too, that I was another woman.

While working on her new film, Andréa (Paule Baillargeon) meets a mysterious woman, Estelle David (Louise Marleau). Enigmatic and elusive, Estelle wanders aimlessly in the hotel where she and Andréa stay. The filmmaker quickly becomes fascinated, if not obsessed, with the ethereal woman, who unwittingly helps both Andréa and her leading actress (Marthe Turgeon) shape their fictional character.

Not unlike Pool's first film, *La Femme de l'hôtel* relies on a certain degree of abstraction, and "it is the moodiness of her film that is so subversive of typical Hollywood narrative" (Melnyk, 176). The three women are less conventional fictional characters evolving within a precise narrative framework than human-shaped concepts. This intellectual exercise on celluloid shows the director's attempt to portray her protagonists outside gender categories. Andréa is working on her film, and although she is confident about her story she struggles to find and understand her female protagonist's inner motivations. Andréa embodies consciousness and intellectuality. As far as Estelle is concerned, she has fled from her family (about whom we know nothing) and, after a failed suicide attempt in her lonely hotel room, she aimlessly wanders through the hotel and the anonymous streets of Montreal: she is primarily a passive woman who belongs nowhere; she represents intimacy, internalized feelings, and spirituality. Her uprooting is never challenged: "she exists within a marginality that does not question itself, its own strangeness" (Gaulin, 7). Then there is the nameless actress who is, on one hand, "the link between the unconscious and the conscious" and, on the other, "the carnal woman" (Gaulin, 8). Thus, the three women form the interlocking parts of the same whole, and their individual interaction fruitfully leads to the creation of the fictional character made up of Andréa's intellectuality and Estelle's interiority and ultimately brought to life through the actress's physicality.

Interestingly, Andréa, Estelle, and the nameless actress are portrayed as independent individuals free from power relations with men: the women exist by themselves outside patriarchy. One of the film's first scenes shows Andréa breaking up with her male partner. "I thought I was the only one to feel this way," she says. To which the man enigmatically adds off-screen: "Our paths just crossed, they just crossed. Why are you making this film?" "Because it's become impossible," Andréa replies. The only man to benefit from some screen time in *La Femme de l'hôtel* is Andréa's gay brother, Simon (Serge Dupire), who also, in his first scene, separates from his lover (who is reduced to an off-screen voice).

Estelle, as previously mentioned, has run away from home, but her past, her personal history, remains unknown. Even less is known of the actress. Indeed, an aura of mystery surrounds Andréa and more so Estelle and the actress. Such elusiveness is represented by some of the characters' incessant wandering through sterile non-places and the "presence of endless symbols of this transitoriness and wandering: train stations, hotels, airports, one-ways tickets, highways with traffic coming and going, subway trains, taxis, automobiles" (Pallister, 124) as well as deserted wintry streets (and an asylum: the fictitious character that the actress interprets in Andréa's film experiences an uprooting and nervous breakdown similar to Estelle's and is forced to check into an asylum): "Montreal is a city occupied, but never inhabited by these women, a city represented only by anonymous places of passage ... all bounded by the haunting and recurring image of the river. This image, compulsively repeated throughout the film, suggests the possibility of return and an escape, evokes, indeed, the sea as the imaginary horizon of desire, as the primordial memory of plenitude and oneness" (Longfellow, 275). Indeed, Pool's portrayal of individuals in the city and its non-places is less dystopian than it may appear at first, partly because the director's "success is in working against a desolate background— yet never letting the viewer lose sight completely of the distant horizon of meaning and hope. The hotel then becomes less a place than an emotional eddy, which one passes through before once again connecting with the world outside" (Winch, 10). In sum, the three women do not belong to a world dominated by gender hierarchies or individual relations marked by a binary mode of identification/ categorization (man versus woman, heterosexual versus homosexual, etc.). On the contrary, these women's passivity "is oppositional, indifferent to the stupidity of the world" (Gaulin, 7). Thus, *La Femme de l'hôtel* operates a displacement: the women do not fight the system head-on, they "exist outside [it]. These are not women of power. They have chosen neither the weapons nor the methods of the people in power" (Gaulin, 7).

That said, Pool's rejection of social structures is taken to an abrasive extreme. The love triangle in *La Femme de l'hôtel* concerns less the three women than the mysterious Estelle, Andréa, and the latter's gay brother, Simon. The triangular relation exists through Andréa's persona: not only does the woman experience a compulsive fascination tinged with lesbo-eroticism for Estelle, she also seems to entertain a close, if not sexual, relation with her brother. Thus, as Lucille Cairns has noted in her *Sapphism on Screen*, the representation of lesbian desires is here rendered problematic because of "the collocation of lesbian desire with sibling incest" (78). She is a desiring woman par excellence (in an early scene, Andréa accompanies with her singing a song on the radio whose final and insistent lyrics are "Touche-moi"), and her feelings are directed first to Estelle and then to her brother. It is not entirely clear whether her desires are assuaged; Pool instills her depiction of sibling relationships with much ambiguity. Their connivance is punctuated with smiles and silences; their physical proximity is stamped with sexual tension. Moreover, with his sensuous postures and objectified body, Simon exudes sexuality. Whether Andréa and Simon have an incestuous relation is a question left unanswered, however. The fact is that Andréa's desires for Estelle cohabit with one quasi-universal sexual taboo (incest); the two types of desire seem to collapse into each other, potentially leading to a conceptual conflation between homosexuality and forbidden sexuality. Ultimately, Andréa is shown as an individual obliged to "realize [her desires] vicariously" (Cairns, 79). Thus, not only is lesbianism here alluded to through the specific relationship pursued by the three ethereal protagonists, it is paired with (non-realized?) sexual taboos, the latter displacing same-sex desires with non-realizable sexual fantasies.

Not unlike Estelle in *La Femme de l'hôtel*, Anne Trister, the deeply con-fused eponymous heroine of Pool's film, is a character who has lost her refer-ence points, metaphorically crumbling from the inside and on the verge of mad-ness.[11] Having just lost her Jewish father, Anne (Anne Guilhe) emigrates from Switzerland to Quebec, where a friend of hers, a child psychologist named Alix (Louise Marleau), agrees to put her up. Thanks to some friends of her late father, Anne, who is a painter, finds a large derelict studio, which she undertakes to ren-ovate and turn into a gigantic piece of art. The walls are covered with murals of the desert (these are reminiscent of the location, in Israel, of her father's funeral as well as Alix's story of her trip to the desert), and, as Pallister underlines, "the journey of the protagonist is one from Israel to the West and back again; it is a quest for another/a(m)other country, a quest that fails at the end" (Pallister, 129).

Alix looks after Anne, who struggles to relate to her family/Jewish roots; she also tries to help an abused young girl, Sarah (Lucie Laurier), to whom she introduces painting as a cathartic/therapeutic mode of expression.[12] As the nar-rative unfolds, a strong relationship develops between Anne and Alix, the for-mer becoming smitten with the latter. Although Alix too seems attached and attracted to her friend, she decides to remain with her male partner and move in with him. Anne then accidentally falls from scaffolding in her studio. Forced to let go of her love for Alix, Anne starts to rebuild her life after her release from hospi-tal. *Anne Trister* ends with home-movie images of a smiling and seemingly happy Anne in the Israeli desert, apparently having succeeded in reconnecting with her family and personal history, and with the suggestion that the two women's attraction and relationship were transitional.

In *Anne Trister*, then, Pool turns her camera to women outside the patri-archal system and to power relations reliant on gendered opposition and other-ness. However, the film represents a break in Pool's work, as she becomes more explicit in her depiction of lesbo-erotic relations. Already in *La Femme de l'hôtel*, same-sex desires/attraction were alluded to through the figures of Andréa and Estelle. However, in Pool's second film, there is no visual representation of sexual desires, nor any overt demonstrations of homosexual tenderness/gratification. In contrast, *Anne Trister* lays greater emphasis on the two female characters' shared complicity and lesbo-erotic relation.

However, Pool positions her two characters less as lesbians than as individuals who happen to feel attracted to each other. Indeed, the director first delineates the two women's relationships with their respective male partners. Both Anne and Alix are involved in seemingly stable heterosexual romances (Anne's boyfriend remains abroad when she decides to move to Montreal); thus, their developing attraction to each other contributes to the blurring and questioning of sexual/gender-based categories. The director represents the women's physical attraction through a non-voyeuristic representation of their kissing and hugging, which first occurs in Anne's studio. It is Anne who takes the plunge, and although Alix does not strenuously reject her friend's advances, nor does she want to commit herself. As the narrative unfolds, the relation develops, and one of the last scenes of the two women together suggests post-intercourse complicity (lying on a bed, the two women kiss and hug, in a scene exuding tenderness but also self-restraint). However, Pool's representation of lesbo-erotic affection excludes scenes with more sexually explicit content. Homosexuality is here limited to the private sphere and—this is another recurrent feature of Pool's works—remains unnamed: words such as "homosexual," "lesbian," and "queer" are never uttered by any of Pool's characters (with the notable exception of the melodramatic *Lost and Delirious*, which is discussed below).

That said, Pool problematizes Sapphic love, in much the same way as she did in *La Femme de l'hôtel*, by including references to sexual feelings for a family member—more precisely, a mother figure. *Anne Trister* makes references—although not as directly as Pool's second film does—to incest, through Alix's character (some fifteen years older than Anne). As stated earlier, the film opens with the funeral of Anne's father. As the protagonist's mother unsuccessfully tries to console her daughter, who is lying sobbing on a bed (only the young woman's back is visible), she admits she has failed to give her daughter the love she wanted. This unsatisfying mother–daughter relationship has repercussions throughout the film, and in particular on the relationship between Anne and Alix. Here, same-sex attraction can be understood as a compensation for insufficient motherly love: "the relationship between Alix and Anne has widely been construed in the mother–daughter mode, with a wounded Anne seeking from Alix the love unforthcoming from the real mother, and Alix responding with the sort of maternal, healing affection she also displays toward her seven-year-old patient Sarah" (Cairns, 84). Indeed, the film draws several parallels between Sarah, Alix's young patient, and Anne: their use of painting as a personal and cathartic mode of expression, as well as their relationship to Alix, who, for both the painter and the little girl, represents an alternative to the absent mother (or at least motherly love). Pool also establishes direct connections between Sarah and Alix by portraying the girl as a sexed being. The little girl tries to touch Alix's breasts, for example; she also caresses her lips, a gesture repeated by Anne toward the end of the film.

In sum, the two films from the In-Transit Trilogy that I here examine offer a portrayal of woman-to-woman attraction seen through the prism of sexual taboos (incest). Both feature films have recourse to homosexuality as a *transitional sexuality*. Same-sex feelings become the expression of a deeper frustration and take the form of a quest for fullness and plenitude—that is, the (re)creation and the idealization of mother–daughter relations. In other words, same-sex desires do not (perhaps cannot) exist per se but are the metaphorical expression of an existential crisis.

The Shifting Trilogy

The feature films included in the Shifting Trilogy are to be understood as both continuity with and a break from the first triptych. As mentioned above, the In-Transit Trilogy focuses mostly on women who are wandering through sterile, if not desolate, non-places and are in the process of reconstructing their shattered selves. It is in the Shifting Trilogy that, for the first time, Pool dedicates screen time to male homosexuality and heterosexual romances. The examination of same-sex desires in Pool's films being the main focus of this chapter, I will only skim through the films concentrating on male–female relationships (*La Demoiselle sauvage*, *Mouvements du désir*) and present briefly their respective storylines.

La Demoiselle sauvage is set in the director's country of origin, Switzerland. Marianne (Patricia Tulasne) is involved in a domestic altercation that claims her husband's life. After a failed suicide attempt, Marianne escapes to the surrounding mountains where, exhausted and half starved, she is taken under the wing of Élysée (Matthias Habich), an engineer who spends most of his time in an isolated shack. Élysée sets Marianne up again and hides her from the police; as the film unfolds, the two individuals fall in love. Pool's *Mouvements du désir*, partly inspired by Roland Barthes's *Fragments d'un discours amoureux*, focuses on the love that develops between Catherine (Valérie Kapriski) and Vincent (Jean-François Pichette). The setting—a fast train—allows the director to take her protagonists even farther from human communities and the possibility of physical and psychological settling.

Undoubtedly Pool's masterpiece, *À corps perdu* has recourse to similar themes; however, the film calls particular attention to the psychological collapse experienced by the bisexual protagonist, Pierre Kurwenal (Matthias Habich), who plays a Montreal-based reporter/photographer. Following a traumatizing experience in Nicaragua, where he witnessed and photographed the cold-blooded killing of several individuals (including a four-year-old child), he discovers on his return to Quebec that David (Michel Voïta) and Sarah (Johanne-Marie Tremblay), the man and woman he has loved and shared his life with for the previous ten years, have deserted him. After one of Pierre's failed attempts to ingratiate himself into his former lovers' good graces, David tells his former lover: "At the beginning, we were three, even when you were away. And then we realized we were two even when you were physically with us." Gruesome images of the brutal killings in Nicaragua haunt Pierre, who embarks on a new professional project, which focuses on Montreal and some of the city's derelict urban spaces. Pierre meets the angelic Quentin (Jean-François Pichette), a dedicated and handsome deaf man, with whom he starts an affair. However, as he spirals into depression, Pierre withdraws to a convalescent home. When he eventually discharges himself, he finds that David and a heavily pregnant Sarah are waiting for him. It is to Quentin, however, that Pierre returns.

À corps perdu is characterized by its non-conventional love triangle (a bisexual ménage à trois) as well as its expressionist *mise en scène*, which includes many visual leitmotivs. Throughout *À corps perdu*, Pool uses a certain amount of forward tracking shots through disused and deserted non-places, which both mirror and respond to Pierre's psychological prostration. A direct connection exists between Pierre's inner turmoil and his surroundings: "The essence of the heartbreak felt after the split-up comes from all these places abandoned since that moment. This rift is overly metaphorized through the use of images of an abandoned city, thanks to the analogy, both visual and auditory, between city life and the chaos of human feelings unique to the director" (Prud'homme, 273–74; my translation).[13]

In *À corps perdu*, as well as in Pool's other works, there is no dramatic crescendo toward the revelation of a protagonist's same-sex desires. Nor are there paroxysmal moments in which characters articulate the nature of their sexual desires. The coming-out scene (or its impossibility) is given great importance in many gay-themed cinematic works, such as *Mambo Italiano* (Émilie Gaudreault, 2003) and *C.R.A.Z.Y.* (Jean-Marc Vallée, 2005), but in Pool's films the expression of homosexuality is typically done through the depiction of sometimes suggestive displays of same-sex affection (hugging, kissing, fondling). One notices a progression from the first to the second trilogies (the third trilogy being even more suggestive and straightforward in its depiction of teenage sex/ love). In *La Femme de l'hôtel*, for example, Andréa's obsession for Estelle has lesbo-erotic undertones but without overt sexual expression between the two women; spectators are informed of Simon's sexual orientation almost indirectly (Simon's first scene is of his breakup with his partner, who remains off-screen). *Anne Trister* is more explicit in that it does not limit itself to suggested homosexuality but visually represents same-sex affection. However, same-sex desires do seem to retain a chaste quality; although Alix and Anne kiss and hug, no nudity is involved, for example. If sexual intercourse occurs between the two women, it is only hinted at and takes place off-screen. In sum, homo/bisexuality in *À corps perdu* is taken for granted and is never used as a narrative trick: it inhabits the film the same way that it is inscribed in Pierre's life and identity.

   À corps perdu is more direct than its predecessors and heralds the non-voyeuristic naturalness that Pool used later in representations of same-sex affection, in *Emporte-moi* and *Lost and Delirious*. From the start of Pool's fourth film, Pierre is positioned as an individual involved in a non-conventional love triangle. "I love David and I love Sarah and I love Tristan. A man, a woman and a cat," Pierre tells a slightly bewildered Quebec tourist while travelling on a bus through the Nicaraguan countryside. One of the film's early flashbacks foregrounds Pierre's sexual identity. Stamped with gaiety and tenderness, this short scene shows David and Sarah naked under the shower. They drag Pierre under the flowing water, and the three embrace and kiss. The simplicity of the scene and the tenderness emanating from it contribute to the depiction of this particular love triangle as a relationship that is joyous and unproblematic.

   However, because the narrative starts after David and Sarah's departure, the love triangle can be synonymous only with nostalgia and irremediable loss to a woebegone Pierre. Hence the recurrent flashbacks of the three lovers' bygone happiness. Thanks to its expressionist *mise en scène*, one particular flashback conveys particularly well Pierre's heartache and sexual longing. This scene is a long shot and starts with black-and-white images (as do all flashbacks in the film). Pierre, David, and Sarah make love. Pierre then slowly withdraws from their embrace, and as he lies down he becomes the camera's main object of focus. The man is then the spectator of his two lovers' affection (the two are off-screen), but the shift from black-and-white to colour announces the scene's changing meaning and time frame. Indeed, Pool switches softly from a tender reminiscence to a harsher present, which nonetheless offers an inkling of a hope for Pierre. The camera operates a backward tracking shot within the same uninterrupted scene. Not only are Sarah and David gone, they are replaced by Quentin, who gently rests his head on Pierre's bare chest. But Pierre turns away from his new lover and, while looking through his window, he notices David's silhouette at a distance.

   Thus, one of the major shifts from the first to the second triptych concerns the unmediated and explicit representation of sexuality, in this instance homo/bisexuality. In *La Femme de l'hôtel* and *Anne Trister*, as has already been explained, lesbianism is portrayed through the distorting lens of incest. There is no such thing here; however, it is suggested at different times in the film that if the love triangle implodes it is because of Sarah's pregnancy. There are several hints that David is the father, and it seems that the formation of this traditional father–mother pairing within the triangular relationship contributes to its collapse. In other words, the mother figure and maternity are presented as disruptive forces.

The Passage Trilogy

As mentioned above, the third trilogy focuses on coming-of-age narratives and, more precisely, storylines and characters that deal with young characters' shift from innocence to an often harsh and alienating entrance into the world of adults. *The Blue Butterfly*, for example, tells the true story of ten-year-old Pete Carlton (Marc Donato), a terminally ill child whose ultimate fantasy is to catch the blue morpho, a butterfly with legendary healing powers. Together with his mother (Pascale Bussières) and a famous but at first reluctant entomologist (William Hurt), Pete goes to a South American rainforest and succeeds in making his dream come true (the child also survives his cancer).

However, I am primarily interested in the other two films of this trilogy. *Emporte-moi* and Pool's first anglophone work, *Lost and Delirious*, deal with the lives of teenage girls who struggle to find their place in some of the traditional structures that contribute to individuals' social and personal positionings, namely the nuclear family. *Emporte-moi* deals with protagonists rooted in a precise historical context—the Quiet Revolution. The film starts in 1963. Tomboyish thirteen-year-old Hanna (Karine Vanasse) hits puberty and awakens to love. She lives with an artistic and nationality-less father of Jewish descent (Miki Manojlovic), an exhausted and depressive Catholic mother (Pascale Bussières), and an older brother, Paul (Alexandre Mérineau), with whom Hanna entertains a close but ambiguous relationship. Her difficult and often tense family life motivates her to look for solace in art, in this case, cinema. There she discovers Jean-Luc Godard's then muse, the beautiful Danish actress Anna Karina, in her famous performance in *Vivre sa vie (My Life to Live)* (1962). Hanna projects her developing obsession for Karina onto one of her schoolteachers (Nancy Huston), with whom she attempts to develop a privileged rapport. Simultaneously, Hanna feels attracted to Laura (Charlotte Christeler), a French girl of her own age.

Thematically speaking, *Emporte-moi* needs to be understood in line with the problematic representations of female homosexuality in *La Femme de l'hôtel* and *Anne Trister*. Once again, *Emporte-moi* proposes a love triangle in which three individuals (Hannah, Paul, and Laura) desire each other—a love formation recalling the ménage à trois in *À corps perdu*. Thus, this particular love triangle relies both on same-sex and incestuous desires: after having turned down several male suitors at a party (during which Hanna's discomfort with boys is evident), Hanna catches a glimpse of short-haired Laura. Forming an immediate bond of complicity, the two girls hold hands and finally kiss in an alley "outside in the moonlight, standard signifier of romance" (Cairns, 168). However, Hanna's burgeoning desire for her troubling friend is soon hindered by Paul's attraction to the same girl. During a kissing game, Paul is quick to express that he likes the adolescent girl, and Hanna finds herself forced to take a back seat to the other two. This is further problematized by the two siblings' relationship. In effect—and not unlike Simon and Andréa in *La Femme de l'hôtel*—brother and sister entertain a relationship with incestuous undertones: in their first appearance together at Montreal's train station, the two teenagers show much affection and connivance, but the film offers no clue as to the true nature of their relations with each other. Are they friends? Lovers? Siblings? Interestingly, it is only after their kinship is revealed that Pool chooses to show Hanna and Paul's physical proximity and tenderness for each other: in an enigmatic underwater scene, the two teenagers unexpectedly kiss on the lips. The shifting dynamics of the love triangle find their expression in one scene in particular: following a violent fight with their father, Paul and Hanna take refuge at Laura's place, where they share the same bed. First Hanna and Laura hug, but the latter slowly turns to Paul. Paul and Laura kiss and share a tender embrace. The girl eventually moves away from her teenage brother and rolls toward the other side of the bed, but Hanna has already left. It is important to underline that Laura, not unlike Hanna, feels alienated from her mother: "The narrative thus promotes a reading of the mutual lesbo-erotic attraction between Hanna and Laura as isomorphous with their mother-love and fear of losing that mother" (Cairns, 86). In other words, same-sex desires are framed and justified by the traumatizing loss, be it literal or metaphorical, of the mother figure. Moreover, as in *Anne Trister*, *Emporte-moi* proposes a portrayal of the mother figure tainted with sexual ambiguity. Hanna's mother is depicted as an exhausted and depressive woman[14] on whom the whole family relies: she is the one who makes ends meet, her husband being an unemployed poet who has never been published.

Much of Hanna's screen time is dedicated to her (failed) fusional relationships with different women: Laura, of course, and also the teacher who reminds her of Anna Karina, her idol, and, crucially, her mother. The love that Hanna has for the latter is unconditional and is often expressed with body language. In an early scene, Hanna rests her head on her drugged mother's shoulder and says: "I'm like you, I'm sick too." It is not clear what Hanna's own sickness is: is it related to her first menstrual periods—or, in other words, to her place as a woman in the world of adults (the film opens with a seaside scene during which blood is seen dripping from Hanna's legs onto the beach's greyish rocks)? Is Hanna's sickness about her relation to her brother and/or Laura? Or is it about all this at the same time? Whatever the answer to the question is, it is interesting to note that Hanna pathologizes her place within human relations.[15] The film's final scene stresses the "imbrication of mother–daughter love and eroticism" (Cairns, 86). This is achieved with a powerful close-up in which, after a long stay in a convalescent home, the mother is finally reunited with Hanna, the former looking intensely at the latter as if they were about to kiss on the lips (the mother then kisses her daughter on the neck).

In sum, the representation of same-sex desires in *Emporte-moi* is rendered problematic in specific ways: it is mingled with attraction for different family members and melancholic feelings for the lost mother figure. Thus, same-sex attractions seem to be the result of unsettling circumstances and existential uprooting and are consequently denied both an empowering portrayal and an existence per se.

Let us move to the last film under consideration here, Pool's first English-speaking work, *Lost and Delirious*. Formally speaking, this film sharply contrasts with its predecessors. Here, Pool abandons her usual slow-paced and introspective narratives for a more accessible and conventional form of storytelling. The uprooted individuals wandering through urban non-spaces commonly found in the director's earlier works (e.g., *La Femme de l'hôtel, À corps perdu*) are gone and are replaced by a small community anchored in its environment. As far as subject matter is concerned, the director explores familiar territory—same-sex desires and the disturbing/traumatizing absence of the mother figure—in this uneven but touching tale of impossible love. However, moving away from problematic portrayals of same-sex desires as in, for example, *La Femme de l'hôtel* and *Emporte-moi*, Pool does not portray lesbo-erotic feelings through the lens of incest.

Lost and Delirious takes place in an all-girls boarding school and deals with a trio of teenage girls: the wide-eyed newcomer Mouse (Mischa Barton) and her senior roommates, the beautiful Tori (Jessica Paré) and the explosive Paulie (Piper Perabo). Mouse soon finds out that Tori and Paulie are lovers. However, when Tori's sister discovers the two girls naked and asleep in the same bed, things start to change: Tori feels under pressure from her peers and particularly fears her "super-super-straight" parents' reaction. Despite intense feelings for her lover, the teenage girl rejects Paulie and abruptly ends their affair. After several unsuccessful attempts to win Tori back, Paulie becomes increasingly desperate and out of control. After one particularly violent altercation with Tori's new male partner (whom she cruelly injures with a stolen sword during a traditional fencing duel), Paulie kills herself by jumping from the school's stately main building.

Once again, then, Pool uses a triangular relationship, but in contrast with her previous productions, particularly *Emporte-moi*, this trio is not based on a three-way love relation. Tori and Paulie are lovers, but the relationship they have with the younger Mouse is a caring one, a quasi mother–daughter relationship that will be inverted by the end of the story. Indeed, the trio allows for the establishment of a substitute for the nuclear family, albeit with a difference, as there are no men. That said, Pool is careful to underline the traumatizing absence of the mother figure in her young protagonists' lives. One quiet evening, the three girls share their frustrations, which are related to their relations with their respective mothers. Mouse had lost her mother to cancer three years prior to her arrival at the boarding school and she is resentful that her father has remarried. Paulie, an adopted child, has never known her real mother, whom she unsuccessfully tries to contact through an adoption agency. As a result of her personal uprooting, the girl—at least verbally—rejects her "fake" mother, the woman who brought her up. As far as Tori is concerned, she stands in awe of parental authority and her ambivalence toward her mother is nowhere more apparent than when she says: "I'm addicted to you, like chocolate.... Sometimes I wish you were dead." On a positive note, the absence of the mother figure in the girls' lives allows them to bond. The mother (as was not the case in either *Anne Trister* or *Emporte-moi*) is not portrayed through the prism of incest; rather, it is her structuring presence—or absence—that is emphasised in *Lost and Delirious*.[16] The absent mother figure does not account for same-sex desires, which are portrayed as sensual and tender.

The collapse of the substitute for the nuclear family occurs when the two girls' love affair is made public. Tori is quick to deny the affair and abandons Paulie. Paulie's resulting emotional despair is in line with other characters that Pool has focused on throughout her filmmaking career (such as Estelle in *La Femme de l'hôtel*, Anne in *Anne Trister*, Pierre in *À corps perdu*, as well as Hanna's mother in *Emporte-moi*). That said, in all the films just mentioned,[17] the protagonists' trajectory is an ascending one: death desires and mental/physical exhaustion are presented as a necessary and ultimately productive phases before reconstruction and regeneration. In *Lost and Delirious*, Paulie's emotional trajectory is inverted: most of the film's first half is dedicated to Tori and Paulie's secret but intense relationship. The two girls' love is taken for granted: in this sense, the numerous kissing scenes and a beautifully filmed, non-voyeuristic love scene confirm the representation of same-sex love as fundamentally unproblematic. Here, Sapphic love is not portrayed as a transitional sexuality, and it is crucially *after* the accidental discovery of Tori and Paulie's "illicit" relationship that Pool's usual themes of uprooting and alienation resurface. *Lost and Delirious* is actually less a story about same-sex love than one of self-hatred and self-repression. Pool's film can indeed remind one of Ang Lee's epic melodrama *Brokeback Mountain* (2005). However, if Lee's character Ennis del Mar (Heath Ledger) eventually evolves toward commitment and self-acceptance (expressed by the enigmatic final line, "Jack, I swear ..."), Pool's young protagonist Tori quickly bows to social and family pressure and sacrifices her love in the name of patriarchal convention. In contrast, Paulie is caught in a whirlwind of unstoppable rage and despair that eventually leads her to self-destruction. However, the teenage girl never stops to theatrically claim her love for Tori and courageously faces lesbophobia (interestingly represented by ignorant young girls).

However, this by no means signifies that Paulie embodies a gay identity as such. For one major characteristic of Pool's cinematic oeuvre is a constant refusal to adhere to gender-based categories. The story of *Lost and Delirious* is told by "the slightly shell-shocked Mouse," who finds Tori and Paulie's love affair "tender and natural" (Tousignant, 22). For the young girl—and probably for most viewers, too—Tori and Paulie's doomed relationship is undeniably seen as a gay one. However, Pool is adamant about staying away from identity categories and prefers to give her story a universalist sheen. This is nowhere more evident than in one of the film's final scenes: Mouse questions the motivations of an increasingly erratic Paulie. Not unlike a mother lecturing her offspring, Mouse advises Paulie to get over it, because "Tori is not a lesbian." To which Paulie replies: "A lesbian? Are you fucking kidding me? You think I'm a lesbian? ... I am not a lesbian, I'm just Paulie who's in love with Tori. Remember? And Tori, she is in love with me because she is mine and I am hers and neither of us are lesbians!"

For the first time in Pool's film career, some twenty years after her first feature film, a word explicitly referring to gender/sexuality-based identities is used. And when the utterance finally appears, it is by a process of self-denial: the word is pronounced in order to underline both its lack of pertinence and its reductive aspect. Pool attempts here to transcend all-embracing identity categories and stay away from the gender oppression that these supposedly entail, by focusing on the universality of human experiences and the mechanisms of love. In the case of *Lost and Delirious*, this means that the director's interest is less on Sapphic love per se than the economy of desire between two individuals; that is why Tori defines herself in negative terms (by stating what she is not rather than what she is).

Such a universalist approach evidently bears traces of Pool's European/francophone background. The French language is deprived of specific terminologies and expressions that would allow speakers to positively set forth their sexual identities during the coming-out process; consequently, French/francophone speakers usually make ambiguous claims regarding same-sex preferences (Provencher, 85–148). Such ambiguity is symptomatic of a specific system of beliefs based on a de-historicized, all-embracing understanding of human experiences (as opposed to a conception of human experiences based on particularities usually found in multicultural nations). Pool's approach is indeed an atypical (and contested) one in North America (see Nadeau 1991, 1997), where sexual, gender, and ethnic particularities are usually brought to the fore. In contrast, Pool's take on identities is based on fluidity and elusiveness, and puts much emphasis on the flimsiness of sexual/gender categories. This fluidity is valid for categories based on sexual orientation, as has been argued throughout this chapter, as well as gender (both men and women supposedly share identical experiences, which are not gender-induced but are related to human condition). For example, religion is used in *Emporte-moi* to confirm characters' uprooting. Hanna's teacher asks her what her religion is. "It depends," the teenager answers. "My father is Jewish, not my mother, she is a Catholic.... For Jews, religion is transmitted by the mother, so I am not Jewish. For Catholics, it is the contrary. Religion is transmitted by the father. I am not a Catholic either." The same can be said about nationality. *Emporte-moi* again: Hanna's father no longer has a nationality: "He is not from here, he is not from elsewhere either." In *À corps perdu*: Pierre is a Quebecer with a strong German accent. This refusal to be categorized is well expressed in an early scene in Pool's second film, *La Femme de l'hôtel*: Estelle and Andréa cross paths at the hotel reception for the first time. When the filmmaker gives her name ("Andréa Richler") to the hotel employee, Estelle asks, "Vous êtes juive?," simultaneously positioning Andréa as a woman and as an individual from a particular religious group.

Although the willingness to transcend identity categories is not necessarily questionable in itself and has been done successfully in some French feature films (Grandena, 63–86), it is far from being without problems. What seems dubious is Pool's systematic refusal to acknowledge some of the specific experiences lived by certain groups and communities, defined in part by their relations to other (dominant) collectives. Can one aspire to the transcendence of identity categories if the latter are denied an existence? Can one ignore the specific relations of, say, gender nonconformists to the so-called traditional family without running the risk of misrepresenting or even obscuring the individuals in question? The cure may in some cases be worse than the disease, and there might not be much difference between the closet and freedom.

Léa Pool's filmography

Laurent Lamerre, portier, 1978

Strass Café, 1980

La Femme de l'hôtel, 1984

Anne Trister, 1986

À corps perdu, 1988

Hotel Chronicles, 1990

La Demoiselle sauvage, 1991

Rispondetemi, 1991

Mouvements du désir, 1994

Lettre à ma fille, 1996

Gabrielle Roy, 1998

Emporte-moi, 1999

Lost and Delirious, 2001

The Blue Butterfly, 2004

Other Films Cited

À qui appartient ce gage? (Suzanne Gibbard, 1974)

Au printemps (Dorothée Brisson and Suzanne Caron, 1958)

La Beauté même (Monique Fortier, 1964)

Brokeback Mountain (Ang Lee, 2005)

Camp Marie-Victorin (Dorothée Brisson, 1956)

Ça peut pas être l'hiver, on a même pas eu d'été (Louise Carré, 1980)

C.R.A.Z.Y. (Jean-Marc Vallée, 2005)

De mère en fille (Anne Claire Poirier, 1967)

Les Filles, c'est pas pareil (Hélène Girard, 1974)

Les Filles du Roy (Anne Claire Poirier, 1974)

La Fin des étés (Anne Claire Poirier, 1964)

J'me marie, j'me marie pas (Mireille Dansereau, 1973)

Mambo Italiano (Émilie Gaudreault, 2003)

Marie s'en va-t-en ville (Marquise Lepage, 1987)

Mourir à tue-tête (Anne Claire Poirier, 1979)

Qui a tiré sur nos histoires d'amour? (Louise Carré, 1986)

Rien qu'un jeu (Brigitte Sauriol, 1983)

Sonatine (Micheline Lanctôt, 1983)

Souris, tu m'inquiètes (Aimée Danis, 1973)

Le Temps de l'avant (Anne Claire Poirier, 1975)

La Vie rêvée (Mireille Dansereau, 1972)

Vivre sa vie (Jean-Luc Godard, 1962)

Zoo (Dorothée Brisson, 1957)

Notes

1
I want to thank Rhea Halfnight Leflufy for her logistic help.

2
For a discussion on the cultural mix in Quebec cinema, see Denis Bachand and Annie Lise Clément's "La Rencontre des cultures dans le cinéma québécois: violence et altérité," *Le Cinéma au Québec: entre tradition et modernité*, ed. Stéphane-Albert Boulais (Montréal: Éditions Fides): 271–81.

3
The first instance of an independent film made by a Québécoise filmmaker from Quebec occurred as recently as 1972 (*La Vie rêvée*, Mireille Dansereau).

4
According to Marcel Jean, the importance of women in documentary making can be explained in different ways. On one hand, documentaries imply a smaller budget than feature films and remain more accessible to upcoming filmmakers, be they men or women (as early as 1973, Helen Doyle, Nicole Giguère, and Hélène Roy laid the foundation of what was to become Vidéo-femmes, a company specializing in the production and distribution of videos for and by women). On the other hand, the increasing number of women directing documentaries accompanied the rise of feminism: "This close relationship implies an activism that, at first, seemed more fitting for documentaries than feature films.... The construction of a new society in which relationships between men and women would be equal; the recognition of the rights of women: they all imply a very close relation to the real" (Jean, 81). Also, a strong tradition of documentaries in the film industry of Quebec can explain the penchant of many a woman cinéaste for non-fiction works. Jean underlines the fact that male producers were slower to acknowledge the relevance of a feminine style of fiction film-making than they were to admit the necessity of a female take on documentaries' subject matter (Jean, 81–84).

5
In 1968, Robert Forget and Fernand Dansereau set up the Groupe de recherche sociale within the ONF. The Groupe's aim was to explore problems emerging in Canadian society, and it produced two feature films, including Dansereau's *St-Jérôme* (1968). The Groupe was then managed by Forget solely and changed its name to Société nouvelle. It was under that name that the "En tant que femmes" program operated (Lever, 235–36; Poirier, 111).

6
In 1974, Kathleen Shannon created the anglophone counterpart of the "En tant que femmes" program: "Shannon's goal was to use Studio D to train women to make films and then have these professionals focus on subjects of interest to women, presented from a feminist perspective. The studio emphasized the concept of 'community filmmaking,' which had three distinct components: it encouraged a group approach to film work as opposed to auteur individualism; it took as a focal point communities of ordinary women and how they supported one another in their struggles; and it highlighted the practical

successes of the women's movement" (Melnyk, 168). Studio D was operative until 2002.

7
Somewhere between documentary and fiction, *Mourir à tue-tête* is a harrowing work that takes rape as its main subject. Its *mise en scène* and its multi-layered narrative are experimental: "'editorials' interrupt the story, and panning, tracking, and freeze-frame are used most effectively; the ultimate realization of the viewer, who sees the entire rape from Suzanne's [the victim's] point of view, and thus is forced into the position of identifying with her, is, in a sense, that the rapist can be anyone, as can the victim. It is a highly political film that criticizes the society and its institutions for victimizing, even criminalizing, the victim" (Pallister, 109).

8
For an excellent in-depth discussion of women cinéastes from Quebec, see Bill Marshall's chapter "Women's Cinema," in his *Quebec National Cinema* (2001), 208–38.

9
Pool has made a number of documentaries, including *Rispondetemi* (a segment of the 1991 collective work *Montréal vu par ...*) and *Gabrielle Roy* (1998). However, the present chapter focuses only on her feature films.

10
In *À corps perdu*, Pool uses a panorama of Montreal virtually identical to this one. Both shots underline the urban alienation experienced by their respective protagonists.

11
Pathology is a recurrent theme in Pool's films and a common feature in many a lesbian-themed feature film. See Cairns, 52–90.

12
Music (*À corps perdu, La Femme de l'hôtel*), literature (*Lost and Delirious*), cinema (*La Femme de l'hôtel, Emporte-moi*), and painting (*La Femme de l'hôtel, Anne Trister*) are all presented as ways of transcending or sublimating one's sorrow.

13
Leitmotifs also concern the uncanny apparition of a glider. The glider's five appearances in the film are stamped with metaphorical meaning. Typically, the glider refers to Pierre's happy childhood days and has indeed an introspective, Proustian quality (flashbacks invariably use black-and-white film stock). The recurrent image of the glider allows Pool to link Pierre's past (about which we know little) and his present. This strategy suggests that Pool's characters are potentially able to root themselves in the present only if they turn to their own personal stories (as opposed to collective stories/histories).

14
The numbness and growing isolation that Hanna's mother experiences are underlined by the earplugs and sleeping pills that the woman uses at bedtime.

15
Hanna's uneasy relation both to others and to sexuality is taken to an abrasive extreme when, following the example of her role model, Karina in *Vivre sa vie*, the young girl finds herself in Montreal's red-light district and descends briefly into prostitution. Here, Pool carefully models Hanna's encounter with a male client on the famous Godard sequence showing first-time prostitute Karina struggling with a customer who is trying to kiss her on the lips.

16
Mouse dedicates her final words to motherly love: "Dear mother, I almost got lost too, didn't I? The pure love you gave me till you died was like a flame always there burning. And just like the rapture, that little flame was all I needed in order to see in the dark. You saved me, Mama, from that deep dark. Paulie, she didn't have that. The darkness took over her so she had to fly away ..."

17
This point is valid also for those works of Pool's that have been touched on only lightly in this chapter. *La Demoiselle sauvage* and *Mouvements du désir* also lay emphasis on female protagonists in moral and emotional crisis. However, unlike most characters in Pool's oeuvre, the heroine of *La Demoiselle sauvage* finds solace only in death.

Works Cited

Bachand, Denis. "What Cinema! Québec: A Different Cinema." *Bridges* 17.2 (1990): 24–30.

Beaulieu, Janick. "Interview." *Séquences* 70 (mars 1994): 12–16.

Cairns, Lucille. *Sapphism on Screen*. Edinburgh: Edinburgh UP, 2006.

Dorland, Michael, and Seth Feldman, eds. *Dialogue: Cinéma canadien et québécois/Canadian and Quebec Cinema*. Montréal: Canadian Film Studies/Études cinématographiques canadiennes, 1987. 269–81.

Gaulin, Suzanne. "Pool's Femme Makes a Splash." *Cinema Canada* 111 (octobre 1984): 7–9.

Grandena, Florian. "L'Homosexuel en dehors de l'homosexualité." *French Contemporary Civilization* 30.2 (2006): 63–86.

Green, Mary Jean. "Léa Pool's *La Femme de l'hôtel* and Women's Film in Québec." *Québec Studies* 9 (fall/winter 1989–90): 49–62.

Grugeau, Gérard. "Cinéma et exil. Interview avec Léa Pool.

L'exil intérieur." *24 images* 106 (printemps 2001): 16–21.

Jean, Marcel. *Le Cinéma québécois*. Montréal: Les Éditions du Boréal, 1991.

Lever, Yves. *Histoire générale du cinéma au Québec*. Montréal: Les Éditions du Boréal, 1988.

Longfellow, Brenda. "The Search for Voice: La Femme de l'hôtel." *Dialogue: cinéma canadien et québécois*. Ed. Michael Dorland, Seth Feldman, and Pierre Véronneau. Montréal: Mediatexte Publications, 1987, 269–81.

Marshall, Bill. *Quebec National Cinema*. Kingston: McGill-Queen's UP, 2001.

Melnyk, George. *One Hundred Years of Canadian Cinema*. Toronto: U of Toronto P, 2004.

Nadeau, Chantal. "Les Femmes frappées de disparition." *24 images* 56–57 (automne 1991), 60–62.

—. "La Représentation de la femme comme autre: l'ambiguïté du cinéma de Léa Pool pour une position féministe."

Québec Studies 17 (1997): 83–96.

Pallister, Janis L. *The Cinema of Quebec: Masters in Their Own House*. Cranbury, NJ: Associated University Presses, 1995.

Poirier, Christian. *Le Cinéma québécois: à la recherche d'une identité?* Sainte-Foi: Presses de l'Université de Laval, 2004.

Provencher, Denis. *Queer French: Globalization, Language, and Sexual Citizenship in France*. Aldershot: Ashgate Publishing, 2007.

Prud'homme, Anne. "Léa Pool : la marginale universelle." *Le Cinéma au Québec: entre tradition et modernité*. Ed. Stéphane-Albert Boulais. Montréal: Éditions Fides, 2006. 271–81.

Tousignant, Isa. "Forging New Paths: Léa Pool's Latest Film Leaves Her Lost and Delirious." *Take 1* (September 2001): 22.

Winch, David. "Léa Pool's *La Femme de l'hôtel*." *Canada Cinema* 111 (October 1984): 10.

4

Transiting Nationality and the Battlefields of Otherness

On the Field of Battle: First Nations Women Documentary Filmmakers
Anthony Adah

How have First Nations women filmmakers imagined the Canadian nation? How has their work in the documentary mode perpetuated, abrogated, or subverted traditional imaginings of what constitutes the Canadian polity and its cultural identity? An examination of films from the 1990s by three women Native Canadian directors provides the basis of an answer to this question. The films include *Kanehsatake: 270 Years of Resistance* (dir. Alanis Obomsawin, 1994), *Keepers of the Fire* (dir. Christine Welsh, 1994), and *Forgotten Warriors* (dir. Loretta Todd, 1996). This selection represents some of the most important works by Native filmmakers acclaimed in Canada and overseas. Frequently screened at local and international festivals, these films function as a resource for learning about First Nations self-representations in relation to Canadian cinema.

Aboriginal peoples appeared in Canadian cinema from the early twentieth century and were the subject of several films in the 1940s under the National Film Board's filmmaking practice.[1] As land and human rights agitation grew in Canada and the activism of the American Indian Movement (AIM) became prominent, the NFB initiated Challenge for Change in the 1960s. Challenge for Change, a program that utilized film to stimulate social change and political agency, brought the first Aboriginal film crew into the NFB. One of its results was *The Ballad of Crowfoot* (1968), the first documentary directed by an Aboriginal person, Willie Dunn. Although few from this pioneering group went into further filmmaking, the success of the project paved the way for Studio One, the First Nations unit. The NFB launched Studio One in 1991 to enable Aboriginal peoples to take control of the making of their own films. As one of its members put it,

"Our greatest concern is in audio-visual.... We are trying to know what it is about our people that we should keep" (Mitchell, 2). Studio One was a cultural activist project and, according to Loretta Todd, "Studio One was intended as part of the tradition of storytelling: of how Native Nations speak to one another about what it means to be part of a nation, a territory, a cultural belief system" (de Rosa, 328). It is obvious from these declarations that Native Canadian cinema invests in interrogating the history of images that Native Canadians perceive as distorted representations of their identity in mainstream cinema and media. Common stereotypical images include those of squaw, child of nature, victim, noble savage, warrior, and the sexually voracious woman (Miller, 64). What is significant about these stereotypical images is that they all depend on images of the body. The following analyses demonstrate that Native Canadian filmmaking critiques and mediates previous stereotypes and also accounts for contemporary Aboriginal experiences. In addition, the films contribute to the critical debate on Canadian national cinema and culture.

Alanis Obomsawin's *Kanehsatake: 270 Years of Resistance* (1994)

Kanehsatake documents the Oka crisis of 1990, when the Mohawk nation blocked access to reserve land that had served as ancestral burial grounds for thousands of years and was then being expropriated by the local municipal government for use as an eighteen-hole golf course. In the ensuing confrontation with the provincial police (and, later, the national army), the Oka Mohawks were joined by the Mohawks of Kahnawake, who proceeded to barricade access to Montreal's Mercier Bridge.

The documentary not only offers a lucid chronology of the events themselves but, through clever storytelling techniques, brings the weight of history to bear on the events, producing a complex argument that enables the viewer to access a fuller understanding of the crisis and how it relates to other aspects of Native Canadians' issues, including self-determination and representation. Because it is the subject of many articles, both scholarly and popular, that detail the political significance of the events at Oka, it is not the intention here to relate this aspect of the film. Instead, the intention is to fill some of the analytical gaps in existing commentary and show how the relationship between storytelling and the body offers a valuable perspective on some of the meanings in the film.

Alanis Obomsawin (Abenaki) is a singer, songwriter, poet, storyteller, activist, and, primarily, a filmmaker (White, 365). She stands as the most prolific and respected Native filmmaker in Canada. *Kanehsatake* is one of her three documentaries on the subject of the Oka crisis, the others being *My Name Is*

Kahentiiosa (1995), and *Spudwrench, Whiskey Trench* (1997). Prior to directing the Oka trilogy, she made notable films such as *Incident at Restigouche* (1984), which tells of two raids by the Sûreté du Québec (the provincial police force) on the grounds that Mi'qmaq people were overharvesting salmon, and *Richard Cardinal: Cry from a Diary of a Métis Child* (1986), a biographical account of an adolescent who commits suicide after living in multiple foster homes. Since *Kanehsatake*, Obomsawin has made other documentary features, most notably *Is the Crown at War with Us?* (2002), which revisits the Mi'qmaq people's right to fish in their own waters, and *Our Nationhood* (2003), a film that brings the Mi'qmaq cycle to a close. What sets *Kanehsatake* apart from the other films is its range and depth, both at the level of subject and, more specifically, cinematic technique, with the film functioning almost as an encyclopedia of cinematic devices found in all her other films.

In *Kanehsatake*, both Obomsawin's aesthetics and socio-political activism are explicit. Using interviews, official documents, news clips, animated graphics, photographs, Native objects, and her own voice-over, Obomsawin constructs a film that worries the judicial system and calls into question Quebec's struggle for sovereignty. Jerry White notes that Obomsawin's documentary practice is linked to that of John Grierson, who advocated a vision of films engaged with the "needs and interests" of their audiences. However, there are major points of divergence between the Griersonian documentary and Obomsawin's filmmaking. White stresses that, in spite of the emphasis on evidentiary realist footage in Obomsawin's films, they are marked by "a pronounced subjectivity" (White, 66). "This subjectivity," according to White, "is most clearly expressed by her own voice, which forms the soundtrack of almost all her films. The voice-over is far from the voice-of-god variety that has been used to convey a false objectivity; instead, it has the effect of identifying whose eyes are seeing the action" (White, 366). In *Quebec National Cinema,* Bill Marshall makes similar remarks, acknowledging that Obomsawin's works disavow "exnominated objectivity" and opt instead for the use of "active interviewee-participants" (Marshall, 261). What is apparent from these comments is that Obomsawin's signature style insists on her corporeal and/or aural presence in the films. It is a presence that highlights the intersection of her cinematic practice with social and political activism.

Zuzana Pick's exploration of this connection between film form and identity politics provides insight into the pivotal role that the oral storytelling tradition plays in Native historiography as demonstrated by the films of Alanis Obomsawin.[2] Pick observes that as storyteller, Obomsawin belongs to a Native tradition where the art of storytelling through voice, image, word, and activism is tied to the custodianship of history and culture, and helps shape contemporary identities of Native peoples (88). This observation has ramifications for critical analysis, because as a storytelling filmmaker Obomsawin is, by implication, influenced by salient features of oral compositional structures and performance techniques. These textual features highlight the connection between storytelling and the body, and this link facilitates a reading of the film as a formally astute documentary that is not only relevant to Native Canadian identity but also fully engaged with the Native body's role in the reconstruction of Canadian national cinema.

When the film opens, the director's own voice-over narration situates the locations of the confrontation (Oka and Kanahwake) with the aid of an animated drawing. Following this, a somewhat tight framing of the golf course lingers onscreen until, through backtracking, the shot widens to reveal the Pines. Obomsawin's narration then provides some backstory to the sit-down protest by the Mohawks in March 1990. Periodic standoffs over the expropriation of land in the 1930s, 1947, and 1961 foreground the historical significance of the Pines, which is the setting for the current action. Intercut with this narration are shots of Oka Mayor Jean Ouellette addressing the press and Mohawks sitting in a circle in the Pines. An extended tracking shot maps the length of the Pines, like a panoptic topographical survey of a piece of land as if it were up for acquisition. Accompanying these opening shots is flutelike music, which balances (by contrast) the gravity of the voice-over exposition. The opening sequence ends with a low-angle shot of the trees that tilts down to reveal a tombstone followed by a close-up of an eagle feather, a symbol of balance in opposites, honour, strength, and healing.

Through a combination of animated graphics, symbolism, camera angle and movement, and the director's own voice-over narration, this opening segment of *Kanehsatake* suggests how the body, in relation to the discourse on golf as a bourgeois recreational activity, becomes a site of power. "Power," Michel Foucault suggests, "must act while concealing itself beneath the gentle force of nature" (*Discipline*, 106). The opening moment of the film is an example of the nation's expropriation of the natural environment—in this case, for sporting purposes and housing development—in order to control the "other" by manipulating the way Native Canadians think about the land and their relationship to it. The segment also operates to map the development arc of the documentary. Oral composition tends to follow a structure where a single theme becomes the core from which the composer makes other elaborations. The narrative core that *Kanehsatake* articulates is the perpetuation of historical injustices done to First Nations people by the nation-state. Around this theme, Obomsawin gathers evidentiary material from events at Oka, examples from history, and other heterogeneous materials that elaborate on, comment on, and accentuate this theme.

While the specific subject here is the expropriation of Mohawk land at Oka, in another sequence Obomsawin uses animation and a map to represent the mapping and carving up of Mohawk territory, marking the dislocation of the Mohawks first by the French, in 1787, and then by the British, in 1868. The segment documents one moment of truce during the confrontation when both parties decide to meet behind the Sulpician church. The documentary does not stay with the meeting; it cuts away to introduce historical materials to contextualize the event. This material includes a re-enacted recitation of the Iroquois Confederacy Longhouse's Great Law of Peace over a painting of Chief Joseph (Sosé) Onasakenrat and a wampum belt that recorded the territorial boundaries made during Treaty agreements at the time.[3] Using these devices effects a contestation of the nation-state's narrative that aims to alienate the Mohawks from place—severing, as it were, the Native world view of the relationship between land and people.

Moreover, the segment highlights a theme of broken promises by Christian churches and state. The Sulpician church, for instance, looms large in the literature of Aboriginal Canada, and wherever it appears the fervour and faith of Native peoples for the Christian faith is always betrayed, often through the use of diverse forms of violence on the part of state and church. Just before the meeting between the Mohawks and the state, a lyrical cutaway prepares the ground for understanding this ambivalent role of church and state as protector-punisher. This poetic shot holds the image of a porcupine clambering down a tree and innocently scurrying away for rescue under a police vehicle. The voice-over accompanying the image states: "Many residence of Kanehsatake have left fearing another attack." The porcupine is a Native totem symbol of trust, faith, and innocence. Like the porcupine, the people of Kanehsatake moved from one besieged zone for safety in another—the Treatment Centre. Ironically, therefore, just as the porcupine's vulnerable body is under threat from the police vehicle, which is likely to crush it in this moment of crisis, the image, by association, extends and amplifies the theme of colonized Native bodies that flock to Christianity for succour but then return, bruised and disillusioned.

This interplay between body and senses in relation to technology works through the film in several forms, sometimes literal and at other times suggested. Indeed, in some instances, it appears that this interplay is the basis of the confrontation. In one scene, for instance, the tension between the two sides escalates over a matter of vision. One night, in order to block the army's search-lights, the Mohawk leader of operations, Robert "Mad Jap" Skidders, with the help of other protesters, puts up a large piece of fabric. The next scene shows the jittery response of Major Alain Tremblay. who frantically and nervously threatens the Mohawks, much to the amusement of Mad Jap and his colleagues. To invoke

Foucault's concept of the panopticon, in this nonviolent sequence of the struggle, the Natives' ability to neutralize the power of the government forces' scopic
apparatus is cited as almost a violation of the law, inciting the state's prompt
coercive intervention. Further, while the industrial/military lights of government
forces illuminate the soldiers and isolate them from the landscape, the poor light
source on the Mohawk side appears to blur the human figure and the landscape.
Remarkably, it is the Mohawks' familiarity with and ability to blend body and
environment that the government soldiers find frightening. In this instance, the
state responds to an innocuous piece of cloth as if it were a lethal weapon.

The ascription of violent behaviour to the Mohawks and their allies is
a subject the film cleverly unpacks. In another confrontation segment outside
the barricade, a CBC reporter describes the possession of a lethal arsenal by
the Mohawks. Obomsawin does not fail to register the political implications of
this media claim. The media, especially television, has been at the forefront of
Native peoples' critique of mainstream (mis)representation of their peoples.
Kanehsatake, however, contests the veracity of CBC's reporting, since the
on-screen images contradict the reporter's claim. An ironic situation is created
whereby it is the state that mobilizes excessive weaponry against the low-
powered guns of the Mohawks and their supporters.

Two-thirds into the film, there is a negotiation meeting between the
Mohawks and Quebec officials. Speaking for the Mohawks, Ellen Gabriel ends
her speech with the declaration that this is an ongoing struggle: "The circle is
not finished. It is not finished." But what, indeed, does it mean to have the circle
continue? It would appear that this is where the vision of the filmmaker coincides
with the agonistics of subalternity. The struggles of Native Canadians have continued even as it is apparent that their political autonomy is not in sight. In his
interpretation of Hegel's concept of agonism, Foucault provides a possible explanation for such seemingly endless struggles. Since power does not reside at any
one point for all time, the end point of some forms of struggle is the charting of
the possibilities of their future re-enactments. On the basis of this interpretation, Foucault suggests that the repressive and enabling aspects of power need
to be reconfigured so that power is "constructed as a productive network which
runs through the whole social body, much more than as a negative instance
whose function is repressive" (*Power*, 119). Native Canadian struggles over land
rights, however, are not merely discursive, as Roxann Prazniak and Arif Dirlik
assert.[4] Even when these struggles fail to achieve all their demands and entitlements, they demonstrate materialist, place-based practices of survival, which
Kanehsatake demonstrates by articulating the body's relationship to land.

One of the obvious benefits of an oral performance structure is that
it enables other stories to be told. The formal technique of *Kanehsatake* opens

spaces within the tale for heterogeneous voices and alliances. It is like the inter-orientating body, in the Bakhtinian sense, with all its orifices receptive to others' voices. The documentary shows, for instance, how effecting the blockade and bringing it to national and international attention was the result of alliances among several Native and non-Native groups in Canada and spiritual elders from Mexico. Overall, this use of multiple political actors to tell the story produces that texture of the craft of storytelling that Walter Benjamin describes as a "slow piling one on top of the other of thin, transparent layers which constitutes the most appropriate picture of the way in which the perfect narrative is revealed" (93). This layering effect in oral storytelling functions as a structural device that triggers other histories that solicit the viewer's ability to track their meanings. It is as if, to paraphrase Benjamin, the human body of the storyteller, in conjunction with the narrative, becomes a passage for humanity to liberate itself from the "ruins" and "progress" of national history.

This understanding is crucial to grasping the layers of *Kanehsatake*. While the centre of the Oka conflict was the Pinelands, the location itself and the purpose for which the municipality sought the land has another history of crisis inscribed by power. Until recently, golf was an elitist sport and has often in the Americas been a privileged pastime of the white male community. But perhaps more important is that while the state often invokes sport as a value-neutral activity, "sports reflect the larger society, particularly its social arrangements, types of inequality, and social dynamics" (Dawkins and Kinlock, 5). As social dramas that "may appear open and democratic, they reflect the inequality predominant in the larger society, whether racial, ethnic, gender-based, class-oriented, or age-defined" (Dawkins and Kinlock, 6). In this sense one can describe the crisis at Oka as a secular exercise of power on sacred Aboriginal land in which the Native community was at the receiving end.

The constant cinematic shift away from simply recording the events in vérité style to an embrace of heterogeneous images shows another influence of oral narrative technique. The art of the oral composer is not merely to recount earlier stories or construct the heritage of a person or community with absolute accuracy. The task is always to choose from a common matrix that functions as a point of departure, and from which the artist is free to improvise, re-enact, and open up to other texts and voices. Similarly, as *Kanehsatake* advances, the use of voice-over becomes less frequent, allowing voices from the action itself and from interviews with people on both sides of the confrontation to enter as agents in the dialogue. Evidently, the documentary provided Obomsawin an opportunity to account for the Oka stand-off from a Native Canadian perspective of the events. As she states in her interview with White, "There had to be a document that came from us.... That was crucial" (368). In a way, Obomsawin was responding judiciously and mockingly to the Griersonian injunction of representing "what Canadians need to know and think about if they are going to do their best by Canada and themselves" (Hardy, 26). White makes the assertion that "a good deal of aboriginal [sic] media has focused on training people to make their own films and video by way of countering imposed representations of their lives" (369).

Like most Aboriginal films, *Kanehsatake* highlights the ethical and material effects of image production and, in the process, it rectifies and restores Native peoples' place in history. To achieve this, the film adopts a formal textual body that is a site of inter-orientating discourses of politics, sports, religion, texts, and the media, as well as the relationship between these discourses to Native Canadian identity.

Christine Welsh's *Keepers of the Fire* (1994)

Christine Welsh's film oeuvre is committed to unravelling marginalized stories of First Nations women. *Women in the Shadows* (dir. Norma Bailey, 1991), her first major film engagement (as producer and writer), is a personal journey into her Metis heritage. This autobiographical film reveals how official accounts of early encounter between Europeans and Native peoples undermine or silence the role of women in interracial unions. Welsh's *The Story of the Salish Coast Knitters* (2001) combines archival footage with interviews with women spanning three generations to recuperate the stories of Native women of the Salish Coast who knitted rare sweaters well known around the world. Her latest film, *Finding Dawn* (2006), takes the viewer across Canada to witness the tragedy of hundreds of Native Canadian women reported missing or found dead.

Narrated in the first person, *Keepers of the Fire* opens with sepia-toned photographs of women from the past. Shown in order from the oldest subjects to the youngest, these photographs suggest a continuum one might describe as traditional Native to contemporary Native. Accompanying the photographs is the voice-over that declares: "No people is broken until the hearts of its women are on the ground. Only then are they broken." The photographs are quickly followed by a montage of news-footage clips depicting violent scenes of burning effigies, soldiers storming a barricade, Native "warriors" making up their faces, and a woman who describes briefly how Mohawk women came together to defend their land during the Oka crisis. Following a straight cut to the director/narrator, who is seen driving toward the Mercier Bridge, the voice-over states: "I want to find out what turns ordinary women into warriors. And for me the story begins in Oka." Welsh narrates Native women's stories to re-articulate a new understanding of the term "warriors" within the context of the much publicized confrontation at Oka and at the scenes of other Native Canadian women's struggles.

The events documented in the first episode of *Keepers of the Fire* begin three years after the Oka crisis. A cut from the travelling shot takes the film into a serene village, where slow, sweeping tracking shots provide dramatic contrast to the violent images they follow. The next shot is an on-camera interview with Ellen Gabriel, a news reporter for a radio station and a major actor in *Kanehsatake*. Gabriel bemoans the destruction of the earth in the name of progress. Her place-based imagination and activism are anchored in a commitment to teaching ways of Aboriginal peoples' survival—with an emphasis on harmony with the earth. Gabriel contrasts Aboriginal interests in maintaining harmony with the earth with the state's interest in economic investments that position Mohawks as dispensable and as having to accommodate what are ironically called "development" initiatives.

Arif Dirlik describes place-based imagination as the "radical other" of the logic of global capitalism, which dislocates and abandons places and peoples on the bases of their market potentials (151). Similarly, Asfar Hasain observes that "for many displaced, homeless, and landless people in the Third World and the Aboriginals—the land is not only the site of oppression as such but is also the site of opposition, the site of continuous struggle" (43). This struggle is taken up after the interview with Ellen Gabriel. The women who were once on the front lines at Oka are now in another kind of front line: a domestic one, the kitchen. The scene that takes place on the dawn of the third anniversary of the Oka confrontation relates the crucial roles of women in Mohawk society. Women, states the voice-over narrator, determine the head of the Longhouse and it is to them that land is entrusted. The sequence alternates between archival footage that foregrounds women's physical involvement in the Oka confrontations and on-camera comments from women reminiscing about those events. The shots are mixed with cutaways to the kitchen where the anniversary is in progress. Thus, by articulating the two fronts of interaction (Oka protest and kitchen). the episode presents expositional information and traces a temporal continuity from past to present. Food is a vehicle of memory, Laura Marks claims (225), and the film makes clear that cooking, laying the table, and eating become a preferred mode of remembering the Oka crisis—as well as a way to facilitate a healing process that binds community and place. The beauty of the sequence derives from the affective and spectatorial pleasures from both: while one concentrates on destruction, wounds, and conflict, the other dwells on feeding, health, and healing the body.

Welsh's films are structured simply and straightforwardly. Yet a closer look reveals intricate nooks that reward exploration. Their structure, consisting of transitional straight cuts and fades, is often balanced by the alternating of diverse images that ceaselessly call for the viewer to construct associations from disparate elements. Further, the juxtapositions in her documentary films draw attention to the role of memory. For instance, the archival footage that is intercut with Ellen Gabriel's on-camera description of the weaponry used during the Oka crisis performs complex functions. The footage includes images of grenades hurled from positions that would have been impossible for Gabriel to access. The footage could be Gabriel's fragmented recollection of different phases of the confrontation or the director's use of archival footage to reinforce Gabriel's remarks. It is equally significant that Welsh's voice-over, which follows immediately, declares that there are many versions of what happened. Regardless, since the interview with Gabriel frames these images, one could argue that they suggest a mode of remembering, recuperating, and assembling an archive of women's experiences at Oka and thereby creating a collective memory.

The next episode builds on this construction of an imagined community of women and nation. The documentary moves to Haida Gwaii, where the issue is logging. Visual details in the episode include vérité shots of women harvesting seafood and archival footage of the 1985 protest in which women confront police over logging issues. Welsh's interview with Diane Brown, who participated in the 1985 protest, occupies most of the episode. Midway through the interview, as they walk through the bushes in a long shot, Brown emphasizes the relationship between bodies, objects, and the environment when she declares that "everything has feelings." In terms of style, the voice over-narration and intimate two-shots deployed in the interviews are interspersed with wide shots and long takes in which the director/narrator and Brown casually stroll and explore aspects of the landscape, plants, and leaves, providing an affective dimension to a moving environmental story.

In the third episode of the film the action moves to New Brunswick, where there has been an eight-year crusade against changes in the Indian Act that made it possible for non-status Indians to be evicted from reserves. More painful to the women was that the band council, composed mostly of men, was indifferent to the gender discrepancies in the Act. Under the Indian Act, if women married white or non-status husbands, they lost their position as status Indians and the right to confer status on their children. The viewer learns that one of the interviewees, Sandra, was at the forefront of those who took the women's case before the UN, part of a series of actions culminating in a decision that made the Indian Act conform to the Canadian Charter of Rights and Freedoms.[5] This segment shifts the lines of confrontation from Native versus white nation-state to that of Native women versus (white) state in collaboration with Native males. As the filmmaker narrates in this episode, "Being a warrior can also mean confronting tradition and finding the courage to listen to your own heart." Through the voice-over narration the viewer learns some of the reasons women have been excluded from the realms of modern politics: menstruation, child-bearing, and breastfeeding. Such a social configuration in modern life excludes women and creates a relationship of dependency, and as one of the interviewees, Shirley Bear (a.k.a. feminist Bear), declares: "Sometimes the battleground isn't a place, it's a state of mind, a place within."

The episode highlights the materiality of women's bodies as a complex site of reproduction and disenfranchisement countered by women's activism. Women's struggle in this episode disrupts conventional understandings of marginalized national struggles by drawing attention to gendered dependency and the continuity of oppression of Native women. In other words, the battle for equity is drawn along the lines of inter-Native gendered relationships and within each individual in that larger relationship.

The last episode of the film opens at a Soroptimist gathering at the Royal York Hotel in Toronto. At the helm is a woman, Catherine Brookes, who is leading a fundraising drive for a Native women's shelter in downtown Toronto. The episode includes a car ride through the city that reveals areas where home-less Native people can be found. The travelling shot terminates in a shelter where an on-camera interview takes place with one of the residents, Julie Penasée. In a confessional mode, Penasée discusses troubled spousal relationships she has had, her travails with alcoholism and violence, and ways the shelter helped her to concentrate on healing as a process. More importantly, the sequence stresses—for Penasée, the filmmaker, and the viewer—the hope that will come to those who make the effort to overcome challenges. Aptly, the voice-over asserts: "A warrior is every one of us who dares to dream."

Keepers of the Fire follows different categories of women activists in order to expand the viewer's understanding of the Native concept of "warrior." Through gradual articulation of different aspects of Native struggles, Christine Welsh weaves together a clever, highly nuanced definition of what the word means to Native peoples and how women may be seen within broader under-standings of the term. Each episode comprises interviews, live-action, and archi-val footage. In terms of form, this combination of images activates an internal dialogue with other aspects such as the verbal information from the intervie-wees or from the voice-over narration, providing a form of meta-commentary. Furthermore, this formal strategy makes possible, in *Keepers of the Fire*, the construction of a comprehensive and grounded understanding of the concept of warrior among Native peoples, especially in relation to women. Overall, the gov-erning premise for Native peoples is that a warrior is "one that bears the burden of peace." For that reason, they must look ahead to the future of their children.

Obomsawin and Welsh's films complement one another. The dominant vérité-style cinematography of *Kanehsatake* draws the viewer into the events recorded at Oka and facilitates "the circulation of affect between protagonist[s] and viewer" (Pick, 77). The conventional documentary format of *Keepers of the Fire*, consisting of talking heads and *mise en scène* emphasizing body–landscape relationship, highlights the collective effort of diverse Native peoples drawn from different strata of society and the recuperation of women's intervention in social action. Both films sunder the fixed stereotypical representations that circulate in mainstream media and recontextualize the Native body's participation in ethnic and national struggles.

Loretta Todd's *Forgotten Warriors* (1997)

Loretta Todd's interest in filmmaking began at community college, where she parlayed her talent in writing into video essays. In the late 1980s she studied film at Simon Fraser University. Todd works in video, installation, and film, and her oeuvre covers socio-political subjects such as the plight of Native convicts in *Halfway House* (video, 1986); displacement and migration in *Breaking Camp* (installation, 1989); alcoholism in *Blue Neon* (installation, 1989); and the art of storytelling—by way of relating a biography of Len George, the son of Native Canadian icon Chief Dan George—in *The Storyteller in the City* (installation, 1989). In 1991 Todd took on the task of making *The Learning Path*, which was the first documentary feature from NFB Studio One and part of a four-part television series, *As Long as the River Flows*, produced by the NFB and Tamarack Productions. *The Learning Path* concerns stories of trauma and recovery by Native Canadian women who spent time in residential schools. The use of archival footage and re-enactments makes the film, in stylistic terms, a precursor to *Forgotten Warriors*. Carol Geddes's remarks about the significance of filmmaking to Native identity and national participation[6] are pertinent to understanding the aesthetics and politics of *The Learning Path*. That Todd's oeuvre explores issues of health, physical displacement, history, and memory is indicative of her engagement with the body's imbrication with Native Canadian struggles and identity.

While the term "warrior" functions primarily at a discursive level in *Kanehsatake* and *Keepers of the Fire*, the subject of *Forgotten Warriors* is Canadian soldiers returned from overseas battlefronts. Organized, for the most part, around on-camera interviews with WW II veterans, the documentary has three main parts: the call to national duty, the disjuncture between Native veterans' commitment to national duty and their abandonment by the state upon their return, and the Native peoples' re-inscription of their histories and memory into the narratives of the nation.

Narrated by Gordon Tootoosis, *Forgotten Warriors* spotlights issues around Native WW II veterans' rights to land and their dispossession from lands after returning from the war. To flesh out this aspect of Native people's history within multicultural Canada, Loretta Todd relies on several stylistic strategies, including re-enactments, archival footage, interviews with women who were on the home front, and war veterans. The pre-credit sequence consists of a fluid panning shot that follows an eagle as it soars from the left to the right of frame, a motif repeated toward the end. Since the eagle signifies healing among most Native Canadians, the shot traces the emotional trajectory of the film from crisis to understanding and peaceful resolution.

The first part of the documentary addresses the enthusiasm and expectations of Native Canadian men and women who joined the armed forces to fight in WW II. It opens with a re-enactment in which a mother discourages her son from fighting in the war but later sends him to protect "country and family." The shift from family to country as the first term of social and cultural relationship is significant because it emphasizes that Native peoples joined the war on the grounds that it was more their war than non-Natives' war—that is, it was their political and spiritual duty to defend their homeland. In addition, the voice-over suggests, Native Canadian enlistment was motivated by economic need, because the trapping season then was poor. The cinematic highlights of these opening moments are several long shots dissolving into one another but concentrating on tracing the young man's path through the landscape.

The next segment elaborates on the subject of Native participation through one of the interviewees, Leroy Littlebear, who stresses that Native involvement in the war was not for imperialist goals but for defence, which in the world view of many Native peoples is often the only legitimate ground for war. The segment introduces another significant element: archival footage of return-ing soldiers that draws attention to their racial diversity. This alliance of races is reinforced by the voice-over, which through its emphasis on the relationship among people, land, and animals elaborates on the theme of collaboration. In Littlebear's reflections it is not only war that demands corporeal investment. Photographic stills of war heroes foreground bodily efforts not only at the front but in sports, as in the case of the Native veteran Tom Longboat, who was an Olympic athlete. By offering diverse images that are sutured by a veteran's recol-lections, the documentary highlights the collaboration of multicultural bodies in all spheres of a multicultural Canada. In foregrounding Native participation, Todd is able, later in the documentary, to demonstrate to the viewer the injustice suf-fered by Native veterans on their return. Early on, then, the film puts a historical spotlight on race relations in the face of what, in this context, the film suggests to be the ambivalent and contradictory practices of a hegemonic white Canada.

Canadian multiculturalism is framed by certain morally and ethically charged keywords such as "acceptance" and "tolerance." This is not the space to rehearse buzzwords that pervade Canadian social and cultural discourse, but suffice it to say that Eva Mackay observes that Canadian multiculturalism "appears to advance a national identity based on acceptance, but in practice this is often not the case" (Mackey, 2–3). Through the interviews with the veterans, *Forgotten Warriors* reminds the viewer that WW II was sold on the propaganda that labour is an edifying and worthy human endeavour for all citizens.[7] *Forgotten Warriors* attests to this sense of belonging through the generous screen time it devotes to the interview with the first Native woman to enlist in the Canadian Women's Auxiliary, Mary Greyeyes, who expounds on the role of Native women in the war effort. Her testimony indicates that the war effort did not discriminate along racial, gendered, and classed bodies. Thus, although the war mobilized every national body, upon their return from battlefronts, Native bodies were denationalized. As the segment moves to its conclusion, archival footage of battle fronts, ruins, and corpses support the voices of veterans Gordon Ahenakew, John Bradley, and Harry Lavalle, who narrate their experiences, with the last shot lingering on decaying bodies and the smell of war. Laura Marks observes that there is strong link between smell and memory, noting that it is an embodied experience that animates the cinematic image. Smell is a sense that is markedly diffuse (unlike sight, which provides hard boundaries), and by invoking it, Lavalle's olfactory memory suggests the oneness of humanity's loss in times of war and reinscribes Native involvement in Canadian national causes.

The middle section of the film returns to the home front by concentrating on the isolation of the women left behind. Through a combination of voice-over and interview, the film argues that the war occurred at a time of cultural deprivation for Native peoples. One of the interviewees, Bernelda Wheeler, describes the feverish manner in which Native women listened to war events on radio, prayed for their loved ones at the front, and sneaked out to the sun dance, which at that time was forbidden. Toward the end of this interview, the frequency of voice-over diminishes significantly and three successive shots dominate: an extended lyrical shot dominated by images of floating telegrams; archival black-and-white footage of arriving soldiers; and finally a continuation of the re-enacted scene, this time with the young man dancing with a girl—a potential bride—against a black background on an empty stage. The shots fuse the zeal and commitment at the opening with the hopes and aspirations of return. Furthermore, the staged dance not only marks the soldier's welcome home but announces his social reintegration into the nation he fought to protect. However, while the *mise en scène* and cinematography at the opening of the film place the body in relation to landscape and community, the empty stage on which his dance takes place suggests displacement from the "national" stage. Furthermore, the difference in age between the young man and the interviewees before and after his dance suggests that the theme of inequalities is not only a matter of the past but continues in the present.

The second part of the film opens on an upbeat note. Sounding bugles accompany footage of veterans receiving war medals from Canada and, in the special case of Tommy Prince, international recognition, when he is presented with the Silver Medal by the United States. However, the euphoria of the moment is undercut by another interviewee, Senator Len Marchand, who laments that although Canada "owe[s] a great debt to these veterans," there was great disappointment among Natives about the way things evolved when the soldiers returned from the war: loss of status, loss of reserve land, which was cut up and given to white veterans, and land given to Native veterans in their own reserves.

This disconnect between official rhetoric and painful experience marks the narrative shape of the next sequence as well. For instance, while the Director of Veteran Affairs, Gordon Murcherson, in news footage, extols the government's efforts to resettle veterans and declares, "There is no place like home," interviewees such as Fred L'Hirondelle and Sam Sinclair highlight the deep frustration and dispossession they faced on their return from war: they were not informed about their entitlements, were offered unproductive land on Slave River, and were sometimes accused of violating the law because they dared to own property, which, under the law, they could not. Images supporting their on-camera testimonies include slow lingering pans of Native land annexed by the state for electrical cable road, poorly compensated Native communities displaced from oil-rich lands, and Ontario reserve land expropriated for use by the military.

The documentary takes on a developmental discourse by calling attention to the tension that exists when place-based struggles face off against the developmental discourse of "national" projects. The representation of the veteran's traumatic experiences reaches an affective coda when one veteran, Al Thomas, who had become an alcoholic, testifies to the feelings of segregation and humiliation Native veterans collectively feel. However, the documentary offsets this gloom with the veterans' decision to undergo a healing process. Thus, subsequent segments highlight self-initiated efforts of the veterans to undergo this healing, and these activities constitute the narrative core of the final part of the documentary.

The first scene of the third part takes the veterans to a Vancouver pow-wow, where they carry the Veterans Flag in the Grand Entry and offerings of eagle feathers. The subsequent scene takes place in a gallery where two young men are guided through photographs of Native families that fought in the war. Museums and exhibitions, Sharon J. Macdonald asserts, are "material performative." Drawing from J.L. Austin and Judith Butler's theorizing of performativity, Macdonald argues that "having a museum was itself a performative utterance of having an identity" (11). In this context, images of Native children looking at Native Canadian heroes suggest a re-inscription of this "unknown" history and pride of the people in the minds of the future generations. The import of the museum "as a site for staging, spectatorship and enactment" (12) of Native identity becomes even more significant because, in the laying-of-the-wreath archival footage that follows, the voice-over narration states that fifty years passed before Native veterans could lay a wreath on national Remembrance Day.

The closing moments of *Forgotten Warriors* concentrate on memorialization and veteraniation as sites for constructing and contesting identities. Canadian veterans were rewarded under the Canadian Soldier Veteran's Act, and after WW II they were rewarded by the federal government under the Canadian Soldier Veteran's Settlement Act. As Benedict Anderson asserts, "No more arresting emblems of the modern culture of nationalism exist than cenotaphs and tombs of Unknown Soldiers.... Yet void as these tombs are of identifiable mortal remains or immortal souls, they are nonetheless saturated with ghostly national imaginings" (Anderson, 10). Recent criticism of the war memorial dedicated to the Unknown Soldier in Ottawa, around which the discourse of Canada's multicultural policy is woven, comes to mind. Around this figure, the Governor General Adrienne Clarkson once declared: "We do not know whose son he was. We do not know his name. We do not know if he was a MacPherson or a Chartrand. He could have been a Kaminski or a Swiftarrow."[8] Here, Clarkson offers an abstracted and de-corporealized identity. However, in her critique of Remembrance Day ceremonies in relation to Canada's multicultural policy, Kirsty Robertson points out that "while the remains of the Unknown Soldier could be that of any ethnicity it was nevertheless propagated as a white body,"[9] one that is described elsewhere as "a young Apollo, golden haired."[10] Thus, the government-sanctioned multicultural policy aimed at facilitating and promoting the national mosaic belly-flops every so often into "a single definition of 'Canadian,' offering only a classic unified (Apollonian) body, and classifying a core group as 'Canadian-Canadians,' against whom everyone else is defined as a hyphenated, or multicultural Canadian" (Mackey, 2–3).

Forgotten Warriors offers the viewer an intersubjective critique of the Canadian nation by highlighting the contrast between the equality of the war burden on all bodies (across race and gender) and the unequal treatment along racial bodies once the war was over. It is a documentary that dwells on a "silenced'" and "repressed" part of white Canada's past relationships with Native Canadians. However, the film undercuts this silence by selecting memories and histories from diverse sources and persons to chronicle a continuing history of dispossessions. This diversity of narrative sources is equally supported by a heteroglossic style in which a careful selection of archival footage, lyrical cinematographic moments, still photographs, and Native Canadian interviewees combine to create an emotional affect. In staging a young man in the first part and emphasizing a young boy in the exhibition scene in the third (healing) part, the film ensures that a continuing history of discriminatory practices in multicultural Canada is superseded by greater understanding and a determination to heal the wounds of history. This stylistic choice also makes possible a deeper historical and contextual scrutiny of the events. Because the subject is war, where lives and bodies are implicated at an affective level, it is not only the evidentiary status of the events that is significant but how these situations connect with Aboriginal memory and how this memory enacts an imagined Native Canadian community and Canadian nation.

The term "warrior" in the films of Obomsawin, Welsh, and Todd is liberated from its colonialist stereotypical usage and becomes a mobile sign, offering new meanings. As V.N. Volosinov suggests, there is always a struggle over meanings of words and signs, and groups may accentuate a particular word or sign in order to respond, control, or dialectically subvert its officially sanctioned meaning by accenting contradictory alternatives (84). In the bodies of Native "warriors" confronting the state at Oka in *Kanehsatake*, in the bodies of women in their practices of everyday life in *Keepers of the Fire*, and in the bodies of Native combatants serving the Canadian nation in WW II in *Forgotten Warriors*, the viewer apprehends how the word "warrior" functions to respond, contest, and "dialectically subvert" the official stereotypical meanings. As *Kanehsatake*, *Keepers of the Fire*, and *Forgotten Warriors* reveal, there is an epistemic disjuncture between Native Canadian and "national" understandings of the relationship between land and peoples. The economic developmental discourse that frames the nation's approach marginalizes other knowledges. However, as Foucault suggests, subjugated knowledges "allow us to rediscover the ruptural effects of conflict and struggle" that the functionalist national model "is designed to mask" (*Archaeology*, 81). This epistemic disjuncture is equally relevant at the level of style. The adoption of cinematic devices such as the long take and tracking shots do not signify itinerancy and placelessness as much as they facilitate a fusion of place and memory in the Groszean sense that suggests that the body extends beyond itself and its being depends on provisional contacts and relations with surrounding objects (Grosz, 100). Unlike the cinema of empty landscapes, a cinema where the nation is "absent,"—a cinema where even in its infancy, an expeditious editing protocol defines the environment as unwelcoming[11]—the cinematographic and editing strategies of Native filmmakers insist on full exploration of the body's senses and the physical environment.

The films also reveal diverse cinematic styles from which the filmmakers opt for narrative and formal devices that best suit their projects. What appears to be common to them is genre blending and transformation. In this regard, these filmic texts exemplify, to a remarkable degree, Grosz's concept of texts: "A text is not the repository of knowledges or truths, the site for the storage of information ... so much as it is a process of scattering through; scrambling terms, concepts, and practices; forging linkages, becoming a form of action.... Texts, like concepts, do things, make things, perform connections, bring about new alignments ... generate affective and conceptual transformations that problematize, challenge, and move beyond existing intellectual and pragmatic frameworks" (57–58). If for a moment one understands genres as fixed textual bodies with predictable syntax, the films this chapter analyzes reveal how Native Canadian films carnivalize and unmake these generic cinematic grammars to new ends. What might these ends be? By unpacking fixed stereotypical images of the Native in mainstream film and media, by unscrambling the conventional national genres, these films foreground Native Canadian identities, re-situate their contributions to the Canadian polity, and recontextualize received understandings of Canadian national cinema.

Notes

1
Such films include *Northwest Frontier* (dir. James Beveridge, 1942) and *Land of the Long Day* (dir. Douglas Wilkinson, 1952).

2
Zuzana Pick, "Storytelling and Resistance: The Documentary Practice of Alanis Obomsawin," *Gendering the Nation: Canadian Women's Cinema*, ed. Kay Armatage et al. (Toronto: U of Toronto P, 1999), 76–93.

3
The wampum belt is a document, a text that, like every other text, requires reading skills. The presence of the wampum belt is a critique of what qualifies as "document" and is therefore "evidence" in so-called literate cultures. See Edward J. Chamberlin, "Hunting, Tracking and Reading," *Literacy, Narrative and Culture*, ed. Jens Brockmeier, Min Wang, and David, R. Olsan (London: Curzon Press, 2002), for a critique of theories of orality and literacy and the connections between these assumptions and power.

4
6 Roxann Prazniak and Arif Dirlik, eds., *Places and Politics in an Age of Globalization* (Boulder, CO: Rowman and Littlefield, 2001).

5
Part of the success of their struggle led to the enactment of Bill C-31. It is important to stress that this "success" is very partial and that it is pertinent to the documentary only insofar as it illustrates a case of women's intervention as "warriors" in Native Canadian welfare. Bill C-31 has come under scathing attack from the Native community. The former president of the Congress of Aboriginal Peoples calls it the "Abocide Bill." The bill forms the focus of an extended satirical segment in the third chapter ("What Is It about Us That You Don't Like?") of Thomas King's *The Truth about Stories.*

6
Geddes, who was the studio's first producer, offers three reasons: "affinity between film and storytelling," "a more balanced view of historical events," and "an opportunity to enjoy the rewards of ownership and profit accruing from stories and filmmaking practice."

7
To a large extent, the war effort in Canada was helped by the Popular Front, a leftist movement for which members of the NFB at the time had a lot of sympathy. Following Germany's invasion of the Soviet Union, the Popular Front reconfigured "the war against fascism as one in which labour had to fight in order to guarantee future progress, democracy, and peace, and ultimately to achieve socialism. NFB films implicitly echoed how the Popular Front advocated the need to create a wide class alliance to fight against fascism." See Malek Khouri, "Counter-Hegemonic Discourse on the Working Class in the National Film Board World War II Films," 2 January 2005, http://www.ucalgary.ca/hic/hic/website/2001vol1no1/articles/khouri_article_2001.pdf.

8
Adrienne Clarkson, quoted in "He Is Every Soldier in All of Our Wars," *Ottawa Citizen* 29 May 2000: A5.

9
Kirsty Robertson, "'We stand on guard for thee': Protecting the Myths of Nation in 'Canvas of War,'" *Journal of American & Comparative Cultures* (Fall/Winter 2000): 99–108.

10
"Canvas of War" exhibition label, Canadian Museum of Civilization, Hull, QC, 2000.

11
These ideas were rehearsed in the introduction to the chapter. Additionally, see Kay Armatage on Nell Shipman's films in Kay Armatage, *The Girl from God's Country: Nell Shipman and the Silent Cinema* (Toronto: U of Toronto P, 2003), 115.

Works Cited

Anderson, Benedict. *Imagined Communities: Reflections on the Origin and Spread of Nationalism* London: Verso, 1983.

Benjamin, Walter. *Illuminations: Essays and Reflections.* New York: Schocken, 1968.

Dawkins, Marvin P., and Graham C. Kinloch. *African American Golfer during the Jim Crow Era.* New York: Praeger, 2000.

de Rosa, Maria. "Studio One: Of Storytellers and Stories." *North of Everything: English Canadian Cinema since 1980.* Ed. William Beard and Jerry White. Edmonton: U of Alberta P, 2002.

Dirlik, Arif. "Place-Based Imagination: Globalism and the Politics of Place." *Review: A Journal of the Fernand Braudet Center* 22.2 (1999).

Foucault, Michel. *Archaeology of Knowledge.* London: Tavistock, 1972.

—. *Power/Knowledge: Selected Interviews and Writings 1972–1977.* Ed. Colin Gordon. New York: Pantheon, 1980.

—. *Discipline and Punish: The Birth of the Prison.* New York: Vintage, 1995.

Grosz, Elizabeth: *Volatile Bodies: Towards a Corporeal Feminism.* Bloomington: Indiana UP, 1994.

Hardy, Forsyth, ed. *Grierson on Documentary.* London: Faber and Faber, 1966.

Hasain, Asfar. "Joy Harjo and Her Poetics of Praxis." *Wicazo Sa Review* 15.2 (2000).

Macdonald, Sharon J. "Museums, National, Postnational and Transcultural Identities." *Museum and Society* 1.1 (2003): 1–16.

Mackey, Eva. *The House of Difference: Cultural Politics and National Identity in Canada.* London: Routledge, 1999.

Marks, Laura U. *The Skin of the Film: Intercultural Cinema, Embodiment and the Senses.* Durham, NC: Duke UP, 2000.

Marshall, Bill. *Quebec National Cinema.* Montreal: McGill-Queen's UP, 2001. Melnyk, George. *One Hundred Years of Canadian Cinema.* Toronto: U of Toronto P, 2004.

Miller, Mary Jane. "The CBC and Its Presentation of the Native Peoples of Canada in Television Drama." *Screening Culture: Constructing Images and Identity.* Ed. Heather Nicholson. Landham, MD: Lexington Books, 2003.

Mitchell, Michael. "Indian Education Today." *Pot Pourri* (1974).

Pick, Zuzana. "Storytelling and Resistance: The Documentary Practice of Alanis Obomsawin." *North of Everything: English Canadian Cinema since 1980.* Ed. William Beard and Jerry White. Edmonton: U of Alberta P, 2002.

White, Jerry. "Alanis Obomsawin, Documentary Form and the Canadian Nations." *North of Everything: English-Canadian Cinema since 1980.* Ed. William Beard and Jerry White. Edmonton: U of Alberta P, 2002.

Volosinov, V.N. *Marxism and the Philosophy of Language.* New York: Academic Press, 1986.

Eradicating Erasure: The Documentary Film Practice of Sylvia Hamilton
Shana McGuire and
Darrell Varga

An acclaimed African Nova Scotian filmmaker, writer, educator, and activist,
Sylvia Hamilton is dedicated to excavating and exposing the buried history,
experiences, and contributions of Black Canadians. Throughout a career in
film now spanning two decades, Hamilton has written, directed, and/or produced six award-winning documentary films along with an array of commissioned work, earning both critical and popular praise.[1] Her films have been
screened all over North America as well as in Mexico, Jamaica, Paris, Norway,
Sierra Leone, Guadeloupe, and Mauritius. She also co-created, with former
Studio D executive producer Rina Fraticelli, the New Initiatives in Film program for the National Film Board of Canada, which fostered the board's Reel
Diversity Program, substantially assisting Aboriginal filmmakers and filmmakers of colour to gain access to means of film production. Hamilton's contributions to Canadian film have garnered her numerous prestigious awards,
namely the Portia White Prize for Excellence in the Arts, a Gemini Award,
the Japan Broadcasting Corporation's Maeda Prize, the Progress of Women
Excellence Award for Arts and Culture, the CBC Television Pioneer Award, and
the Expression Awards Trailblazer Award, among others. She has also held
the distinguished Nancy's Chair in Women's Studies at Mount Saint Vincent
University, is a visiting professor at King's College both in the School of
Journalism and in the Contemporary Studies Program, holds two honourary
doctorate degrees, and has an impressive list of publications in both scholarly and non-fiction writing. Hamilton identifies herself as much as an educator
as a filmmaker, with the subject of education resonating throughout her body

of work—explicitly so in the trilogy of *Black Mother Black Daughter*, *Speak It! From the Heart of Black Nova Scotia*, and *Little Black Schoolhouse*.

Despite the impressive list of accomplishments and contributions to film culture in Canada, scant critical attention has been paid to Hamilton's work—but then the pattern of scholarship is to follow industry, and this filmmaker's work does not fit the template of box-office-oriented narrative fiction. Unfortunately, the neglect of the African Canadian experience in the historical and cultural narratives of this country is long-standing—and this is precisely the impetus behind Hamilton's documentary film practice. In "Our Mothers Grand and Great: Black Women of Nova Scotia," Hamilton writes: "Very little of what one reads about Nova Scotia would reveal the existence of an Afro-Nova Scotian population that dates back three centuries. Provincial advertising, displays and brochures reflect people of European ancestry: the Scots, the Celts, the French, and the Irish.... There is occasional mention of Nova Scotia's first people [the Mi'kmaq]. Yet Afro-Nova Scotians live in forty-three communities throughout [the] province" (45). Echoing this sentiment, Shingai Nyajeka, the teenage narrator of Hamilton's film *Speak It! From the Heart of Black Nova Scotia* (1992), points out: "There's been a black community in Nova Scotia for over three hundred years, but you wouldn't know it from the history books. You won't find our faces on the postcards. You won't find our statues in the parks. My attitude is you don't have to be from Scotland to have a history." Shingai's sentiment is echoed in Hamilton's short film *Keep on Keepin' On* (2004), in which the director asserts the continuity of Black presence in Nova Scotia in a lyrical expression of place accompanied by a Black bagpiper. Together, these films are a reclaiming of space through the exercise of oral culture and dispossessed history. Absences in the national memory regarding Black history include the disturbing realities of racism and segregation that African Canadian people have had to endure for centuries and that persist today. Many Canadians do not realize—or are not willing to acknowledge—that slavery existed in this country or that segregated schools operated in Canada long after the 1954 US Supreme Court ruling (*Brown v. Board of Education*) that overturned laws establishing separate public schools for Black and white children. In fact, Hamilton tells us in her most recent film, *Little Black School House* (2007), that the last segregated school in Nova Scotia did not close its doors until 1983. How is it possible to expunge an entire people, culture, and way of life from the pages and images of Canadian history? Sylvia Hamilton's documentary films represent an important step in opposing and eradicating this erasure.

In "Four Black Documentary Moments," Leslie Sanders emphasizes the important role that filmmakers have played in addressing the cultural and institutional silence that has surrounded the Black historical narrative: "The virtual silence in Canadian history concerning the presences, contributions and experiences of people of African descent in Canada now finally is beginning to trouble the dominant 'national narrative.' Its ability to do so is greatly assisted by the work of black filmmakers, whose contributions, at least at this point and time, collectively comprise the most sustained discourse on black Canada's history in any genre or medium" (196).[2] Our aim in this chapter is two-fold: first, to highlight the ways in which Sylvia Hamilton's body of work has contributed to this discourse, calling attention to central themes and issues in her films; and, second, to assert that Hamilton's films provide an alternative model for film authorship and challenge the ways in which the concept of "nation" has been traditionally understood. A critical interrogation of the twin concepts of authorship and nationhood revitalizes these tropes for a politically informed art and pedagogy. By engaging in a participatory process of filmmaking—or what Bill Nichols describes as the Interactive mode of documentary (Nichols, 33)—Hamilton occupies both subject and object positions in her films; there is a strong autobiographical element to her work, yet the people we meet and the stories we hear therein are clearly representative of the African Nova Scotian—indeed African Canadian—experience. As an extension of this reciprocal process, she also posits new ways of perceiving and recording history through the acknowledgement of everyday people, places, and events as alternative repositories of memory.

Hamilton's films belong to a well-defined, cohesive project in which she unearths missing pieces of Black history—a history that runs against the grain of the Canadian myth of tolerance and multiculturalism—and exposes the myths and prejudices to which African-descended Canadians have been subjected in this country. More importantly, perhaps, she pays tribute to those who have ensured their survival as a people and celebrates the heroines and heroes who have surmounted enormous social, economic, and institutional obstacles to gain personal and professional success. The films celebrate the vitality of Black experience and participate in the oral culture of these communities while serving as a warning that much progress is yet to be made.

The filmmaker grew up in the community of Beechville, outside of Halifax, and attended a segregated school. Among her filmmaking credits is director of the Ontario production *Hymn to Freedom: Nova Scotia against the Tides* (1994), a straightforward and compelling television documentary on Black immigration to the province, featuring long-time community activist Rocky Jones, who, at age fifty, graduates from Dalhousie law school. Jones is seen as an outspoken radical activist in an early NFB Challenge for Change film *Encounter at Kwacha House-Halifax* (dir. Rex Tasker, 1967), made when he was under surveillance by the RCMP. *Hymn to Freedom* relays how Black institutions provided spiritual, social, and political support to the family and also provides stories of family life and mischievous children, which serve to normalize the family rather than posit Black history as all about suffering. Racism does, however, pervade experience in subtle ways that are just as oppressive as any "white only" sign. On growing up in Truro, Nova Scotia, Rocky Jones says: "I knew that if I stayed, that town would destroy me." The style of the film continues the legacy of oral history to tell stories that would otherwise have remained untold. We also see images of Halifax Harbour, a place better known as a naval base and tourist destination; but in the context of the film it is more important to remember that slave ships travelled to this same harbour—and to understand the social conditions of place and identity as integrated with global patterns of trade and immigration.

Sylvia Hamilton, having long felt a disconnect between what she experienced in her own life and saw in her community in relation to the visual representations propagated by the media and educational systems, seeks to re-appropriate the Black image, especially that of the Black woman, in order to offer an alternative vision of African Canadian realities. Shortly after being awarded Nova Scotia's highest recognition of artistic excellence, the Portia White Prize, Hamilton explained: "I wanted to see images of Black people, and came to understand that if I wanted to see images I had to take them myself. [There were] precious few on television or in the movies.... There is such power in the image. Writ large. I wanted to see Black people writ large" (2004b, 113). She made her first steps toward this goal in 1975 by joining the Reel Life Film and Video Collective, a women's group in Halifax, in a move that brought her into contact with women who would become important local filmmakers: Lulu Keating, Cheryl Lean, and Pat Kipping, among others. Although the collective disbanded after completing only a few projects, several former members reunited in the late 1980s to initiate a process that would soon see women making films with the NFB Atlantic Centre for the first time. The organization was very male-dominated at the time, with the important exception of the late producer Shelagh Mackenzie, who was executive producer of *Black Mother Black Daughter*. Women generally did not, at that time, have access to board resources, nor were they a significant part of NFB production crews. Yet these determined women, Hamilton among them, were persistent in vocalizing their desire to tell their own stories on film, and from a uniquely female perspective. Once the NFB allocated a small amount of money to fund a single project, the group decided to get behind Hamilton's film proposal, recognizing the need to focus on women in the Black community and the issues and obstacles that they faced. This project became Hamilton's first documentary, *Black Mother Black Daughter*—and it was the first film made at the NFB Atlantic Centre to have an all-female production crew, a full decade and a half after the formation of the Board's Studio D.

One of the vital threads connecting Hamilton's films is this focus on the feminine,[3] especially the desire to recognize and pay tribute to the African Nova Scotian women who have played such a crucial role in the survival and growth of their communities and in the preservation of Black cultural history in the province. Three of Hamilton's films specifically portray Black women "writ large": *Black Mother Black Daughter* (1989), *No More Secrets* (1999), and *Portia White: Think on Me* (2000). Each of these films is structured on what Gloria Gibson-Hudson[4] calls a "female-centred narrative":

> The female-centered narrative takes cognizance of women in relation to the convergence of race, sex, and class. This cinematic perspective in turn provides an authentic historical and socio-cultural context to address specific thematic issues such as cultural identity, social invisibility, and economic marginalization. Within this cinematic and aesthetic structure evolves a framework in which individuals or characters exhibit a resilience to oppression and subsequently develop an increased sense of self-determination and an acknowledgement of "woman-self." (1991, 80)

Gibson-Hudson contends that films fitting within this framework "call for Black women to redefine their own image through introspection and cultural activism," and cites *Black Mother Black Daughter* as a key example. She also sees in Hamilton's cinematic cultural expression the manifestation of "an emancipatory aesthetic" (1991, 79) in that it successfully portrays women's resourcefulness and solidarity in the face of racial, sexual, and class oppression.

The project for *Black Mother Black Daughter* began out of a need to redress a blatant omission in the narrative of Canadian history: the absence of stories about Black women's lives. Their experiences, struggles, and victories have ostensibly been unworthy of study, as their presence is nowhere to be found in textbooks or other accounts of our nation's past. Hamilton contends that "we can and need to find different ways to document and preserve women's history in all its richness and diversity" (1995, 167). Undoubtedly one of Hamilton's most personal films, *Black Mother* recounts, in an intimate interview format, the stories of several women in the Black Nova Scotia community who have had an indelible impact on the director's own life, and where the personal has great political efficacy. These stories and experiences serve as lessons to be passed down through future generations of women with the filmmaker as intermediary and participant across generations of lived history.[5] These lessons are a vital part of the tradition of oral storytelling that up until this point had been the primary means of transmitting this history. Hamilton explains: "African people have a long tradition of oral history; stories about their heroes and heroines have therefore gone unrecorded.... The making of cultural heroes and heroines is an act of unification and empowerment. This process, just beginning among Afro-Nova Scotians, is integral to the survival of a people" (1982, 45).

Although Hamilton calls it "a modest, unassuming short film" (2004a, 9), *Black Mother* nevertheless accomplishes a great deal. By inviting these women to share their stories of hardship and resilience, the voices of generations of · Black women are rescued from centuries of institutionally and culturally imposed silence. It renders visible the formerly invisible lives of Black women in a personal, authentic, and creative way. Combining family photos of women through several generations, oral histories from a number of female elders in the Black community, and a haunting soundtrack of powerful female voices, Hamilton creates an atmosphere of solidarity, pride, and purpose. She impresses her own presence directly into the film, implicating her individual, autobiographical investment in the narrative. As we hear the filmmaker's voice-over personally inviting the viewer into the filmic space to meet these ordinary yet extraordinary women, we see a contemplative exterior shot of Hamilton staring wistfully out at the Halifax Harbour. Although there is no counter-shot to show the viewer what she is looking at, one might assume she sees Seaview Park in the distance—the former site of Africville, home to the city's Black community until its demolition by the provincial government in 1967.[6] Later in the film Hamilton takes us to Seaview Park, and this visit, taken together with the aforementioned opening scene, invokes the deep-seated sense of loss—of land and identity—keenly felt by the African Nova Scotia population. As in *Hymn to Freedom*, the harbour here is a place of reflection but also a space that witnessed the flow of transnational capital and its attendant histories of displacement and of slavery.

There are several examples in Hamilton's films of a desire to reclaim this lost sense of identity through the re-appropriation of lost (or stolen) space. Along with *Black Mother Black Daughter*, *The Little Black School House* is especially representative in this sense. Production on this film began after the making of *Speak It!*, with footage of a reunion of retired teachers from Nova Scotia's segregated schools. That footage was unfortunately lost in the 1992 fire that consumed the NFB's Halifax headquarters, and the film took many years to re-emerge (it was finally released in 2007 without funding from the NFB). *Black Schoolhouse* tells the personal stories of the women, men, and children who attended and taught at segregated schools in Nova Scotia and Ontario and begins, as does *Black Mother Black Daughter*, with a personal invitation to enter the space of the film. The image of a school bus barrelling down the road toward the viewer is followed by a pan that reveals a decrepit old building. The camera slowly zooms in to a broken pane of glass, through which we begin to perceive images of Black children and teachers—those who formerly inhabited this space. As this montage of archival footage and photos appears onscreen, we are transported back in time and space by Hamilton's voice-over: "For fifty years, one hundred and fifty years, two hundred years, I've been sitting here, a witness to obstacles, to victories, to the desire to mould the promise of freedom into reality. I'm the Little Black School House. Many stories are buried in these walls ... listen ..." The space is revealed as a unique repository for decades of memories evocative of the experiences and struggles that the Black community has had in gaining equal access to education. Run-down schoolhouses, school buses, plots of scrubland, deserted country roads—Hamilton invests these unassuming spaces and places with special meaning, stirring up powerful emotions in the people she interviews. The school buildings and rough-hewn surrounding terrain also function as an important visual structuring device in the film. Hamilton describes the film's use of space:

> In *Little Black Schoolhouse* it was really important to be in a number
> of locations where people had lived for hundreds of years and actually
> see those spaces, because those spaces were the ones that created
> the situation we are in. The reason we have these small communities
> sprinkled throughout Nova Scotia is not by happenstance or by accident
> at all. They were established because of the way the land was granted
> from the earliest period of colonization and settlement in Nova Scotia.
> For me, embedded in the soil, embedded in the rock and lakes of all of
> these places are these stories of African people.... So the physicality of
> the rock is really important because that's where people were landed
> and they made what they could out of nothing. (Varga 2008)

Geography thus becomes a character in the film, and we learn that the location of schools is a consequence of segregation, since Black settlements are situated on the province's more marginal lands. While school segregation was the product of law, segregation in the larger community was not officially legislated but instead built into the economic system—Black villages would be in close proximity to a white town, separate but close enough for labour exploitation. This spatial relation functions to legitimize the location of white colonial power and the subsequent lack of resources for Black schools; consequently, the antiquated infrastructure of rural areas assists in limiting the aspirations of youth to move beyond this spatial regime. In this film we are provided with a pedagogy of space whereby the process of education is linked with physical territory. As Jennifer Nelson describes in her book *Raising Africville: A Geography of Racism*, the use of space follows the ideological construction of race: "The dispossession of spaces deemed marginal bolsters the development of 'respectable' white space" (Nelson, 22).

The film provides a sweeping history of the country not through the more typical nation-building narratives of industrialization, immigration, and war but through the fact of school segregation where the space of the nation is created through ideological effects such as education policy. Past and present are integrated through interviews with young Black students expressing their aspirations juxtaposed with testimony from older people recalling how their own hopes were diminished. Individual stories of strength and perseverance are set against a social context of systemic discrimination. What the film does is inscribe Black presence in the pages of Canadian history and help articulate the integration of past in the formation of the present. *Black Schoolhouse* is not simply a narrative of progress. First of all, what is described is not ancient history; the experience of segregation in schools continues to affect the lives of those involved, and racism remains a structural fact of life in Nova Scotia, not the least through the physical space of Black communities in the province. This is not to diminish the real gains made through progressive struggle, but the point is that the struggle is ongoing.

We are acutely aware of Hamilton's authorial presence throughout *Black School House* as her voice guides us through the complex narrative, connecting the various threads; at one point she appears briefly onscreen in her role as interviewer, initiating a discussion among a small group of Black community members about their past experiences with educational segregation. Hamilton's brief appearance serves as a subtle reminder that she knows and understands their tales of obstacles that prevented African Nova Scotians from getting an education. The scene also reminds us of Hamilton's authorial voice and the pedagogical and communal process informing her work. During an intimate kitchen scene in *Black Mother Black Daughter*, Hamilton appears with her mother, Dr. Marie Hamilton, as the latter shares her experiences with racial barriers to education. Due to the colour bar that existed in the nursing profession until after WW II, Marie, along with many other Black women, was rejected when she applied to nursing school; she then became a teacher, one of the few careers deemed acceptable for Black women at the time. The presence of the daughter-filmmaker at the table is important here, as it highlights Hamilton's desire for this discussion to be an inclusive, participatory experience—a distinctive characteristic of all her films, and one that encourages a more nuanced conception of film authorship. As she visits various church and community leaders and ordinary women who simply have valuable experiences to share—both tragic and heart-wrenching, touching and inspiring—Hamilton situates herself in a long line of Black women whose desire to share their life lessons, both positive and negative, serves the greater purpose of instilling in present and future generations an understanding and appreciation of the women who got them to where they are today. This communal sharing urges African-descended women to continue a culture of resistance and to oppose discriminatory behaviours and actions that strip them of their dignity.

Another example of Hamilton's communal form of inquiry is a scene in *Black Mother* in which several women, young and old, sit around a large table weaving baskets, talking animatedly, their hands constantly in movement as they discuss the importance of the basket-weaving tradition to their community and of the sense of duty they feel to keep this practice alive.[7] It is in this manner that they, along with the other women in the film who have passed on their stories and lessons, can be understood as unique and necessary repositories of memory for safeguarding African Canadian culture. Oral culture is integrated with the experience of work, with the quotidian rhythms of women's labour. This film also underscores the reciprocity integral to Hamilton's project and is a means of allowing her to engage directly with her community:

> The films, I hope, promote engagement, allow people to see themselves. Over the years ... there have been many theses written about the African Nova Scotian community. Most people I know have never seen them.... They've just been limited to an academic exercise. Over the years it has been people from outside the community who come, do their research, then go away. There is little, if any, reciprocity. With film, I can make something with what people are telling me, and they'll see it. They are the subject and the audience. And others will see it too. The film then becomes a communal act, in that broader public way. (2004b, 116)

In fact, *Black Mother Black Daughter* reached far beyond the Black communities that figure at the centre of the documentary. The audience response to Hamilton's first film was overwhelmingly positive in a number of national and cultural contexts. Over a thousand people attended the opening screening in Halifax and similarly large numbers were present at screenings in Toronto and other cities across the country; the film was screened at more than forty international film festivals. Hamilton reflects on its success: "I have often thought about the varied reasons why this film has been so well received. Perhaps it taps the elusive concept we call the 'universal'; it carries stories that travel past race, gender, class, time and geography" (2004a, 9).

A subject broached by Hamilton that crosses these social and spatial boundaries is that of violence against women. While recording the stories of the women who appeared in *Black Mother Black Daughter*, the filmmaker realized that this part of the narrative needed to be tackled separately and accorded the space and time to be explored fully. Developed, directed, and produced by Hamilton, the two-part documentary *No More Secrets: Part I, The Talking Circle* and *Part II, Understanding Violence against Women* (1999) addresses this insidious problem. Produced for the African United Baptist Association Women's Institute (AUBAWI), *No More Secrets* exposes the myths behind the reasons why many Black women tolerate living in dangerous and abusive relationships. Violence and abuse are of course not issues exclusively within Black communities; they invade families all over the world. Why, then, create a film with this specific focus? "Confronting violence against women in the Black community is prickly and difficult," Hamilton writes. "For a variety of complex reasons, including racism and fear of stigmatization, it has been rarely talked about publicly. It took a group of African Baptist Church women to 'stand up and be counted'" (2004a, 10). These 'Church women' exert a powerful influence in the Black community and have occupied this central position since at least the beginning of the twentieth century. In 1917 the women of the African Baptist churches in Nova Scotia formed a Ladies' Auxiliary, a group that would take responsibility for the "stimulation of the spiritual, moral, social, educational, charitable and financial work of all the local churches of the African Baptist Association" (Hamilton 1999, 3). With little means and a strong will, African Nova Scotian women took it upon themselves to build and sustain better communities. The church, however, had no space in which they could meet; they chose instead to gather around the community well in the village of East Preston and thus became known as the "Women at the Well."[8] Some of these same women, along with others who had joined the cause, organized the inaugural Convention of Coloured Women in Halifax in 1920—the first gathering of its kind in Canadian history.

Women of this lineage continue to this day the legacy of protecting the social, educational, and spiritual life of their community members. It therefore comes as no surprise that the African Baptist Women's Institute spearheaded a research project to investigate the gravity, pervasiveness, and implications of violence perpetrated against Black Nova Scotian women. The results of this investigation were heard loud and clear: Black women in Nova Scotia did not feel they were reflected in any of the existing print or visual material dealing with violence and domestic abuse. Even in this, they were made to feel "other," despite the vast scope of the problem. Hamilton was then commissioned by the ABWI to produce a documentary addressing the issue of violence against Black women so that it could be used as an educational tool in their communities across the province. In the hope of breaking the code of silence surrounding an issue so devastating to the women and families of Nova Scotia's Black population, Hamilton created documentary *No More Secrets*.

The first part of the film, titled *The Talking Circle*, features ten courageous women representing multiple generations of the African Nova Scotian community who have gathered, for the first time, in a safe, private, and supportive environment so that they may openly discuss the abuse that they and other Black women they know have suffered. One of the group members begins by saying that their "survival as a Black community depends on addressing this issue with passion," a declaration that sets the tone for the difficult yet necessary conversations that follow.[9] They address a number of issues at the core of violence against women: the myths that pervade their communities and keep the issue shrouded in silence; their first memories of experiencing abuse and the devastating impact it has on children; and their observations on the continued objectification and abuse of young women by young men in contemporary Black communities. The second instalment of *No More Secrets* transforms the personal into the political. Several prominent members of the Afro–Nova Scotian community take the discussion into a wider sphere by making a public call for action and transformation.[10] They discuss the essential role that the church must play in addressing and solving these problems, and they come up with productive strategies that highlight the ways that women, men, the church can come together to combat violence against women.

The testimonies and conversations in both parts of *No More Secrets* often have a didactic tone and intent, but it is not in the same propagandistic, exploitative vein as the "victim tradition" outlined by Brian Winston, which he sees as characteristic of much social documentary work. In his essay "The Tradition of the Victim in Griersonian Documentary" (246), Winston notes that socially conscious films and filmmakers tend to focus on oppressed groups as victims, demarcating the strict separation between the privileged gaze of the filmmaker and the marginal subject or "other." He criticizes documentary studies for their neglect of the ethical issues surrounding the power imbalance between filmmaker and subject, insisting that filmmakers are co-participants, along with their subjects, in the power dynamic involved in documentary filmmaking. The relationship between filmmaker and subject is one of central importance to Hamilton, and she is clearly cognizant of the need for moral accountability in the making of documentary films:

> Documentary filmmaking holds within it this special responsibility of dealing with "truths." Since such films feature actual people and their stories, one has to take special care in how the story will be told.... Films have long lives and their impact is much different than other media. Choosing who will be in a film and then carrying out the interview and the process of editing are two of the major areas where a filmmaker feels the enormous weight of responsibility.... You strive for honesty, fairness and integrity. (Hamilton 1995, 166)

In *No More Secrets* Hamilton creates a space in which Black women participate in their own transformation into active agents of social and political change. Although the women who take part in the talking circle have suffered from various forms of physical and emotional abuse, Hamilton does not ask the viewer to pity them; instead, she encourages us to see their speaking out as an act of courage with socio-political implications. As we see in their dignified faces and hear in their determined voices, these women do not classify themselves as perpetual victims condemned to a life of subordination and degradation. On the contrary, due to their unwavering belief in the power of family, church, and community (a theme prevalent also in *Black Mother Black Daughter*), they have hope that through cooperation—among women *and* men—profound change is possible. The key issue underlying *No More Secrets* is the necessity for women to break free from the socially and culturally imposed silencing of their voices, a problem that has haunted feminist debates for decades as well as the art of cinema from its very beginnings.

One particular woman's voice that Hamilton felt a strong desire to resurrect from its historical and cultural grave was that of the gifted African Canadian contralto Portia White. Born in Truro, Nova Scotia, in 1911, the third of thirteen children, White dared to dream big—and immense international success followed. In the film *Portia White: Think on Me* (2000), which Hamilton wrote, directed, and produced,[11] the spectator is taken on a lyrical journey through the life of this singular artist who faced incredible odds in achieving her ambition of becoming an opera singer during the tumultuous decades of the 1940s and '50s. White had accomplished the unthinkable: a young Black woman from a small Maritime town, motivated by nothing other than childhood dreams and an insatiable creative drive, overcame many discriminatory obstacles to become one of the most celebrated and internationally prominent classical singers in Canadian history. Despite that White won renown over half a century ago, Hamilton's cinematic tribute is the first major work about the singer's groundbreaking life and career. As is the case for the lives of many Black women, both ordinary and extraordinary, Portia White occupied no space in the Canadian cultural memory.[12]

Portia White: Think on Me is the product of a decade-long research project during which Hamilton retraced the footsteps of the woman who had haunted her own cultural memory since she was a child. "I grew up with the myth of Portia. My uncle had a crush on her," she reveals in an opening scene as she sits at a table sifting through the piles of news clippings, photos, concert programs, and memorabilia she had managed to unearth. Once again making her authorial presence felt from the beginning, Hamilton moulds these traces of White's past into a remarkably cohesive vision of a life that had heretofore gone undocumented, unheard, and unseen by the vast majority of Canadians. "I felt I was on a rescue mission," asserts Hamilton, "an effort to restore her memory, her presence, her image and her voice" (2007, 220). Hamilton effectively rescued several of White's performance recordings, a CBC television interview, radio interviews, rare archival footage of concerts, family photos, and the personal scrapbooks White filled during her tours around the world. The most significant portion of the narrative is the numerous interviews with the many people whose lives Portia White touched: her surviving siblings and other family members, her former accompanist, musicians with whom she had worked over the years, people who had seen her in concert as a child, and former pupils (White spent years as a music teacher after her public singing career ended). Often referred to as "Canada's own Marian Anderson," White was known for her resiliency of spirit, fierce independence, a regal stage presence, and, above all, a voice that lingered long in the memories of her listeners, students, and colleagues, as the many touching interviews in the film demonstrate. Hamilton uses that voice as the "spine of the film," as she puts it, and lures the spectator into the narrative by sharing these words uttered by the singer during a radio interview: "Nobody ever told me to sing. I was born singing. I think that if nobody had ever talked to me, I wouldn't be able to communicate in any other way but by singing. I was always bowing in my dreams and singing before people and parading across the stage as a little girl."

The film demonstrates how both the expressive power of the voice and the international language of music allowed White to cross racial and geographical boundaries. Her performances became a means of rising above the scorn of racism and discrimination. A discernable tension is evident in the film's narrative, however—a push–pull struggle between an emancipatory tale on one hand and the weight of North American racism and prejudice on the other. While White was being trained by prestigious European musical directors, travelling the globe, appearing onstage in regal attire before prestigious and discerning audiences, she was not allowed to eat at what was then the Nova Scotia Hotel or at other dining establishments in the city of Halifax. While her physical presence in and relation to ordinary places was strictly regulated by a racist society's rules, the seemingly confined space of the stage provided White an opening onto the world that the vast majority of African Canadians would never experience. Racism, in guises both subtle and overt, is a contemptible fact of Canadian life, both past and present. By clearly situating Portia White's story within the cultural and social climate of the 1940s and '50s, Hamilton gives an intimate view of the ways in which race defines and limits an individual's existence.

In her perceptive personal essay "Searching for Portia White," Hamilton reiterates the need to revisit and recast historically stereotypical and derogatory representations of Black women and to reclaim their rightful place in the narratives that define the Canadian nation-state. Her persistent interrogation of "the erasure of events, organizations, communities, and people such as Portia White from narratives about Canadian history and society" (264) is informed by a sense of responsibility and an almost urgent need to create a visual space in which to express both the complex and quotidian aspects of life as an African Canadian—a need for images that come "from 'inside' the experience." Highlighting once again her profound respect for the relationship between film-maker and subject, Hamilton explains: "I work against 'problematizing' the people I work with. They are not to be stripped of their humanity and reduced to sociological constructs. Rather, I strive to see people as 'whole'—I try to find the beauty in the experiences, and in the people, as an antidote perhaps to the ugli-ness of some of the experiences that come with the negotiation of daily survival" (2007, 217). This approach is indicative of an approach to authorship that is com-munal and pedagogical, through which the space of the nation can be dialecti-cally reconfigured. By prioritizing personal, human experience in her creation of an African Canadian counter-history, Hamilton transforms her subjects into alter-native repositories of cultural memory. Generations of Black mothers and daugh-ters, the courageous women who share their stories of abuse, the trail-blazing Portia White—as well as, we assert, Sylvia Hamilton herself—all become what French historian Pierre Nora terms *lieux de mémoire*, or sites of memory. Memory in this sense is not simply of the past but is a lived experience in the present that in turn migrates between past, present, and future. In her discussion of her search for Portia, Hamilton borrows the concept of *lieux de mémoire* to provide a culturally and historically relevant context for the reception of the work. For example, many members of the African Nova Scotian community had heard of Portia White, but a clear picture of her life and contributions simply did not exist. "Who is responsible for remembering," Hamilton asks, "when the memory keep-ers are gone?" (2009, 268). Nora asserts that we have not attributed enough cultural relevance to memory, that history has become the universal authority. What does this mean, then, for populations and communities that have not been part of a nation's official historical record? Do the stories about real people and the lived experiences of African Canadians as passed down through generations carry no "official" cultural or historical currency? Nora explains the split that has opened between memory and history through which we can begin to grasp how sites of memory may inhabit the spaces between:

> Memory is life, borne by living societies founded in its name. It remains in permanent evolution, open to the dialectic of remembering and forget-ting, unconscious of its successive deformations, vulnerable to manipula-tion and appropriation, susceptible to being long dormant and periodi-cally revived. History, on the other hand, is the reconstruction, always

problematic and incomplete, of what is no longer. Memory is a perceptu-
ally actual phenomenon, a bond tying us to the eternal present; history
is a representation of the past.... Memory is blind to all but the group it
binds—which is to say ... that there are as many memories as there are
groups, that memory is by nature multiple and yet specific; collective, plural and yet individual. History ... belongs to everyone and no one, whence
its claim to universal authority. Memory takes root in the concrete, in
spaces, gestures, images, and objects; history binds itself strictly to
temporal continuities, to progressions and to relations between things.
Memory is absolute while history can only conceive the relative. (285–86)

By privileging those oral histories that are of importance to Black communities, stories that are vital and affirmative but also about struggle and vulnerabil-
ity and that are absent from the mainstream discourse, Hamilton makes a decisive
move toward lessening the gap about which Nora speaks—toward eradicating the
erasure of Black Canadian stories and histories. She effectively exposes the defi-
ciencies in the Canadian conception of who and what make up the nation by highlighting previously untold stories, unheard voices, and unseen faces in her films—
the people, places, and events that the Black community had already long understood as part of their official history, as their collective sites of memory.

Hamilton's films exemplify the *mise en scène* of memory—or rather
of a counter-memory—as an alternative form of recording and comprehending
history, and place African Nova Scotian women squarely at the centre of this
endeavour. Although the following words are spoken by Hamilton at the end of
Portia White: Think on Me, they can also be understood as a tribute to the many
women in her films who have touched the lives of those in their communities and
who leave a legacy of resistance for future generations of African Nova Scotians:
"I marvel at all her accomplishments in the face of the barriers that would break
even the bravest of souls. Her life showed me the dream is worth dreaming."

Notes

1
Speak It! and *Black Mother Black Daughter* are available through http://www.nfb.ca. For inquiries on all other films, contact maroonfilms@ns.sympatico.ca.

2
Sanders's essay appears in *Multiple Lenses: Voices from the Diaspora Located in Canada*, David Devine, ed. This valuable contribution to the literature on African Canadian history is the result of a three-day conference held at Dalhousie University, Halifax, Nova Scotia, in October 2005. Over 428 delegates—from disciplines as varied as law, history, film, literature, music, sports, education, and from community organizations—gathered to explore "what it means to be black and Canadian" (foreword, x).

3
Hamilton has done extensive research into the experience of Black women in Nova Scotia. See also "Naming Names, Naming Ourselves: A Survey of Early

Black Women in Nova Scotia," in Peggy Bristow, Dionne Brand, Linda Carty, Afua P. Cooper, Sylvia Hamilton, and Adrienne Shadd, eds.,"*We're Rooted Here and They Can't Pull Us Up": Essays in African Canadian Women's History* (Toronto: U of Toronto P, 1994), 13–40; and *African Baptist Women as Activists and Advocates in Adult Education in Nova Scotia*, Hamilton's master's thesis, Dalhousie University, Halifax, 2000.

4
Gibson-Hudson, assistant director of the Black Film Center/ Archive at Indiana University, has lectured and written extensively on the images of Black women in film. See in particular "Aspects of Black Feminist Cultural Ideology in Films by Black Women Independent Filmmakers," *Multiple Voices in Feminist Film Criticism*, Diane Carson, Linda Dittman, and Janice R. Welch, eds. (Minneapolis: U of Minnesota P, 1999), 365–79; and "The Ties That Bind: Cinematic Representations by Black Women Filmmakers," *Quarterly Review of Film and Video* 15.2 (1994): 25–44.

5
Sylvia Hamilton, her mother, Marie, and her daughter, Shani, all appear in the film.

6
See also Jennifer J. Nelson, *Razing Africville: A Geography of Racism* (Toronto: U of Toronto P, 2008); and Sheilagh Mackenzie's film *Remember Africville* (1991).

7
Edith Clayton, the last of the Black basket-weavers in Nova Scotia, is descended from the Black Refugees, a group of about two thousand former slaves. Hamilton elaborates:

"Basket-maker Edith Clayton learned her craft from her mother, who in turn learned it from her mother. Edith passed on this family and community legacy by teaching her daughters how to collect the maple wood and to weave baskets. The Black Refugees of the War of 1812 carried this unique tradition, along with the African Baptist faith, to Nova Scotia; they are the ancestors of Edith Clayton, the Hamilton family and of many others in African Nova Scotian communities." Across Cultures, http://www.nfb.ca/ acrosscultures.

8
"Women at the Well" is also the title of a Studio D series "by and about black women," created by former executive producer Rina Fraticelli. The three films in the series are Claire Prieto's *Older Stronger Wiser* (1989), *Sisters in the Struggle* (dir. Dionne Brand and Ginny Stikeman, 1991), and another Dionne Brand project, *Long Time Comin'* (1993).

9
The concept of the talking circle is borrowed from an Aboriginal sacred ceremony. Although the gathering in the film does not adhere strictly to all of the special protocols attached to the Aboriginal ritual, the members of this circle pass around a symbolic object that is to be held by the person speaking; other important elements include the idea of mutual respect and the practice of prayer. See Hamilton 1999, 11.

10
These include Doreen Paris, president of the AUBAWI; Dr. Wanda Thomas Bernard, professor of social work; Rose Fraser,

public health nurse; Rev. Tracey Grosse, Dr. Lionel Moriah, and Brian Johnston, three leaders in the African United Baptist Association; and two women who speak publicly about their personal experiences with abuse.

11
The film won the Craft Award for Sound Design at the 20th Atlantic Film Festival.

12
Official recognition of White's important role in Canadian history did not arrive until the late 1990s, though some significant gestures were eventually made in this vein, as Hamilton points out. In 1997, the Historic Sites and Monuments Board of Canada designated White as a person of historical significance. Canada Post included White in their Millennium Collection series of postage stamps; and in 1998 the Nova Scotia government created the Portia White Prize to honour her artistic accomplishments. See Hamilton's essay "Searching for Portia White," which deals both with her subject and her work process, weaving together themes of history and memory along with the personal and the political, in Darrell Varga, ed., *Rain/ Drizzle/Fog: Film and Television in Atlantic Canada*, 259–87.

Works Cited

Devine, David, ed. *Multiple Lenses: Voices from the Diaspora Located in Canada.* Newcastle: Cambridge Scholars Publishing, 2007.

Gibson-Hudson, Gloria. "Aspects of Black Feminist Cultural Ideology in Films by Black Women Independent Filmmakers." *Multiple Voices in Feminist Film Criticism.* Ed. Diane Carson, Linda Dittman, and Janice R. Welch. Minneapolis: U of Minnesota P, 1999. 365–79.

—. "Through Women's Eyes: The Films of Women in Africa and the African Diaspora." *Western Journal of Black Studies* 15.2 (1991): 79–86.

—. "The Ties That Bind: Cinematic Representations by Black Women Filmmakers." *Quarterly Review of Film and Video* 15.2 (1994): 25–44.

Hamilton, Sylvia. "A Daughter's Journey." *Canadian Woman Studies/Les cahiers de la femme* 23.2 (Winter 2004a): 6–12.

—. *African Baptist Women as Activists and Advocates in Adult Education in Nova Scotia.* Master's thesis, Dalhousie University, 2000.

—. "Film as a Medium to Reflect Research about Women's Lives." *Atlantis* 21.1 (1995): 163–67.

—. "Memory Writ Large: Film and Inquiry." Sylvia Hamilton interviewed by Lorri Neilsen. *Provoked by Art: Theorizing Arts-informed Research.* Ed. Ardra L. Cole, Lori Neilsen, J. Gary Knowles, and Teresa C. Luciani. Halifax: Backalong Books and Centre for Arts-informed Research, 2004b. 112–19.

—. "Naming Names, Naming Ourselves: A Survey of Early Black Women in Nova Scotia." *"We're Rooted Here and They Can't Pull Us Up": Essays in African Canadian Women's History.* Ed. Peggy Bristow, Dionne Brand, Linda Carty, Afua P. Cooper, Sylvia Hamilton, and Adrienne Shadd. Toronto: U of Toronto P, 1994. 13–40.

—. *No More Secrets: A Workshop Guide.* Maroon Films Inc. and the African United Baptist Association of Nova Scotia, 1999.

—. "Our Mothers Grand and Great: Black Women of Nova Scotia." *Canadian Woman Studies/Les cahiers de la femme* 4.2 (1982): 45–48.

—. "Searching for Portia White." *Rain/Drizzle/Fog: Film and Television in Atlantic Canada.* Ed. Darrell Varga. Calgary: U of Calgary P, 2009. 259–87.

—. "Visualizing History and Memory in the African Nova Scotian Community."

Multiple Lenses: Voices from the Diaspora Located in Canada. Ed. David Divine. Newcastle: Cambridge Scholars Publishing, 2007. 214–21.

Nelson, Jennifer J. *Razing Africville: A Geography of Racism.* Toronto: U of Toronto P, 2008.

Nichols, Bill. *Representing Reality.* Bloomington: Indiana UP, 1991.

Nora, Pierre. "Between Memory and History: Les Lieux de Mémoire." *History and Memory in African-American Culture.* Ed. Geneviève Fabre and Robert O'Meally. New York: Oxford UP, 1994. 284–300.

Sanders, Leslie. "Four Black Documentary Moments." *Multiple Lenses: Voices from the Diaspora located in Canada.* Ed. David Devine. Newcastle: Cambridge Scholars Publishing, 2007. 196–203.

Varga, Darrell. Personal interview with Sylvia Hamilton, Halifax, Nova Scotia, March 2008.

—. ed. *Rain/Drizzle/Fog: Film and Television in Atlantic Canada.* Calgary: U of Calgary P, 2009.

Winston, Brian. "The Tradition of the Victim in Griersonian Documentary." *New Challenges for Documentary.* Ed. Alan Rosenthal. Berkeley: U of California P, 1988: 269–87.

Women, Liminality, and "Unhomeliness" in the Films of Mina Shum
Brenda Austin-Smith

Mina Shum prefers to be known as an independent filmmaker rather than a Canadian one, seeing this label as one way to get people to see her films "without prejudice."[1] What she seems reluctant to do is to signal belonging in a way that creates a sense of obligation, whether her own (to somehow brandish her national status in her films) or her audience's (to fulfill their civic duty by watching them). Nevertheless, her resistance to having her work classified as what Christopher Gittings calls "the national product" engages with redefinitions of the relationship between film and nationality.[2] Kass Banning points out in an essay in which she considers Shum's work that "minoritarian" films "perform a corresponding mutuality with the state.... Canada requires them for self-definition." [3] As Ella Shohat puts it, "all films are in a sense national," for they all "project national imaginaries."[4]

In Shum's case, that imaginary is indirectly articulated through her depiction of ironic, discontented young women who want to leave wherever they are for somewhere or something else. For these women, home in particular is a site of conflict, boredom, and disappointment, a place that makes material the familial, societal, and sexual pressure to accommodate themselves to the demands and expectations of others. The desires of these characters for something other than what is "home" link these films to the "unhomeliness" Homi Bhabha describes as a "paradigmatic . . . post-colonial condition," and marks them with traces of Hamid Naficy's independent transnational film genre.[5] Eva Rueschmann writes, "The question of home and belonging has historically been a vexed one for Asian Americans and is doubly so for immigrant women who have had to negotiate their relationship to different cultural definitions of female roles and the gendered meanings of home."[6] Rueschmann herself discusses *Double Happiness* in this context, and the observation is usefully extended to all three of Shum's feature films.

Mina Shum was born in Hong Kong in 1966 and came to Canada with her family before her first birthday. The Shums left Maoist China and settled in Vancouver as part of the first wave of predominantly working-class Chinese immigrants that Jacqueline Levitin thoroughly historicizes in her recent essay on Shum's work.[7] Even in her early school years, Mina was interested in acting and theatre, and pursued these interests in the face of her parents' disapproval, an experience that informed her first and most lauded feature, *Double Happiness* (1994). Mina attended the University of British Columbia, where she earned a B.A. and then received a Diploma in Film and Television Studies. She followed this with a stint in the director's program at the Canadian Film Centre, in Toronto.

Shum released her first successful film, a short documentary called *Me, Mom & Mona*, in 1993. It is an overture of sorts for her first feature, introducing the themes and character types that would appear in fictionalized form in *Double Happiness* the next year. As *Me, Mom & Mona* begins, we see what looks like a talk-show set, with three women sitting at a table, drinking mugs of coffee, and sharing details of their lives and relationships. The presentational format reminiscent of television works in comic-ironic contrast to the topics the women proceed to discuss for the next twenty minutes, which are the complexities of their familial histories and connections, and each woman's sometimes strained relations with the patriarch of the family, "Dad." Shum uses this setting, associated with very public celebrity chit-chat, to air the private tensions of her family with both amusing and serious results.

As the structuring absence of the film, the elder Mr. Shum is a figure of anxiety, affection, and fun. "You're totally worried about telling Dad," says Mina at one point to her sister, referring obliquely to Mona's live-in relationship with her boyfriend, Nelson. The comment initiates a discussion of how family members cope with the clash between their ambitions, desires, and actions and their father's attitudes toward those same things. Mr. Shum's views of family life are inflected by his desire to head a family shaped by Confucian traditions and his expectations of women. He expects his children to remain loyal to the family—to abide by his wishes, in other words—and to choose partners and careers in keeping with that loyalty. What emerges in the back-and-forth conversation that follows is that each woman in the Shum family has made concessions to the father's views of just how the family should run. At the same time, they use a combination of secrecy, diplomacy, and their father's own pride—which makes him loath to admit any suspicion that he is being fooled—as strategies to get what they want.

Interleaved with the often raucous talk between Mina, her sister, and her mother are cutaway shots, many from old films that illustrate Mina's voice-overs. In these sequences she recounts the childhood of her mother, So Yee, or describes her own childhood fascination with Lawrence Welk as the perfect father: "soft-spoken, stern, and asexual." On a more oblique note, a recurring shot shows a woman's hands wringing water from a piece of clothing into a basin. It is an image of forbearance, and it suggests as well the timeless and unchanging nature of woman's work. The shot gains resonance as this short film moves from the humorous contemplation of how children and wives manoeuvre around the obstacle of a patriarch, to a more serious recounting of So Yee Shum's childhood before she married and moved to Canada from China. As a young girl So Yee was beaten for her defiance of her grandmother, and was a witness to domestic violence in the home she shared with her father, mother, and a mistress who ordered her around. She recalls never having seen herself in a mirror until she was six years old, and even then was unsure of how to regard her own reflection: "I don't know if I was pretty or not." Now, as an adult, she is a buffer between her husband and their children, saying at one point to Mina, "If I didn't lie to him, I think your relationship with your father would be very bad."

Speaking sometimes in English and sometimes in Mandarin, So Yee looks directly into the camera, comparing her life to that of her two daughters. "They have to be independent, not like their mother," she says. After this emotional climax, the film returns to a closing focus on the physically absent, but psychically ever-present father, whose influence seems at this point no real match for the combined determination of the three women onscreen. Mina, Mona, and their mother are smiling as the film ends, even though their closing declarations—"We've accepted him, and love him" and "It doesn't mean we won't get our way"—predict anything but an easy future together as a family.

Mina Shum is not a perfect example of Naficy's transnational filmmaker, having spent virtually her entire childhood in Canada. While he acknowledges that "it is not necessary to leave home to enter the spaces of liminality and transnationality," and that "not only filmmakers but people all over the world are always already transnational," Naficy does say that "those filmmakers who journey beyond their homelands constitute more fully the type of exilic transnationals whom I have in mind."[8] Still, Shum's work expresses an ambivalence toward both her ethnically Chinese family traditions and expectations and to aspects of her ethnically Canadian life in a post-colonial, officially multicultural country in a fashion congruent with Naficy's notion of a transnational genre. This is most true of *Double Happiness*, a film that exhibits "self-narrativization with specific generic and thematic conventions," and which is also a product "of the particular transnational location" of the filmmaker "in time and place and in social life and cultural difference."[9] Jade Li, the protagonist of *Double Happiness* who channels the experiences of both Shum and the actress Sandra Oh, thus stands as a cinematic figure of the "liminar."[10] Writing about the "slip-zone of fusion and admixture" inhabited by the transnational subject, Naficy describes these subjects as "deterritorialized," but still "in the grips of both the old and the new, the before and the after. Located in such a zone, they become interstitial creatures, lininars suffused with hybrid excess."[11]

The release of *Double Happiness* in 1994 confirmed that Shum had not exhausted the material of *Me, Mom & Mona*. In this first feature, though, the semi-autobiographical details of a young woman who craves independence from the stifling expectations of her strict family take the shape of a *Künstler* film—a story of the development of an artist. The film's "ethnic plot" is entwined with what Levitin identifies as the "gender plot" of love and conflict between a daughter and a father.[12]

Jade, the Canadian-born eldest daughter of the Li family, chafes against the rules and requirements of her immigrant Chinese parents, especially those of her father. Jade wants to be an actress and to lead her own life, unrestrained by the traditional patriarchal attitudes embodied in her father's banishment of Jade's brother from the family and in the deferential behaviour of Jade's mother toward Mr. Li. Jade struggles to please her family and to become independent— to achieve the "double happiness" of the film's title, a reference to the Chinese character for unity and marriage.[13] While dutifully dating the young Chinese men her parents regard as suitable mate material, Jade rehearses scenes from plays in her bedroom, tries out for film roles, and begins a relationship with a non-Chinese boy named Mark. Complications multiply during a visit from her paternal uncle, Ah Hong, a sympathetic figure who shares his own family secrets with Jade and in so doing fortifies her for a confrontation with her father. The rupture occurs over an elaborate dinner, and Jade announces tearfully that she is leaving home. As she packs her things to go and passes her father on her way down the side stairs, he demands that she surrender her house key, a symbolic turning in of her family identity and belonging. In the final shots of the film, Jade is in the disarray of a new beginning in her own apartment, pinning up colourful curtains printed with a cartoon image of Marilyn Monroe.

What could have been an overly earnest and predictable drama of intergenerational misunderstanding with a sentimental ethnic flavour is instead thoroughly animated and refreshed by the filmmaker's ironic yet affectionate approach to Jade and her family. Kass Banning refers to the "playful formalism" that characterizes the film, and cites touches such as its strong colour sense and bold camera moves.[14] Banning, Levitin, and Gittings all comment, for example, on the disruptive and energizing effect of a dinner sequence shot from the vantage of a Lazy Susan in the middle of the Li's dining table.[15] As the Lis gossip about neighbours and then discuss the subject of Jade's marriageability, our perspective swivels back and forth as family members serve themselves, as if the camera itself were a source of sustenance.

The camera certainly seems to sustain Jade, who seeks it out both as character and as aspiring actor within the diegesis. The camera provides her with a means of self-expression and of validation, as over the course of the film she fashions a self she can live with and through. The self-narrativization begins in the first shot of the film, in which Jade holds a clapper designating her own scene. "I want to tell you about my family," she says. "They are very Chinese, if you know what I mean. But for the moment, just forget they are a Chinese family. Just think of them as any old family, any old, you know, white family." The phrase "If you know what I mean" signals the multiple audiences Jade has in mind, including those whose knowledge arises from similar experiences of family membership and those whose "knowledge" is, perhaps, rooted in stereotypes. This direct address functions as a way of allying viewers, whether "insiders" or "outsiders," with Jade's perspective, which is itself both inside and outside, detached and implicated.

In a sense, the camera *does* feed this family, supplying each member of it with an opportunity to speak to it, in moments of direct address that flesh out their histories and inner lives for the viewer. As Jade's sister, mother, and father each take their place alone in the frame, there is a pause in the flow of the plot that allows these characters a few moments of unguarded self-representation before he or she is incorporated once again into the forward momentum of the film. Jade's father, Quo, takes his place at the centre of the camera's gaze for his soliloquy, as befits a character who demands attention and to whom all the other characters must adjust. Standing with his hoe in his hand, he recalls the figure in Grant Wood's painting *American Gothic*, as Eleanor Ty points out.[16] He seems an ironic version of Jade's desire to have a more Americanized family, though Puritanism rather than the Brady Bunch is the nightmare outcome of her wish. Looking sternly at the camera, Mr. Li describes the life he lived in China before the Revolution—an ordered, privileged existence he is nostalgic for. The other two characters, Pearl and Jade's mother, each appear at the left-hand side of the frame for their non-diegetic speeches. Pearl recalls the presents she used to get from her now-disowned brother, Winston. Mrs. Li's story is the most poignant of the three, as she recalls her own life in China, connecting memories of a woman traumatized after the murder of her baby girl to her current fear of losing contact with another of her children. She is thinking of Winston, whom the family never refers to in the presence of the father, but is also dreading the possibility that Jade too will leave home and become a ghost to the family.

Performance, whether before family members or cameras, is central to Jade's life and indeed to the doubleness of her life, for she attempts to pacify her parents and to fulfill her own ambitions through acting. Eva Rueschmann argues that acting is the film's "central metaphor ... for the negotiation of [the] cultural spaces" of Jade's hyphenated identity, "the interstitial meaning of being both Chinese and Canadian."[17] In a similar vein, Ty sees performance—in Judith Butler's sense of a "forced reiteration of norms"—as the core of the film's questioning of ethnic and cultural essences. "Many of the characters in the movie lead 'double' lives," she writes, "acting parts and changing identities, thereby critiquing both Euro-American and Chinese cultures and ideologies in the process."[18] We see Jade acting like a meek and dutiful daughter when she is at home, and like a feisty, sassy young woman when she is not. In her first interactions with Mark, as they both stand outside the No-No! club, she dips her head shyly and doesn't answer when Mark first speaks to her, as if indulging in the sort of stereotypes described by critics Marilyn C. Alquizola and Lane Ryo Hirabayashi, before morphing into a sexually assertive woman confident enough to sleep over with a man she has just met.[19] Her costume changes highlight these shifting roles: in auditions and when she is out with Mark, Jade wears tailored suits or funky short dresses, tights, boots, and a denim jacket. At home she usually wears high-necked tops and muddy-coloured cardigans. We see her change in the car from a nightclubbing outfit to "family wear" during her desperate attempt to get home from Mark's apartment before her parents learn she has been out all night.

Jade is most obviously and uncomfortably acting when she goes out on dates set up by her parents. For these events she dresses in shapeless shifts, with her hair done up by her mother in the formal style of Connie Chung. The dates are auditions for a part Jade does not want, and they contrast both comically and seriously with the dramatic roles she dreams of. Twice we see Jade in the privacy of her bedroom, once reciting lines from Williams's *A Streetcar Named Desire* and another time from Shaw's *Saint Joan*. The frame itself is caught up in the intensity of her concentration and fantasy, transformed by lighting and special effects into Blanche DuBois' boudoir and Joan of Arc's burning stake. Though the scenes poke fun at Jade's pretentiousness and youthful self-dramatization, there is something about the two parts she rehearses that comment on Jade's situation. Blanche is ultra-feminine, dreamy, and dependent "on the kindness of strangers," while Joan is a gender-rebel, a leader whose faith and will brook no obstacles. Both, though, are ultimately sacrificial figures. Jade confides early on in the film that what she really wants is to win an Academy Award, and not just for any role but for "something really hard and real."

The arrival of the second family-sanctioned Chinese date has interrupted one of Jade's upstairs rehearsals. The grim, resigned look on her face as she prepares to leave drains the residue of humour left over from the earlier date with the closeted Andrew, even as her family is filmed in slow motion gathering yet again at the window to watch her drive off with a faceless man in an expensive car. This time, though, as if inspired by her late-night talk with her uncle, Ah Hong, who confessed that the weight of his secret life sometimes makes him feel as if he is about to disappear, Jade makes her date stop the car, and we see her get out. As she strides along the sidewalk, music swelling along with her emotions, she finally breaks into a run, gaining momentum that does not stop until she has left her family. Though she is shot running with arms outstretched, Jade is not running home but rather *beyond* home, reaching for an "unhomely" life, an effort both hard and real.

Bhabha writes of the "unhomeliness" of "extra-territorial and cross-cultural initiation," referring also to the "recesses of the domestic space" that become "sites for history's most intricate invasions."[20] Citing the domestic as a place of disorientation in this way summons in turn Naficy's description of the "phobic spaces" typical of the independent transnational genre.[21] The claustro-phobic spaces he associates with transnational films are evident here too, as they are also in *Drive, She Said* and *Long Life, Happiness, and Prosperity*, though they take the form of domestic spaces rather than the carceral spaces Naficy focuses on. Very few outdoors scenes in *Double Happiness* take place in a setting that is in any way expansive, and the interior shots tend to reinforce the restriction, and not just the intimacy, of Jade's family life. In the climactic dinner scene, for example, Jade's body is not fully contained in the crowded frame for the first few seconds. Her face is not visible at first, much as it wasn't visible in the film she watched on television with her mother and sister, in which she had a role as a waitress. She is outgrowing the confines of her family and at the same time being pushed away by her father's authoritarianism. But the shelter Jade finds at the film's conclusion is not utopic, no more so than her family life is completely dystopic, which again aligns her with figures of transnationality, whose relations with the spaces of both homeland and host country are charged with ambivalence.

Shum's second feature, *Drive, She Said*, was released in 1997. Though Shum had planned to use Sandra Oh once again in the lead role, the actress was unable to participate in the project, and Moira Kelly was cast in the role of Nadine Ship. Levitin writes of this film that without Oh to give the plot an "eth-nic nuance," the conventional storyline attracted no positive interest from either viewers or critics. "Perhaps everyone in the audience was surprised that Mina Shum had produced a 'non-Chinese' film."[22] On the other hand, Steve Gravestock describes the film as "underrated," and discusses it as one of several Canadian romantic comedies that in their own "cautious and forlorn" way, subvert the conventions of the genre.[23] In Canadian takes on this quintessentially American genre, Gravestock especially notes the way in which the Canadian version "leaves its participants alone and somehow fulfilled," rather than happily coupled at the end of the reel.[24]

In the first shot of *Drive* we hear a voice, talking over a slow-motion shot of two girls jumping on a trampoline in a yard separated from the camera by a white picket fence. The voice belongs to Nadine Ship, who works as a bank teller in First City. Nadine's voice sounds languorous, as she recalls her mother telling her that if she "kept walking straight enough, long enough, and hard enough," she would eventually reach China. Nadine would walk around her neighbourhood, stopping to make friends in pretend countries along the way, but in her imagination she was always on her way to somewhere else: "One day Egypt, another day Africa. I never wanted to stay. I would say to them, 'I'm on my way to China.'" The memory establishes Nadine as a restless young woman with a strong sense of destination. It is a surprise, then, when we see her for the first time onscreen, still part of a narrated flashback, wearing her prim bank teller outfit and with a hairstyle that recalls Jade Li's Connie Chung 'do. What we see is someone who has given up her youthful sense of imaginative exploration and who has become too quick to settle for what is in front of her.

Nadine gets the first job she applies for, and finds her Prince Charming as well. Jonathan is a co-worker who daringly thwarts a bank robber on Nadine's first day of work, impressing her mightily. We see all this reconstructed in Nadine's memory—tinted blue, as are all the scenes shot in the bank, suggesting that even recollections of Jonathan's gallantry in saving Nadine from harm have faded into the general monochromatic lifelessness of the daily grind. The flashback ends, and we learn that five years after taking the first job and the first man available, Nadine is bored and restless. She and Jonathan are in counselling.

Then one day an interesting customer, who introduces himself as Tass Richards, appears at Nadine's wicket to open an account, and shows obvious interest in her. Their flirtation continues when they meet at the local grocery store, in which everyone seems to know everyone else. A few days later, the bank is robbed again, and this time Nadine is taken hostage. In the getaway car, the robber reveals himself as Tass, who apologizes for having taken her along but who asks Nadine to help him escape. Tass reassures her that she will still technically be a hostage, an offer Nadine agrees to, since it is a way to continue the adventure without taking any responsibility for it. The days of fugitive life on the road with Tass are a much-needed tonic for Nadine; they recast Tass as a white knight in a rubber LBJ mask, a saviour in abductor's clothing who absolves Nadine from having to take any initiative for changing her life.

The goofy outfits Tass and Nadine don as part of their getaway plan include a dye job for Nadine, whose hair is now a vibrant red and worn loosely

curled around her face. This "disguise" is really more a revelation of self for
Nadine, a release from the staid blue tones of the bank into a world of colour,
improvisation, and adventure. Meanwhile, rather than sit morosely in the
apartment and wait for news of Nadine from the police, Jonathan becomes an
amateur investigator, piecing together clues that finally lead him to the motel
where the couple, who have become lovers, are holed up. "Goin' to get my girl,"
he says to anyone who asks what he is up to. The climax of the film is a chase
scene in which Tass and Nadine are pursued by a cop on a motorcycle. Grabbing
a gun from Tass, Nadine fires wildly "like a Peckinpah wannabe" from the car,
hitting the cop.[25] Her belief that she has killed someone shocks Nadine into
responsibility. She contacts Jonathan and turns herself in, letting Tass escape.
Nadine returns to the intrepid Jonathan, but, still dissatisfied with her life, leaves
him once again a year later. In the final scene of the film, she drives to a fork in
the road. Pausing, she turns right before stopping once again, reversing the car,
and taking the left-hand fork. In voice-over once again, Nadine muses on her
childhood desire to walk to China: "I know I'll get there."

Drive may be a romance dressed up as an action flick, but it is also,
Sandra Oh's absence notwithstanding, a film in which ethnicities are connected in suggestive ways to ideas of home and belonging. In fact, the ethnically
Chinese material of the film works provocatively with the non-Asian protagonist
of the story, Nadine Ship, in ways that it might not have had Oh appeared in the
film as planned. The presence of a white actor in a film seeded with references
to China can unsettle the assumptions of viewers who might have seen the connection between Asian actors and Asian themes as obvious, a cultural given.
Instead, Drive bears more complicated traces of "ethnicities-in-relation." Ella
Shohat uses this phrase to draw attention to the ethnicity at work in all films, not
just those "where ethnic issues appear on the 'epidermic' surface of the text."[26]
Viewers cannot assume, for example, that the phrase "walking straight enough
and hard enough" to reach China is an expression of ethnic nostalgia, either felt
by Nadine or displaced from her parents. It might indeed communicate heritage
longings, but we do not know this for certain.

On the other hand, neither does the motif of China that runs throughout
the film participate uncritically in the kind of imaginative exoticization associated
with orientalism. Though the idea of China enters the film through Nadine's wist-
ful voice-over, it reappears in connection with Tass. He comes from China City, a
place presumably located in the US because he needs money to cover his
mother's hospital bills, the ostensible reason for the bank heist. Tass and Nadine
set out for China City along a highway ranged with signs that communicate
pointedly on their existential road trip, such as the one that reads "We Are Not
What We Seem." Scenes involving Tass and Nadine are intercut with those of

the pursuing Jonathan to build and reinforce a sense of synchronicity as well as of cosmic commentary on the action. In one scene an ad for travel to China—a place for "those who really want to get away"—plays on TV in Jonathan's apartment and in Nadine and Tass's car. In another, Jonathan decides to get something to eat just as Nadine, in China City, is resisting Tass's suggestion that they eat at Wing's Motel and Chinese Restaurant, a sign for which is visible in the frame as they cross the border. Walking up to the entrance of Wing's they see what looks like a ticket booth, and as they enter the building the image spins around in a way reminiscent of the beginning of the "Girl Hunt" number in *The Band Wagon* (1953), heralding the self-reflexive, artful experience they are about to have.

When they stop at Wing's, Tass and Nadine enter a truly liminal space, one in which Chinese and non-Chinese North American ethnicities are in kitschy rather than exotic relation. Shum has said that she conceived of Wing's as a place where Tass and Nadine "could shed their own baggage," and that its surreal and performative quality upsets assumptions about Chinese Canadian restaurants.[27] The hosts, Sloan and Chen, are an ambiguously gendered pair who shepherd Tass and Nadine into the dining room after dressing them in costume. The silhouettes of swaying bodies are visible on the curtains behind them as Tass and Nadine eat, drink, and flirt over suggestive fortune cookies. In providing Tass and Nadine with a respite from life on the road, and with a chance to admit their growing fondness for each other, Wing's becomes a place of comic "unhomeliness." Likewise, Sloan and Chen are gender and cultural liminars who have set up shop in erotic transnationality. It seems useful to remark here that though theories such as Bhabha's and Naficy's are usually applied to grimmer films than Shum's, we shouldn't overlook the points Shum makes about similar matters in her work simply because comedy is her preferred mode.

The attraction of "unhomeliness" to her is made explicit in Nadine's voice-over as she drives with Tass. "I did not want to get caught," she says. "I did not want to go back. Not yet. I was living every minute." It is in being "unhomed" with and through Tass that Nadine is reconnected with her childhood fantasy of walking to China, a place that by the end of the film has become a metaphor for selfhood. This unhomeliness also confirms the fairy-tale quality of the interlude with Tass. He is himself an unlikely figure: a cute, somewhat shy bank robber who loves his mum, has never really hurt anyone, and who falls in love with his hostage. His is a permanently liminal life, without direction or gravity, until someone pulls out a gun. When Nadine calls Jonathan to turn herself in, Tass disappears completely from the film.

Tass is a catalyst for Nadine's movement from passenger in a getaway car to driver of her very own bright-red punch buggy. Even so, he shares with Jonathan a tendency to efface her agency. As Gravestock writes, each man in her life tells her she's not responsible for what happens to her "and that things are going to be fine—even when they won't be."[28] What Nadine wants, though, is to have an effect on the world, something she achieves when she shoots the cop. It is when Nadine steps fully into the role of accomplice to Tass that she regains a sense of responsibility and choice, something her mother had always reminded her of. It is not really surprising, then, that the relegation of Nadine's adventure to the realm of "closed cases" by the detectives who interview her, and her behaviour as symptomatic of Stockholm Syndrome, does not resolve anything. Nadine is as restless, as discontented, as ever, and as the film closes she seems happiest in her own company.

The conventionality of *Drive, She Said* in terms of plot affected its reception. Critics decried its reliance on the caper film as a means of exploring a woman's self-actualization. Also problematic is the characterization of Nadine herself. Though Kelly's performance is good, the character is difficult to know, or at least care for. Nadine's tone of voice, like Jade's, is often ironic and wisecracking, and it descends on occasion into the sullen, which seems to stand in for rueful self-reflection. Like Jade, she is diffident toward and often irritated by the men who desire her, as if being somewhat rude is the way to communicate independence and sophistication. Though this tactic signals the neediness of both characters, at least Jade is emotionally vulnerable to the people who care for her, and the use of effects such as slow motion and theatrical lighting gives us a sense of her inner life and pokes fun at her flair for the melodramatic. Nadine, though older than Jade, seems emotionally younger and more self-indulgent. We overhear her talking to a friend on the phone about "a husband, a life, blah, blah, blah," but that is as close to articulate self-expression as she gets. Neither does the camera offer us a glimpse through framing, colour, or other effects, of what is going on inside Nadine's head. She doesn't really open up to anyone—Jonathan, Tass, the camera, or us—and remains a curiously opaque protagonist.

This is true as well of Kin, the central character in the "happiness" plot of Shum's 2002 feature, *Long Life, Happiness and Prosperity*. In this film, set in a Vancouver "of village-sized proportions" that is as charming as it is self-enclosed,[29] Shum wove together three stories of family conflict. In one, Shuck Wong, a security guard, loses his job and considers suicide. In another, the local butcher, Bing Lai, tries to keep hidden the truth about his estranged relationship with his father in China, even as his behaviour threatens to drive his own son away from the family. And in the third, twelve-year-old Mindy Lum wanders through the neighbourhood, practising Taoist magic in order to make her mother rich and to match her up with an interested young man named Alvin. Mindy's mother, Kin Lum, is overworked and stressed by her job in a Chinese restaurant, where she routinely ignores Alvin's attempts to make nice. Kin is another of

Shum's cranky women, whose irritability seems out of proportion to the cute Mindy's ability to annoy, even given her mother's job-induced weariness.

Kin shares with Jade and Nadine a kind of temperamental discontent that seems, like theirs, to be exacerbated by her life situation but not entirely explained by it. Kin is the woman and mother we might imagine Jade or Nadine to have become had Jade not found her "unhomeliness" in a life of art, or if Nadine had returned to Jonathan instead of lighting off on a female picaresque. In Kin, Jade's and Nadine's attempts at mordant wit have become even more bitter, as when she says about buying a lottery ticket, "Yeah, I've got horseshoes up my butt." Kin looks overripe for the kind of rebellion and flight that Shum's other films depict, and perhaps if she were not a mother, she too might have kicked over the traces of her life. Alvin certainly appears to be the kind of safe and unexciting man Jonathan is in *Drive*, someone who embodies conventionality. Such a film would not have been much of a comedy, though, unless Mindy were to join her restless mother on the road.

Sticking safely to comedy, then, the film makes Mindy the mechanism through which Kin overcomes her anger at the world and her disdain for Alvin. By the film's conclusion, though Mindy's magic has gone haywire, it seems to have worked all the same to bring various interlocking crises to resolution. What is lost though is any convincing plot line that explains the transformation of the grumpy, restless spirit of Kin into the satisfied homebody she becomes by the end of the film. What the film appears to say is that nothing short of a magic spell could convince Kin to be happy with Alvin and with life in the small, tightly knit ethnically Chinese community she lives in.

Commenting on the homogeneity of the community depicted in *Long Life*, Levitin remarks on the effect of this portrayal on the themes of ethnicity and identity that have been prominent in Shum's work. She writes that the film presents "a vision of Chinese-Canadian existence in which the tension between the two poles—Chinese and Canadian—is eliminated because the implications of the second term are missing.... A Canada of non-Chinese barely exists."[30] Motivated by Shum's desire to pay homage to her parents' experience in Canada, *Long Life* dispenses with what Naficy calls the "consent relations with the host society" and concentrates exclusively on the "descent relations with the homeland."[31] The liminal spaces of transnationality are effaced here, and the unhomely qualities of life amid cultures and ethnicities repressed. Instead we see domesticated, nostalgic, and romanticized versions of Chinese customs and attitudes, to which women like Kin are expected and, it seems, finally happy to accommodate themselves.

Mina Shum has described her next project, tentatively entitled *The Immortal Immigrants*, as a "fantasy" about tensions within a family of Chinese immortals trying to fit into life in present-day Vancouver. The daughter, in her early twenties, wants to give up her immortality in order to date a mortal, which is one way for the film to address inter-ethnic relationships. The scenario suggests the attraction Shum still feels for these stories of restless women caught between expectation and desire. "This is about trying to find a definition of family and home and trusting," she says.[32] It is in her wry but affectionate depiction of familial negotiations around these fraught subjects that Shum initially found her audience. Whether immortality will interact thoughtfully as well as playfully with ethnicity, gender, and genre in her next work will be of interest to viewers and scholars curious about the multiply negotiated subjectivities of contemporary Canadian film.

Notes

1
In an interview with Pamela Cuthbert, Shum says, "Although I'm proud of my personal identity and I'm proud that it's a Canadian film, the best way to make sure people see it without prejudice is to say it's an independent film." "Mina Shum Drives On," *Take One*, Spring 1998, http://www.findarticles.com/p/articles/mi_moJSF/is_19_6/ai_30066448/print.

2
Christopher Gittings, *Canadian National Cinema: Ideology, Difference, and Representation* (New York: Routledge), 127.

3
Kass Banning, "Playing in the Light: Canadianizing Race and Nation," *Gendering the Nation: Canadian Women's Cinema*, ed. Kay Armatage, Kass Banning, Brenda Longfellow, Janine Marchessault (Toronto: U of Toronto P, 1999), 292.

4
Ella Shohat, "Introduction," *Multiculturalism, Postcoloniality, and Transnational Media*, ed. Ella Shohat and Robert Stam (New Brunswick, NJ: Rutgers UP, 2003), 10.

5
Homi Bhabha, *The Location of*

Culture (New York: Routledge, 1994), 9; Hamid Naficy, "Phobic Spaces and Liminal Panics: Independent Transnational Genre," Shohat and Stam 203–26.

6
Eva Rueschmann, "Mediating Worlds/Migrating Identities: Representing Home, Diaspora and Identity in Recent Asian American and Asian Canadian Women's Films," *Moving Pictures, Migrating Identities* (Jackson: UP of Mississippi, 2003), 183.

7
Jacqueline Levitin, "Mina Shum: The Chinese Films and Identities," *Great Canadian Film Directors*, ed. George Melnyk (Edmonton: U of Alberta P, 2007), 271–91.

8
Naficy, 207.

9
Naficy, 204–5.

10
Both Mina Shum and Sandra Oh shared the experience of leaving home at the age of eighteen, and for very similar reasons. See Levitin, n25, 290.

11
Naficy, 208.

12
Levitin, 281. In this light it is interesting that when Jade first meets the young grad student who becomes her lover, he asks her if she is "emotionally attached to a guy other than your dad."

13
Levitin, 275.

14
Banning, 300.

15
See Banning, 302; Gittings, 40; Levitin, 279.

16
Eleanor Ty, "Rescripting Hollywood: Performativity and Ethnic Identity in Mina Shum's Double Happiness," in Ty, *The Politics of the Visible in Asian North American Narration* (Toronto: U of Toronto P, 2004), 80.

17
Rueschmann, 191.

18
Ty, 70.

19
The list of stereotypes of Asian women includes exotic, sexual, beautiful, mysterious, dutiful, polite, quiet, and conservative. Alquizola and Hirabayashi, "Confronting Gender Stereotypes of Asian American Women: *Slaying*

the Dragon," *Reversing the Lens: Ethnicity, Race, Gender, and Sexuality through Film*, ed. Jun Xing and Lane Ryo Hirabayashi (Boulder: UP Colorado, 2003), 157.

20
Bhabha, 9.

21
Naficy, 213.

22
Levitin, 272.

23
Steve Gravestock, "Love Hurts: Canadian Romantic Comedy," *Take One*, Spring 1999, http://www.findarticles.com/p/articles/mi_moJSF/is_23/ai_30001087/print.

24
Gravestock, 1.

25
Cuthbert, 1.

26
Ella Shohat, "Ethnicities-in-Relation: Toward a Multicultural Reading of American Cinema," *Unspeakable Images: Ethnicity and the American Cinema*, ed. Lester D. Friedman (Chicago: U of Illinois P, 1991), 215–17.

27
Miya Davar, "Interview with Mina Shum: The Director's Question," http://www.film.ubc.ca/ubcinephile/cinephile/davar-shum.pdf.

28
Gravestock, 2.

29
Levitin, 283.

30
Levitin, 284.

31
Naficy, 208.

32
Davar, n.p.

Works Cited

Alquizola, Marilyn C., and Lane Ryo Hirabayashi. "Confronting Gender Stereotypes of Asian American Women: *Slaying the Dragon*." *Reversing the Lens: Ethnicity, Race, Gender, and Sexuality through Film*. Ed. Jun Xing and Lane Ryo Hirabayashi. Boulder: UP of Colorado, 2003. 155–68.

Banning, Kass. "Playing in the Light: Canadianizing Race and Nation." *Gendering the Nation: Canadian Women's Cinema*. Ed. Kay Armatage, Kass Banning, Brenda Longfellow, Janine Marchessault. Toronto: U of Toronto P, 1999. 291–310.

Bhabha, Homi K. *The Location of Culture*. New York: Routledge, 1994.

Cuthbert, Pamela. "Mina Shum Drives On." *Take One*, Spring 1998. http://www.findarticles.com/p/articles/mi_moJSF/is_19_6/ai_30066448/print.

Davar, Miya. "Interview with Mina Shum: The Director's Question." http://www.film.ubc.ca/ubcinephile/cinephile/davar-shum.pdf.

Gittings, Christopher E. *Canadian National Cinema: Ideology, Difference, and Representation*. New York: Routledge, 2002.

Gravestock, Steve. "Love Hurts: Canadian Romantic Comedy." *Take One*, Spring 1999. http://www.findarticles.com/p/articles/mi_moJSF/is_23/ai_30001087/print.

Levitin, Jacqueline. "Mina Shum: The Chinese Films and Identities." *Great Canadian Film Directors*. Ed. George Melnyk. Edmonton: U of Alberta P, 2007. 271–91.

Melnyk, George, ed. *Great Canadian Film Directors*. Edmonton: U of Alberta P, 2007.

Naficy, Hamid. "Phobic Spaces and Liminal Panics: Independent Transnational Genre." *Multiculturalism, Postcoloniality, and Transnational Media*. Ed. Ella Shohat and Robert Stam. New Brunswick, NJ: Rutgers UP. 203–26.

Rueschmann, Eva. *Moving Pictures, Migrating Identities*. Jackson: UP of Mississippi, 2003.

Shohat, Ella. "Ethnicities-in-Relation: Toward a Multicultural Reading of American Cinema." *Unspeakable Images: Ethnicity and the American Cinema*. Ed. Lester D. Friedman. Chicago: U of Illinois P, 1991. 215–50.

—. Introduction. *Multiculturalism, Postcoloniality, and Transnational Media*. Ed. Ella Shohat and Robert Stam. New Brunswick, NJ: Rutgers UP, 2003.

Ty, Eleanor. *The Politics of the Visible in Asian North American Narratives*. Toronto: U of Toronto P, 2004.

Beyond Tradition and Modernity: The Transnational Universe of Deepa Mehta

Christina Stojanova

When I visited India, my first thought was that its impoverishment was actually external and material, while the internalized spiritual impoverishment of the West was the much graver one. I found many of the themes and questions I have been grappling with ever since discussed in Mehta's films, and this was my inspiration for this article.

Much has been written of Deepa Mehta's in-between experience of the "old" country, India, and the "new" country, Canada, and of her dual displacement as a woman of colour and as an immigrant.[1] However, as a versatile visual thinker and film auteur (she has scripted six of her twelve films), Mehta resists confinement to any single discursive paradigm, for she has succeeded in destabilizing and transcending them all.

Although Mehta has been making films in Canada and the US since 1975,[2] she became established as a filmmaker with an original voice with *Fire* (1996, India/Canada), a story about a lesbian love affair between two sisters-in-law that she both wrote and directed. It was, however, the controversy generated by its release in India in 1998 that made her famous internationally and that has until recently dominated most journalistic[3] and scholarly texts devoted to her oeuvre.[4] Not that directors who never left their countries have been immune to controversy when tackling the sensitive issue of homosexuality in traditional cultures. A case in point is Chen Kaige and his remarkable film *Farewell, My Concubine/Bàwáng Bié Ji* (1992, China), an internationally acclaimed film that has been consistently dismissed by nativist critics, who accused the director of selling out to the West. These accusations were obviously fuelled in part by Kaige's iconoclastic references to the tragedy of the Cultural Revolution but largely for introducing a homosexual character as one of the principals in his poignant drama.

While the *Fire* controversy prompted the re-release of the film in Canada, its numerous festival exposures and awards facilitated Mehta's access to

Canadian funding for her subsequent projects. In addition, the resultant intense discussions circumvented the limitations of Canadian multicultural cinema and even those of the South Asian diasporic cinema, and Mehta became increasingly identified as the quintessential transnational filmmaker.[5] She has, however, repeatedly described herself a "hybrid person who can move from continent to continent" (Levitin 2003, 277), canvassing diverse economic, cultural, and political milieux from North America to India. And although she enjoys her growing international reputation, she seems prepared to risk being called either insufficiently Canadian or insufficiently Indian, which basically means dwelling in a perpetual state of controversy.[6] In this she is not unlike her European colleague Emir Kustirica, another high-profile transnational filmmaker, who got into trouble with critics both from his native Bosnia and from his adoptive country, France, because of his ingenious film *Underground* (1995, France/Federal Republic of Yugoslavia/Germany/Hungary). An uncompromising condemnation of the Yugoslav Communist establishment for lying to the people and keeping them literally "underground" for more than forty years, the film was slated for its ferocious (and brilliantly visualized) criticism of the Yugoslav people for complying with their own demise and, mostly, for mourning the founding myth of the failed federation. Kustirica's next film, *Black Cat, White Cat/Crna macka, beli macor* (1998, France/Germany/Yugoslavia), on the other hand, was attacked for its escapist, nostalgic, and apolitical idealization of rural gypsy life. The most serious accusation levelled against Kusturica, however, seems to be his lack of a discernible adherence to any national entity, whether traditionally religious or newly formed, on the territory of former Yugoslavia. Instead, almost twenty years into the breakup of Yugoslavia, the director stubbornly insists on identifying himself as secular and Yugoslav (and, as of late, as a mischievously self-proclaimed Serbian).

Kusturica's is a textbook case of the growing complexity of transnational filmmaking (and the inevitable challenges of its critical interpretation), where volatile politics seem to override and often eclipse the artistic merits of the project. It is becoming increasingly difficult for transnational artists like Mehta and Kusturica, who come from religiously and ethnically diverse states with a history of bloody conflicts and economic hardships, to insist on their sacrosanct right to forge a particular artistic vision and espouse passionate views, as anything they create with foreign funding is considered suspicious in the old country and by definition hurtful to its national image. Since any significant work is bound to be personal, visionary, and therefore potentially controversial, the crunch becomes even more intolerable when dealing with the diverse interests of international film financing. For there could be no work of art capable of appeasing all aesthetic, emotional, and political concerns simultaneously and still remain a work of art.

The *Fire* controversy did, however, bring Mehta closer to Satyajit Ray, one of the best-known Indian filmmakers, whose influence she has repeatedly acknowledged. For many years Ray's name was synonymous with Indian cinema internationally. Yet Ray's realistic, even tragic, representation of the impoverished life in colonial and post-colonial rural India in such masterful works as the Apu trilogy (1955–1959), *Devi* (1960), and *Charulata* (1964) was severely condemned for "tarnishing India's image in the eyes of the world" by none other than Nargis, the megastar of Bollywood from the 1950s, known also as "Woman in White" and a symbol of Mother India since her starring role in *Mother India/Bharat Mata* from 1957. The condemnation is hardly surprising, bearing in mind that Ray's Italian-neo-realism-inspired films about the quiet struggle of both men and women for rational and moral agency at the turn of the twentieth century have never enjoyed the domestic popularity of a *Mother India*. Similarly, Mehta was harshly taken to task by Madhu Kishwar, a prominent Indian women's-rights activist, who accused her of misrepresenting the India's urban middle class in *Fire* for the sake of achieving fame and material gains in the West (qtd. in Levitin 2001, 280–81).

On the positive side, Mehta's transnational credentials have undoubtedly helped her to appeal to some of the best Bollywood actors, such as the superstar Aamir Kahn (*Lagaan*, 2001, India; *Raja Hindostani*, 1996, India), who starred in the principal role of Dil Navaz, the Ice Candy Man, in the second film of her trilogy, *Earth* (1998, India/Canada). Mehta works on a regular basis with the famed Indian actresses Nandita Das and Shabana Azmi, who both shone in *Fire* and *Earth*. For *Water* Mehta assembled another all-star cast, this time including Seema Biswas, Lisa Ray, John Abraham, and Kulbhushan Kharbanda. In addition, Mehta's Canadian connection has also secured her the collaboration of famed cinematographers like Guy Dufaux (*Sam & Me*, 1991; *Camilla*, 1994), who is the director of photography for the Oscar-winning *Barbarian Invasions* (2004, Canada). Certainly Mehta's work has been tremendously influenced by the vision of Giles Nuttgens, the British cinematographer who shot the Indian trilogy and whom she met on the set of the segments and episodes she shot for George Lucas's TV series: *The Young Indiana Jones Chronicles* (1992, USA) and *Young Indiana Jones: Travels with Father* (1996, USA). Paradoxically, this experience was Mehta's ticket to a more universalized kind of art cinema and to the world of politically charged transnational cinema.

In view of the transnational mode of production of her films and their multinational reception by North American, Indian, and South Asian diasporic audiences, Mehta's specific artistic pedigree begs a more precise definition, since her most powerful films are Indian in subject matter, sensitivity, and imagery and have therefore yielded a specific scrutiny (and even accusations of Hindu cultural bias) appropriate to an Indian director working in Canada (or out of

Canada). On the other hand, Mehta's candid way of representing female subjectivity, in a break with a century-old Indian tradition, has undoubtedly been facilitated by her Canadianness, which has added a new creative dimension to her
feminist vision. This outsider's perspective has informed her take on the rapidly
developing Indian society of the last two decades, its unusual angle akin to that
of Ray, inspired by his passion for the themes and aesthetics of Italian neo-real-
ism, in his low-key portrayals of human struggle for dignity amid often unpredict-
able social and cultural tensions.

In her Indian films, Mehta does question and deconstruct the attempts
of the post-colonial nation-state to perpetuate and mobilize tradition (or the collective archetype) in the name of what fundamentalist Hindu parties perceive as
national survival vis-à-vis the economic and cultural threats brought on by globalization, Western individualism, and consumerism. In her North American films,
however, she probes the exclusivity of said individualism and consumerism as the
only desirable way to go, and thus implies, if not points to, a possible hybrid ideal,
one that combines the best of both worlds. These two discourses, the Indian and
the North American, meet, as it were, in her latest film, *Heaven on Earth* (2008),
a dramatic story of a young and imaginative Punjabi bride who, after an arranged
marriage, is trying to fit into the crowded family home of her grumpy husband in
Brampton, Ontario.

Mehta's Indian Trilogy, Part One: *Fire*

By foregrounding Mehta's Indian trilogy, this study concentrates on two main
aspects within the broadly defined areas of tension between tradition and
modernity: the painful emergence of the individual out of the archetypal depths
at the cross-section (or *chronotope*, in Mikhail Bakhtin terms)[7] of historical and
metaphorical time and space. In his Indian journals, Joseph Campbell reflects:
"The individualistic (modern)] experience of history and life is not that of the
round (*yugas* and rebirth: a changeless society since the millenniums of the
Neolithic), but that of the destiny shaping decision, and that of conflict of values
implicated in every decision—the rejected continuing to assert their claim, if not
in our consciousness, at least in our unconscious (172)."

Mehta's elemental trilogy—*Fire, Earth,* and *Water*—focuses on the
plight of women caught in the centre of this "conflict of [traditional and modern]
values." And her interest is certainly prompted by her feminist concerns
about those Indian women, who happen to suffer most and benefit least
from the major changes that have affected Indian society since the time of its
independence in 1947. On the other hand, the women's gradual but irreversible
extrication from traditional societies is dramatically charged and usually

impelled by some kind of personal drama or tragedy, which is extremely cinematic. When women start taking "destiny shaping decisions," they tend to be punished more severely for challenging the "changeless society" out of its millennial cocoon. The emergence of women as rational and moral agents is the surest (and therefore most threatening) sign of the irreversible transition from mythological into historical time.

While structured in a linear fashion, inviting even accusations of didacticism,[8] of all three elemental films, *Fire* is most deeply rooted in the three intertextual layers, so typical of Mehta's Indian films: the mythological, the cultural, the historical. Even her choice of a warm "colour palette [of] green, orange and off-white" alludes subconsciously to the colours of the Indian flag (Comer, 99). According to Hindu mythology, Fire or *Agni* is the eternal purifier. Like the other four elements (Earth, Water, Air, and Ether) it is associated with one of the five senses, namely *vision-light* (Zimmer, 204 fn).

Fire tells a story of two middle-class sisters-in-law, Radha (Shabana Azmi) and Sita (Nandita Das), who become attracted to each other emotionally and sexually after having being rejected for too long by their husbands. Radha, the older one, is the middle-aged, motherly type—soft, submissive, hard-working. She is a devoted wife to her husband (Kulbhushan Kharbanda) and a good daughter-in-law to his infirm mother. She quietly endures her husband's pursuit of spiritual perfection and obediently joins him on the couch whenever he decides to check whether sexual drives are still bothering him. The young one, Sita, has recently joined the family in a loveless arranged marriage to the husband's young brother. She is the woman-child, sparkling, tom-boyish, and vivacious, and the active party in the growing closeness between the two. But no secret could be guarded for long in the closed quarters of an Indian family, and all hell breaks loose when the servant denounces them. Radha and Sita, however, survive the trial of fire (or *agnipariksha*) in the literal and metaphorical sense: Radha's sari gets caught in the kitchen stove, but in spite of her husband's betrayal (he runs away, leaving her to a certain death), she is transformed and purified, and joins Sita in their flight to a more than uncertain future together.

The generic link to the "changeless" world of mythological tradition, traced through the etymology of the heroines' names, is skilfully subverted by Mehta. While the name *Radha* has an intense sensual ring to it (the mythological Radha, albeit married to another man, is one of the favourite consorts of Lord Krishna, his *shakti* or Supreme Goddess), playing on the mythological meaning of *Sita* is of much more importance to the film.[9] Sita Devi is Lord Rama's devoted soul mate, whom he loses to another ruler, wages a battle to release from captivity and then marries. While loving her unwaveringly, Rama nevertheless rejects his pregnant wife under the pressure of his loyal subjects on the grounds that she had spent too much time in another man's domain and "will have a bad effect on their own wives" (Macfie, 134–41). Ever since, Sita has been worshipped as a symbol of female resilience and power, silent sacrifice, and an example for Indian girls to follow. Especially powerful is her willingness to pass the *agnipariksha* as a proof of her chastity, although in the film it is Rhada, not Sita, who is tested by fire and survives (Desai, 169). This re-rendering of the *Ramayana* symbolism further destabilizes the binding mythological references, revealing the director's intention to seek a more universal interpretation of the passage through fire as "transcendence of the human condition" by both Rhada and Sita (Cirlot, 106).

Coming to terms with the cruel betrayal of Sita by Rama, on the other hand, and "recognizing and bringing to consciousness a 'dark side' of Indian mythos—the traditional 'sins' of [...] of Rama vis-à-vis Sita"—was one of the favourite themes of post-independence Indian poets and writers in their attempt to somehow explain and make up for the millennial neglect and oppression of Indian women (Campbell, 173). It is a theme brought to the screen first by Satyajit Ray and now, in an audacious manner, by Mehta. *Fire* is indeed strongly reminiscent of Ray's 1964 gem, *Charulata* (or *The Lonely Wife*), based on the Rabindranath Tagore's literary classic *The Broken Nest*, written during the time of the Bengal Renaissance in the late nineteenth century. *Charulata* tells the story of the forbidden love of a neglected wife, Charu, who finds a response to her emotional and intellectual yearnings in her husband's younger brother-in-law (actually cousin), Amal. Says Ray: "There is a Bengali convention about the relations between a wife and her *debar*, her younger brother-in-law. It is always a very affectionate relationship ... always verges on a kind of intimacy ... where the younger brother-in-law is attracted to the sister-in-law.... So there is always the possibility that a relationship of a rather deep nature might develop" (Robinson, 160).

But the parallels to Ray's work are not limited to the narrative level—they run on a much deeper, structural one. Like *Charulata*, *Fire* demonstrates a "complete fusion of eastern and western sensibility" in the light of the above discussion of the transnational (Robinson, 157). In *Fire*, Mehta displaces this highly charged "family romance" onto another taboo terrain—that of the homoerotic attraction between Rhada and her sister-in-law Sita. In addition to exploring the contemporary dimension of such a forbidden love affair, Mehta adds her voice to the ongoing and lively debate about the role of Indian women: Should the Indian woman be *Prachina* (a Conservative, or traditional woman) or *Nabina* (a Modern woman)? Tagore's elegant prose registered this argument in a number of works, and later inspired some of the best works of Ray (from *Charulata* and *Devi* to *Mahanagar* [1963, India]). The heated resuscitation of the century-and-a-half-old argument is reflected in the above-mentioned reception of Mehta's films.

Obviously, while Rhada is definitely a Prachina, who transcends into Nabina via the transformative fire of love, Sita is a Nabina through and through.

The drama of this painful transformation to an enlightened *vision* is condensed in the fundamental *chronotope* of home and extended family—the protective but also repressive cocoon, where Indian women have been caught in the cobweb of the circular time of tradition and where the intrusion of the linear, historical time of modernity has had the most tangible effect. Both Ray and Mehta explore with unusual artistic intensity the attempts of their characters to *carpe diem*—to grasp the unique moment when tradition and modernity intersect, and reveal how, if captured, it sets them on a difficult but rewarding path toward individuation and subjectivity. Judging by the vehement reaction to *Fire* in India, it seems that the quest of Rhada and Sita has succeeded in grasping this unique moment, putting the Indian patriarchal tradition to a test. Indeed, the trial by fire of *Ramayana*'s "Sita is more a testing of Rama than of her" (Shulman, 93), triggering an identity crisis in Lord Rama, who begins asking himself the question "Who am I"? (Shulman, 110). Similarly, the cinematic ordeal of Rhada and Sita—by getting the viewers on two continents passionately involved in the complexities of their all-too-human experience—has triggered an identity crisis of epic proportions in India.

Mehta's Indian Trilogy, Part Two: *Earth*

Mehta's script of *Earth* is based on a well-known memoir—Bapsi Sidhwa's *Cracking India* (1991)—about the violent partition of India in 1947, which explains the straightforward metaphor of the film's title: according to Hindu mythology, Earth or *Prithvi*, is associated with *smell-fragrance* (Zimmer, 204 fn) and *Prithivi Mata* (Mother Earth or Earth Goddess) is its deity.

Personalizing the film's narrative through the eyes of a child is an excellent artistic device, tested for the first time in *Earth* and then successfully repeated in *Water*. Casting seven-year-old Lenny (Maia Sethna) as the mediator of the spiritual agony and physical terror of partition allows Mehta to intensify the film's emotional impact, to justify its straightforward symbolism, and to stay away from the politics of partition. The recurring image of the caged lion, for example, signifies the masculine principle in Asiatic ornamentation, "pertaining to the element of Earth" and also "the danger of being devoured by the unconscious" (Cirlot, 189–90). Indeed, the repressed destructive impulses released from the collective unconscious by the partition interregnum threaten to engulf victims and perpetrators alike in the ensuing suicidal storm of ethnic hatred. In *Earth*, as in *Fire*, the film negotiates serious social issues within the claustrophobic confines of a family home using the heightened emotionality of narratives, propelled by complicated love stories.[10] However, the flashback structure—featuring a world long gone through the nostalgically naive reminiscences of an infirm child—forestalls the hostile reception[11] that might have arisen yet again from critics who perceived an "idealization of a lost united India" and a "national bias ... far more palatable to an Indian audience than to a Pakistani [one]" (Herman, 142). The fact that Lenny belongs to a well-off Parsee family—the ethnic group that, in the words of Lenny's mother, declared itself neutral "like Switzerland" in the bloody conflict between Muslims, Hindus, and Sikhs in the once cosmopolitan city of Lahore—allows for yet another degree of distance from the evolving horrors. The historical truth, however, refuses any easy rationalizations (or politicization) of the characters' tragic lot, and, as in *Fire,* the motif of rejection and betrayal takes centre stage. Under the pressure of thunderous tensions, the harmonious multi-religious community quickly unravels, victimizing any and all. Lenny's flashbacks are dominated by her Hindu Nanny, the luminously beautiful and educated Shanta (Nandita Das, Sita from *Fire*). In the ensuing chaos, Shanta is betrayed—partly out of jealousy, partly out of revenge for his massacred family—by one of her Muslim suitors, who happens to be Lenny's favourite friend, Dil Navez, the Ice Candy Man (Aamir Kahn). In the most powerful scene in the film, Shanta is dragged away by the mob, with Lenny, her parents, and their servants watching from the wings. Yet *Earth* is arguably Mehta's most serene film, shot predominantly outdoors and tenderly enwrapped in the yellow-reddish colours of the torn Indian soil, whose alluring fragrance is almost palpable. Its tragic beauty is strongly reminiscent of Ray's forgotten masterpiece *Thunder/Ashani Sanket* (1973), about the Bengali famine, "triggered by another ineptitude of the Raj," in which, in Ray's words, "people died and suffered amidst a great beauty" (Kemp, 41). *Earth*'s sunlit nostalgia for a paradise lost is compellingly epitomized in one of the most stunning love scenes ever captured on film: that of Shanta and her beloved Hassan (Rahul Khannaher) — the Muslim suitor she has chosen—making love on the eve of their demise.

In *Earth*, the clash between the "changeless rounds" of tradition and the linear impetus of modernity is resolved in favour of the former, since at that time modernity's "destiny-shaping" decisions were taken not in the process of personal individuation but in the treacherous realm of (post-)colonial politics. In other words, modernity here is seen as a form of divisive alien intrusion into the almost idyllic life of pre-partition India, where Sikhs, Muslims, Hindus, British, and Parsees live in harmony and respect. And yet, as rightfully stated by one insightful author, "With one hand Mehta offers the familiar gesture of memory as commemoration and forgetting—the neat national narrative of partition as the cost of independence, as part of a national history that exists only in the past— and with the other hand she takes away the comfort of resting in this narrative ... [b]y refusing to resolve Shanta's abduction or Lenny's experience of loss and trauma" (Herman, 143–44). Therefore, in the context of Mehta's Indian oeuvre, *Earth* could be read as a balancing act in her keen scrutiny of tradition and modernity; a compensation, to quote Campbell once again, for the "the rejected [values] continuing to assert their claim" in the mythological domain of the Indian collective memory.

Mehta's Indian Trilogy, Part Three: *Water*

In *Water*, the mythological time of the millennial tradition and the historical time of India on the eve of major changes toward the end of the 1930s run parallel and converge at points during the film. Mehta follows a little widowed girl, who loses her husband almost immediately after her betrothal, to a shelter for widows where, according to tradition, widows spend the rest of their lives in prayer and asceticism in an attempt to improve their bad karma.[12] This situation is in itself archetypal, and was until recently still fresh in other traditional cultures, such as that of rural southeastern Europe, for example, where severe social restrictions and stigma were imposed on unfortunate women who had lost their husbands. Prompted by the utter hopelessness of their predicament, Mehta's narrative highlights four female characters at different stages of individuation. Certainly the most vivacious is Chuyia (Sarala), the eight-year-old who is also the narrative motor. Because of her youth, little Chuyia is unable to accept the finality of her lot and lives in the hope that one day she will be able to go home to her mother and father and once again be their favourite playful child. While at the ashram, she behaves as a curious outsider, stubbornly refusing to abide by the rules and—except for a few scenes—it is through her incredulous and innocent eyes that we observe this closed world.

Then comes Kalyani (Lisa Ray), who was brought to the ashram at approximately the same age as Chuyia and has grown into a gorgeous young woman, the only one who is allowed to keep her hair long, as she is forced into prostitution, the only source of income for the fourteen women.

There is also the middle-aged Shakuntala (Seema Biswas, the star of *Bandit Queen*, Shekhar Kapur, 1994, India), whose silent but intense presence and wisdom have established her undeniable spiritual and moral authority in the ashram. The actual power, however, is the hands of the much older Madhumati (Manorama), a self-appointed "mother superior" in charge of the physical survival of the women. She is the most vital, the biggest, and the greediest. There are a few other women, who step in and out of their quiet anonymity at dramatic junctures, but the narrative focus remains on these four.

Similar character economy could be found in any group portrayal of women, but Mehta's contribution is in her unique blending of the universal and the specific, the global and the local, in the portrayal of her four principal characters and their evolution. In Hindu tradition, the *Maha-Yuga* (or the Great Cycle) comprises four *yugas* or secondary periods, which are "comparable to the four ages in Greco-Roman antiquity," with both traditions implying "involution" of the relative "virtues of the period ... [the] progress of individual existence being tantamount to gradual surrender of the golden values of childhood," a process characterized by William Blake as "the punishment of God" (Cirlot, 5–6). In India, the *yugas* "are called after the throws in a dice game: *krita* (winning dice of four; the perfect *yuga*), *treta* (one fourth loss of perfection), *dvapara* (half loss, but balanced) and *kali* (the losing dice or the age of darkness)" (Zimmer, 13–16).[13] However, the unusually challenging circumstances of stigmatized widowhood subvert in a dramatic way the essentialist mythological symbolism of those four ages/*yugas* as perceived in Hindu and Western traditions. Chuyia's "golden" childhood, her "perfect" *krita*, is poisoned by forced confinement, cruelty, deceit, and sexual exploitation; Kalyani's "silver" beauty cannot be saved even by the "winning *treat*" of true love that unexpectedly comes her way; Shakuntala's "bronze" experience, her *dvapara*, fails to balance her striving for perfection with the calls of earthly desires. And ironically, only the shocking tragedy of the elderly Madhumati fits into the dire classification of her "iron" or *kali* age as the worst, stripped of all and any illusions but physical survival, which she can ensure only by pimping out the bodies of the young and beautiful with the help of her sidekick, the eunuch Gulabi (Raghubir Yadav).

Water is by far Mehta's most mature and resonant work,[14] where she succeeds brilliantly in capturing the numinous duality of the third element, Water or *Jal*, linked to the sense of *tasting-taste* (Zimmer, 204 fn) and its power, like that of tradition, to both nurture and destroy. And while *Agni*, the perennial purifier, is associated with the "the devouring sun ... regarded in India as a deadly power ... the moon, the controller of waters, confers the refreshing dew" (Zimmer, 60). Here, as in *Fire* and *Earth*, Mehta has teamed up again with Nuttgens, whose masterful "white highlights," described by her as "incredibly subtle and warm," capture the tired beauty of the parched Indian landscape in stark contrast with the cool waters of the Ganges (Comer, 99). The visual poetics throw into high allegoric relief the suffering of the four women in the ashram, emerging from the depths of the millennial rounds of changeless archetypes at a precarious transitional moment in India's history, which they could either seize or miss, sinking back into the still waters of tradition.

Kalyani's story is at once the most banal and the most gripping. Her astounding beauty attracts the love interest of Narayan (John Abraham), a law graduate and a Gandhi pundit, who sees his plans to marry an untouchable widow, a social outcast with bad karma, as an opportunity to prove the validity of his beliefs in spite of the tearful protests of his Brahmin mother. Abraham's

overall *raisonneur* presence, further depleted by the thin psychological motivation of his character's defiant intentions, is compensated for to a large extent by
Lisa Ray's excellent performance and Nuttgens's camera. When Kalyani finds out
that the boat is taking them to a mansion she has visited many times before to
meet a client, she softly asks (off camera), "What is the full name of your father?"
and immediately demands, again off camera and again *sotto voce*, to be taken
back to the ashram. Her suicide is one of the high points of the film: after her
prayers and ritual washing, she slowly enters the holy waters of the Ganges until
they cover her head, with the camera almost tenderly focusing on her modest
earthly belongings, neatly folded on the bank.

Little Sarala (Chuyia) and the veteran star of Indian cinema, Manorama
(Madhumati), are real treasures, demonstrating Mehta's skill at integrating children and old people into her films. Here again she works with both the negative
and the positive aspects of the archetype. In her Indian trilogy, the elderly are
rarely sympathetic. Chuyia's friend, the charming toothless old woman perennially
dreaming of her wedding feast, where she obviously ate her delicious full for the
last time, is a rare exception and a direct tribute to Ray's unforgettable Pishi, the
toothless cheeky aunt from his 1955 masterpiece *Pather Panchali*. Usually, Mehta
construes her senior characters as fierce custodians of tradition, too zealous to be
considered sympathetic. The "Indian woman looks forward to the day when she is
a mother-in-law. The repressed impulses, when they break out, let loose the horror of massacres" (Campbell, 10). One need think only of demonic figures like Biji,
Rhada's infirm mother-in-law in *Fire*, who is pleased to see her on fire as divine
retribution, or Madhumati, who, after Kalyani's death sends Chuyia to "play" with
her most generous client, Narayan's father, to accept this harsh statement.

In *Water*, as in *Earth,* the hope is with the child as a symbol of the anticipated political and social changes yet to be brought on by Gandhi and his fol-
lowers. After discovering Chuyia in Gulabi's boat, devastated by what seems
to have been a horrific night of sexual and physical abuse, Shakuntala delivers her to a railway-station meeting with Gandhi. This act of rebellion is beautifully built into Seema Biswas's performance, whose Shakuntala finally turns her
back on the Ganges and the eternal hypnotic power of its waters to help Chuyia
onto Gandhi's train, which she sees as the only salvation for wretched souls like
theirs. The train as a symbol of linear progress and modern enlightenment is yet
another tribute to Ray's visual symbolism—to his particular fondness for trains
as a sign of transformation and hope.... Shakuntala is the only one who reaches
this advanced stage of individuation, allowing her to take "destiny-shaping decisions." And yet again the paradox of her transformation, so typical of the advent
of modernity, is elegantly subverted by Mehta, revealing the "conflict of values
implicated in [this] decision." It is not only her suffering, exceptional intelligence,

and stoicism but also the long years of discussion with her aging guru (Kulbhushan Kharbanda) by the Ganges that have brought Shakuntala to the realization that if she has attained any spiritual wisdom, she should act against the horrible injustice here and now, in this world, not in the next. In other words, her agency has been achieved as a result of the uneasy but rewarding interaction of tradition and modernity.

Mehta's 'Canadian' films

> Q: Do you think that your films are distinctly Canadian?
> DM: Oh, yes, I think they're really Canadian. They are idealistic. They are self-deprecating. I think they have a lot of suppressed anger.
> (Dale and Cole, 140)

Dramatically charged intergenerational relationships similar to those informing her Indian films are to be found in two of Mehta's Canadian films: her debut fiction *Sam & Me* (1991, Canada) and *Camilla* (1994, Canada/UK). Both films stand or fall on her belief that the young and the old belong together not so much pragmatically—that is, to teach each other the wisdom of life, or paradigmatically, capitalizing on the visual and psychological clash of what Shakespeare describes as "summer morn" and "winter weather," but to nurture each other emotionally. With one major difference, of course: in her North American oeuvre Mehta deals with hyper-individualized personalities, who, in the twilight of their days crave the warmth of the collective—whether extended family or clan or just a friendly neighbourhood. While their existential drama stems from that impossible yearning, her Indian elders, Biji and Madhumati, ultimately take their revenge on the inevitable and inescapable collective by terrorizing it. The moment of reckoning, in which the growing generational tensions in *Water* are released, comes when Chuyia kills Madhumati's favourite pet bird. The moment is made all the more powerful by the little girl, who spends her precious dime to buy a *ladoo* for the toothless dying woman, who craves the traditional sweets she recalls from her wedding banquet.

As mentioned above, Mehta is not unequivocally supportive of Western (post)modernity either, and firmly points out alienation and the unravelling of familial and communal ties as one of Western modernity's most detrimental effects. In her North American oeuvre she attempts to explore—artistically less successfully than in her Indian films, one has to admit—the flip side of late modern (or postmodern) individualism or of what the Polish-born social philosopher Zygmunt Bauman calls the "agony of choices," following Hannah Arendt's idea of the "tyranny of choices" (Bauman, 5). Late modern "moral life," he writes, is "a life of continuous uncertainty ... loneliness and ambivalence, predicated on

the agony of responsibility over making the right choice" and so doing no harm
to one's material well-being.[15] The "agony of choices" could be alleviated only
by a "life lived in a succession of episodes ... free from the worry about consequences" (Bauman, 5). It is enough to look at the derailed love affair of the professional couple—Tom (Bruce Greenwood) and Fay (Emilia Fox)—in *Republic of Love*
(2003, Canada) to see the effect of a life cushioned from "worry about consequences." The longing for passionate commitment reaches a point of sentimental
triteness in *Sam & Me*, and especially in *Camilla*—a danger that haunts every film
featuring the elderly and children. Both films are based on unusual friendships:
respectively, between a young Indian immigrant, Nikhil (Ranjit Chowdhry), and
an old Jewish man, Peter Boretsky (Sam Cohen); and between a young frustrated
woman, an aspiring musician (Bridget Fonda), and an old one, Camilla, once a
hopeful violinist (the last role of the late Dame Jessica Tandy). And while Mehta's
criticism of Western values is rather timid, it does come through in the rebellious
nature of these bizarre bondings. Her septuagenarian characters vehemently
reject the spiritual aloofness of their cocooned environment, closely controlled by
their children. The frustration of the Holocaust survivor Sam (Peter Boretski) with
his materialistic son threatens his sanity. Thus, death among his new-found immigrant friends comes as a relief from a disenchanted world, where the audacious
pursuit of individual freedom has turned into egotism, prosperity into pragmatism, and happiness into the immediate gratification of fleeting desires. Magnetic
Camilla seizes the chance to dump her boring existence and rush up North to meet
her old flame in Canada. For life, Mehta insists, is much more than financial security, and the characters of her Canadian films demonstrate real personal courage
in transcending the mundane and venturing into the realm of the spiritual, usually
symbolized by warm companionship.

Mehta's ambivalence about both traditional Indian and (post)mod-
ern Canadian values is fully revealed in the passionate detachment (as Laura
Mulvey would have it) of the elegant ironic mode in *Bollywood/Hollywood* (2002,
Canada), enhanced by the episodic structure of the film and sustained by shrewd
intertitles. In it, the omnipresent mythological narrative about Cinderella and her
Prince Charming unfurls against the backdrop of present-day Toronto, that perfect chronotope of postmodern life, and is delivered as a delicious mélange of a
Hollywood romantic comedy and a Bollywood formula film, featuring stars, songs,
and dance routines. An educated and enterprising Canadian Indian beauty, Sue
(Lisa Ray), from a humble Sikh background, agrees to pose for a price as the fian-
cée of a rich Canadian Indian heir, Rahul Seth (Rahul Khanna), so that, in keeping
with Indian tradition, his younger sister is free to marry. However Rahul cannot
get over the departure of his gorgeous Caucasian girlfriend, the blond Kimberly
(Jessica Paré), a split precipitated by his mother's and grandmother's vehement

disapproval of her. A string of events involving Sue and mistaken ethnic identities follows (she pretends to be a Latin American who impersonates an Eastern Indian girl), but finally she gets her Prince Charming, only to have their budding love put to the test by Rahul's accidental revelation of her steamy past as a consort for hire. The story, richly immersed in self-conscious, even campy performances and art direction, ends with the couple's happy reunion. But the film would not truly be Mehta's if it did not reveal another level of meaning beneath this rather predictable (à la *Pretty Woman*) narrative: in this case, her ascerbic social observations about the hilarious incongruity of Indian tradition and Canadian values and of the brazen class and gender inequality within the Indian community her characters are trying to negotiate. On the other hand, casting Indian megastars-on-the-rise—such as Lisa Ray (who was yet to shine in *Water*) and Rahul Khanna (who had appeared in a main role in *Earth*)—is yet another nod by Mehta to the Indian cinema, to Bollywood, and to entertainment cinema in general. Mehta's film thus falls comfortably in the recently emergent genre of the *masala* film—defined as "the return of the bourgeoisie" [Desai, 216–17])—which genre comprises works such as Srinivas Krishna's *Masala* (1991, Canada), Mira Nair's *Mississippi Masala* (1991, UK/USA), and *Monsoon Wedding* (2001, India/USA/France/Italy/Germany). These films revel in the clash between a displaced, albeit resilient cultural tradition and Western values. The absurdities of this clash have become extremely attractive for filmmakers in multi-ethnic societies, prompting the success of the paradigm far beyond the Indian diaspora.[16]

Mehta's Accomplishment

There is no indication so far that Deepa Mehta plans to make a film about Air (*Vayu*), linked to *touch-tangibility*, or Ether (*Akasha*), the divine "fifth Element" (Zimmer, 240 fn), the element related to *sound-hearing* and the only eternal one of the five. Perhaps this is so because her work has already been informed by this "creative breath of life," which "for one of its eminent worshippers, Nietzsche, was a kind of higher matter ... the very stuff of human freedom" (Cirlot, 6). Mehta, not unlike Shakuntala, makes her "destiny-shaping decisions" at the precarious divide between (Indian) tradition and (Western) (post)modernity, where resides the sometimes irresolvable "conflict of values implicated in those decisions" (Campbell, 172). She is blessed, however, with the ability to counterbalance the values that are banished or repressed by these two very different cultures. By interweaving them together in her films, Mehta releases from the Indian and Canadian collective unconscious painful memories, longings, and images that transcend their origins and inspire viewers worldwide to expand their spiritual and emotional universe. And isn't this the noblest goal for any transnational filmmaker?

Notes

1

In her detailed study of her Mehta's work, "Deepa Mehta as Transnational Filmmaker, or You Can't Go Home Again," Jacqueline Levitin reiterates the difficulties Mehta—as someone who, in the words of Kass Banning, is "pegged by race"—has encountered in Canada in getting *Fire* funded, as it did not correspond to Telefilm Canada's guidelines of what constitutes a Canadian movie (qtd. in Levitin, 2001, 284). See also Monk, 183, 200–2; Pearson; Cuthbert.

2

Her first film was the short documentary *At 99: A Portrait of Louise Tandy Murch* (1975, Canada).

3

For more on the controversy, see Stackhouse and Padgaonkar.

4

Levitin's study focuses mostly on *Fire* (270–93), while Jigna Desai devotes a chapter, "Home on the Range: Queering Postcoloniality and Globalization in Deepa Mehta's *Fire*," to the controversy the film generated in India, where its vehement, even violent, rejection by the right-wing Shiv Sena (Shiva's Army) and the Hindu nationalist BJP sparked equally passionate liberal responses. Among the special features on the *Fire* DVD (2000) are the ransacking of theatres in New Delhi and Mumbay (Bombay) in November 1998 and an interview with a female defender of Indian women's values.

5

Levitin 2001; 2003; Desai; Herman.

6

The shooting of *Water* created yet another public-relations storm, resulting in the destruction of the original film set in Varanasi (Benares) in 2000 by Hindu fundamentalists, who threatened ritual suicide in opposition to Mehta's alleged unreceptive attitude toward Hindu religion. This protest caused tremendous financial losses, a production delay of almost four years, and the relocation of the shoot to Sri Lanka.

7

"A term taken over by Mikhail Bakhtin from 1920s science to describe the manner in which literature represents time and space. In different kinds of writing there are differing chronotopes, by which changing historical conceptions of time and space are realised.... Chronotopes can become condensed in fundamental organising metaphors ... by which basic conceptions of time and space get translated into narrative terms. Chronotopic analysis thus seeks to address literary history at a very fundamental level; it mediates between historically created and thus changing conceptions of time and space, and their realisation in the underlying narratives of literary texts." "Chronotope" entry, by Simon Dentith, in *The Literary Encyclopedia*, 18 July 2001, http://www .litencyc.com/php/stopics .php?rec=true&UID=187.

8

See Stone (*Ottawa Citizen*).

9

Indeed, so important is the symbolism of the name Sita in India that, in the approved for release version of the film, she is renamed Nita (Desai, 160).

10

Herman argues that Earth belongs to the melodramatic genre, referring to Charles Affron and Christine Gledhill, among others. I am not convinced that the emotional excesses they associate with (Western) melodrama can be equated to the inherent emotionality of Indian cinema, especially of Ray's neo-realist cinema, whose influence is strongly felt throughout Mehta's oeuvre, including her North American films.

11

According to Herman, the "film has received widely varying responses from Western, Indian, and South Asian diasporic viewers ... from deeply affected and enthusiastic to unmoved and critical ... and the reception does not divide easily along national, regional, or cultural lines" (Herman, 111–12).

12

In *Ramayana*, "widows are considered dangerous and inauspicious ... unable to bear children ... [with] their chastity suspect ... since women are believed to have insatiable sexual appetites ... In North Indian languages, the word *randi* can mean both widow and a whore" (Erndl, 84).

13

See also Macfie, 307.

14

Her 2007 Oscar nomination for Best Foreign Film is an eloquent proof of this proposition.

15

Bauman goes on to say that

"pre-modern times provided a religious 'ex post facto cure ... in the form of redemption and repentance' for the sin of choosing evil over good, 'guaranteeing freedom from worry in exchange for obedience'" (3). The modern project proudly promised to "prevent evil from being done ... eliminating sin (now called guilt) from choice ... simplified to the straightforward dilemma of obedience and disobedience to the rule," prescribed and proscribed by supra-individual agencies "endowed with exclusive moral authority" (Bauman, 4). In postmodern times, however, with the "state ethical monopoly in abeyance ... the supply of ethical rules is abandoned to the care of the marketplace" (Bauman, 5).

16
For example, Joel Zwick, *My Big Fat Greek Wedding*, scripted by the Canadian Nia Vardalos (USA, 2002).

Works Cited

Bauman, Zygmunt. *Life in Fragments: Essays in Postmodern Morality*. Oxford: Basil Blackwell Publishers, 1995.

Campbell, Joseph, et al. *Baksheesh and Brahman: Indian Journal, 1954–1955*. New York: HarperCollins, 1995.

Cirlot, Juan Eduardo. *Dictionary of Symbols*. 2nd ed. New York: Philosophical Library, 1971.

Comer, Brooke. "*Fire* Sets Traditional Indian Family Ablaze." *The International Journal of Film and Electronic Producton Techniques* 78.1 (1997): 99–100.

Cuthbert, Pamela. "Deepa Mehta's Trial by *Fire*." *Take One: Film in Canada*. Winter (1997): 28–31.

Dale, Holly, and Janis Cole. *Calling the Shots: Profiles of Women Filmmakers*. Kingston, ON: Quarry Press, 1993.

Desai, Jigna. *Beyond Bollywood: The Cultural Politics of South Asian Diasporic Film*. New York: Routledge, 2004.

Erndl, Kathleen M. "The Mutilation of Surpanakha." *Many Rāmāyanas: The Diversity of a Narrative Tradition in South Asia*. Ed. Paula Richman. New Delhi: Oxford UP, 1992.

Herman, Jeanette. "Memory and Melodrama: The Transnational Politics of Deepa Mehta's *Earth*." *Camera Obscura* (2005): 107–47.

Johnson, Brian D. "Forbidden Flames." *Maclean's* 19 September 1997: 86.

Kemp, Philip. "*Earth*." *Sight and Sound* January (2000): 40–41.

Levitin, Jacqueline. 2001. "Deepa Mehta as Transnational Filmmaker, or You Can't Go Home Again." *North of Everything: English-Canadian Cinema since 1980*. Ed. William Beard and Jerry White. Edmonton: U of Alberta P, 2002.

Levitin, Jacqueline, Judith Plessis, and Valerie Raoul. *Women Filmmakers: Refocusing*. Vancouver: U of British Columbia P, 2003.

The Literary Encyclopaedia. 18 July 2001. The Literary Dictionary Company. http://www.litencyc.com/php/stopics.php?rec=true&UID=187.

Macfie, John Mandeville, and Ashok Banker. *Myths and Legends of India: An Introduction to the Study of Hinduism*. New Delhi: Aryan Books International, 1992.

Monk, Katherine. *Weird Sex & Snowshoes: And Other Canadian Film Phenomena*. Vancouver: Raincoast Books, 2001.

Padgaonkar, Latika. "'Shadows and a Cloud of Light': Deepa Mehta's *Water*." *Osian's Cinemaya* [The Asian Film Quarterly] 1.2: 45–47.

Pearson, Peter. "*Sam & Me* Speaks for Those Trapped by Multiculturalism." *The Gazette* 24 August 1991: H10.

Robinson, Andrew. *Satyajit Ray: The Inner Eye*. London: André Deutsch, 1989.

Saltzman, Devyani. *Shooting Water: A Mother–Daughter ourney and the Making of a Film*. Toronto: Key Porter Books, 2005.

Saunders, Doug. "Furor Sparks Re-Release of *Fire*: Mehta Film to Hit Canadian Screens." *The Globe and Mail* 11 December 1998: A18.

Shulman, David. "Fire and Flood: The Testing of Sita in Kampan's *Iramavataram*." *Many Rāmāyanas: The Diversity of a Narrative Tradition in South Asia*. Ed. Paula Richman. New Delhi: Oxford UP, 1992.

Stackhouse, John. "Canadian Film Stirs Outrage in India: Fundamentalists Force Shutdown of Popular Story about Lesbian Love." *The Globe and Mail* 4 December 1998: A1:14. Stone, Jay. "*Fire* Burns Beautifully despite Obvious Agenda." *The Ottawa Citizen* 5 December 1997: D3.

Zimmer, Heinrich Robert, and Joseph Campbell. *Myths and Symbols in Indian Art and Civilization*. New York: Harper Torchbooks, 1946.

Les Québécoises
Jerry White

Let's leave aside questions of national cinema aside for the moment. It is important in the context of an anthology about women's filmmaking in Canada[1] to discuss how we have seen in the last twenty years the emergence of a group of women filmmakers working in Quebec who have redefined and in some cases moved entirely beyond traditions in Quebec cinema. It is equally important to examine the others who have produced relatively conventional work that is historically significant and clarifies significant aspects of Quebec film history itself. Among the filmmakers from the 1990s who are advancing the form in a way deserving of the term "avant-garde" are Catherine Martin and Lucie Lambert, while those who have sought a middle ground between the popular and the unconventional include Louise Archambault and Manon Briand. Other filmmakers more oriented toward pop forms include Denise Filiatrault. There are of course many other women filmmakers worthy of discussion, including Michka Saäl with *La position de l'escargot* (1999), Guylaine Dionne with *Les fantômes des trois Madeleine* (2000), and other films by veteran filmmakers such as Micheline Lanctôt (1993's *Deux actrices*) and Anne-Claire Poirier (1997's *Tu a crié LET ME GO*). This is also true of the important work going on in Quebec animation, exemplified by short work as Martine Chartrand's *Âme noire/Black Soul* (2001) and Torill Kove's *My Grandmother Ironed the King's Shirts* (2000) and her Oscar-winning *The Danish Poet* (2006). The prominent filmmaker Léa Pool, who in some ways blazed the trail for filmmakers like Archambault and Briand, is the subject of a separate essay in this volume. The five filmmakers I have chosen to highlight here—Martin, Lambert, Archambault, Briand, and Filiatrault—represent three key streams: semi-experimental, narrative, and popular cinema. Despite the apparent divergence in formal practice there is throughout their body of work a *very* loose sense of national belonging (giving the lie to the stereotype that all Quebec artists ever talk about is nationalism) and a vigorous attempt to give cinematic life to the way that women see the world (illustrating the degree to which gender is a core part of communication, no matter what form that communication takes). We can also see through each set of filmmakers (popular, narrative, semi-experimental) the degree to which they are each led by some important aspect of Quebec cinema, showing just how central women filmmakers are to the important historical back-and-forth that characterizes contemporary Quebec cinema *as a whole*. The Quebec cinema of the 1940s and '50s is too easily forgotten, but it does lay important groundwork, work that filmmakers like Filiatrualt genuinely expand upon. It's just as easy to think of the Quebec cinema of the 1960s and '70s as a sort of gold standard for more ambitious filmmaking, but Briand, Archambault, Lambert, and Martin all take in important innovations from that era—a vigorous interest in cultural criticism, formal ambition, and so on—and *expand* on that; they are inheritors of Quebec cinema's traditions, but they are not mere imitators.

Pop

It has become something of a truism that English Canada has no real popular cinema and that Quebec does. Paul Gross's successes with *Passchendaele* or *Men with Brooms* is one thing; the mass-culture phenomenon *Les Boys* is something else entirely. The turn of the twentieth century saw a sort of "back to the future" effect for that cinema. Quebec (also unlike English Canada) has a pre-war popular cinema (twenty films were made between 1942 and 1954) that is not well known in English Canada (largely because the material has only rarely been subtitled), and a several of its most famous (infamous?) films were remade in the 2000s. The most notable of these were Luc Dionne's 2005 *Aurore*, a remake of Jean-Yves Bigras' 1952 *La petite Aurore: l'enfant-martyre*, and Charles Binamé's 2002 *Séraphin: un homme et son péché*, a sort of remake of Paul Gury's Séraphin films *Un homme et son péche* (1949) and *Séraphin* (1950) (themselves based on Claude Henri-Grignon's 1933 novel *Un homme et son péché*, which was also adopted for radio starting in 1939). This revival of Duplessis-era popular cinema is, I think, the relevant framework in which to view the films of Denise Filiatrault.

Filiatrault actually has had more of a career as an actor than as a director. She was in some important films of the 1970s and '80s, including Denys Arcand's *Gina* (1975), French filmmaker Claude Sautet's lone Quebec production *Mado* (1976), and Gilles Carle's masterpiece *Les Plouffes* (1981). She did a fair bit of television acting as well, including series such as 1975's *Rosa*, 1977's *Chez Denise*, 1984's *Le 101, ouest, avenue des pins* and 1995–97's *Moi et l'autre*, all of which she also wrote. She was also an actress in the original version of *Moi et l'autre*, which aired from 1966 to 1971. No doubt the kind of writing work that she did during this period helped lead her into her work as a director, which began at the end of the 1990s.

Her first film as a director was 1998's *C't'à ton tour, Laura Cadieux*. Based on a 1973 novel by Michel Tremblay, it was co-written by Filiatrault and Tremblay. It was basically the first work she did after finishing *Moi et l'autre*, and so it's not surprising that it seems consistent with the highly efficient, linear narrative style of television comedy and drama. It tells the story of a group of women who go to the same doctor, ostensibly for weightloss but really for the pleasure of each other's company. The catalyst for the film's drama is the loss of one of the women's sons, who seems to be wandering around Montreal's metro system. When he turns up after another woman has gone is search of him, comical misunderstandings and misadventures follow. That the film was followed by a sequel (1999's *Laura Cadieux... la suite*) and a TV series (*Le petit monde de Laura Cadieux*, 2003–7) indicates the degree to which the vision here is not so much that of the nationalist, working-class playwright Tremblay as it is of someone formed by the commercialism of Quebec's vibrant popular cinema and television. Indeed, Bill Marshall writes of the relationship between the first and second Laura Cadieux films that "The second film ... based on the same characters but leaving Tremblay's authorship behind, is paradoxically rather freer to explore this all-female popular genre, reminiscent of TV sitcoms and *The First Wives' Club* (Hugh Wilson, 1996)" (206).

Indeed, one aspect of the Laura Cadieux phenomenon that it is important to point to is the fluidity with which it moves between film and television. Part of this is characteristic of Quebec cinema and indeed of small cinemas generally. Martin Allor wrote of this sense of Quebec audiovisual métissage in 1993; viewers tended to see the same faces on Quebec screens, be they cinemas or televisions, he noted, and added:

> This organizational and occupational hybridity is, I assume, relatively common in small countries. But, in other ways, the sector of audiovisual production is integrated into the peculiar political economic system in Québec (and Canada)—what one Canadian critic has called a permeable Fordism. In one form or another, the entire sector of cultural production is characterized by structures of coproduction. More importantly, this system of production almost always involves provincial and federal investment or subvention. (72)

This sort of "permeable Fordism" is characteristic of Quebec cinema in the 1990s and the '00s, as it was in the 1940s and '50s. Writing of that period in Quebec's national cinema, Pierre Véronneau recalled that film production began to wind down toward the end of the 1950s because "most of its artisans moved into working for television, or for private companies that produced series for television" (1992, 45).[2] I agree with Allor's sense that the barriers between these forms have never been very strong in Quebec, as in most small countries; the system there is Fordist without a doubt (the Laura Cadieux films and TV shows are, like many of the Quebec films of the 1940s and '50s, formally conventional audiovisual products that can be efficiently produced and easily consumed), but it is a highly porous form of Fordism. That sense of a nimble yet basically industrial model is something that commercial Quebec cinema seemed to recover with a vengeance in the early 1990s. "Since 1990, Quebec has produced an annual minimum of 30 feature films," Christian Poirier has written. "This gives it one of the highest ratios (as a function of population) in the world, after the United States" (Tome 2, 258).[3] The chart that Poirer includes to illustrate this point places Quebec after France, the UK, and Australia in terms of production from 1994 to 1998, but the accomplishment is formidable nonetheless. The Laura Cadieux phenomenon allows us to see clearly some key elements of that accomplishment, as well as some of its historical precedents.

Filiatrault's next film was also her most critically acclaimed—2004's *Ma vie en cinemascope*. This biopic of the Quebec chanteuse Alys Robi won Pascale Brussières the 2005 Jutra Award for Best Actress and also probably led to Filiatrault getting a special lifetime-achievement Jutra in 2006. More than the Laura Cadieux work, though, this is the film that really connects to the filmmaking of the Duplessis era. Part of this connection comes at the simple level of subject matter: Robi was at the height of her popularity in the 1940s, and although she was internationally famous she was also part of a locally grown entertainment industry that also included popular radio dramas and films.

And consistent with that sense of being part of a home-grown entertainment industry, *Ma vie en cinemascope* is very much a melodrama/bio-pic. It tells the story of Robi's rise from scrappy child star to international singing sensation, a rise that was ended by her increasing mental instability and her eventual committal and lobotomy. Following a classic melodramatic formula, she achieved a great deal, was impeded by forces not of her own making, and although she struggled heroically to get back on track, she was never the same, and ended up losing everything.

Thus the real connection between *Ma vie en cinemscope* and the cinema of the Duplessis era is ideological. Although I don't want to understate the complexity of the Quebec cinema of the 1940s and '50s (or the complexity of that historical period generally), the consensus among Quebec film scholars is that it is defined by a sort of masochism that is typical of the most reactionary elements of Duplessisism. Writing specifically of the characters of Séraphin and Aurore, Christiane Tremblay-Daviault argued in her 1981 history of Duplessis-era filmmaking that "some of these characters (like Séraphin or Aurore) became Quebecois 'types,' perceived as sadomasochistic social referents" (43).[4] Pierre Véronneau has been harsher. Describing "weepy melodramas" like *L'esprit du mal* (1953), *Coeur de maman* (1953), and *La petite Aurore* (1951) as "films [that] epitomize the collective morbidity that marked our darkest period, suffocated by Catholic values of penitence, atonement, forbearance and self-sacrifice. They reflect with great insight the sick imagination of our society and are valuable today more for their sociological connotations than for their cinematic qualities" (1980, 63).[5] Christian Poirier offers a different emphasis:

> It's necessary ... to not only take account of negative reactions. It's necessary to clearly understand the context of the period: cinema in Quebec was almost completely foreign. Furthermore, the cinema examined by these authors [critics of the 1950s] as a means of understanding, paved the way, I believe, for the cinema to be understood as an instrument of national affirmation, a sort of representation that would really blossom in the 1960s. (Tome 1, 51)[6]

Watching *Ma vie en cinemasope*, it is hard to avoid the impression that it is part of the early 2000s resurgence of neo-Duplessist politics that shaped the politics of Quebec generally, but it is equally difficult to avoid thinking of theorists like Laura Mulvey and their work on feminist possibilities for melodrama. "Melodrama as a safety-valve for ideological contradictions centred on sex and the family may lose its progressive attributes," she wrote in her 1977 essay "Notes on Sirk and Melodrama," "but it acquires a wide aesthetic and political significance.... There is a dizzy satisfaction in witnessing the way that sexual difference under patriarchy is fraught, explosive, and erupts dramatically into violence within its own private stomping ground, the family" (39). So this is the question that *Ma vie en cinemascope* presents: Is it a film that visualizes that "type québécois" of the masochist, so central to the culture of *la grande noirceur*, or is it a film that provides a dizzying satisfaction by visualizing the violence that is part of that patriarchy-defined historical moment, and manages to do so by visualizing this fraught, explosive sexual difference in one of patriarchy's other private stomping grounds, the entertainment industry? This is a genuinely open question.

What is clear, though, is that *Ma vie en cinemascope* shows the degree to which Filiatrault is central to the understanding of Quebec's popular cinema in the late 1990s and '00s. What defines popular cinema of that period is fluidity between film and television, an emphasis on convention mixed with locality, and a clear sense of neo-Duplessisism without a clear sense whether the emphasis should be on the *neo-* or the Duplessisism. Filiatrault's work is an excellent starting point for an examination of recent Quebec popular cinema.

Art

A great deal of what generates critical discussion of Quebec cinema in English Canada is not the popular cinema in which Filiatrault labours but an ambitious narrative cinema, along the lines of Léa Pool. Pool's films are being dealt with elsewhere in this volume, so I will forgo discussion of them here. The 1990s and 2000s saw the emergence of a number of younger filmmakers in the Léa Pool mould, a mould colloquially known as "art cinema."[7] The films of Louise Archambault and Manon Briand are especially useful as examples of what can be done in a semi-conventional practice like Pool's, both in terms of formal complexity and social critique.

Briand is the more famous of the two, and the one with the longer filmography. After studying film at Concordia and making a few shorts, she came to wide attention as part of the 1996 anthology film *Cosmos*. This was produced by Roger Frappier, who was acting as a sort of mentor for a group of young Quebec filmmakers, and indeed the list of directors reads like a generational roll call: Briand, Arto Paragamian, André Turpin, and, most famously, Denis Villeneuve (the other two women on the project—Jennifer Alleyn and Marie-Julie Dallaire— did not go on to direct features). Briand's segment of *Cosmos*—called *Boost*— was a modest character study, about an automotively challenged young woman who tries to cheer up a friend of hers as he waits for the results of an HIV test. It was a low-key, closely observed, and visually modest work, one that is utterly unrepresentative of what would come later. For Briand has become one of Quebec cinema's more visually stylish filmmakers, someone whose eventual collaboration with Luc Besson would seem almost inevitable.

Her first feature film, *2 Secondes* (1998), was also produced by Roger Frappier, and pointed in some ways to the aesthetics of Luc Besson. This film tells the story of a young female mountain-bike racer who becomes a bicycle courier in Montreal. During a slightly deranged downhill mountain-bike race, she hesitates for the titular two seconds and is kicked off of her team. Once re-established as a different sort of cyclist in Montreal, she is taken in by a wise and grouchy former cycling champion who now owns a bike shop, has troubles with women, and tries to get along with her goofy little brother, whom she has had to move in with. If this feature represented the sum of Briand's career, I would without question have grouped her with Denise Filiatrault in the popular-cinema part of this essay. The characters of *2 Secondes* seems to be taken right off of the television sitcom: the grouchy but loveable old-timer who wants to help the new kid, the eccentric roommate who can't deal with women, and the soulful but difficult heroine who can't quite get her life in order. The film is, to be fair, visually arresting in a way that TV sitcoms rarely are; Briand makes a real effort to create a sense of vertigo as she moves us through Montreal at a genuinely breakneck pace. The film is far more visceral at the level of visuals than, say, *Quicksilver*, the utterly mediocre 1986 film starring Kevin Bacon to which it is also tempting to compare *2 Secondes*. Briand continued her interest in women's athletics with her next film, the Marilyn Bell biopic *Heart: The Marilyn Bell Story* (2001).

Briand's third feature, though, was something quite different. *La turbulence des fluides* (2002) was again produced by Frappier, but one of its other producers was Luc Besson. Besson has become practically synonymous with the "Cinéma du look" of '80s French cinema, a movement—which is equally defined by the films of Jean-Jacques Beineix's, such as *Diva* (1984) and *37°2 le matin* (a.k.a. *Betty Blue*, 1986)—that Susan Hayward defines as "belief in the image as pure surface seduction, the image for and of itself" (244). *Turbulence*'s opening sequence in Japan—which is full of bustle, light and dark, and neon in a way that recalls Besson's 1985 *Subway*—seems to give the sense that the film will be primarily about slick, beautiful images. Even when the narrative shifts to Baie-Comeau in the Gaspé, there is a sense that this could still be the case; these opening sequences are defined by sharp, colourful images such as a plane lumbering over the forest as it douses a fire and, a few shots later, its buff pilot (played by Jean-Nicholas Verreault) wandering through the small regional airport as the film's heroine, Pascale Brussières, ogles him with a mild smirk. But as the film's narrative of a young, cosmopolitan scientist returning to her hometown to watch over seismic irregularities advances, it becomes clear that Briand is interested in more than pure surface seduction.

Part of what she's interested in here has to do with the portrayal of the quiet, comfortable alienation that is at the heart of small-town life. One particularly vivid image of this is that of a young girl, Verreault's daughter (played by Ji-yan Seguin), sleepwalking through the streets of Baie-Comeau, inevitably past the diner owned by the character played by the genuinely iconic Quebec actress Geneviève Bujold. This is the first symbol of melancholy that Briand gives us, and it is an expressive one. This young child, obviously a symbol of a new, métis Quebec (Verrault's character is still mourning the death of his Chinese wife, the girl's mother), is very much present in the life of the community, but she is unable to settle herself, wandering comatose rather than resting peacefully. The rumours of a newer generation of more internationally aware, less historically weighed-down Québécois is, as we see here, more complicated than an ideal-ist vision might suggest. A similar and particularly affecting scene comes mid-way through the film, as Brussières and her friend Catherine (played by Julie Gayet) go to the archives of the local newspaper in search of information about this death. The editor's office is dimly lit and furnished all in brown, and the edi-tor, the memory of the community, is played by Gabriel Arcand, a veteran Quebec actor and brother of Denys Arcand. When Brussières says everyone in the town seems more focused on golf than death, Arcand waves his hand dismissively, wearily: "They pretend," he says.

Thus *La turbulence des fluides* may be consistent with the imagery of "Cinema du look" but not with the ideology. Briand is presenting three genera-tions of Québécoises—embodied by Seguin, Brussières, and Bujold; the lat-ter two are authentic celebrities in Quebec—as, in their different ways, asleep and alone. She is presenting the landscape as simultaneously wild—the forest fires are clearly not far away—and built up to the point of benumbing the citi-zenry. Briand's Baie-Comeau has boreal forest on one side and the St. Lawrence River on the other, and in between its landscape is defined by the golf course. But Briand presents certain elements of the story with a matter-of-factness that is refreshing; here and there we find a genuine cause for optimism. The Chinese heritage of the Verreault's Asian daughter is barely remarked upon, and the les-bianism of Brussière's friend Catherine seems a matter of no particular interest. Whatever serious melancholy defines the life of Quebec at the turn of the cen-tury, the place has, in Briand's vision, made discernable progress in the integra-tion of different ethnicities and sexualities. Hayward writes of the play between history and image that defined French cinema of the 1980s that "while nostal-gia culture harkened back to earlier myths and thereby functioned cryptologi-cally as transparence for past ideologies, the 'cinéma du Look' refracted purely and solely upon itself. Narcissus had come of age" (244). This is half true in the Quebec context. The presence of a "nostalgia culture" in the form of an ADQ-led neo-Duplessism was a very real part of Quebec politics of the turn of the twenty-first century (although Baie-Comeau sits in a fairly safe PQ riding, one that is called "Comté René Lévesque"). This nostalgia culture certainly harkened back to earlier myths and past ideologies, such as the essentially stable and pleas-ant qualities of small-town life. But the refraction of the film itself is not simply on "itself" in the form of imagery, but "itself" in the form of Quebec. *La turbulence des fluides* is indeed a film that is turned inward, but not in a narcissistic way. It is a portrayal of the sometimes imperceptible seismic shifts that are remaking Quebec culture, sometimes for the better, and sometimes not.

Louise Archambault offers a similar critique of Quebec's fully post–Quiet Revolution existence in her first feature, 2005's *Familia*. Here the key metaphor embedded deep in the narrative is not sleepwalking but bigamy, although the overall analysis is similar. Archambault's only feature to date (her *Atomic Saké* won the 2000 Jutra for best short, and its opening shots, many of which are of a woman on a bicycle, strongly recall the visual frenzy of *2 Secondes*) shows just how wracked by materialist anxiety a lot of Quebec culture is, just how shallow and alienating a lot of everyday life has become. Its main characters are all women, young and old, and although Archambault shows them each to be terribly lonely in their own way, they are also all notable for the flexible and compassionate way they approach family and its associated obligations. Like Briand's Baie-Comeau, the green suburb where Archambault sets the better part of the film's action is the stomping ground of hollow people trying to fill themselves out and failing as often as they succeed. But like Baie-Comeau, it is also the place where we find sometimes unnoticed but nevertheless seismic shifts in the culture.

The narrative mostly centres on the relationship between the interior designer Janine and her childhood friend—and sister-in-law—Michèle, who is working-class and perpetually in some kind of trouble. Their daughters—thirteen-year-old Gabrielle and fourteen-year-old Margot—are at first hostile but quickly bond over a shared interest in teenage chaos-making; this is the mirror image of the disintegration of their mothers' relationship. All of these women are desperately lonely, and the most visceral evocation of this is via Janine's relationship with her husband. Early in the film we see that he is perpetually away on business, but as the film progresses it becomes clear that he is leading a double life, complete with a new baby, with a British woman who lives in Montreal's plateau district. Michèle befriends the woman only to ambush her at the end of the film by inviting her and the baby out to her suburban house to meet her entire family, including of course her—their—husband. Meanwhile, Margot discovers that she is pregnant, as a result of a post-rave date rape of which she has no memory, and a subplot about teen pregnancy and abortion ensues.

All of this is the stuff of high melodrama and strongly recalls the ideological complexity of the genre that I invoked by way of explaining *Ma vie en cinemascope*. Here, though, the degree to which the emotional release of melodrama is being marshalled by the film's director to visualize the paradoxes of domesticity is *a lot* more explicit. In a 1986 essay called "Melodrama Inside and Outside the Home," Mulvey traced melodrama's narrative evolution by noting that "the theatrical tradition of popular culture constructed its 'post-proletarian phase' around a process which dovetails money and morals" (68), and a better summary of the broad narrative pattern of *Familia* one could hardly find. This is indeed a Quebec narrative cinema in its "post-proletarian" phase inasmuch as it is not in the mould of those grubby, 1950s-inspired films like *Ma vie en cinemascope* or, for that matter, *Aurore*; the visuals here are far more expressive, the treatment of sexuality and modernity far more explicit. And that intersection of money and morals is at the core of the story; Janine is just as clearly upper-middle-class as Michèle is underclass, but the moral economy here ends up being more complex than it at first seems. For while Archambault dwells on Michèle's general fecklessness (she is a compulsive gambler and is essentially sponging off of Janine until she can get together enough cash to move to California to flop with her sister, who, as we see in an early scene in the film, wants nothing to do with her), the film concludes with her helping her daughter through an abortion in a way that emphasizes her tough, quiet parental responsibility (a dimly lit scene in the recovery room is especially evocative), whereas Janine's narrative—and indeed the entire film—climaxes with the aforementioned ambush, where she announces she is leaving the family to go smoke pot and hitchhike through Europe.

Like the melodramatic pattern *of Ma vie en cinemascope*, this use of the narrative bones of melodrama is mostly about evoking the repressed ideological nuttiness of the nuclear family. Mulvey's "dizzy satisfaction in witnessing the way that sexual difference under patriarchy is fraught, explosive, and erupts dramatically into violence within its own private stomping-ground, the family" is also an excellent way of summarizing *Familia*, and the final scene is especially dizzy, especially explosive, and especially repudiating of the hypocrisies of the nuclear family. In the final analysis its critique is as open-ended as that of *Ma vie en cinemascope*; again, the primary difference is on the level of form and structure. Archambault's narrative is far more complex—encompassing far more sub-narratives—than Filiatrault's, and her visuals are a lot more deliberate about evoking place. This is especially true of the way that she represents the leafy ease of the suburbs, the run-down quality of the campground where Michèle and Margot go after alienating Janine, and the comfortable urbanity of the plateau's condos. Filiatrault's visual palette is not comparably complex; even the images of Montreal in *C't'à ton tour, Laura Cadieux* feel bland in comparison. *Familia*, like the work of Manon Briand, is formally ambitious, but not in a way that could be labelled disruptive or really even eccentric. Like Léa Pool, these filmmakers are serious and committed, while still in a basically accessible cinematic pattern.

Stylo

Much less accessible are filmmakers like Catherine Martin or Lucie Lambert, even when they are working in ostensibly conventional forms like narrative or documentary. These are two filmmakers who illustrate the inadequacy of labels such as "art cinema" and "popular cinema," and offer instead a version of what Alexandre Astruc, writing in 1948, hoped would be "a new avant garde." In his celebrated essay "The Birth of a New Avant-garde: La caméra-stylo," Astruc wrote that "the term *avant-garde* savours of the surrealist and so-called abstract films of the 1920s. But that *avant-garde* is already old hat. It was trying to create a specific domain for the cinema; we on the contrary are seeking to broaden it and make it the most extensive and clearest language there is" (22).[8] That sense of forward-looking pragmatism, and of clarity, is at the heart of both Lambert's and Martin's oeuvres. More than any other Quebec filmmakers, male or female, they are the inheritors of the caméra-stylo ideal.

In many ways Lucie Lambert is writing back to another giant of the Quebec caméra-stylo, Pierre Perrault. Her films are set in a maritime Quebec landscape that strongly recalls his Île aux Coudres films; they are shot just past Perrault's beloved Charlexoix, in the part of the St. Lawrence known as the Côte-Nord. She has made only a few films—1996's *Paysage sous les paupières*, 1999's *Avant le jour*, and 2005's *Père de Gracile*—but they are major works, wondrous interventions in contemporary documentary. And yet they remain mostly unknown in English Canada. "Is it in spite of its artistic achievement or because of its artistic achievement that *Paysage sous les paupières* was rejected by the programmers of Perspective Canada at the Toronto International Film Festival?" was Peter Harcourt's acidic question in the wake of the film's rejection and the distributor's subsequent refusal to strike a subtitled 16mm print (32). Harcourt sees this not only as a matter of a lovely film not getting as much exposure as it deserves but also as an example of Quebec cinema's historically engaged evolution being kept hidden: "What Pierre Perrault did for his male society on Île-aux-Coudres, Lucie Lambert has done for her female society at Ste-Anne-de-Pontneuf is La Haute-Côte-Nord in 1995" (30). This is true of her other films as well.

Paysage sous les paupières has, in its opening minutes, disembodied shots that wander through a house, close-up images of feet walking along sand and trails, and a through-a-rainy-window shot of logging trucks driving past that might make it seem as through this is to be a semi-abstract study in details; but Lambert's canvas is wider than that. Because the film is really a study of the whole community, Lambert's voice is in a number of cinematic registers. There is a good deal of interview footage, especially with the film's protagonist, Diane O'Connor, who acts as a kind of foster mother for a lot of the town's troubled young people (like many Québécois, she is a francophone with an Irish name). But even this is a deceptive statement, since the interview strategies are variable; in some places she draws on talking-heads-style imagery, in other places on a more interactive style. This is especially effective early in the film when she interviews a teenage girl, Cathy, who is working at the local fast-food place. We never see Lambert's face, but we hear her voice, as she speaks gently to Cathy from behind the camera, asking her about the special program for at-risk kids that she's part of, and of the oddball nicknames that the foster kids wind up with. She tells Lambert that hers is "Greluche" (a French word that is the rough equivalent of "chick" but also connotes someone who's a bit simple), but that she doesn't mind as long as it's friendly. This is a minor scene, but it's remarkable. Cathy never stops moving, always hustling behind the counter and clearing tables; Lambert's voice is almost ghostly. This is followed by very different but equally remarkable sequences. In the first, Guylaine Girdard (a professional singer who has come back to her hometown to give a concert) is rehearsing "Ave Maria" in a church. Her voice is powerful and other-worldly, but she slumps over into her music, occasionally stopping to confer with the accompanist and generally looking utterly earthly. It's *work*, Lambert shows us, this sort of beauty; it may sound divine, but its origins are imperfect, human. Cutaways to the church's statuary come as the pianist stops suddenly and then sort of trails off, only emphasizing the divine–earthy/transcendent–imperfect duality of the task and indeed of the place. This is followed by a montage of kids on swings and then of the town's front yards. On the soundtrack is a young girl, first muttering repeatedly, "Jamais jamais jamais, toujours toujours toujours," and then telling of how she would get scared when she would hear the wind at night. Then there is a medium shot of Diane and two girls in the front yard, chattering about the school bus, and then Lambert cuts to the talking-head interview with Diane.

I recount this sequence to give a sense of the visual and structural complexity of the film. No doubt *Paysage*'s subject matter—a remote community seen through the eyes of marginalized women—is of crucial importance. But a big part of what makes the film significant is formal and indeed occurs at the level of montage, both within a sequence and sequence-to-sequence. Lambert is using montage here to open up the complexity of Ste-Anne-de-Pontneuf, to show the ways in which the quotidian and seemingly plain—a young woman hustling from table to table, a kid mumbling a story about a rainstorm—coexist with the clearly beautiful or expressive—a woman singing "Ave Maria," the staccato repetition of a few words, a woman in an interview recalling her struggle with abuse. These strategies are interlaced with one another—the artificial "jamais jamais" sounds are put over simple images of front yards, "Ave Maria" may be on the soundtrack, but slumping is on the image track—and they exist side by side, showing how the complexity that defines this community can be understood only as a mosaic.

This sort of complexity is an equally important part of Lambert's second film, *Avant le jour* (1999), which is shot in an area north of Ste-Anne-de-Pontneuf and the Haute Côte-Nord, in the region known as Basse Côte-Nord. As though confirming that this is a continuation of her engagement with (and advancement on) the Perrault project, she told Gérard Grugeau in a 1999 interview with the Quebec film magazine *24 Images* that "I wanted to once again dig into the relationship between a territory and its inhabitants…. So I started on the adventure, into the unknown, for a first research trip, with Nadine Beaudet, my collaborator for the whole project. We stopped at Tête-à-la-Baleine, where Pierre Perrault had shot in the 1960s" (12).[9] As with *Paysage*, though, this is a genuine *advance* on Perrault, with sounds of English and French mixing as freely as images of interiors and maritime landscapes, as freely as the repeated 180-degree pans over those images mix with the voices of the inhabitants retelling aspects of their everyday lives. Again we see an ethic of montage at work here, an impulse occasionally visible chez Perrault but here given a real ethical imperative as Lambert slowly unfolds the dizzying intricacy of the region. Something similar is going on in her most recent film, *Père de Gracile* (2005), which mixes documentary, fictional, and home-movie footage to create a similar sort of vertigo.

In that 1999 interview, Lambert gave a lot of credit to her editor. She told Grugeau that "our editor René Roberge's real gift was to manage to link it all together. We tried to never give the impression that you were turning a page at the end of a scene. Each image has to call another." Grugeau responded by asking "Do you sense in montage all these meanings that open up, all this back-and-forth between reality and fiction?" Lambert's answer really does illuminate her entire cinematic project: "That's the distinguishing quality of poetry" (14).[10]

Catherine Martin's oeuvre also bears the marks of a career-long search for a new form of poetic cinema. As a filmmaker she is flexible, having made both features and documentaries. When I participated in the jury for the Toronto Film Festival's Top Ten Canadian Films of 2002, I wrote in my citation for Martin's film *Océan*, "With this film, Catherine Martin has become 'our' Chantal Akerman, but a truly Québécoise, truly North American Chantal Akerman." Recently I've started to rethink that assessment. Across her features and documentaries, Martin has looked for the revelatory in the everyday, finding in cinema's photographic essence a sort of neo-Bressonian spirituality, a means by which ineffable sensations and concepts can be evoked. She is becoming our Gus van Sant, without the occasional pieces of Hollywood drivel.

Martin's first major film was the feature-length *Mariages* (2001), which tells the story of Yvonne, a young woman in the nineteenth century who falls in love for the first time and experiences a host of intense emotional sensations that are implicitly linked to the film's lush, wild, back-country setting. These sensations run the gamut. One particularly affecting scene comes when Yvonne sees her dead mother's recently exhumed and almost perfectly preserved body for the first time. It is laid out before the altar in a church, and after Yvonne walks in, kneels and crosses herself (an image that is shot from behind). Martin cuts to a frontal medium shot of Yvonne; she walks a bit toward the camera to turn this into a close-up and starts to talk to her mother, softly telling her that she had a dream that the angels had been carrying her in their arms. Martin then cuts to a brief high-angle shot of the ghostly white mother and then back to that close-up of Yvonne. On the image of the dead mother, we hear Yvonne say she sees her everywhere; when Martin returns to the close-up of Yvonne, the soundtrack is completely silent. There is an intense simplicity at work here; the editing strategy is not exactly classical (Martin lingers on Yvonne for quite a while), but it is clear, realist, and gently insistent on pauses, duration, and silence. It feels Bressonian because of the way that Martin is using plainness, almost blankness in montage to evoke the most mysterious of sensations, the perpetual presence of the dead. An intense, open-ended spiritual exchange is being evoked here in just a few shots, a few shots whose editing pattern draws almost no attention to itself. "Expression by compression," Bresson wrote in the section of *Notes sur le ciné-matographe* called "De la fragmentation." "Put in one image that which a writer would lay out in ten pages."[11] Martin takes this to heart in another very different scene just a few minutes past this one, where Yvonne goes to see her mysterious aunt, an old-style *sage-femme* who lives by herself in a cabin in the woods. The two women sit on a log by a pond, and the older one gives the younger woman a pipe (it helps with pains, she tells her, and it's good for the dreams) that had belonged first to her grandmother and then to her mother. They go on to talk about the presence or absence of her mother's soul in her body. This is all shot in a still, tableau-like long take lasting about three minutes. Again, the sense of stillness, of semi-blankness, is unmistakeable. But the *mise en scène*, the complex soundtrack in this single image—defined by the green messiness of the woods, of the ever-present burble of unseen water—and the way that this visual–sound relationship connects to the film's themes of spiritual mystery and women's experiences of them would, to say the least, take a skilled writer ten pages to lay out.

A comparable economy of form, and a comparable ambition, is evident in her 2002 film *Océan*, which to my mind is her masterpiece. This is simply a portrait of the *Océan*, the last train to run between Montreal and Halifax. It is thus literally a linear film—we follow a voyage straight down the tracks—but it is in fact a deeply elliptical film, concentrating on the gestures, rituals, and landscapes that characterize a form of travel that is starting to die.

A key sequence midway through the film illustrates *Océan*'s formal link to *Mariages*. Martin lingers in Padoue, a small town that used to be an important rail hub. Like the sequence with the mother's body in *Mariages*, the montage here is simple, slow but not self-consciously so, and evokes the ineffable with a plainness that makes it clear how impossible it is for cinema to really visualize such concepts as death or permanence. The sequence begins with the camera placed about at table height, pointed at the window of a shop at night; the train rolls past the window. Once it is all the way by, Martin pauses for a few seconds, cuts to an extreme long shot of the town in the daytime, and then returns to the same set-up, this time in daylight. This serves as an introduction to a series of interviews, first with the show owner (in a medium shot from the side, as he looks away from the camera) and then (following a few images of the town that recall Yasujiro Ozu's "pillow shots") with a middle-aged woman and a younger man who recall the now irrelevant train station. The woman does all the talking, but it is the young man who holds an old photo of the station. The camera wanders hand-heldedly between the two of them, documentary-style, but the sequence ends by lingering, in an odd-but-not-too-odd way, on the photo of the station. This is followed by a very dark shot of an old desk, presumably from the station, which is itself a prelude to an interview with an older woman, where large photos of the woman's ancestors, who had worked at the station, loom imposingly on the wall above her. Martin cuts away to one of them, briefly. Like the sequence that I described in *Mariages*, Martin is dealing here with death and what remains, memory and affection, loss and persistence. She is doing so in a way that is steady, almost rhythmic; there are no flashes of cinematic or narrative extravagance, and only the most indirect invocation of the sequence's clear concern—the degree to which landscapes remain haunted by memory. She calls attention to old photographs by way of explicitly evoking death—the camera that wanders to the photo of the station, the brief cutaway to the ancestor—but mostly she accomplishes this invocation at the level of composition: by setting the interview with the middle-aged woman beside the tracks where there is now only a small stop, or the interview with the older woman in a dark, warm interior that is filled with traces of older forms of domesticity. This is expression by compression; it is as evocative as any passage in a novel.

In Astruc's sense of the camera as pen, then, Lambert and Martin really are the writers of Quebec's women's cinema. Bresson, of course, has something similar to say about the relation between cinema and writing. Drawing on the root of "cinématographe" in the word "graph," to write, he distinguishes between a narrative/theatrical cinema and what he favours: "Theatre and CINEMA: alternating between believing and not believing. *Cinématographe:* continually believing."[12] To write with a camera, for both Lambert and Martin, is to continually believe both in the possibilities of cinema as a dynamic, fluid means of expression and in the world as a place where genuine mysteries remain, mysteries that sustain us through their basic inaccessibility.

Conclusion

What I have been trying to show here is not only that Quebec has a vibrant group of women filmmakers but also the degree to which their films are at the heart of the national cinema. The ease with which Denise Filiatrault moves between film and television, and the degree to which her films are based in conventions of both forms, is an important starting point for an understanding of Quebec popular cinema generally. Briand and Archambault may look like they are drawing on the same conventions as Filiatrault, but their films are important in no small part because of the way they nudge *idées reçus*—both aesthetic and cultural—just slightly off-centre, speaking in a relatively accessible register but at the same time encouraging critical viewers in a way that popular cinema rarely does; this in-betweenness is typical of a lot of Quebec cinema since the 1970s, from Denys Arcand right through to Léa Pool. And the intense, rigorous cinema of Catherine Martin and Lucie Lambert shows the degree to which Quebec's contributions to the building of a "new avant-garde" must not be understood as a matter of "the 1960s and its imitators." Quebec's best filmmakers (and this includes Filitrault, Archambault, and Brand as well as Lambert and Martin) are well aware of what came before them, and integrate those advances into their own work. But they build on that history, taking it in genuinely new directions. Understanding Quebec cinema since the 1990s is to understand these sorts of issues; understanding what is going on with Quebec's younger filmmakers in unimaginable without discussion of the filmmakers I have focused on here. Women's cinema, however marginal it may sometimes seem, has, at the levels of both form and ideology, set the agenda of Quebec cinema since the 1990s.

Notes

1
Quebec cinema has a volume that is comparable to this one, although it badly needs updating. See Louise Carrière's anthology *Femmes et cinéma québécois* (Montréal: Boréal Express, 1983).

2
"Il faut souligner que plusieurs de ses artisans passent au service de la télévision ou de ses compagnies privées qui réalisent des séries pour celle-ci."

3
"Depuis 1990, il [le Québec] s'est produit une moyenne annuelle de trente longes métrages pour le cinéma. Cela donne un des ratios (par millions d'habitants) les plus élevés au monde."

4
"Certains des personnages (tels Séraphin ou Aurore) sont devenues des types québécois perçus comme des référents sociaux sado-masochistes."

5
"Ces trois films poussent à son sommet la morbidité collective qui était celle de l'époque de notre grand noirceur, étouffée par les valeurs catholiques et ses ersatzs : la souffrance, la pénitence, le châtiment, le rachat, le sacrifice, etc. Ces films correspondent bien à l'imaginaire malade de notre société et valent aujourd'hui davantage pour ses connotations sociologique que pour leur qualités cinématographies" (1978, 44).

6
"Il ne faut toutefois pas, comme nous l'avons vu, ne s'en tenir qu'à ces réactions négatives. Il faut bien saisir le contexte de l'époque : le cinéma au Québec était presque totalement étranger. De plus, le cinéma considéré par ses auteurs comme outil de connaissance a pavé la voie, selon nous, au cinéma conçu comme instrument d'affirmation nationale, une représentation qui prendra son véritable essor durant les années 1960."

7
This is a term that I personally detest as redundant in the same way that "literary fiction" is; all cinema is art, just as all literature is, ahem, literary.

The real question these terms seem to answer (to beg, really) is whether it is ambitious or distinctive art or literature. But like the term "literary fiction," I acknowledge that the term "art cinema" has considerable currency and thus considerable explanatory power. For an uncharacteristically frustrating legitimization of this term, do not see David Bordwell, "Art Cinema as a Mode of Film Practice," originally published in *Film Criticism* 4.1 (1979): 56–64, and recently reprinted in his collection *Poetics of Cinema* (New York: Routledge, 2007).

8

"Je sais bien encore une fois que ce terme d'avant-garde fera penser aux films surréalistes et aux films dits abstraits de l'autre après-guerre. Mais cette avant-garde est déjà une arrière-garde. Elle cherchait à créer un domaine propre du cinéma ; nous cherchons au contraire à l'étendre et à en faire le langage le plus vaste et le plus transparent qui soit" (328).

9

"Pour ce film, qui est ma deuxième, j'avais envie de creuser à nouveau le rapport qui existe entre un territoire et ses habitants…. Je suis donc partie à l'aventure, dans l'inconnu, pour un premier voyage de recherche, avec Nadine Beaudet, ma collaboratrice tout au long du projet. Nous sommes arrêtés à Tête-à-la-Baleine, là où Pierre Perrault avait tourné dans les années 60."

10

"Le grand mérite de René Roberge, le monteur, est d'être arrivé à tout enchaîner. On cherchait à ne jamais donner l'impression de tourner une page avec la fin d'une scène. Chaque image doit appeler une autre. *Sentiez-vous au montage tous ces sens qui s'ouvrent, tout ce va-et-vient entre le réel et la fiction?* C'est le propre de la poésie."

11

"Expression par compression. Mettre dans une image ce qu'un littérateur délaierait en dix pages."

12

"Théâtre et CINÉMA: alternance de croire et de ne pas croire. Cinématographe : continuellement croire."

Works Cited

Allor, Martin. "Cultural *Métissage*: National formations and productive discourse in Québec cinema and television." *Screen* 34.1 (Spring 1993): 69–75.

Astruc, Alexandre. "The Birth of a New Avant-Garde: La caméra-stylo." *The New Wave*. Ed. Peter Graham. New York: Doubleday, 1968. 17–23.

—. *Du stylo à la caméra et de la caméra au stylo: Écrits (1942–1984)*. Paris: L'Archipel, 1992.

Bresson, Robert. *Notes sur le cinématographe*. Paris: Gallimard, 2002. [1975].

Grugeau, Gérard. "Avant le jour: Entretien avec Lucie Lambert." *24 Images* 98–99 (Automne 1999): 12–14.

Harcourt, Peter. "Paysage sous les paupières." *Point of View* 30 (Fall 1996): 30–32.

Hayward, Susan. *French National Cinema*. 2nd ed. New York: Routledge, 2005.

Marshall, Bill. *Quebec National Cinema*. Montreal: McGill-Queen's UP, 2001.

Mulvey, Laura. *Visual and Other Pleasures*. Bloomington: Indiana UP, 1989.Poirier, Christian. *Le cinéma québécois: À la recherche d'une identité? Tome 1: L'imaginaire filmique*. Sainte-Foy: Presses de l'Université du Québec, 2004.

—. *Le cinéma québécois: À la recherche d'une identité? Tome 2: Les politiques cinématographiques*. Sainte-Foy: Presses de l'Université du Québec, 2004.

Tremblay-Daviault, Christiane. *Un cinéma orphelin: Structures mentales du cinéma québécois (1942–1953)*. Montréal: Québec/Amérique, 1981.

Véronneau, Pierre. "1944–1953: Première vague du long métrage québécois." *Les cinémas canadiennes*. Ed. Véronneau. Paris/Montréal: Lherminier/Cinémathèque Québécois, 1978. 37–46.

—. "Quebec's Feature Wave: 1944–53." *Self Portraits: Essays on the Canadian and Quebec Cinemas*. Ed. Véronneau and Piers Handling. Ottawa: Canadian Film Institute, 1980. 54–63.

—. "Le Québec : De la fiction, dirent-ils. Des origines à 1960." *Les cinémas du Canada*. Ed. Sylvain Garel and André Pâquet. Paris: Centre Georges Pompidou, 1992. 35–49.

Contributors

Anthony Adah is an assistant professor in film studies at Minnesota State University, Moorhead, Minnesota. He specializes in post-colonial cinemas, especially those from settler states (Australia, Canada, and New Zealand) and Africa. He is published in *Postscript* and *Film Criticism* and has a forthcoming article in *Pompeii*. His current research projects include theoretical exploration of authorship and genre in Nollywood as well as land and memory in Aboriginal cinemas.

Kay Armatage is a professor cross-appointed to the Cinema Studies Institute and Women and Gender Studies Institute, University of Toronto. She is the author of *The Girl from God's Country: Nell Shipman and the Silent Cinema* (University of Toronto Press, 2003) and co-editor of *Gendering the Nation: Canadian Women's Cinema* (University of Toronto Press, 1999). She has also directed documentary films, including *Artist on Fire: The Work of Joyce Wieland* (1987). Her current research is on film festivals.

Brenda Austin-Smith is an associate professor in the Department of English, Film, and Theatre at the University of Manitoba, where she teaches a variety of courses, including Cult Film, Film and the City, and Film and Affect. She has published on emotional responses to film melodrama, symbolism in American literature, adaptation, the late novels of Henry James, Patricia Rozema, Manitoba feature films, cinema memory and World War II, and Lars von Trier.

Jean Bruce teaches film theory and cultural studies at Ryerson University in the School of Image Arts, where she is currently the associate chair. She also teaches visual culture in the joint graduate Program in Communication and Culture at Ryerson and York universities. Her research interests include melodrama, consumer culture, sexuality and the cinema, and the home-improvement genre of reality television.

Andrew Burke is an assistant professor in the Department of English at the University of Winnipeg, where he teaches critical theory, cultural studies, and British literature and culture. His current project is on representations of modernity and modernization in contemporary British cinema, part of which is forthcoming in the journal *Screen*. His recent articles on contemporary cinema and cultural theory have appeared in *Historical Materialism* and *English Studies in Canada*.

Kathleen Cummins is a Ph.D. candidate in the graduate program in women's studies at York University. Her doctoral research focuses on the reconstruction of frontier histories in women's/feminist cinemas. Kathleen has taught film production, screenwriting, and media studies in a variety of institutions, such as the Department of Film at York University, the Media Arts Department at Sheridan College, and the Department of Communication, Culture and Information Technology at the University of Toronto–Mississauga/Sheridan College. Her short films have been screened and broadcast internationally.

Florian Grandena is assistant professor in the Department of Communication of the University of Ottawa, where he teaches film studies. He researches gay-themed French-speaking films, particularly the films of Olivier Ducastel and Jacques Martineau, on which he is currently writing a book. He is the author of *Showing the World to the World: Political Fictions in French Cinema of the 1980s and the early 2000s* (Cambridge Scholars Publishing, 2008) and co-editor of *New Queer Images* and *Cinematic Queerness* (Peter Lang Publishing Group, 2010), which focus on the representations of homosexualities in contemporary visual cultures in France and in Quebec.

Shana McGuire is completing a Ph.D. in French at Dalhousie University in Halifax, Nova Scotia. Her doctoral research, funded by both the Killam Foundation and the Social Sciences and Humanities Research Council, examines representations of the body in contemporary French cinema, namely the films of Catherine Breillat, Claire Denis, and Bruno Dumont. She has taught film studies at Mount Saint Vincent University and at the Nova Scotia College of Art and Design in Halifax.

George Melnyk is associate professor of Canadian Studies and Film Studies in the Department of Communication and Culture, University of Calgary. He is a cultural historian who has authored and edited over twenty books on cultural and political issues relating to Canada. In the field of Canadian cinema he has authored *One Hundred Years of Canadian Cinema* (2004) and edited *The Young, the Restless, and the Dead: Interviews with Canadian Filmmakers* (2008) and *Great Canadian Film Directors* (2007). He is currently completing a manuscript on urbanity in postmodern Canadian cinema.

Lee Parpart is a Toronto-based writer and lecturer whose work on Canadian cinema and visual culture has appeared in *Canadian Art*, *POV*, *The Globe and Mail*, *The Whig-Standard*, *The Canadian Journal of Film Studies*, and *Essays on Canadian Writing*. Her essays on gender and cinema and television (including critical writings about Canadian filmmakers Lynne Stopkewich, Patricia Rozema, and the American TV series *Buffy the Vampire Slayer*) have appeared in numerous anthologies, including *North of Everything: English-Canadian Cinema since 1980*, *Gendering the Nation: Canadian Women's Cinema*, and *Athena's Daughter's: Television's New Women Warriors*. After a care-giving hiatus of several years, she is completing a dissertation that explores feminist film and new-media adaptations of Canadian women's fiction.

Agata Smoluch Del Sorbo is a Toronto-based film programmer and writer who has programmed Canadian feature films for the Toronto International Film Festival since 2005. She holds an M.A. in film studies from York University and has written articles on Patricia Rozema, Canadian cinema, and women's filmaking. She has served on a number of film juries, including the Imagine NATIVE Film Festival and the National Screen Institute and was a lecturer in American cinema at the University of Genoa, Italy. Currently she is completing a research project on national cinemas and cultural identity

Christina Stojanova is an academic, curator, and writer who focuses on cultural semiotics, gender, genre, and ethnic representation in Canadian multicultural cinema, the cinema of Quebec, and Russian and Eastern European cinema. As a member of the Association of Quebec Film Critics, she writes for a number of critical journals and sits on international film festival juries. She also sits on the editorial boards of Rhodopi Publishing House and of Studies in Eastern Europe Cinema. She is an assistant professor in the Department of Media Production and Studies at University of Regina. Among her major publications are chapters in *Making It Like a Man: Canadian Masculinities* (Wilfrid Laurier University Press, 2009), *European Nightmares* (Wallflower, 2009), *Berlin Culturescapes*

(University of Regina Press, 2008), *The Cinema of Eastern Europe* (Routledge, 2005), *Traditions in World Cinema* (Edinburgh University Press, 2005), *Horror International* (Wayne University Press, 2005), *Cinema of Central Europe* (Wallflower, 2005); *Alternative Europe: Eurotrash and Expoitation Cinema since 1945* (Wallflower, 2004). She is currently co-editing an anthology on Wittgenstein on Film and a monograph on New Romanian Cinema.

Darrell Varga is associate professor and Canada Research Chair in Contemporary Film and Media Studies at the Nova Scotia College of Art and Design in Halifax. He is the co-editor of *Working on Screen: Representations of the Working Class in Canadian Cinema* (2006) and editor of *Rain/Drizzle/Fog: Film and Television in Atlantic Canada* (2007).

Jerry White is associate professor of Film Studies at the University of Alberta. He is author of *The Radio Eye: Cinema in the North Atlantic, 1958–1988* (Wilfrid Laurier University Press, 2009) and *Of This Place and Elsewhere: The Films and Photography of Peter Mettler* (Toronto Film Festival/Indiana University Press, 2006). He is the editor of *The Cinema of Canada* (Wallflower Press, 2006), co-editor (with William Beard) of *North of Everything: English-Canadian Cinema since 1980* (U of Alberta Press, 2002), and the former editor of the *Canadian Journal of Irish Studies*.

Index

Books in the Film+Media Studies Series
Published by Wilfrid Laurier University Press

The Young, the Restless, and the Dead: Interviews with Canadian Filmmakers /
George Melnyk, editor / 2008 / xiv + 134 pp. / photos /
ISBN 978-1-55458-036-1

Programming Reality: Perspectives on English-Canadian Television / Zoë Druick
and Aspa Kotsopoulos, editors / 2008 / x + 344 pp. / photos /
ISBN 978-1-55458-010-1

*Harmony and Dissent: Film and Avant-garde Art Movements in the Early
Twentieth Century* / R. Bruce Elder / 2008 / xxxiv + 482 pp. /
ISBN 978-1-55458-028-6

He Was Some Kind of a Man: Masculinities in the B Western /Roderick McGillis /
2009 / xii + 210 pp. / photos /
ISBN 978-55458-059-0

The Radio Eye: Cinema in the North Atlantic, 1958–1988 / Jerry White / 2009 /
xvi + 284 pp. / photos /
ISBN 978-1-55458-178-8

The Gendered Screen: Canadian Women Filmmakers / Brenda Austin-Smith and
George Melnyk, editors / 2010 / x + 272 pp. /
ISBN 978-1-55458-179-5